RAF
HAWKINGE

For my dear wife who has supported me throughout the research and preparation of this book.

RAF
HAWKINGE

RAF'S WARTIME FRONTLINE AIRFIELD;
FROM DUNKIRK TO THE BATTLE OF
BRITAIN AND D-DAY

ANTONY J MOOR

AIR WORLD

RAF HAWKINGE
RAF's Wartime Frontline Airfield; From Dunkirk to the Battle of Britain
and D-Day

This Edition in Great Britain in 2024 by
Air World
An imprint of
Pen & Sword Books Ltd
Yorkshire – Philadelphia

Copyright © Antony J Moor, 2024

ISBN 978 1 39907 146 8

The right of Antony J Moor to be identified as Author of this work has been asserted by him in accordance with the Copyright, Designs and Patents Act 1988.

A CIP catalogue record for this book is available from the British Library.

All rights reserved. No part of this book may be reproduced or transmitted in any form or by any means, electronic or mechanical including photocopying, recording or by any information storage and retrieval system, without permission from the Publisher in writing.

Typeset by SJmagic DESIGN SERVICES, India.
Printed and bound in the UK by CPI Group (UK) Ltd.

Pen & Sword Books Limited incorporates the imprints of Atlas, Archaeology, Aviation, Discovery, Family History, Fiction, History, Maritime, Military, Military Classics, Politics, Select, Transport, True Crime, Air World, Frontline Publishing, Leo Cooper, Remember When, Seaforth Publishing, The Praetorian Press, Wharncliffe Local History, Wharncliffe Transport, Wharncliffe True Crime and White Owl.

For a complete list of Pen & Sword titles please contact

PEN & SWORD BOOKS LIMITED
George House, Units 12 & 13, Beevor Street, Off Pontefract Road,
Barnsley, South Yorkshire, S71 1HN, England
E-mail: enquiries@pen-and-sword.co.uk
Website: www.pen-and-sword.co.uk

or
PEN AND SWORD BOOKS
1950 Lawrence Rd, Havertown, PA 19083, USA
E-mail: uspen-and-sword@casematepublishers.com
Website: www.penandswordbooks.com

Contents

Introduction vi

Acknowledgements viii

Chapter 1   Flights of Fancy 1910–1914 – Barnhouse
Flying Ground 1

Chapter 2   World War I 1915–1919 – The RFC arrives
at Hawkinge 7

Chapter 3   RAF Hawkinge During the 1920s – Airmail Flights 19

Chapter 4   The Halcyon Days of 1930s –
Summer Camps and Training 30

Chapter 5   RAF Hawkinge Goes to War 1940 –
The Phoney War Ends 66

Chapter 6   The Battle of Britain 1940 – Hawkinge Frontline Airfield .. 76

Chapter 7   A Year of Change 1941 – 'Jim Crow' and
Air Sea Rescue 113

Chapter 8   Hawkinge During 1942 – Flying for their Lives 135

Chapter 9   Taking the War to the Enemy 1943 – Rescue and Patrols ... 162

Chapter 10   Air Sea Rescue 1944 – The V1 and the Fleet
Air Arm Arrive 203

Chapter 11   The Last Year of War 1945 – Peace Returns to Hawkinge ... 238

Chapter 12   The WAAFs – An Uncertain Future 1946–1961 251

Bibliography 271

Index 274

Introduction

Airfields often adopted the name of its local village and Hawkinge was one such location; an appropriate name which derived from the Northumbrian word 'hafoc' meaning a 'hawk', and 'ing' relating to a 'place or settlement' – a 'place frequented by hawks'. Originally named Uphill, high on the downs overlooking Folkestone and the coast. In 1910 two aircraft landed at Barnhouse, Uphill – the first to land at the site. By 1912 the field was called 'Megones' after William B. Megone, an amateur aviator, and was later known as Barnhouse Flying Ground. When in the War Office surveyed Kent for suitable airfield locations, the landing ground was owned by the 7th Earl of Radnor, Jacob Pleydell-Bouverie KG, KCVO, DL, who he agreed to allow the RFC to establish an airfield.

Initially used for transporting aircraft to France, by 1917 hangars appeared along with administrative buildings. Hawkinge Aeroplane Dispatch Station flew supplies to France and Belgium, and mail was delivered. Hawkinge expanded following the reorganisation of the RAF in 1923, No.25 Squadron was now based at Hawkinge, squadrons arrived for annual Summer Camp, fighter training continued. In December 1939, too close to French coast for training, it became a Fighter Station in No.11 Group, Hurricanes No.3 Squadron arrived.

Hawkinge took part in the Dunkirk evacuation in 1940 – Operation *Dynamo,* aircraft provided air-cover for retreating forces. Hurricanes and Spitfires used the airfield as a forward base, refuelling and rearming before heading off to France. The possibility of invasion increased following Dunkirk and anti-aircraft guns were placed around the perimeter.

Hawkinge was first attacked on 12 August 1940, and during a raid on 7 September that year, six villagers died. Throughout the Battle of Britain, many aircraft were kept airborne, fending off attacks. Six Spitfires were based at the airfield, three in the air patrolling at any given time.

September 1941 Nos.277 to No.278 Squadrons arrived, for Air Sea Rescue (ASR) which operated Walrus amphibious aircraft, Spitfires,

INTRODUCTION

Hurricanes and Defiants, rescuing crews from the Channel. By early 1941, the daylight raids by the Luftwaffe had subsided; fighter-bomber sweeps ended in December 1941, resuming in February 1942, when No.11 Group airfields, Hawkinge, Lympne and Manston were targeted. Between 1 February and 29 May 1942, the RAF recorded 283 day and night attacks. No.91, No.41 and No.501 Squadrons, escorted ASR patrols and flew 'Jim Crow' sorties patrolling the coast, intercepting enemy aircraft crossing the coastline. Several squadrons moved to Hawkinge from permanent bases, for frontline operations. USAAF and RAF bombers landed at Hawkinge when returning home damaged or low on fuel. Hawkinge played a diversionary role for D-Day in June 1944, convincing the Germans an invasion would be in the Calais area. FAA aircraft, equipped with depth charges helped clear the Channel of U-boats.

Hawkinge was officially closed on 3 September 1945 but used by WAAF technical training unit and glider training. In 1964 the MoD sold the land, in 1968 the airfield played a role during the making of the classic film *Battle of Britain*. The Kent Battle of Britain Museum Trust, dedicated to all who served at Hawkinge and the Battle of Britain, survives on the site, but sadly the airfield has long gone.

Acknowledgements

I would like to express my gratitude to people, organisations and museums who have assisted in producing this book. Kent Aviation Historical Research Society, RAF Museum Hendon, Imperial War Museum, Kent Battle of Britain Museum Hawkinge, National Archive Kew, Skyfotos Ltd, David Brocklehurst MBE, Peter Dunn, Graham Pitchfork MBE, BA, FRAes, Mrs Shelia Pearce (née Moor), Alan E. Wright, Paul Leva (family), Edward McManus, Battle of Britain London Monument, Romney Marsh Wartime Collection (Brenzett). Other photographs Kent Aviation Historical Research Society and Authors Collection unless shown otherwise.

Pilot Officer J. Gillespie Magee was killed on 11 December 1941 flying with No.401 (RCAF) Squadron, leaving a poem 'High Flight' often quoted. But he left another, unfinished, 'Per Adua' (through adversity):

> They that have climbed the white mists of the morning
> They that have soared, before the world's awake
> to herald up their foeman to them, scorning
> the thin dawn's rest their weary folk might take.
> Some that have left other mouths to tell the story
> of high, blue battle, quite young limbs that bled
> How they had thundered up the clouds to glory,
> Or fallen to an English field-stained red.
> Because my faltering feet would fail, I find them
> Laughing beside me, steadying the hand.
> That seeks their deadly courage
> Yet behind them
> the cold light dies in that once brilliant Land …
> Do these, who help the quickened pulse run slowly
> Whose stern, remembered image cools the brow
> till the far dawn of Victory, know only
> Night's darkness, and Valhalla's silence now?

Chapter 1

Flights of Fancy 1912–1914
Early Flying at Barnhouse

During 1910 Edmund Kettle was in the vicinity of Uphill (Hawkinge) near Folkestone when his attention was drawn to the sky. Flying sedately towards him from the direction of Terlingham Farm were two aircraft which descended onto fields, later known as Barnhouse Flying Ground, Edmund watched the two fragile machines take off. Both may have flown from Whitfield airfield near Dover. The identity of the two pilots is unknown, but by coincidence, an aviation meeting took place at Folkestone Racecourse,

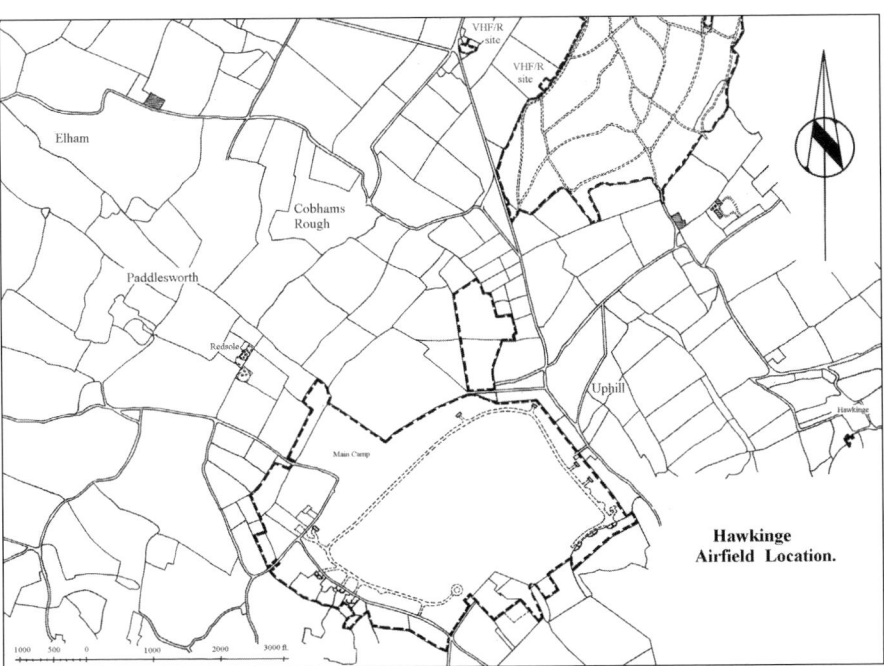

The airfield close to the village of Hawkinge, was once known as Uphill, set high on the downs above Folkestone. An ideal location for an airfield but would later be vulnerable to attacks by the Luftwaffe.

Westenhanger, on 14 September 1910 where J.B. Moisant, Cecil Grace and C.G. Barnes demonstrated their Bleriot aircraft. Whether these events are connected is uncertain, but Edmund was undoubtedly fortunate to have witnessed the first aircraft landing and taking off from Barnhouse, for it was here that the famous airfield at Hawkinge would be sited.

In 1912 one gentleman who fits the category of 'pioneer aviator' is William B. Megone, allegedly a Dutchman. William erected a workshop, on land belonging to Lord Radnor's estate near Folkestone, which had been leased to a farmer for grazing sheep. The shed was erected close to Bijou Cottage, both adjacent to Barnhouse Lane. It was at the cottage that Megone prepared his designs, aided by the owner of a local cycle shop named Harding.

Both had little understanding of aviation and materials required for aircraft construction, a problem for many such pioneers of this new industry. Megone's early attempt was constructed of metal tubing, the engine mounted between the wings where the pilot sat, housed in a metal canopy; flying surfaces were covered with mutton cloth stretched over a spruce structure.

Megone had been experimenting with a biplane, the outcome of several types of aircraft that he discarded. Finally reaching a design at Barnhouse

In 1910 two monoplanes flew over the village pond at Barnhouse, near 'Terlingham Farm'. Edmund Kettle watched as they landed, later taking off. The nearest a Bleriot, the other is thought to be an early Deperdussin. (Kent Battle of Britain Museum, Hawkinge)

FLIGHTS OF FANCY 1912–1914

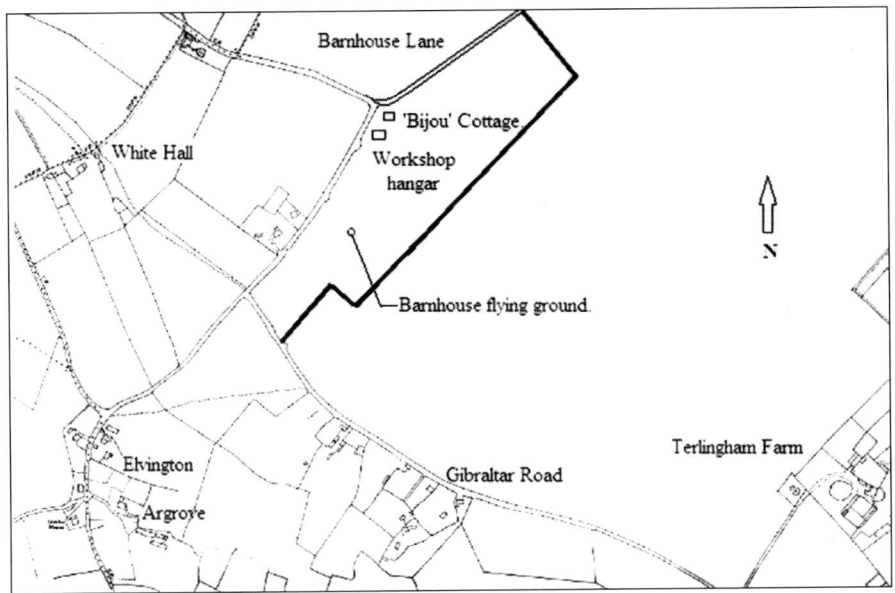

A general layout of Barnhouse Flying Ground as it was in 1912, here William B. Megone constructed his aircraft shed close to Bijou Cottage.

Flying Ground, Uphill in 1912. The 'Mayfly', a pusher type, was powered by a 60 hp Green engine mounted in the front of the nacelle, driving the propeller via an extension shaft at the rear. Control wires for the tail were taken through the propeller boss. The passenger, seated behind the pilot on an adjustable seat like the pilot, had a good view downwards through the celluloid panels in the lower wings. Unfortunately, the Mayfly refused to rise more than a few feet from the ground.

Megone recruited Victor Hunt in 1913, having responded to an advertisement in *Flight* magazine of 9 October 1913 for a mechanic. Hunt had been working on motorcycles and was delighted when Megone offered him the job. Perhaps somewhat apprehensive, he was informed that he would be flying the biplane! The engine was problematic, a few types were tried, producing very low horsepower; a large wooden propeller was over engineered, hand-carved, and heavy.

During a trial run, the engine blew its cylinder pots. Victor threw himself sideways onto the lower wing to avoid being struck by debris. Some years later Victor recalled that the aircraft would run up and down the field, in a series of fits and starts, much to the amusement of onlookers. The aircraft never achieved a successful flight, and so it was decided to approach the

RAF HAWKINGE

The two-seat pusher biplane, or *Mayfly*, with its propeller mounted similar to the Graham White Type 6 and the F.E3. The machine had several unorthodox features. Its final fate is unknown, as is that of William B. Megone. (A.V. Russell)

Victor Hunt proudly displays a propeller used on his *Mayfly*, which had little success, but is an important part of the airfield's history. (A.V. Russell)

FLIGHTS OF FANCY 1912–1914

'Green Engine Co. Ltd'. Their engines were manufactured by the Aster Engineering Company, Wembley, who produced a range of water-cooled, mostly inline engines. Green engines powered many British aircraft, including those of AV Roe, Samuel Cody, and Short Brothers.

During September 1914 'Mayfly' was ready, with extended lower wings and modified propeller. A Hele-Shaw Clutch was fitted, enabling the engine to be de-clutched from its propeller. Megone thought this reduced engine noise, allowing the machine to fly 'soundlessly over an enemy army'. Megone began a design for a monoplane, but his interest gradually faded, concluding when Victor arrived to start work one morning, and found the workshop locked and William B. Megone – gone.

Rumours circulated that Megone was a spy; 'locals' pointed to his secretive ways: the locked room where he developed photographs, frequent visits to the surrounding countryside with his camera. In the frenzied atmosphere of 1914, anyone with a foreign name was suspect. It is not surprising that locals were suspicious, as he often drove his Schneider motor car locally taking photographs; if he was a spy, he did little to conceal the fact. The shed remained at Barnhouse Flying Ground until the RFC took

Designed to carry two people, the passenger seated behind the pilot on a raised seat. Both had a good downward view by means of celluloid windows located in the lower wing. (A.V. Russell)

over the site in 1915, becoming Hawkinge Aerodrome. As to the fate of the Mayfly, nothing is known. Whether Megone was a Dutchman is debateable, as War Office records suggest there was a William B. Megone who joined a YMCA Battalion, serving in France in September 1918; could this account for his disappearance in 1914?

The *Daily Mail*, keen to promote aviation and encourage public and government interest, organised flying demonstrations around Britain, with the 'Wake Up Britain' tour of 1912/13. They recruited aviators, such as Claude Grahame-White, William Hugh Ewen, Louis Noel, Herbert Travers, Jules Fischer, Gustav Wilhelm Hamel, Bentfield Charles Hucks (who invented the Hucks starter) and M. Salmet. Having flown to many coastal towns around Britain, by the beginning of August 1912 Salmet was in Essex. Following the coast, he visited major seaside towns in Kent and Sussex. He flew a Blériot XI-2, a two-seater, enabling him to have a paying passenger – the first 'joy-rides'. Salmet visited Folkestone on 12 August, remaining until 17 August 1912; there is no conclusive evidence he used the site known as Barnhouse Flying Ground, but a postcard suggests he possibly boarded at Cherry Tree Garden Avenue, visiting Folkestone again in 1913.

Chapter 2

The First World War 1915–1919
The RFC Arrives

On the 18 August 1914 the Aircraft Park was formed at Farnborough, Hampshire, from which an Aeroplane Dispatch Section was detached to Hawkinge from September 1915. In September 1915 the RFC arrived at Hawkinge looking for the flying ground at Barnhouse Lane, which the War Office had taken an interest in as a site for an airfield. It is known that No.1 Squadron RFC used Barnhouse landing ground, as a stepping off point to France in March 1915.

No.1 Squadron flew to France without mishap, but No.7 Squadron lost an RE8 which burst into flames at Folkestone, and two BE2cs of No.8 Squadron crashed on the airfield a week later. Compasses were in their infancy and to assist pilots who had to fly to St Omer, two circles were cut into the ground. When lined up, they pointed directly at St Omer airfield France.

Many airfields had been developed in southeast England. These were essentially for Home Defence purposes following the public outcry of the Zeppelin raids, and later Gotha Giant bomber raids, which terrorised the population of London and towns such as Folkestone, killing many civilians and damaging property. On arrival, equipment and stores were unloaded, and within a few days the RFC began clearing trees and hedges in preparation for the arrival of aircraft. By the time they had completed this task, the original area of the flying field had doubled, having removed hedges dividing the largest of two fields.

Three Bessonneau hangars, canvas covered, used by the RFC were erected close to Barnhouse Lane. Although vulnerable to damage from high winds, cheap and easy to construct, many were used in France, some remaining in use until the expansion of the RAF in the 1930s. By the time the RFC had established themselves on their new airfield it was known as Folkestone, later to become RAF Hawkinge, following the formation of the RAF on 1 April 1918.

Sergeant/Pilot Trompton who served at Hawkinge during the First World War, is seen here in front of an Avro 504K, note the Bessoneau hangar in the background. The Avro 504 was a popular biplane, and many pilots gained experience on the type, which flew throughout 1914–18 and was still in use in the 1930s. (E. Young)

The only aircraft to appear at Folkestone were BE2cs of No.12 Squadron, formed at Netheravon, Wiltshire on 14 February 1915. BE2cs were delivered to the squadron in June 1915; prior to this they had operated Avro 504 aircraft. Arriving at Hawkinge in September 1915, they flew on to St Omer on 6 September 1915, commanded by Major C.L. Norton Newall (later becoming, Marshal of the RAF, The Right Honourable Lord Newall GCB, OM, GCMG, CBE, AM).

Arriving at the windswept airfield, pilots were delighted to learn they were to have lunch at the Metropole Hotel, Folkestone, as there were no suitable facilities at the site. Their BE2cs were checked, refuelled, and made ready for the hazardous flight over the Channel to St Omer, where they were based until 28 February 1918. Unbeknown to those having lunch, high winds and driving rain had torn canvas on the hangars, and a few

THE FIRST WORLD WAR 1915–1919

aircraft were damaged. An urgent appeal for help was sent to Lympne, and fitters, riggers and armourers arrived at Hawkinge to repair the aircraft.

By April 1916 an Examination Ground was established as part of the 6th Wing Eastern Command, formed to handle and despatch aircraft in transit to the British Expeditionary Force (BEF). On 3 January 1917 a directive was issued by HQ to the 21st Wing RFC that to avoid confusion between many airfields set up in the southeast, the name of the village or town nearest to the site had to be adopted (occasionally Hawkinge had been mistaken for the RNAS airship base at Capel-le-Ferne).

Previously known as Folkestone, the site became the Aircraft Despatch Section, Hawkinge, later No.12 Aircraft Acceptance Park, formed on 27 August 1917 (ex-Dispatch Section and Examination Ground), for aircraft in transit overseas (disbanded in December 1919). On completion, AAP Hawkinge became the final Despatch Station for all machines going overseas, relieving the duties of No.8 AAP at Lympne. There were 424 airmen, thirty officers, twenty-eight WOs and NCOs, and forty-one corporals; staff included no less than 129 women. The Motor Transport section had twenty-eight vehicles, including two aircraft trailers, motor bikes, an ambulance, and a touring car.

The airfield now covered 2,400ft (732m) EW and 2,000ft (610m) NS, but there were delays in the erection of hangars. In 1918 two sheds based on the

Sopwith Snipe 7F1 F2346 at Hawkinge in 1918 outside one of the Bessoneau hangars on the airfield, used extensively by the RFC. (C.J. Bass)

design of those at Handley Page Aircraft Co. Ltd, were constructed on the NE side, to accommodate larger aircraft and/or increased numbers of machines. Many aircraft were in transit to France, some stored or scrapped, stripped of any useful items. A large, encamped area now existed at Hawkinge, on the other side of the road between Hawkinge and Paddlesworth. As the number of aircraft arriving increased, so did the problem of where to park them as there was little free space in the hangars. It was decided to locate several aircraft around the airfield's perimeter, tying them down with ropes secured to the ground with spiral stakes. High winds were a constant problem at Hawkinge, on one occasion a Bessoneau hangar, under construction, was severely damaged and two aircraft inside were badly damaged.

Ferry pilots were recruited both from the RFC and RNAS – their attire was quite irregular and visitors who entered the 'Pool Room' – where pilots and gunners waited for their next flight – were amazed at the types of flying gear worn. Ground crews, usually recruited from the RFC and Royal Engineers, wore more familiar uniforms. Unlike Lympne airfield, from where ferry pilots on occasion would take off to try to locate German bombers attacking coastal towns such as Folkestone, there is no record of this occurring at Hawkinge. During 1916 the airfield was expanded by the RFC in the direction of Terlingham Manor Farm to the south. The following year a Belfast-type hangar, with massive lattice wooden trusses supporting

A Bristol Fighter F1 attached to No.1 School of Aerial Gunnery, based on the airfield near the redoubt at Dymchurch. The school moved to New Romney during 1918. Seen here during a visit to Hawkinge. (E.F. Cheeseman)

THE FIRST WORLD WAR 1915–1919

the roof and brickwork walls, was constructed. Several other permanent structures replaced tented accommodation, followed by barrack rooms and workshops.

Unlike Lympne, which was blessed with a railway line which came from Westenhanger onto the airfield, all materials and equipment for Hawkinge airfield arrived at Folkestone railway depots. Here it was loaded on to traction engines and transported to the airfield. In November 1917 it was proposed that a new road should be laid because the surface of Barnhouse Lane was unsuitable for constant heavy traffic on the airfield. Earl Radnor offered the War Department a suitable new location for a public highway, which would include fencing and gates; legal and surveyor's costs were borne by the War Department. On 24 November L.C.A. Collins, the agent acting on behalf of Radnor Manor Office, was directed by the Road Board to begin work. New huts in the vicinity of the proposed road caused problems for the erection of boundary fencing. Despite setbacks, Aerodrome Road, the diversion from Canterbury Main Road to Hawkinge Airfield, was completed under the Defence of the Realm Act by 21 December 1918.

Looking rather pleased with themselves, airmen mounted Avro 504K E3798 onto a trailer, which was taken back to the workshops at Hawkinge and restored to flying condition. This aircraft was destroyed in a mid-air collision with Avro 504K E2914 over Manston on 16 December 1925. L.A/C W.E. Parrish in Avro 504K E3798 was seriously injured and taken to Ramsgate Hospital with injuries to head and right ankle, where he recovered. (C.G. Culvin)

RAF HAWKINGE

Two large hangars were erected on the east boundary of the site, 300 yards (275 metres) distant from Hawkinge village. These were used to house Handley Page O/400 large twin-engine biplanes – it was proposed to bomb Berlin! This did not happen, but if the war had continued, there was a plan to bomb Berlin with Handley Page V/1500 aircraft flying from bases near Prague.

No.274 Squadron formed at Bircham Newton in May 1918 and was based at Hawkinge to develop methods of coastal patrol and long-range transport that would be relevant to the peacetime duties of the RAF. Two V/1500s were ferried into Hawkinge on 13 and 24 May 1919 flown by Clifford Prodger, the well-known test pilot employed by Handley Page Aircraft Company.

The first RAF flying unit based at the airfield was No.120 Squadron, commanded by Major A.R. Stanley Clarke MC. They moved from Wyton on 20 February 1919. No.120 Squadron also operated from Lympne, between 17 July and 21 October 1919. Formed as a day bomber squadron equipped with the de Havilland DH9A biplane, they had been scheduled for service with the Independent Force. Before they could be moved to France, the Armistice of 1918 intervened. They were sent to Hawkinge not as a bomber squadron, but to carry mail between the UK, France (Maisoncelle) and Germany (Cologne), from here other units distributed mail to the British Army of Occupation.

They began their new role on 1 March 1919, when four DH9s of 'B' Flight flew the first of the squadron's regular Air Mail services to Maisoncelle. They carried twenty-three bags of mail between them, leaving Hawkinge at 0900hrs in formation, returning later that afternoon. In May 1919, they had extended their range by flying direct to Cologne, operating DH10 'Amiens', a twin-engine aircraft. On 14/15 May that year, Captain Barret, Lieutenant Fitzmaurice, and Lieutenant Oliver took off from Hawkinge at 2215hrs on a trial night service, flying non-stop, arriving at Cologne at 0130hrs. The flight covered 300 miles, at an average speed of 100mph in strong head winds.

On 24 May Hawkinge hosted a visitor from Belfast, a Handley Page V/1500 had to land to refuel. The reason for the flight was to determine if such enterprises could be a commercial success, eventually leading to passenger and freight services. Despite early proposals by Handley Page to convert the V/1500 for commercial use, none were civil-registered and only three 'near civic' demonstrations were made.

However, the Handley Page V/1500, being a large aircraft, was selected by the RAF to deliver much needed food and clothing for the unfortunate

THE FIRST WORLD WAR 1915–1919

Right: One of the pilots who flew with No.120 Squadron between Folkestone and Cologne. The aircraft is a Bristol Fighter during 1920, not of No.120 Squadron but possibly a visiting aircraft of No.4 Sqdn. at Hawkinge. (D.G. Collyer)

Below: DH9 serial D597 of No.120 Squadron, takes on bags of mail to be flown to Cologne 1919–1920. In the background is one of the canvas covered Bessoneau hangars. (E.F. Cheesman)

Belgians, their government having asked Britain for help. The result was the formation of a parcel service in early 1919, flown and organised by the Aircraft Transport & Travel Ltd with DH9 biplanes, used by the RAF and flown by service pilots. By summer of that year, the need for such a service was infrequent, with mail being handled by civilian aircraft so a detachment moved back to Hawkinge on 2 August 1919.

At Hawkinge more thought had been given to the general layout of the airfield, which helped newly arrived airmen find their way around various buildings occupied by their squadron or unit. Engaged in their new role of delivering mail to France, airmen of No.120 Squadron worked hard to ensure their new task was successful, made easier as both officers and airmen knew one another, a great advantage and good for morale.

By July 1919 the number of HP O/400 aircraft on the airfield increased to twenty-five, causing overcrowding which led to an accident. That day, aircraft were taking-off parallel to the hangars. Lieutenant Barlow was taking off in DH9 E8995, thinking he had plenty of room to taxi he opened-up the engine. Suddenly, a gust of wind caught Barlow's aircraft, just a few feet from the ground and almost level with the wings of an HP O/400; it flew straight into the wing bay, damaging wing-struts, and wires. The DH9 twisted on its side at full throttle and charged along the ground, wiping off the undercarriage, wrecking its wings but leaving the tail plane and rudder intact. The Medical Officer Captain S. Pritchard wrote:

> The first thing I knew about it was Barlow appearing at my sick parade. He came in the door without so much as a by-your-leave. I just glanced up, saw who it was and said, 'half a minute' I am just doing something'. Barlow said, 'I've crashed' – just like that. At once all my professional instincts came uppermost and I looked at him. He was holding a handkerchief over his face, and it was very gory indeed. But it only came from a very bloody nose. Not even a broken nose, he was a bit shaken and no wonder, for it was indeed a hell of a crash!

If the medical officer was not to be found in his sick quarters, he could often be seen wandering around the aircraft chatting to everyone and looking for a chance to have a flight. He often approached aircraft which landed with engine trouble, and if no mechanic was in sight would greet the pilot by saying: 'Oi – do you want someone to swing your prop!' On one occasion, he nearly got ploughed into the ground for his trouble.

THE FIRST WORLD WAR 1915–1919

A DH10 of No.10 Squadron, another unit given the task of delivering service mail to units based in Europe. Both engines are running up shortly before leaving Hawkinge bound for the city of Cologne. (E.F. Cheesman)

Another amusing incident involving No.120 Squadron occurred on a very foggy day in October 1919. An officer wandering around the airfield heard an aircraft approaching, the engine coughing and spluttering. The pilot landed but only just avoided wrecking the aircraft. Unimpressed by such a poor attempt to land, the officer ran over to the aircraft and proceeded to tell the pilot what he thought of it, asking whether he even knew where he was. By this time mechanics had arrived to help; the pilot had managed to taxi in with mechanics trying to hold the wing tips and the irate officer running along shouting at him. With the aircraft safely parked, the pilot removed his flying gear – it was none other than General Sir Sefton Brancker, RAF.

His response is unknown, but he may have had a few choice words to say. Sir Sefton, then Secretary of State for Air, was one of the passengers, killed when the R101 airship crashed in France during its maiden overseas voyage on 5 October 1930, killing forty-eight of the fifty-four people on board. The R101 was one of two British rigid airships built in 1929 as part of a British government programme to develop civil airships capable of service on long-distance routes within the British Empire. A course was planned, departing from Cardington, which would take R101 over London,

Paris, and Toulouse, crossing the French coast near Narbonne. During the flight in poor weather, the R101 suffered engine problems. With the increasing winds and the fact that the airship was flying east of Beauvais near Paris, not to the west as planned, R101 lost height and crashed into high ground at Allonne southeast of Beauvais.

Because Hawkinge was frequently covered by low clouds, No.120 squadron transferred to Lympne on 16 July 1919; this also freed up the hangars for Handley Page bombers returning from France. On 17 July 1919, Lieutenant Murphy almost lost his life on his air mail flight, carrying mail from Lympne to Marquise for No.110 Squadron to Cologne. Leaving the English coast in poor weather, with no sight of France, he realised his compass was unserviceable. Murphy had no idea whether he was flying down the Channel or over the North Sea.

Finding a ship, he circled around firing red distress rockets to alert the ship, landing on the sea; the wings of the DH9 were damaged and, as the aircraft started to sink, Murphy made his way to the aircraft's tail. When the vessel came alongside, he was on the top-plane and the mailbags were under water. The vessel turned out to be a Dutch tug, and as he clambered aboard the sailors attempted to recover some of the mail bags. Being a short distance off the Dutch coast, they headed for Brunsbüttelkoog, but upon arrival the captain wouldn't let Murphy leave his boat without payment! As there was no British Consul available, Murphy wrote a cheque, which he cancelled on return to Lympne. Two days later he obtained transport for himself and eight mail bags continuing onto Cologne. German Customs officials demanded 1,000 marks from the British Postal Services in the city, the sum was recovered in a diplomatic manner.

Pilots of No.120 Squadron who flew Air Mail delivery flights were obliged to have an Aerial Post identification card, as they often force landed due to mechanical problems, shortage of fuel or poor weather. Each had been instructed to apply to the nearest unit for transport to take the pilot and mail bags to a military post office. These flights could provide the opportunity to buy certain products, such as cigarettes and drink often found in Cologne, bring them home for customers at Hawkinge, a well-known 'perk of the flight'.

Lieutenant Watten had just reached the sands at Zeebrugge and (taking-off with a senior officer) ran out of sand, tipping the aircraft on its nose. The propeller stopped, his passenger struggled out of the DH9, climbing down cursing. Returning from a delivery to Marquise, Lieutenant Pearce-Gervis in DH9 serial E9026 was alarmed at noise and vibration coming from the

THE FIRST WORLD WAR 1915–1919

engine, and opened the throttle to head for the French coast. Turning off the engine in fear off it shaking itself lose from its bearings and rapidly losing height, there was no chance of landing at Wissant Sands.

The tide was out so he tried to reach Gris-Nez and crashed on rocks; the DH9 was a write-off, but fortunately Pearce-Gervis was uninjured. At the time these aircraft were without wireless equipment, so a pilot in difficulty was unable to let anyone know of his plight. It was felt that if a wireless was fitted to the DH9s it would save delays and possibly lives. Not long after this episode a Wireless Maintenance Section was established at Lympne to fit all aircraft with wireless.

On 12 August 1919 orders arrived from HQ Cologne: No.120 Squadron was to be disbanded under GOC Southeastern Area. Airmail delivery was taken over by No.18 and No.110 Squadrons as No.120 Squadron were needed to ferry aircraft back from France. Mail flights were taken over by Air Transport & Travel Ltd in August 1920, operating a civilian DH9A G-EAHF delivering mail, freight, and newspapers.

Before the Versailles Treaty, signed on 28 June 1919, the RAF intended to order fifty Lion engine V/1500s serials J6523 to J6572, but

In all weathers, including the winter snow of 1920, No.120 Squadron continued their mail flights. In the background is a DH9 with open cockpit, extremely cold during flights over the Channel. (E.F. Cheesman)

the Air Ministry purchased only J6573 for trial purposes, test flown at Aldergrove on 3 September 1919 and flown on 22 September to Hawkinge. Flying the aircraft that day was Major Keith Park, later Flight Lieutenant K. Park RAF, and a Flight Commander with No.25 Squadron during 1919–1920, before taking up duties as a squadron commander at the School of Technical Training. Commissioned as a captain when new RAF officer ranks were introduced in 1919. Park's career is legendary, he later commanded No.11 Group RAF in the Second World War, and was promoted to Air Chief Marshal. He retired on 20 December 1946, finally returning to his native New Zealand.

No.83 (Bomber) Squadron based at Serny, France received orders to move to Hawkinge, arriving on 14 February 1919. Formed at Montrose on 7 January 1917 and equipped with F.E.2bs, they flew night bombing and reconnaissance flights. They moved to Lympne on 19 September, reduced to cadre on 15 October 1919, disbanded on 31 December 1919. A Storage Section was formed at Hawkinge on 28 November 1919, handling unwanted aircraft taken out of service or moved to another squadron. The Storage Section had thirteen Handley Page O/400s, seventeen Handley Page V/1500s, two Avro 504K aircraft and an F.E.2b.

Chapter 3

RAF Hawkinge During the 1920s
Airmail Flights

Many RAF units faced an uncertain future. No.25 Squadron, which since its formation at Montrose, Scotland, on 25 September 1915, had been sent to Europe in 1916, operating from France and Germany, and was expected to be reduced to cadre. Following the war, the RAF was depleted, its future argued over by government. Based at Bickendorf, then Merheim, Germany, in July 1919, No. 25 Squadron moved to South Carlton and finally Scopwick, Lincolnshire, on 3 December 1919 until 31 January 1920.

Wessex Area Storage Unit, the title given to the Aircraft Storage Units at Hawkinge, occupied a lot of hangar space. Aircraft arrived direct from the manufacturers and were stored until being assigned to a squadron. Each was thoroughly overhauled before leaving the airfield, collected by pilots of the squadron involved often arriving in aircraft due to be taken out of service, which remained in storage until disposed of. The Storage Section had been formed on 28 November 1919 at Hawkinge and redesignated No.25 Squadron cadre, taking on charge a selection of aircraft consisting of thirteen Handley Page O/400s, seventeen Vickers V/1500, one F.2.b and two Avro 504K aircraft. Still in possession of DH9a and Avro 504Ks, No.25 Squadron re-formed at Hawkinge on 1 February 1920, having the honour of being the first squadron to have a long association with the airfield.

It is thought that Major G.G.A. Williams, who landed at Hawkinge to refuel in October 1919, met Squadron Leader Sir Norman Leslie, who informed Williams that the Air Ministry had decided to disband fighter squadrons based in the UK, including many Depot stations, such as Hawkinge, with effect from 31 December 1919. As a result, following a period of leave, NCOs and a few other ranks were posted to Hawkinge. Squadron Leader Sir Norman Leslie became CO of No.25 Squadron, replacing Major Williams, who retired from the RAF in December 1919 due to ill health.

The idea was to secure the airfield, still with aircraft parts in the hangars and fully equipped workshops and armoury. After the war many airfields, returned to farmland, often purchased by previous owners. Maintaining a presence at Hawkinge, Squadron Leader Leslie arranged for Avro 504Ks to be flown by No.25 Squadron, one such being Avro 504 K F8794, which remained on charge until early 1926. By 26 April 1920, the squadron was equipped with Sopwith Snipe 7F.1s and experienced pilots on the type arrived as instructors. No.25 Squadron exceeded all expectations by the end of 1920. Hawkinge was a well-equipped airfield with a highly motivated fighter squadron. Of the fifteen officers, eight had the DFC, four the MC. No.25 squadron was the only home-based fighter unit.

On 24 June 1921, Flying Officer H.M. Struben was killed flying Sopwith Snipe 7F.1 E6156. At 1,500ft (1,372metres) the aircraft turned over and spun in, crashing near Folkestone during practice landings at Hawkinge. Struben was buried at St Mary and Eadburg churchyard, Hawkinge. On 24 July 1922, Flying Officer H.E. Walker MC, AFC, was seriously injured and Aircraftman 1st Class F. Kershaw killed, when Sopwith Snipe 7F.1 E6600 (a two-seat trainer), stalled and spun in off a steep turn from 2,000ft (1,829 metres) near Folkestone.

Flying Officer D.M.I. Macarthur took off on 18 January 1922 on a routine flight in Sopwith Snipe 7F.I serial E7423. At 800ft (732 metres), during a sharp turn, the engine failed, Macarthur landed in a snow-covered field near Hawkinge and overturned. The pilot escaped with minor injuries. A similar incident occurred on 18 September 1922. Flying Officer S.G. Williams flying at 1,500ft (1,372 metres) suffered engine failure over Sandgate flying Snipe 7F.I E7558, landing in the sea off Folkestone, Williams was uninjured. Onlookers were kept entertained until the aircraft was recovered, returning by road to Hawkinge. The following day, Flying Officer B.A. Davy was airborne in Snipe F2437 when the engine failed. Flying at low level, Davy landed at Hawkinge, slightly injured, his aircraft a write off.

During 1922 No.25 Squadron became part of No.1 Group RAF, its HQ situated at Kenley, Surrey. Posted overseas to assist in easing the situation between Greece and Turkey, they joined No.207 Squadron at San Stefano on 11 October 1922, returning to Hawkinge on 3 October 1923. Squadron Leader A. Hicks Peck DSO, AFC took over as CO from Squadron Leader Sir Norman R.A. Leslie BT, CBE in February 1923. Known as 'Bushell', Peck had been a successful pilot with No.11 Squadron in Palestine, his last victory being over an Albatross DIII in March 1918. Peck demanded that pilots of No.25 Squadron become experienced in close formation flying, believing this gave pilots skills needed to be a fighter pilot. Such a high standard of formation flying was dangerous, a fact brought home to pilots

RAF HAWKINGE DURING THE 1920s

The Whippet biplane G-EAGS, manufactured by Austin Motor Company during 1919, designed by John Kenworthy under licence in the First World War, visiting Hawkinge in 1924. Only five were built, two sent to New Zealand, a third to Argentina G-EAGS. Just visible in No.3 hangar, is an Avro 504k its markings are of No.17 Squadron. (C.G. Culvin)

Sopwith Snipe 7F.1 serial E6951 '9' of No.56 Squadron based at Hawkinge between November 1922 and May 1923, remaining with the unit until December 1924. (J. Jordan)

of No.25 Squadron on 15 February 1924. Flight Lieutenant G.H. Homer Scutt MC was killed flying Snipe 7F.1E7601 during formation practice, when he struck the leading aircraft while diving, crashing at Hawkinge after losing control at 500ft (152 metres).

No.56 (Punjab) Squadron was formed in 1916, based at Bekesbourne, near Canterbury, for Home Defence duties. Now at Bircham Newton they were disbanded on 22 January 1920, re-formed overseas at Aboukir, Egypt, and like No.25 Squadron, served at San Stefano until returning to England and being disbanded on 23 September 1922. They re-formed at Hawkinge on 1 November 1922. Two flights formed under command of Flight Lieutenant J.S. T Fall DSO, AFC, the adjutant Flight Lieutenant T.C. Luke MC, Flight Lieutenant C.T. McLaing MC and Flying Officer A. Jerrard VC, a celebrated pilot of the First World War. Squadron Leader I.T. Lloyd arrived from No.2 FTS on 22 November as the new CO.

Following a visit to Manston on 15 December 1922, Sopwith Snipe 7F.1E6484, collided with a Hucks starter (a vehicle used to assist start up). On 4 April 1923 Sopwith Snipe E6791 returning from practice flying, overturned and was written off, the pilot being only slightly injured. A similar accident occurred on 18 April 1923, when E6819 struck a ridge and overturned at Hawkinge. In April 1922, No.56 Squadron provided a flying display at Aldershot. Flight Lieutenant J.S.T. Fall DSC, AFC, Flying Officer J.T. Paine, and Flying Officer M.V. Ward took off for Eastchurch, where they practised away from their normal flying duties at Hawkinge; on 7 May 1923 the squadron moved to Biggin Hill as part of the Air Defence.

On 1 April 1924, No.17 Squadron reformed as 'A' Flight at Hawkinge, commanded by Squadron Leader J. Leacroft MC. Two days later, three Sopwith Snipes 7F.1s arrived at Folkestone Junction in crates and were transported to Hawkinge for assembly and test flights. In May 1924 the squadron took part with the Acoustical Section, experimenting in detecting incoming aircraft over the coast, flown by Flying Officer H.W. Taylor.

On 15 September, Pilot Officer A.D. Baillie flew Sopwith Snipe 7F.1 F2484 to Eastchurch, for a training exercise. The aircraft stalled and dived into the ground, killing the pilot. Ballie was buried at Hawkinge on 19 September. By 23 December 1924, the squadron consisted of nineteen officers, twenty-four NCOs and ORs and had three Flights. Flight Lieutenant A.W. Cuddon-Davis, flying Sopwith Snipe E6490, was killed on 24 September 1925 and given a full military burial at Shorncliffe Military Cemetery on 28 September. No.25 Squadron was notified that they were to be re-equipped with the new Gloster Grebe II, in October 1924. On 27 October,

RAF HAWKINGE DURING THE 1920s

One of the many large twin-engine biplanes which passed through the Aircraft Storage Section at Hawkinge during the 1920s. This aircraft is a Vickers Victoria III serial J7921, seen here in July 1927 during maintenance, before moving on to No.58 Squadron.

Gloster Grebe II J7409 of No.25 Squadron crashed on landing at Hawkinge during 1924. Inspecting the damage, on the left, is Leading Aircraftman Albert Moor, who remained in the RAF until retiring as Squadron Leader in 1965. He was one of many airmen whose service life began at RAF Halton, Buckinghamshire as an RAF apprentice. (Squadron Leader A. Moor)

RAF HAWKINGE

Flying Officer A.E.T. Bruce lost control of Gloster Grebe J7411, recovering from a dive with the engine cut. Attempting to land at high speed the aircraft overturned, injuring the pilot. The aircraft was repaired at Hawkinge.

Service trials with Gloster Grebe II J7283 began in September 1924 at Hawkinge. The squadron was the first front-line fighter unit to take charge of this robust, powerful biplane, fitted with the Armstrong Siddeley Jaguar IV engine, which could reach a speed of 162mph at sea level. Pilots and groundcrew were trained at Gloucestershire Aircraft Company, Hucclecote. It was not long before they got used to the Grebe and were in constant demand to perform aerobatics and formation flying throughout England. Flight Lieutenant R.J.A Ford recalls:

> I remember finding I was in great discomfort when diving from about 10,000ft or more. My ears would begin to pop. I went to the station Medical Officer who advised me to 'Pinch your nose and blow hard man!' Evidently it was the normal remedy for such a complaint. I know that I was quite speechless and left his surgery wondering how on earth I could manage to accomplish that while diving at full throttle, in a machine which possessed wing flutter, clutching the control stick with one hand and my nose in the other!
>
> *Hawkinge Airfield 1912–1961*
> R.S. Humphreys

An accident which highlighted a problem of 'wing flutter' when flying the Grebe II occurred on 27 October 1924. Pilot Officer R. Scott-Taylor, flying J7411, experienced severe oscillation when diving at high speed with two other Grebes; he crashed attempting to land at Hawkinge. The aircraft was wrecked, and the pilot injured. Gloster Grebe J7410 was also involved in an accident which occurred on 6 January 1925 – again with Flying Officer R. Scott-Taylor, who experienced 'wing flutter' during a dive; losing control he crashed on approach, the pilot not seriously injured. The Grebe II was later fitted with anti-flutter modifications.

Flying Officer J.H.C. Purvis, nephew of Sir John Gilmour, Secretary of State for Scotland, was killed on 9 December 1926, while taking part in gunnery practice over Hawkinge. The target was a large circle of white stones marked out in a field close by; the Grebe crashed at Terlingham Farm. Bursting into flames, farm workers rushed to the aid of Purvis, but he died on impact. The news of his nephew's death reached him during a debate in the House of Commons concerning the increased number of deaths in the RAF.

RAF HAWKINGE DURING THE 1920s

Right: Following a crash landing in a crosswind at Hawkinge in May 1929, Armstrong Whitworth Siskin IIIA J9312 of No.25 Squadron, was later taken to the hangars where it was repaired, moving on to No.56 Squadron the same month.

Below: FO J.H.C. Purvis No.25 Squadron killed on 9 December 1926 during air to ground firing over the airfield at Hawkinge. Gloster Grebe II J7384 crashed near Terlingham Manor Farm.

RAF HAWKINGE

An eyewitness account of the crash involving Gloster Grebe J7384 stated that the pilot was performing a series of half rolls or stalled turns to left and right. On almost the last one before straightening out, another Grebe appeared below him; trying to avoid this aircraft, he struck the ground.

Gloster Grebe 1 J7412 was involved in an accident on 17 November 1924. During gun camera practice, the aircraft flew into the garden wall of a house on the brow of a hill near Hawkinge, and Flying Officer L.E. Maynard was seriously injured. On 13 June 1927, Flying Officer L.A. Walsh, in J7581, ran onto tarmac landing at Hawkinge colliding with J7402, piloted by Flying Officer R.J.A. Ford who was unhurt. Walsh was again involved in an accident, during a mock dogfight over Capel near Folkestone on 17 February 1928, when two Gloster Grebes collided. Flying Officer L.A. Walsh, flying J7372, parachuted safely, Pilot Officer E.J. Watson was killed flying J7392; both aircraft were wrecked. No.25 Squadron flew Grebes longer than other units: the Grebe IIIDC a two-seat trainer, served with the squadron from July 1925 until April 1926. Conversion to the unpopular Siskin IIIA commenced during December 1928; over a period of five months, pilots and groundcrew grudgingly became used to the aircraft.

Pilot Officer W.K. 'Bike' Beisiegel still in his flying gear on the right, had a narrow escape during 1927, when on landing at Hawkinge Gloster Grebe II K7292 flipped over. This aircraft was repaired and flew with No.29 Squadron. (C.G. Gulvin)

RAF HAWKINGE DURING THE 1920s

In 1925 No.17 Squadron, still based at Hawkinge and flying the Snipe, began training in night flying, not popular with pilots as forward view was restricted. On 25 March 1926 No.17 Squadron was equipped with the Hawker Woodcock II, although a few Snipes lingered on. The Squadron moved to Upavon.

Squadron Leader A.H. Peck DSO, MC, remained with the squadron until September 1926 and was followed by Squadron Leader E.D. Atkinson DFC, AFC. It was Squadron Leader W.H. 'Porky' Park MC, DFC, who had the greatest impact on the squadron's fortunes, arriving at Hawkinge in April 1927. Squadron Leader Park was a popular CO with a light-hearted approach; his greatest attribute was his ability to spot fledgling pilots with instinctive flying skills, and he would also encourage those less confident pilots. Park was well known for inviting local dignitaries and their wives for drinks at the Officers' Mess, thus gaining support from the local population living close to an extremely noisy and active airfield. Mostly he was popular because he led from the front, often taking part in formation flying. Despite being an accomplished pilot, he often had problems landing, fortunately without major incident. Park was admitted to Shorncliffe Military Hospital, Folkestone on 6 September 1928 and died on 19 October 1928 following an emergency operation. Park had requested that, on his demise, his much-loved bullnose Morris car be buried at Hawkinge. Legend has it that the car was buried close to the landing 'Tee'. As a final tribute to their CO, the squadron's Grebes formed in a square facing outwards and their guns opened fire. Squadron Leader L.G.S. Payne MC, AFC became CO of No.25 Squadron in September 1928. It was during his command that the squadron re-equipped with the Armstrong Siddeley Siskin. Flying Officer L.A. Walsh was again involved in an accident, during a mock dogfight over Capel near Folkestone on 17 February 1928, when two Gloster Grebes collided. Flying Officer Walsh flying J7372 parachuted safely, Pilot Officer E.J. Watson was killed flying J7392, both aircraft wrecked.

No.25 Squadron flew Grebes longer than other units, the Grebe IIIDC, a two-seat trainer, served with the squadron from July 1925 until April 1926. Formation flying was continually practised. On 18 February 1929, a Siskin IIIA, flown by Sergeant J.W. Pearce, left formation, and crashed on a sports field in Folkestone, the aircraft overturned killing the pilot.

Under the command of Air Chief Marshal Sir John Maitland Salmond, GCB, CMG, CVO, DSO & Bar, who in 1930 replaced ACM Sir Hugh Trenchard GCB, OM, GCVO, DSO, the Air Defence of Great Britain

RAF HAWKINGE

The remains of Gloster Grebe II J7392 which collided with J7372 over Capel, near Folkestone on 17 February 1928. Flying Officer L.A. Walsh baled out of J7392, Flying Officer E.J. Watson was killed when he failed to clear J7372. (C.G. Gulvin)

The Kings Cup race held at Heston on 5–7 July 1929 was won by a twin seater Gloster Grebe II J7520 of No.25 Squadron flown by Flying Officer R.L.R. Atcherley and Flight Lieutenant G.H. Stainforth Navigator, at a speed of 150mph (241kph). This aircraft joined the squadron in July 1925.

RAF HAWKINGE DURING THE 1920s

(ADGB) was reorganised. No.25 Hawkinge, No.1 and No.43 Squadrons Tangmere, became the spearhead of the RAF Air Defence, others were based at Biggin Hill, Kenley, Hornchurch and North Weald. No.25 Squadron still flew the Siskin 111A, the other units were re-equipped with the Bristol Bulldog. Despite this, morale was high, everyone was pleased with the new officers' and sergeants' mess recently completed. Other developments included workshops, and new sick quarters were also to follow on the expanding airfield.

On 25 March 1926 No.17 Squadron was equipped with the Hawker Woodcock II, although a few Snipes lingered on, No.17 Squadron moved to Upavon.

LAC L.H. Weeks No.25 Squadron at Hawkinge pauses for the camera during maintenance on an Armstrong Whitworth Siskin IIIA. This type replaced the squadrons Gloster Grebe IIA in May 1929. (L.H. Weeks)

Chapter 4

The Halcyon Days of 1930s
Gliding, Summer Camps, and Training

An Army Cooperation exercise took place on 8 August 1930 and No.25 Squadron was involved in a mock attack on troops of the 167th Infantry Brigade at Falmer, Sussex. Tragically Sergeant O.H. McNair was killed when his Siskin IIIA J9325 stalled in a steep turn at low level and crashed. In October 1930, Squadron Leader H.M. Probyn DFC replaced Squadron Leader R.S. Aitkin MC, AFC, who had been with the squadron for ten months. Nicknamed 'Daddy', Probyn was a strict disciplinarian who remained CO for two years. His prized possession was Westland Widgeon G-EBRQ, in which he won the Grosvenor Trophy race in 1928 and had flown in the Kings Cup Race of 1929, taking 12th place. It was in this

RAF Hawkinge during 1932, by when the airfield had expanded greatly. Note the chalk landing circle, a common sight on most RAF airfields of the period. Left of centre stands No.4 hangar later destroyed by fire in 1933. (Squadron Leader D. A. 'Max' Upton)

THE HALCYON DAYS OF 1930s

machine during the Army Cooperation exercises, and not his usual Siskin IIIA, that he led the squadron in a Formation Battle Climb, the manoeuvre to maximise the width of the formation so that the outer wing men can reduce the blind spot behind each aircraft. The outer wing pilots covered the rear of the formation and their opposite number on the other side of the formation.

It had been rumoured in April 1930 that No.25 Squadron, with two other units, would soon re-equip with the Hawker Fury I, but due to restrictions of the defence budget the changeover did not take place until February 1932.

Little civil aviation took place at Hawkinge in the 1930s. However, gliding was very popular, and in June 1930 the Channel Gliding Club was formed. The president was Sir Philip Sassoon CBE, CMG, MP, Secretary of State for Air, who owned and flew his own aircraft – a DH Puss Moth G-ACLW, later a DH90 Dragon Fly G-AEDE. Colonel H.T.H. Kenny was the Chairman, F.H. Worral, a local watchmaker and jeweller, with a shop in Folkestone, was Secretary. No.25 Squadron took a keen interest in the club, one of the instructors was Major C.M.C. Turner, who lived in a windmill at St Margaret's Bay.

Westland Widgeon III G-EBRQ owned and flown by Squadron Leader H.M. Probyn, CO of No.25 Squadron Hawkinge from October 1930 until February 1932, in which he led the squadron during the weekly battle flight. (Air Cdre. H.M. Probyn CB, CBE, DSO)

RAF HAWKINGE

Flight Lieutenant J.C.M. Stewart had written an article in the local paper about gliding and the newly formed club. With public interest in aviation already at a high during of the 1930s, gliding added to their interest and support. Squadron Leader H.M. Probyn DSO, Flying Officer F. Read No.25 Squadron and Norman Derham, a Channel swimmer, were also members. The club flew gliders from fields leased to them by Alfred Aird, on the Downs above Folkestone. One of the gliders a Zogling or RFD Primary, later known as the Manuel Crested Wren sailplane, and designed by Corporal W.B. 'Bill' Manuel No.25 Squadron was built at The Danes, Creteway Downs in 1932.

Several of this type were built during the time Corporal Manuel was a member of the club at Hawkinge. He constructed a replica of the Octave Channel glider (named after the early American aviator Octave Chanute 1893–1910) while with No.25 Squadron during 1927, which he successfully flew. Manuel had formed the link with Hawkinge and the club in 1929, becoming the club's instructor during 1932 and 1933. He was the ideal person for the job, having already designed gliders while with No.25 Squadron at Hawkinge. He often scrounged scrapped aircraft parts, such as a DH4s wing struts, cut to size, using woodworking machinery in a locked hangar, much to the bafflement of the Station Warrant Officer. Construction took place at Terlingham Manor Farm, on completion the

Following some modifications, the Manuel VII Primary, the first glider to be constructed and flown at Hawkinge airfield, finally took to the air. On one occasion a Siskin, chocked up with its engine running, blasted the glider into the air. (W.B. Manuel)

THE HALCYON DAYS OF 1930s

door of the barn had to be removed to take the glider out. Bill made his first flight on 18 May 1929, from the Downs at Newington, Postling, which became the launch site for the Channel Gliding Club. Visitors included Miss Winifred Spooner, who flew Sir Sefton Brancker, Minister of Civil Aviation to Hawkinge, and flew the No.7 Manuel Primary. Bill gained his licence No.111 with the British Gliding Association on 19 January 1931, in one of the club's gliders, a Dagling. He was posted away from Hawkinge in 1933, later assisting with tuition at the Cinque Ports Flying Club in 1937, offering gliding lessons and auto-launching using an Austin 10. Which, believe it or not, was found in a shed at Dane Farm during the 1970s – the shed was used for storing the club's gliders.

Channel Gliding Club Member Flight Lieutenant Read competed in the Daily Express Cup, flying the Manuel VII Primary Glider. Herr Kronfield, the Austrian Glider Ace, was invited to England for the event, an opportunity to promote his Kronfield glider which he designed and built and christened 'Vien' after the city of Vienna. He would take off from the Valiant Sailor pub, pass over Caesars Camp and Sugarloaf Hill near Paddlesworth, remaining airborne for 3½ hours. Hawkinge often

The Daily Express glider and its pilot, a Frenchman, M. Magasoupe with his 'Falke' glider at a meeting sponsored by the newspaper at Home Farm, near Folkestone in July 1930. RAF personnel from Hawkinge willingly volunteered to assist in the event. The Channel Gliding Club had been formed the previous year. (W.S. Manuel)

received phone calls from him checking on weather conditions. During his stay in Kent, he addressed the Channel Gliding Club at the Queens Hotel in Folkestone and visited the gliding club ground with members of the British Glider Association. On 15 July 1938, Peter Davis arrived at Hawkinge airfield in a Rhonalder sailplane during the National Gliding Contests, following a flight of ninety-six miles from Dunstable Downs. In April 1939 G.H. Stevenson in a Slingsby Kirby Kite, flew over the club's grounds, crossing from Folkestone to Calais on route for a record-breaking flight from Dunstable to Boulogne. When war was declared the club closed and did not reopen, but in 1984 the Channel Gliding Club reappeared, having been formed by a former RAF pilot, John Salt, and his wife, who started a motor-glider school and club at Waldershare Park, near Dover, where it can be found today.

After Bank Holiday on 7 August 1930, No.600 (County of London) Squadron RAuxAF moved to Hawkinge from their base at Hendon for Summer Camp. An Advance Party arrived in the morning commanded by Flight Lieutenant Maygothling. With many of their officers from wealthy backgrounds, such as Lord Carlow, the squadron was known as 'The Gentlemen in Blue'. The following day, Hawker Demon Is arrived between 1540hrs and 1730hrs. At 2030hrs that evening, a Road Party with Pilot Officer Maclachlan in charge, arrived with a convoy of trucks.

The squadron comprised of thirty-three regular airmen, five attached for the duration of the camp, and 106 Auxiliary airmen. Officers and other ranks messed in bell tents; although officers had individual tents, the airmen shared tents with a maximum of five men in each. Their biplanes shared No.25 Squadron's hangar. They soon settled in, the following day they set to work preparing and inspecting aircraft and clearing up the stores. On 10 August, while 'A' Flight commenced gunnery practice at Lydd Ranges, Sir Phillip Sassoon arrived in his own aircraft to inspect the squadron.

Rivalry between squadrons of the Royal Auxiliary Air Force, although friendly, was intense. None more so than that of No.601 (County of London) and No.600 (City of London) Squadrons, particularly during the 1930s. Both squadrons felt they should take part in off-duty activities to make life uncomfortable for each other. No.601 Squadron, then at Lympne for Summer Camp, decided to stage a mock bombing attack on No.600 Squadron on Hawkinge, dropping various types of items such as balloons containing milk and soot and flower, even crabs and dead rabbits! With No.601 based at Hawkinge and No.601 at Lympne, opportunities for 'cunning attacks' were frequent. Once when No.600 was at a party in

THE HALCYON DAYS OF 1930s

Folkestone, sheep went missing from Romney Marsh and reappeared in the tents of No.601 Squadron! In retaliation No.600 entered Lympne airfield at night, waited until all lamps went out, and carefully removed all the guy ropes and pegs from the Bell tents. The rivalry continued during the 1930s, even making the national newspapers. One evening during summer camp of 1936, Flight Lieutenant Campbell-Orde No.601 Squadron flew his Hawker Hart from Hawkinge to Lympne; having served with both squadrons he was on good terms with officers of No.600 Squadron. He was plied with drinks, then tied up, his uniform pockets stuffed with fish. Notices adorned his aircraft, such as – 'To and from the boat race' and 'This way to the zoo'. He was flown back to Hawkinge in a private aircraft, and dumped in the middle of the airfield. Flight Lieutenant R. Davies flew his Hart back from Lympne but tipped it up on its nose.

No.601 put every aircraft in the air, bombed tents at Hawkinge with bags of soot and flower, bad eggs, fruit, fish, and potato peelings etc. Attacks ended when they had painted the tents, hanging stockings at the entrance of each, filled with treacle and manure. Both Commanding Officers were summoned by the AOC (Air Officer Commanding). After hearing their accounts, he advised that the matter was now settled to the relief of both COs. However, it is recorded that the feud between the two squadrons continued well into the 1950s.

The Aircraft Storage Section (ASS) at Hawkinge accepted many aircraft ferried to them for disposal. Pilot Officer M. George Warrington RAFVR had been volunteered to fly DH9A J8491 to Hawkinge on 7 November 1930. This aircraft had flown with No.501 (County of Gloucester) Squadron since May 1927, and was one of twelve DH9s, J8483 to J8494, being replaced by Westland Wapitis biplanes, for No.501 Squadron. Pilot Officer Warrington took off from Filton, the weather was fine until approaching the Kent coast, when he met heavy mist.

At 1300hrs he arrived over the area and made his approach, but hit a haystack at Terlingham Farm and somersaulted, catching fire. Warrington was thrown clear, his parachute breaking his fall so he was not seriously injured. The fire tender at Hawkinge was immediately dispatched. The whole front part of the DH9A was destroyed while two hay ricks caught fire when petrol tanks exploded after the crash. A farm worker standing near the rick leaped out of the path of the crashing DH9 but was uninjured.

A Searchlight Tattoo was held at Folkestone football ground on 7 August 1931, a display by the military. Adding to the evening's entertainment, Pilot

RAF HAWKINGE

Vickers Virginia VI J7716 'Y', one of many aircraft which passed through the Aircraft Storage Unit (ASU) at Hawkinge in February 1930. After leaving the ASU, this aircraft was transferred to No.9 Squadron, where it served from June 1930 until February 1932.

Officer Dennis G. Vaughan-Fowler, flew a Siskin III adorned with light bulbs. Returning to Hawkinge the Siskin's engine developed a problem: landing without any power the aircraft flipped over and burst into flames, killing the pilot.

Sergeant R.H.H. Ross No.25 Squadron, taking off in Siskin IIIA J8629 collided with J8632 at Hawkinge on 22 October 1931, the aircraft was a write-off, but he and the other pilot Flying Officer B.W. Knox escaped from their machines unhurt. On 29 October 1931, Lieutenant A. Sucharitkul, born in Siam, lost his life during air-to-ground firing practice at Hawkinge in Siskin IIIA J8881. He had taken evasive action to avoid a collision with another aircraft, he stalled and spun to his death from 700ft (640 metres), crashing into the side of a hill near Folkestone. (This was the last fatal crash involving the Siskins of No.25 Squadron.)

Following German night raids on London in September 1917, it became essential that some means of detecting the bombers' approach was developed. To this end, large concrete spherical dishes were built into the cliffs at Joss Gap, Kingsgate, in Thanet and at Fan Hole, just to the north of Dover Castle. In September 1926 a detachment of the night flying No.56 Squadron was based at Hawkinge to assist in these trials. By 1931 various types of bowls and dishes were constructed around the Kent coast,

THE HALCYON DAYS OF 1930s

at Hythe Greatstone and Lydd. In 1931 these 'sound mirrors' were tested during the Air Defence of Great Britain exercises held in June and July each year. These were manned by the Royal Engineers, responsible for their design and erection, together with newly trained personnel from various RAF units. RAF personnel helped man the mirrors and the control room. One of them, Warrant Officer Sydney Scamp, was serving with No.3 at Upavon, Wiltshire, although his family lived in Folkestone:

> I was pleased to be sent down from Wiltshire to Hawkinge in the summer of 1931 as my home was at Folkestone. Each morning we were taken from Hawkinge to one of the sites, or to the Plotting Room where there was a large table-top map showing the coasts of France and England and the position of the mirrors.
>
> *Kents Listening Ears*
> D.G. Collyer

Bristol Bulldog IIA K2165 of No.54 Squadron, then based at Hornchurch, is seen here at Hawkinge circa 1932, also served with No.19 Squadron at Duxford. (W. Solley)

RAF HAWKINGE

Although microphone equipment mounted in the 200ft (183 metres) long dish at Greatstone could deal with the most difficult engine sounds, details of foreign engines had to be studied carefully. The success of the mirror depended on an understanding of the acoustic properties of aircraft engines. If sound characteristics of a particular engine were known, it was possible to tune the listening microphones to respond to the notes of that engine. Discrimination between the sounds of different engine types would be important in a war situation. If the detection equipment was tuned to respond to the sound of friendly aircraft, it could be assumed that other engine notes came from hostile aircraft.

At a meeting between officers of the ADGB and the Engineers Board in January 1934, Dr Tucker, mastermind behind the experiments, requested the use of aircraft with Rolls-Royce Kestrel engines as their notes gave peculiar scope for study. Hawkinge, only a few miles from the Hythe Acoustic Research Station, was used from time to time by RAF aircraft participating in the exercises. Following Dr Tucker's request, Hawker Harts with Rolls-Royce Kestrel engines were provided, but on this occasion, aircraft were to be based at Manston, because Hawkinge was considered not suitable for two squadrons equipped with a fast type of aircraft over a long period.

During the Air Defence Exercises of 1933, Flying Officer Burke and Flying Officer Nelson, along with fifteen airmen, operated the four existing coastal sound mirrors, five raids by formations of day bombers and seven-night raids were reported. The smaller mirrors were used to give warning and sound bearings up to 10 miles (16 km), while the 200ft (183 metres) mirror was intended to give ranges of up to 25 miles (40 km). Training was undertaken on 26 June until 14 July for five days a week using aircraft from No.9 Squadron at Manston (Vickers Virginias), No.25 Squadron at Hawkinge (Hawker Furies), No.32 Squadron at Biggin Hill (Bristol Bulldogs) as well as Southampton Flying Boats from No.210 Squadron.

No.602 (City of Glasgow) Squadron RAuxAF began their Summer Camp and training at Hawkinge on 15 July 1932, remaining at the airfield until 29 July. During the month the squadron took part in the ADGB (Air Defence of Great Britain) exercise. Of the twenty-one Squadrons which were to form the RAuxAF, No.602 Squadron was the first unit to hold its Summer Camp at Hawkinge in 1931. Based at Renfrew, Scotland, it was a welcome change to relocate for a few weeks. During their stay they took part in the 1931 Air Exercise and Annual Training – they were still flying the Westland Wapati. No.602 Squadron comprised of three flights: 'A'

THE HALCYON DAYS OF 1930s

Right: LAC A. Moor seated centre, during a break from maintenance duties with No.25 Squadron, in the background is a Hawker Fury I close to the squadron hangar. (Squadron Leader A. Moor)

Below: LAC Albert Moor, on the left, with colleagues of No.25 Squadron Hawkinge. Behind them is Hawker Fury I K2079 delivered to the squadron on 31 March 1933. On 3 September 1936, this aircraft force-landed in fog near Canterbury, when its undercarriage collapsed. (Squadron Leader A. Moor)

RAF HAWKINGE

Flight commanded by Lieutenant James Lennox, 'B' Flight commanded by Wing Commander D. Mcintyre AFC, and 'C' Flight commanded by Squadron Leader Clydesdale, Marquess of Clydesdale (he later became CO of the squadron in 1931); they returned in July 1932 for Summer Camp. Clydesdale was highly respected and delighted in leading the whole squadron down to zero feet on cross-country flights to read railway station nameboards, to get his bearings. His reputation was enhanced by often landing in fields to relieve himself in local woodland.

During Summer Camp in July 1932, the whole squadron was airborne from Hawkinge. On the ground, fitters and riggers waited, listening anxiously to the sound of aircraft circling above a mist, then landing 'blind'. LAC John F. Davies remembers:

> Eventually all except one came down safely, the pilot of this machine made several attempts to land, but always at the last moment, apparently unable to judge accurately his height, he roared off again into the white void. Our CO stood for some time at the edge of the tarmac apron in front of the hangar, and then grimly strode to his aircraft, started up, and took off into the mist. Some minutes later we faintly discerned the CO's machine leading in the other pilot, with the aircraft almost nose to tail, and there was a general feeling of relief when they both touched down safely.
>
> *Lions Rampant*
> Douglas McRoberts

In 1931–32 a decision was made to re-equip three fighter squadrons with the Hawker Fury I, an expensive aircraft costing £5,000. Their use was restricted to units based in the south. Nos.1, 25 and 43 squadrons would take on charge some sixty to seventy of this delightful new fighter biplane, the lucky three squadrons selected being based at Hawkinge and Tangmere. On 23 April February 1931, No.25 Squadron received the news that the squadron's first Commanding Officer Major F.V. Holt DSO, RFC (1915–16) had been involved in a mid-air collision between a Siskin of No.43 Squadron, giving a display at Tangmere, and a civilian Tiger Moth, wreckage fell on spectators, a few being injured and killed.

The Under Secretary for Air, Sir Philip Sassoon Bart, CBE, CMG, MP visited Hawkinge, taking a keen interest in the aircraft. He witnessed an accident when Pilot Officer F.P.R. Dunworth flying in formation in

THE HALCYON DAYS OF 1930s

Hawker Furys of No.25 Squadron, the nearest being K2078 joined in 12 January 1933, and K2053 a year earlier on 20 February 1932. (W. Smith)

Fury K2057 collided with K2055. Dunworth parachuted successfully. Hawker Fury K2057 crashed near Hawkinge at Sugar Loaf Hill and K2055 managed to crash land at Hawkinge. Pilot Officer 'Jock' Ross, who returned from Brooklands in his new Fury I, arrived over Hawkinge and decided to show off the aircraft, commencing with slow rolls, but hadn't allowed enough altitude, a common mistake. Managing to complete 2½ rolls, he landed inverted in front of his colleagues, casually dropping out of the cockpit and walking away unscathed. Ross was court-martialled for this offence and grounded, the incident being a serious breach of King's Regulations.

Other duties undertaken by No.25 at Hawkinge during 1931 involved cooperating with Hythe Small Arms School, occasionally giving converging Bombing Demonstration (without bombs) and Line Ahead attacks to students at the school. Another exercise involved carrying out fighter attacks on Supermarine Southampton flying boats of No.201 Squadron. No.25 moved to Gosport on 4 May 1931, returning to Hawkinge on 16 May 1931.

Above: Empire Air Day 1932 at Hawkinge. This Handley Page Hinaidi while with the ASU outside, attracted much attention from the visiting public.

Left: Hawker Furys of No.25 Squadron being prepared for their participation in the RAF Hendon Display which took place on 24 June 1932. (Squadron Leader A. Moor)

THE HALCYON DAYS OF 1930s

Hawker Fury I K2057 of No.25 Squadron May 1932. This aircraft collided with another Fury I K2055 during formation flying on 14 July 1932. The pilot of K2057 Flying Officer F.P.R. Dunworth parachuted safely. Seated in the cockpit is Aircraftman 1st Class A. Moor No.25 Squadron. Note the side panel has been removed for easy access during maintenance. (Squadron Leader A. Moor)

Hawker Fury I K2057, which crashed following the mid-air collision on 14 July 1932. The location is thought to be near Sugar Loaf Hill, Folkestone, on the North Downs. Such events attracted many onlookers. An RAF Corporal chats to locals, prior to a recovery team from Hawkinge arriving. (Squadron Leader A. Moor)

RAF HAWKINGE

The squadron attracted several well-known pilots, one being Flying Officer A.E. Clouston, later Air Commodore CB, DSO, DFC, AFC, and bar. Clouston was New Zealander, and had arrived in England in 1930, joining the RAF and eventually arriving at Hawkinge on 07 April 1931. Clouston was accepted for experimental flying at Farnborough and later awarded the AFC. He became famous for record-breaking flights in the 1930s flying the DH Comet racer 'The Orphan', renamed 'The Burberry' G-ACSS, with Mrs Betty Kirby-Green, taking-off from Croydon for the Cape on 14 November 1937, breaking the record in the time of 45hrs 2 minutes.

> I was posted to No.25 Squadron Hawkinge, generally accepted as one of the elites; and apart from our normal routine, we were regularly called upon for flypasts and aerial salutes on special

A Hawker Fury of No.25 Squadron K2059, taxies out for take-off during an Empire Day display, with hundreds of keen spectators looking on. (D. Rolfe)

THE HALCYON DAYS OF 1930s

ceremonial occasions such as the opening of Speke Airport, and the unveiling of the R.101 memorial at Le Bourget. At the Hendon Air Display we performed the tied-together loop of nine aircraft. We spent five months rehearsing this manoeuvre of supreme co-ordination. It was a tricky business. The pilot's safety depended not only upon his own meticulous flying and split-second timing, but upon the same qualities from each of his colleagues. A slight misjudgement by one man could easily cause a mid-air crash of every aircraft in the formation. It was not the human mistake that we feared, however, so much as the unexpected bump caused by air-pocket or thermal current. With the aircraft linked together, the effects of such a bump were to send them converging into one another. This happened in the early days of our preparation. We had begun by practising in flights of three aircraft. My own flight was roped together upside-down at the top of the loop when a bump sent the aircraft on my left slithering in towards me.

We had no time to check the movement before the wing hit my propeller. Out of the corner of my eye I saw the starboard aircraft bank away unharmed, as I gazed with horror at the wing of the other aircraft. Taking what seemed an incredible time, it slowly buckled up and broke away from the fuselage, which promptly dropped like a stone. I had no time to watch it though, for half my propeller had gone and the ailerons waggled about freely without sufficient slipstream force upon them to bring any reaction on the aircraft. I was stuck upside-down. Still lying on my back, I kicked the rudder hard over. This coarse use of the rudder still produced some effect. The aircraft began to skid round in a flat turn, and then the drag of the wing came into operation, twisting the machine over, so that I was right way up once more. Holding her like that, I glided down and managed to reach the aerodrome. At Hendon everything went beautifully. The tied-together loop and the tied-together rolls in formation, which had never been previously performed, were the highlight of the display. The perfection of co-ordination, however, had been achieved only at the cost of months of rehearsal, and we had no casualties.

The Dangerous Skies
Air Commodore A.E. Clouston

RAF HAWKINGE

During a mock dog-fight Flight Lieutenant Clouston had to make a forced landing due to fuel starvation. Some five miles away from Hawkinge, he noticed a rugby field at Folkestone, and landed successfully. Hawkinge was immediately notified, and within half an hour a mechanic arrived. Checking for any damage, and finding no significant repairs required, fuel arrived courtesy of a local garage. Clouston returned to the airfield without any further problems.

No.504 (County of Nottingham) Squadron held their first Summer Camp at Hawkinge, arriving on 2 August 1931 with ten Hawker Horsley aircraft. On 11/12 August, Group Captain Edmonds and Squadron Leader Baker flew to Eastchurch for Gunnery and Bombing practice. The squadron remained at Hawkinge, returning to Hucknall on 15 August 1931. Having completed a training exercise at Filton on 21 August 1932, an advance party from No.504 Squadron set off for Hawkinge. Familiar with the airfield, they were joined by twelve Horsley and three Avro 504K aircraft. There followed two days of air firing and bombing exercises at Lydd Ranges. On completion they were visited by The Right Honourable Sir Philip Sassoon 3rd Baronet, GBE, CMG Under Secretary of State for Air, who lived at Lympne Place, close to the airfield. Sir Jeffrey Salmond KCB, KCMG, DSO, arrived by air from Lympne to inspect the squadron in his role as CO Air Defence of Great Britain (ADGB).

During 1933 the area surrounding the hangars at Hawkinge was a hive of activity, as office extensions were well underway. New barrack blocks, messes and sick quarters replaced existing wooden buildings. No.504 Squadron, back at Hucknall, still equipped with Hawker Horsley I biplanes, arrived at Hawkinge on 31 July 1933 for Summer Camp. On 7 August Hawker Horsley J8025 flown by Flight Lieutenant Hartridge, overshot the runway when landing. Unfortunately, the Horsley carried out a perfect landing on top of No.4 hangar. Both airmen climbed out of the aircraft and descended from the roof by a maintenance ladder. The Horsley's fuel tank had ruptured, and the escaping fuel ignited. Despite the best efforts of the station's fire tender and Folkestone Fire Brigade, the fire took hold.

Due to the quick response of airmen, there were no injuries or fatalities, they managed to haul a nearby fuel bowser away from inferno. The hangar housed six Fleet Air Arm Blackburn Darts, but the press reported that six Hawker Harts were destroyed. When the both Flight and Aviation magazines heard of the fire, they assumed the aircraft were Furys and, acting on this, the Air Ministry ordered six replacement Hawker Furys – the mistake was

THE HALCYON DAYS OF 1930s

The aftermath of the disaster on 31 July 1933 when Hawker Horsley J8035 crashed on the roof of No.4 Hangar. It was a miracle that nobody was killed.

A scene of destruction, No.4 Hangar caught fire when Flight Lieutenant Hartridge No.504 (County of Nottingham) Squadron RAuxAF, crashed Hawker Horsley J8025 onto the roof on 7 August 1933. Both pilot and observer climbed from the wreckage uninjured.

discovered and the contract with Hawker Aircraft Co. Ltd swiftly cancelled. The Chief Engineer of the construction company was behind schedule due to pressure of work, much to his surprise he was instructed to clear the site and No.4 hangar – which was never rebuilt.

In May 1933, Empire Day was celebrated at airfields throughout the UK, Hawkinge opened its gates to crowds eager to see the flying. Some 2,000 spectators arrived and Flight Lieutenant Clouston and Flight Lieutenant Dainty performed an excellent display of aerobatics. Squadron Leader A. Paxton led a flight of nine Hawker Furys. Each Fury was tied together by a bungee, secured to upper and lower rear inter-plane wing-strut. Two lengths of cord were tied to the middle of the bungee, the end of the cords joined 6ft of kite cord, with flags sewn on the cord. Flying consisted of loops and barrel rolls, flown in a 'V' of nine aircraft, the finale was the Prince of Wales feather (Fleurs- de-lis), when each Fury broke away in various directions.

On 17 July 1933, No.33 (B) Squadron left North Coates for Hawkinge to take part in the Air Defence of Great Britain Command Exercise.

The British public, always fascinated by flying, admiring Hawker Furys of No.25 Squadron. On the left K2059, which taxied into Armstrong Siddeley Siskin J9177 on 21 March 1932 at Hawkinge.

THE HALCYON DAYS OF 1930s

Hawker Fury's of No.25 Squadron taxi out to perform aerobatics and low flying above the seated crowds during Empire Day Hawkinge during the 1930s, the leading aircraft is K2079. (W. Smith)

A regular visitor to Hawkinge was Jeffrey Jordan, who with his father and brother had a keen interest in aviation. The line-up consists of Hawker Fury Is K2041, K2882, K2068 and K2059 – an 'aircraft spotter's' idea of heaven. (J. Jordan)

RAF HAWKINGE

No.504 Squadron returned to Hucknall on 14 August 1933 on completion of their Summer Camp. No.25 Squadron's first performance of aerobatics at the Hendon Air Pageant had taken place in 1925, flying the Gloster Grebe Is. Under the command of Squadron Leader A.H. Peck, they were dubbed by the press as 'Pecks Bad Boys', for their daring aerobatics. Squadron Leader A.L. Paxton DFC took over as CO in February 1933. No.25 Squadron also gave impressive displays at other venues, such as Liverpool Airport and Lympne airfield during 1935.

Vickers Virginia X K2323, originally having been delivered to Hawkinge on 18 August 1931 and taken on charge by No.502 (Ulster) Squadron RAuxAF on 9 February 1932, returned to Hawkinge for storage, or 'reduction to produce' as it was known in the RAF, being flown from Aldergrove by Wing Commander Russell and Flying Officer U.Y. Shannon. Between 1931 and 1936, thirty-eight Virginia Xs passed through Hawkinge, many returning to Aircraft Storage Unit (ASU) Hawkinge for eventual scrapping or sale. Other Virginia types, such as the IA, V, VI, VII were handled by the ASU at Hawkinge during the 1930s, replaced by new biplanes coming

LAC Tong and Hawker Fury I K2079 at Hawkinge during May 1934. This aircraft remained in service until 1936 when scrapped. Note the hangars or General Service Aeroplane Repair Sheds in the background, which dated back to the days of the RFC. (Squadron Leader A. Moor)

THE HALCYON DAYS OF 1930s

into service with the fast-expanding new RAF and RAuxAF squadrons. No.504 Squadron proceeded again to Hawkinge with nine Westland Wallace Is on 22 July 1934, for bombing training and a simulated attack on London. Nine aircraft proceeded to the target on 24 July, via Whitstable and Hatfield, returning to Hawkinge via Selsey Bill. For the next few days Air Firing and Bombing exercises took place at Eastchurch, the squadron returning to Hucknall on 4 August.

Training Camp was commenced on 4 August 1934. No.504 Squadron looked forward to their return to Hawkinge, a regular event on the calendar. They liaised with No.25 Squadron for Gun Camera exercises, the photographs taken being found of great value to the squadron. Individual Air Navigation exercises took place in cooperation with No.2 (cadre squadron). Night Air Bombing Exercises were carried out, following which the squadron returned to Hucknall.

No.33 (B) Squadron at Upper Heyford was the first RAF squadron to fly the Hawker Hart. On 7 May 1935, Sergeant Crawley and Leading Aircraftman Med were detached to Hawkinge with their own maintenance crew to cooperate in acoustical mirror exercises. They returned to Upper Heyford on 28 May 1935. Many such Air Defence exercises were

In 1934 Handley Page Hinaidi K1075 'Y' of No.99 Squadron, was hit by K1073 at Upper Heyford while parked, and sent to No.2 Aircraft Storage Unit (ASU) Hawkinge.

undertaken by units based at Hawkinge during this period, including Army Cooperation exercises using the Lydd ranges for gunnery training.

No.2 (Army Cooperation) Squadron were based at Manston from 27 October 1927 until 30 November 1935. They flew the Armstrong Whitworth Atlas from July 1933 until shortly before moving to Hawkinge, re-equipped with the Hawker Audax I, commanded by Squadron Leader N.L. Desoer and later Squadron Leader W.A. Opie. In November 1935, a road party of vehicles and equipment arrived at Hawkinge and made their way to No.3 hangar. Army Cooperation squadrons worked with Army ground units, infantry artillery and tanks. Their function was to advise the Army of enemy ground force movements and positions, and bombing enemy positions.

On 21 April 1936, Audax K3055, flown by Acting Pilot Officer P.F. Edinger No.2 Squadron, came into land at Hawkinge, from Manston. The aircraft overshot, struck trees, and crashed. Edinger although injured soon recovered, returning to active service but was killed in action over Germany, 8 September 1941. On Saturday 23 May 1936, an air display took place a Hawkinge as part of the Empire Day celebrations.

The day ended in tragedy when Hawker Audax I K3718 No.2 (Army Cooperation) Squadron based at Hawkinge, struck power cables, over the Folkestone Canterbury Road. Flight Lieutenant A.J.W. Geddes saw the display in which aircraft simulated a low-level attack on guns at Hawkinge. One performance started at 1430hrs and finished at 1515hrs; the gunners were firing blank cartridges. A second attack started at 1718hrs when the flight took off. They carried out a mock attack to show how a surprise attack might be launched. Having completed the first, they flew away and prepared for another; it was when returning that the accident happened.

Geddes was leading with Flying Officer Ashton flying about 100yds (92 metres) behind. Turning around Caesar's Camp, on the left side of Sugar Loaf Hill, he climbed steeply to lead the flight up over the wires. Flying Officer Ashton did rise but carried on lower down the valley. Just before reaching the cable, Ashton pulled the nose up and struck the top wires. There was a bright flash, the Audax exploded. Still rising, the aircraft was a ball of fire, it fell into a field beyond the wires, bouncing along the ground into the next field.

Flying Officer P. Wigram Ashton pilot, and LAC J.H. Simpson were killed, both electrocuted; one of them was thrown out of the aircraft before it reached the ground bursting into flames.

THE HALCYON DAYS OF 1930s

Flying Officer Ashton had considerable experience of flying around Hawkinge. Every pilot was aware of the cables, having to dive under them when approaching the airfield by road. If Ashton had flown under them, he would have had about 3ft (0.91metres) clearance above and below. Flying under the wires was forbidden. Witnesses stated he was flying too low and had made an error of judgement in not keeping in line with Flying Officer Geddes. Flying Officer H.J. Shelley RAF, in charge of the Fire Tender on duty, saw a big cloud of smoke, seeing only two aircraft appear he thought there had been a crash. Doctor R.L. Worsley said that in his opinion death was due to electrocution, although the bodies were badly burnt afterwards. The jury at the inquest returned a verdict of death by misadventure.

Flying Officer Ashton was a well-known RAF boxer and rugby player, from Basutoland. LAC Simpson's wife, who watched some of the display, was living in Radnor Park Road, Folkestone. Both bodies were identified by Corporal Harry Emmis of the RAF Medical Service, LAC Simpson only by his boots. Dover's electricity supply was cut-off and trams were stopped, the local cinema shut down. Twenty minutes later power was partially restored, and the Central Electricity Board worked all night and following day to repair the damaged cables.

The Officers' Mess at Hawkinge was a large, modern building. Officers were waited upon hand and foot by staff who served them drinks in the anteroom, beer in silver tankards and attended them at formal dinner each evening. Apart from weekends, when lounge suits were allowed, everyone was required to wear mess dress or dinner jackets each evening, involving the usual struggle with starched shirts, winged collars, studs, and cuff links. During the working day pilots wore smart white flying overalls with the crest of No.2 Squadron sewn on the upper pocket. Half of the Army Cooperation squadron pilots were Army officers, which was not always popular. Pilot Officer Mike Pedley recalls his feelings at Hawkinge in June 1936:

> I was dismayed to find at least half the officers wearing various regimental uniforms. I had just been painstakingly indoctrinated in the traditions of the RAF; my loyalty was exclusively to that service. I later came to understand the philosophy giving rise to the joint service manning of Army Cooperation units, but I never appreciated the need for it, or its desirability. Each of our armed forces had its characteristics and set of values. When Army officers attained positions of authority in their Squadrons, they placed undue stress on

RAF HAWKINGE

matters of 'ceremonial' and to have such inflexible attitudes to discipline as to stifle the initiative and 'press-on' spirit inherent in their RAF subordinates.

Second to none
Hans Onderwater

Squadrons were often allocated an aircraft for communication purposes. No.2 Squadron was a recipient of Percival P.10 Vega Gull W6464 G-AEYC. Flight Lieutenant A.J.W. Geddes, 'B' Flight Commander usually flew this delightful aircraft. On one occasion, he took off from Friday Wood, an Advanced Landing Ground used by the squadron, bound for a meeting at Hawkinge. The stores at Hawkinge received a phone call from an NCO at Friday Wood, requesting tins of paint. During the meeting, the Vega Gull was loaded with the paint, a large sandbag was pushed to the far end of the aircraft's locker. It was common practice to have a sandbag, to act as ballast behind the pilot's seat, when flying solo. Setting off to return to Friday Wood, he embarked on some aerobatics, with the aircraft going into a flat spin, when Geddes realised that the aircraft's centre of gravity was too far aft. From that day onward he always checked the locker.

No.504 Squadron left Hucknall to Hawkinge on 25 July 1936 for Annual Summer Camp, and the usual firing and bombing exercises. On 27 July, during Gun Camera Practice at Hawkinge, Pilot Officer J.A.F. Mertens flying Westland Wallace I K4018 force-loaded on the airfield, Mertens was uninjured, and his aircraft returned to service. Hawker Audax I K3718 No.2 Squadron, was written off on 11 January 1937, when the engine failed on take-off, the wing hit the ground and LAC T.G. Young was killed, the pilot Flying Officer A.C.G. Wimbush escaping uninjured.

In March 1937, pilots of No.46 Squadron arrived Hawkinge, from Digby, for an exercise with No.2 (Army Coop) Squadron which lasted until 9 April. Among those selected for this task was Pilot Officer Ian Gleed, later Wing Commander I. Gleed DSO, DFC, CdeG. Coming into land, Gloster Gauntlet II K7844 wheels hit the top of Gibraltar House, Paddlesworth, near Hawkinge, damaging a chimney, making a hole in the roof and scattering tiles into the garden below. Committed to his landing approach, Gleed realised the undercarriage was a trifle damaged, but decided to continue landing. Part of his undercarriage was torn off, but he touched down gingerly some 200 yards (183 metres) from the house west of the airfield. There was a crunch, the Gauntlet tipped forward, the propeller splintered and the machine turned over. Gleed scrambled

THE HALCYON DAYS OF 1930s

An aerial view of RAF Hawkinge taken between 1935 and 1939, note the hangars and workshops and the airfield recognition circle. To the right is the compass swinging base. (D.G. Collyer)

out unhurt. A report in the local newspaper stated that the aircraft was damaged, but Gleed confirmed to his family that the Gauntlet had been a write-off! It was his first crash and he had walked away from it, thus being able to claim it as a 'good landing'!

Station Headquarters (SHQ) was formed at Hawkinge on 4 July 1935, when control of the airfield passed to the Air Defence of Great Britain (ADGB) Command, to include Area Command No.22 Group. In early 1938 No.25 Squadron, became the first unit to convert to a Night Fighter squadron, eventually equipped with the twin-engine Bristol Blenheim I. Before this could happen, observers who had flown in Hawker Demons were re-mustered for navigational training in preparation to crew Blenheims. Equipped with a selection of camouflaged Gloster Gladiator IIs, these provided experience for pilots in night flying and landing aircraft fitted with flaps. Sixteen Gladiators transferred to No.25 Squadron at Hawkinge, fourteen from No.56 Squadron and No.65 Squadrons, who had converted to Hawker Hurricanes. Delivery began on 21 June 1938, a week later the last

RAF HAWKINGE

A more unusual aircraft to pass through No.2 ASU Hawkinge was this Saro Cloud flying boat K3722 on 25 January 1937, which remained in service until 15 November 1938. (Saunders Roe Aircraft Ltd.)

Officers of No.2 (Army Cooperation) Squadron at Hawkinge during November 1936 arrived at Hawkinge on 30 November 1935. The aircraft is a Hawker Audax later replaced by the Hawker Hector. Note the mixture of Army and RAF uniforms.

THE HALCYON DAYS OF 1930s

Gladiator flew into Hawkinge; all remained with No.25 Squadron until the end of 1938 before moving to No.607 Squadron.

Shortly before the departure of the Gladiators, No.25 Squadron took part in developing the means of early warning of approaching enemy aircraft. Flying from Hawkinge two aircraft patrolled twenty miles (32 km) off the coast, approaching Folkestone and flying along the southeast coast. The newly completed Chain Home (Radar) station at Rye would gain experience of detecting the incoming machines. Conducted in secrecy, not even the pilots knew why they were flying these unusual exercises, logbooks recording them as patrols.

No.603 (City of Edinburgh) Squadron RAuxAF, Turnhouse, arrived for Summer Camp at on 11 July 1937, comprising of twenty officers, 150 airmen and the Westland Wapiti biplane. The weather that July was not good and the squadron were billeted in bell tents, and during one memorable downpour in the early hours, the tents were flooded. This had its compensation, as airmen spent the rest of the stay at Hawkinge in the Officers' Mess. On

A visiting Hawker Hind K6785 of No.504 (County of Nottingham) Squadron RAuxAF at Hawkinge in 1937. Note the hangars and the fuel bowser on the left.

completion of Summer Camp Pilot Officer H. Somerville and Pilot Officer R. 'Bubble' McGregor Waterston were awarded their Flying Wings.

No.610 (County of Chester) Squadron RAuxAF proceeded to Hawkinge from Hooton Park for Summer Camp on 25 July 1936 – a period of intensive training for pilots and groundcrews. Squadron strength consisted of thirteen officers and eighty-three airmen, including NCOs. Leysdown and Eastchurch ranges were used for gunnery practice, and Hawkinge provided opportunity to improve formation flying. Groundcrews gained experience, it also helped to boost camaraderie. On 5 August they were inspected by the Air Officer Commanding (AOC) of No.6 Auxiliary Group Air Commodore J.C. Quinnell DFC. Another reason for his visit was to present them with the squadron badge, granted by the School of Heraldry. Another presentation was for the best maintained aircraft, in this case, a Hawker Hart, whose groundcrew consisted of Aircraftsmen C. Pigdon, E.V. Halewood, J.E. Orford, J.J. Jackson, R.I. Huskinson, A. Alkin and L.H. Bellamy. No.610 Squadron returned to Hooton Park on 7 August 1937. No.504 Squadron had their final visit to Hawkinge during the 1930s, arriving on 24 July 1937 for Annual Training Camp. Over a two-week period, 111 Auxiliary Airmen, two Regulars, fifteen Auxiliary Officers attended that year's camp, returning to Hucknall on 7 August 1937.

No.604 (County of Middlesex) RAuxAF Squadron, arrived from Hendon by air and coach on 31 July 1938 for Summer Camp and Annual Training, equipped with Hawker Demon. At Hawkinge the squadron took part in Home Defence exercises at North Weald, returning to their base at RAF Hendon on 8 August 1938. Avro Tutor biplanes had been in service with No.612 (County of Aberdeen) Squadron at Dyce since formation; under command of Squadron Leader Finlay Crerar, they re-equipped with Hawker Hectors in December 1937. On 18 July 1938, they moved to Hawkinge for Summer Camp, commencing annual training. In competition with No.225, and No.602 Squadrons and Staff Headquarters Hawkinge, No.612 won the Inter-Squadron Sports Cup at the Annual Sports event.

The situation in Europe intensified with the Munich crisis of 1938, the squadron along with others were put on alert moving to their battle stations – in the case of No.25, Northolt. Returning to Hawkinge on 10 October 1938 they were warned that they may take up the role as night fighters. The first Blenheim arriving at Hawkinge was K7058 'RX-K', on loan from the School of Army Cooperation in December 1938. Equipped as a bomber, it was soon being flown with both navigator and gunner, to gain experience.

THE HALCYON DAYS OF 1930s

Three accidents occurred during this period. On 23 May 1938 Blenheim 1, L1241 flown by Pilot Officer Rolfe hit a bank on landing. On 30 January 1939, L1510 made a heavy landing, and the undercarriage collapsed. The first fatal crash for No.25 Squadron happened on 10 December 1938 when L1439 was on night patrol. The pilot became lost in cloud and crashed near Dartford. Sergeant J.C. Lingard parachuted to safety, LAC F.R. Jones was killed. On 4 October 1939 No.25 Squadron, having been at Hawkinge since 1 January 1920, moved to Northolt. They had established Hawkinge as an important front-line airfield, distinguishing themselves as one of the elite squadrons of the RAF.

In preparation for the display at Hawkinge on 20 May, No.2 Squadron practised for the big day, Lysander I, L4702 flown by Flying Officer R.A.G. Petrie and LAC H.A.J. Stacey, crashed during a slow flying demonstration at Hawkinge on 28 April 1939. The aircraft was destroyed by fire in front of spectators. At about 100ft (30 metres) Petrie made a 180 degree turn and stalled. Horrified, the CO, Squadron Leader A.J.W., Geddes, ran over to the wreckage and tried to recover the crew but was beaten back by flames, the Lysander an inferno, both Petrie and Stacey died. Undaunted Geddes, took

Basking in the summer sun at Hawkinge are six Blenheim Is, the first to be delivered to No.25 Squadron at Hawkinge in December 1938. With no squadron markings applied they would soon be coded 'RX'. These aircraft had black and white undersurfaces, dark earth, and dark green upper surfaces of the period. (R.S. Humphreys)

RAF HAWKINGE

By 1937/38 RAF Hawkinge had expanded, the extent of the changes clearly seen. The Officers' Mess is situated in the centre of the camp in front of the tented area. (Wing Commander D.A. Upton OBE)

Lysanders of No.2 (Army Cooperation) Squadron and a Blenheim I of No.25 Squadron are just visible, also noticeable is the distinctive 'dip' in the grass airfield and hangars. (D. Rolfe)

THE HALCYON DAYS OF 1930s

off and performed the same manoeuvres, stalling his Lysander, but managed to recover as he climbed to a safer altitude. As a result of the accident, restrictions were imposed on flying at slow speed and low altitude. Despite all, 16 new Lysanders were delivered to No.2 Squadron, Hawkinge.

Lysanders practised dropping parachute containers in the middle of the airfield, which was followed by a mishap when Acting P/O P.J. Edinger opened his parachute in the slipstream of a parked Lysander, dragging him across the airfield on his back in the wake of a fully opened Irvine parachute. The event was concluded when Squadron Leader A.J.W. Geddes gave a fine demonstration of short take-off and landing abilities of the Lysander.

Rapid development and reorganisation of the RAF, required to repel the Luftwaffe, was underway. The Spitfire had begun to fly operationally in June 1938. Gradually aircraft such as the Gladiator, a front-line fighter, were replaced by the Blenheim, Spitfire and Hurricane. Hawkinge prepared for war, conflict with Germany being inevitable and all RAF ranks were recalled, and gate passes issued. Buildings were camouflaged, blackout curtains fitted to all windows. Thousands of sandbags were stored in the Clerk of Works' building and four 12,000-gallon (54,553 litres) fuel storage tanks installed. These were soon filled, but someone left the valves open. Fortunately there were no explosions or fires, and despite a Court of Enquiry, the culprit was not apprehended. Every building, including paths and roads highly visible from the air, were covered in green and brown paint, gas detector posts installed around the airfield and slit trenches dug.

In September 1939 No.3 Squadron had a brief detachment to Manston before moving to Hawkinge on 17 December. Eleven Hurricane Is of 'A' Flight arrived at Hawkinge, landing was difficult due to the camouflage ground, but all landed safely, and Shipping Patrols were flown. Hurricanes were scrambled before an apparent intruder was identified as an aircraft of the Dutch Airways, KLM. The squadron managed to fly nine sorties on 31 December 1939 from Hawkinge, moving to Croydon on 10 February 1940.

The Radar Defence Frequency (RDF) station opened on 16 January 1939, under the name of RAF Rye, close to the historic Cinque Port town of Rye. This RDF station along with others, such as Dunkirk near Canterbury, and Dover on the Kent coast would be vital in the coming war, particularly during the summer months of 1940. As a result Hawkinge became the administrative centre for RAF Rye. Another important link in the country's Home Defence was the Observer Corps, which provided the eyes and ears of the defence system. With the German escalation of munitions, a Home

RAF HAWKINGE

Defence Sub-Committee headed by Sir Hugh Dowding in 1937 called for forty-five fighter squadrons, 1,200 anti-aircraft guns, 5,000 searchlights, radar, radio, and further expansion of the Observer Corps. By the time of the Munich Crisis in 1938 it was agreed that national coverage by the Corps was essential.

In addition to AA batteries at Hawkinge, the Air Tactical Assault Group (ATAG) based at the airfield used a parachute & cable (PAC) system consisting of a small rocket trailing a steel cable, which shot vertically 300–400ft (91–122 metres) into the air, then descended on a parachute. The rockets were grouped in batteries of nine, launched simultaneously in a curtain pattern. The idea was to create a web of steel cables across the path of a low-flying aircraft, causing it to catch the wires and stall to the ground. The parachute had a dual function: once the rocket burned out, the canopy slowed the cable's fall, allowing the 'curtain' to stay up in the air for a longer time. If the cable caught a bomber's wing, the added drag from the parachute was hoped to be sufficient to foul its flight. There was also a smaller parachute at the lower end of the cable designed to balance the

The Air Tactical Assault Group (ATAG) experimented with parachutes at Hawkinge in May 1939. An RAF pilot undergoes parachute opening experience in the slipstream of a stationary aircraft. (J.A. Hampton)

THE HALCYON DAYS OF 1930s

drag of the first one and thus prevent the cable from sliding off the wing of the aircraft. Later versions had an additional explosive charge hung at the bottom of the cable, intended to detonate on contact with the aircraft.

On 3 September 1939 air raid sirens sounded when a French aircraft which had failed to file its flight plan was located by radar. It flew over the domain of No.1 Group Maidstone and No.19 Group Bromley. That day, Neville Chamberlain informed the nation that it was at war with Nazi Germany. For the next five and a half years all observer posts in Kent would be permanently manned, forming the basis of Great Britain's Home Defence. To familiarise themselves with their Administrative HQ, 274 members of the Observer Corps arrived at Hawkinge on 11 June 1939.

Despite its importance as a front-line fighter base and following the declaration of war, the station CO, Wing Commander W.L. Payne, could not understand why it became No.3 Recruit Training School. From the beginning of August 1939 until mobilisation on 1 September 1939 was a busy period for the airfield, which also hosted Summer Camp for No.613 Squadron RAuxAF.

Air Raid alarms were heard at Hawkinge on 3 and 4 September, but there was no enemy aircraft activity and life on the airfield continued at a relative relaxed pace. On 20 October, a C.39 Autogyro flown by Flight Lieutenant Carroll en route to France, escorted by Squadron Leader Thynn, arrived in a Blenheim 1. At 1014hrs the following morning they took off for France. The Blenheim returned, Squadron Leader Thynn reporting that Flight Lieutenant Carroll had landed in a field near Griz Nez in poor weather, though the Blenheim could not land to assist. Squadron Leader L.S. Weedon took command of Hawkinge on 27 October 1939, and Wing Commander Hanmer was posted to Manston. The month ended with more false Air Raid alarms.

A conference was held at Hawkinge, involving No.24 Group RAF and the 36th Infantry Brigade, to discuss the airfield's defences against parachute troops. Although the 5th Buffs at Canterbury were able to provide airfield defence, Anti-Aircraft guns were established on the airfield. On 21 November 1939, the first enemy aircraft was sighted flying over Hawkinge at an altitude of 3,000ft (914 metres), AA guns did not have time to respond. Sergeant A.C. Banks, born in Folkestone, based at Hawkinge, was killed on 4 December 1940 in a flying accident. Serving with No.5 FTS at Sealand, on a course, he was flying Airspeed Oxford I P1087, which spun into the ground near Chavenage, Tetbury. Sergeant Banks was buried at the Folkestone Cemetery (Hawkinge), an RAF escort firing party attended.

Within twenty-four hours of war being declared on 3 September 1939, pilots of No.2 (Army Cooperation) Squadron were ready to fly their Lysanders to France from Hawkinge. (R.S. Humphreys)

At the beginning of 1940 the Air Ministry turned their attention to subject of 'intelligence war'. At the time there was a thriving peacetime radio industry and large numbers of amateur radio 'hams' in the Royal Air Force Volunteer Reserve RAFVR. Concentration on radio intelligence began in earnest in December 1939, when Flying Officer Scott Farnie, later Group Captain, was recalled from duties as station signals officer Oban, Scotland, reporting to the deputy director of signals at the Air Ministry. Pulse signals had been heard coming from Germany. They were later discovered to emanate from a scientific establishment peacefully engaged in ionospheric research, but they prompted investigation. Flying Officer Farnie was given the job and from this evolved the monitoring system. In February 1940 Scott Farnie, now a Flight Lieutenant, was instructed to set up the first listening post at Hawkinge. He found that there were no suitable high-frequency receivers in the RAF and was forced to bargain with Webb's Radio, Ltd, London, for the whole of their stock of American Hallicrafters model 510 civil receivers. With Flight Lieutenant Allway, a former BBC engineer, Flight Lieutenant Farnie installed the sets in a hut at Hawkinge and began a listening match on the forty-megacycle band. There was no certain knowledge of what waveband the Germans used for radiotelephony. For over two months nothing was heard, but in mid-May, at the height of the Battle of France, German transmissions began to come through loud and clear. Delight in the hut was tempered by the fact that none of the crew spoke German! By chance one of soldiers in the guardroom was a linguist, who was quickly given headphones, and was soon translating. It so happened that on this occasion it turned out to be a formation of Ju87s preparing for a ground attack. The bemused soldier was Private Mattheson, who was quickly transferred to the RAFs Signals Intelligence Service. German radio-telephony frequencies having been established, the Hawkinge unit suffered from an acute shortage of German translators to keep continuous watch. It was decided to recruit women to fill the gaps and to the consternation of the 'queen bees' of the WAAF. Those recruited were given direct entry in the rank of sergeant, and gave great service working six-hour shifts, taking down messages in longhand. One operator, Section Officer A.B. Morris, won a well-earned MBE for her work in 1940, but the citation gave no hint of her job. The success of Hawkinge and the fact that E-boats also worked the 40-megacycle band led to the establishment of a chain of joint RAF and RN monitoring stations along the east coast England.

Chapter 5

RAF Hawkinge Goes to War 1940
The Phoney War Ends

No.3 Squadron were scrambled in January 1940, to escort troopships to France. Flying Officer Boyer Hurricane I N2339, spotting a floating mine, directed an RN ship into the area and the mine was destroyed. No.3 Squadron Hurricanes flew back to Kenley on 4 February, later returning to Hawkinge, where they refuelled and took off to patrol the Channel. Before leaving Hawkinge in January 1940, RAF personnel cleared snow from the runway as there had been another heavy fall during the night. No.3 Squadron were warming up to leave. Three Avro Ansons 'MK-R' and 'CY-Q' of No.500 (Kent's Own) Squadron, Detling, detailed for the Dover Patrol, managed to lose themselves in the snowstorm. They found Hawkinge and were pleased to see the runway area had been cleared. Quickly landing without incident they put down just as the Hurricanes of No.3 Squadron were forming up for a take-off; there were no accidents, and the Hurricanes headed for Kenley. The crews of the Ansons remained at Hawkinge until the weather had improved.

No.1 Pilotless Aircraft Section formed at Henlow on 31 January 1937, moved to Hawkinge, under the command of Squadron Leader P. Bathurst. By 29 February 1940 their aircraft arrived, all coded R2, DH Queen Bee (LF789) R2-K, DH Moth (K1902), Avro Tutor (K3423), Prefect (K5065), Bristol Blenheim (L1144), Westland Wallace II (K6019), Queen Wasp (P5442), DH Leopard Moth, Botha (6238), Miles Proctor (RM170) R2-V, DH Tiger Moth (T7694).

No.416 (Army Cooperation) Flight formed at Hawkinge on 1 March 1940, commanded by Squadron Leader D.J. Eayrs. They were due to be equipped with nine Westland Lysander IIs, with three in reserve. Organisation was delayed as equipment had not arrived, so essentials were borrowed from No.16 Squadron and Hawkinge HQ. By 6 March, notification arrived that their aircraft were ready for collection from No.19 AMU (Aircraft Maintenance Unit) at St Athan. Pilots of No.416 Flight and No.16 Squadron set off by train to collect the Lysanders. On arrival work commenced

RAF HAWKINGE GOES TO WAR 1940

No.16 Squadron equipped with Lysanders Is completed their move to Hawkinge on 17 February 1940, moving to Amiens, France on 13 April 1940. (P.L. Donkin)

preparing the aircraft for operations, although there was some concern raised when it was realised that few pilots had experience flying Lysanders!

During an exercise between Lysanders of No.16 and Hurricanes of No.3 Squadron on 11 March, Sergeant E.A. Lomax Hurricane II L2123 crashed on Folkestone Golf course. Three pilots of 'A' flight had taken-off from Kenley for Hawkinge, Flight Lieutenant Churchill, Sergeant Wilkinson, and Sergeant Lomax. Lomax made a mock attack on a Lysander, going into an uncontrolled spin at 1,500ft (457 metres). He was buried at St Margaret's Church, Edgware, No.3 Squadron provided an escort and firing party.

On 13 March the CO of No.416 Flight led flying practice, but further flights were cancelled due to snow. Two days later, evasive flying practice commenced. Pilots handled the Lysanders much the same as a fighter, although they found it difficult bringing gun sights to bear on aircraft taking evasive action. On 28 March No.16 Squadron were equipped with Westland Lysander IIs, and preparations were underway to move an Advance Party to their new base at Amiens, France, which took place on 1April.

RAF HAWKINGE

On 7 April, Squadron Leader Robinson with an RAF detachment arrived, in connection with trials of Airspeed AS.30 Queen Wasps of the PAU (Pilotless Aircraft Unit) for No.1 AACU Air Armament Gunnery Unit based at Watchet. The Queen Wasp was a British pilotless target aircraft built by Airspeed Limited at Portsmouth. Although intended for both RAF and RN use, the aircraft never went into production. If adopted they would have replaced the existing DH Queen Bee adapted from the DH Tiger Moth pilotless target aircraft.

Spitfires of No.613 Squadron arrived for cooperation work with Hythe School of Small Arms Fire. On 16 April, the Air Party of No.16 Squadron, comprising of sixteen Lysander IIs, took off from Hawkinge to join the main squadron at Amiens. That day, a signal from Fighter Command HQ was received stating that No.416 Flight recently disbanded was to reform at Hawkinge with immediate effect. Squadron Leader D.J. Eayrs temporarily posted to command No.59 Squadron on 17 April was replaced as CO of No.416 Flight by Flight Lieutenant C.R. Beaston. Before the end of April 1940, Lysanders of No.416 Flight had been fitted with an additional fuel tank, modifications took longer than expected, as fitters had little experience. This problem hindered Air Gunners and Signals Officer, all of whom had no experience of Army Cooperation flights, and the flight was poorly equipped. A few Lysanders were fitted with target towing mechanism, and the squadron received Lewis Guns for ground defence and small firearms. Nine Lysander IIs were delivered to No.416 Flight Hawkinge to reform the flight.

On 10 May Hawkinge was on alert, leave was cancelled and airmen recalled to base. Emergency measures for defence were in operation and an emergency platoon of the Queen's Westminsters guarded the Wireless/Telegraph Station. Major Thompson and Captain Cleaver Royal Engineers arranged suitable sites for Anti-Aircraft Bofor guns. No.601 Squadron moved to Manston, No.1 (DBRE) Defence Battalion RE Shorncliffe arrived commanded by 2nd Lieutenant AW. Bentley, attached to Hawkinge for defence. Two Bofor guns were placed into position, commanded by 2nd Lieutenant Wilkinson. Machine gun posts were always armed, awaiting attacks. No.601 Squadron returned to Hawkinge from Manston but took off again that evening. By the end of the day all senior NCOs had been issued with weapons, next day roads surrounding Hawkinge were barricaded, and guards posted. No.17 Squadron moved from Martlesham Heath with Hurricane 1s, personnel arrived in Blenheims of No.29 Squadron at Debden, and some arrived with the Transport Section.

RAF HAWKINGE GOES TO WAR 1940

Eleven Hurricanes were scrambled to Merville. Squadron Leader G.C. Tomlinson had shot down a Ju 87 but stalled and crashed fifteen miles (24 km) from Brussels at Hingene; Hurricane I N2547 was abandoned, attacked by an Me 109 flown by Oblt. Schafer of 5/JG 27. Hurricane I, N2407 was shot down by a Bf 109; Lieutenant Terry, Stab 1/JG 51 victim was Pilot Officer O.P de L. Hulton-Harrop who baled out and was captured; Oberlt. Krafft of 3/JG 51 attacked and destroyed Hurricane I N2403, Flight Lieutenant M.S. Donne killed. Uffz. Scheiter 3/JG 51 forced down Sergeant J.A.A. Luck, who was taken PoW; Hurricane I P2758 was lost, Flying Officer R.V. Meredith Hurricane I N2457 was luckier. Despite being damaged by Bf 109s of 1/JG 51, he returned safely uninjured. Pilot Officer Whittaker destroyed another, Pilot Officer Lines, Sergeant Pavey and Pilot Officer Harris failed to return. The remainder of the flight returned to base, shaken by their initiation in combat, their first week at Hawkinge. Following a joint operation with No.32 Squadron, escorting Blenheims near Arras, No.17 Squadron were ordered to move to Debden.

A rear HQ 'Black Violet' was established at Hawkinge to control operations of the Corps Reconnaissance units returning to England, a sortie being flown that afternoon. When the Air Component Reconnaissance units were withdrawn from France to operate from airfields in southeast England, Hawkinge and Lympne were immediately earmarked.

No.605 (County of Warwickshire) RAuxAF had been defending Scapa, Scotland, so it came as a pleasant surprise when told they were to move to Hawkinge. By 2100hrs all fifteen aircraft had arrived at Hawkinge, the advance party left Wick by train. Having settled into new billets and prepared their Hurricanes the squadron was at readiness. The call came at 0430hrs for the Squadron to scramble and patrol the Calais and Boulogne areas. No enemy aircraft were sighted on this patrol, but later that day after another scramble, a group of Heinkel 111s were sighted. Flight Lieutenant I. Jock Muirhead destroyed one and Flight Lieutenant Mike Cooper-Slipper shared another. While patrolling the Arras area of France the Squadron were jumped by a group of Me 109s. This was not to prove a very successful first encounter with Germany's front-line fighter, with Flight Lieutenant C.F. 'Bunny' Currant having to make a forced landing in France. The enemy fire struck his Hurricane, the engine seized, the propeller stopped. The cockpit filled with fumes hissing noisily, he opened the hood, undid his straps, and climbed out on to the wing intending to jump. He then changed his mind, climbing back in and glided down, and – wheels up – slid into a field. 'Bunny' had no time to do up straps and as the Hurricane skidded rapidly to a sudden stop, he hit the side of the cockpit, breaking his nose, and cutting his face. Clambering out he looked up to see Flying Officer Hope circling round and fly off back to Hawkinge. Hurricane I P3575 landed with a damaged oil system during the combat with Bf109s of 2/JG 3 following an attack on HeIIIs of III/KG 27 west of Douai at 1215hrs. Flight Lieutenant Currant found fame by appearing in the classic film *The First of the Few*, with actors David Niven and Leslie Howard as R.J. Mitchell in 1942.

No.605 Squadron lost two pilots on 22 May, Sergeant Moffat Hurricane I L2058 and Flying Officer G.F.M Wright Hurricane I L2120, attacked by Me 109s near Arras. Flying Officer G.W.B. Austin Hurricane I N2349 was also shot down. With his aircraft on fire, he baled out near Vermelles; his left leg hit, he was evacuated via Dunkirk and sent to hospital. The recent losses suffered by No.17 Squadron meant the squadron was short of aircraft, but were able to continue operations. The Air Component HQ moved to Hawkinge to mount reconnaissance flights from bases in southern England and No.53 Squadron's Blenheims used Hawkinge. On 22 May 1940 Blenheims took off from Hawkinge on a reconnaissance flight to Arras-Perrone; Blenheim R3596 returned damaged by ground fire and crashed. Pilot Officer Triptree, Sergeant Williamson and Leading Aircraftman Jeffrey were unhurt, but the aircraft was a write off. Blenheim IV L9184 crashed alongside the Cambrai Road at Haucourt. Pilot Officer R.L. Saunders, Sergeant S.F. Simmons and Leading Aircraftman G.R. Pirie were killed. The crew were buried close to the crash site but were later transferred to a local cemetery in July 1919 along with the remains of Sergeant Saunders' dog, which he had taken with him on his last flight. Blenheim IV L9246 crash landed at Rouen following a ferry flight, Pilot Officer Herbert, Sergeant Pope and Leading Aircraftman Newberry unhurt. With only one Air Component Flight left in France, tactical reconnaissance and Artillery Observation Flights were impossible without direct fighter support. French Reconnaissance Flights suffered serious losses; the bulk of sorties were made by aircraft of No.53 Squadron based at Hawkinge.

Squadrons based at Hawkinge were again despatched to Bekesbourne, near Canterbury. This was well timed, as the main party of No.605 Squadron RAuxAF arrived, along with two more Bofors guns, sited and quickly manned. Apart from Lysanders of 'B' Flight No.4 Squadron and No.13 Squadron, all that now remained of the RAF Air Component in Northern France were HQ Staff left behind to liaise with 'Black Violet', now established at Hawkinge. On 23 May, No.605 Squadron and No.79 Squadron escorted Blenheims to

Arras. Flying Officer P.G. Leeson, Hurricane I L2121, was shot down at St Pol and taken PoW, remaining in hospital for nine months.

On 23 May 1940, Blenheim R3691 No.53 Squadron was shot down, and Flying Officer S.G.L. Pepys, Sergeant A. Haygreen and Aircraftman H. Spear were captured. Two days later, No.53 Squadron were on a Reconnaissance Flight over Neufchatel-Rethel. Blenheim IV R3694 was damaged by flak; Flying Officer Rochfort, Sergeant Clayton and Leading Aircraftman Roberts were unhurt, but were taken PoW. Blenheim L8863 No.53 Squadron was believed shot down near Bayenghem-lès-Seninghem during a Reconnaissance Flight. Pilot Officer C.M. Bailey, Sergeant W.J.K. Evans and LAC A.A. Gillmore were killed, as were Pilot Officer P.F.C. Villiers-Tuthill, Sergeant D.B. Mearns and Sergeant A.H. Payne No.53 Squadron, shot down by Obfw. Labusga 6/JG 3, crashing near Faumont, Blenheim R8735 destroyed. Returning to Hawkinge, Blenheim R3703 was damaged by fighters and abandoned over St Margaret's Bay. Pilot Officer Aldridge Trafford baled out injured, Sergeant McRae unhurt. Blenheim R3735 was fired on by Bf 109s between Hoogstade–Poperinge–St Omer, Pilot Officer Robinson, Aircraftman Couchen were injured.

Spitfire N3167 No.92 Squadron, force landed at Hawkinge on 23 May, damaged in combat with Bf 110s of II/ZG 76, claimed by Hptmn. Groth Grp. Komm. (Group Commander) near Calais. Flight Lieutenant C.P. Green badly wounded in the thigh was admitted to Shorncliffe Hospital. No.92 Squadron operating from Hornchurch on 23 May 1940, had already taken part in action with Me 109s over the beaches at Calais-Marck, lost Pilot Officer B.H.G. Learmond in Spitfire I P9370. They later engaged He IIIs and Me 110s, escorted by Me 109s, Flying Officer R. Bushell (of 'Great Escape' fame) crash landed, Sergeant P.H. Klipsch was killed. Flight Lieutenant C.P. Green, Spitfire I N3167, was hit in the thigh by shrapnel, but managed to fly his aircraft, despite vomiting and feeling faint. He stuck his thumb into the wound and pressed hard hoping to stop the bleeding, landing at Hawkinge with the cockpit was covered in blood. He was rushed to hospital where the surgeon saved his leg, but he was unable to fly for many weeks.

Seven Lysanders of No.4 Squadron left St Omer–Clairmarais for Dunkirk en route to Hawkinge, the last RAF Component Aircraft in France. During a Reconnaissance Flight to Amiens, a Blenheim of No.57 Squadron, taking off from Hawkinge, crashed on landing at Lympne, following attacks by Bf 110s. Pilot Officer W. Hutchings was wounded in the arm, Sergeant Whitlam and Corporal A. Daley unhurt. Flight Lieutenant A.C. Brown

RAF HAWKINGE

was flying R3605 on 24 May near St Omer when his aircraft was struck by flak, he landed at Manston. Flying Officer Bartlett was also hit by flak on 25 May, L9466, and landed at Hawkinge. No.605 Squadron patrolling Calais–Dunkirk on 25 May, Hurricane I N2577 was hit by flak but limped back to Hawkinge with a damaged wing spar. Pilot Officer I.J. Muirhead was shot down by an Me 110 patrolling Calais/Dunkirk, baling out of Hurricane I N2346 and was fired on by Belgian soldiers but not injured. Returning on a ship from Oostende, they were torpedoed. Muirhead was rescued, finishing up in hospital. In May 1940 No.613 Squadron RAuxAF moved to Hawkinge. On 26 May 1940, Pilot Officer Brown flying Hawker Hector K8111, was one of six detailed to dive-bomb gun emplacements near Calais. En route he test-fired his forward gun, the omission of a split pin caused the muzzle attachment to fly off and penetrate the fuselage, damaging the main fuel-tank. Brown jettisoned his two bombs and turned back, landing at Hawkinge.

Pilot Officer Coleson in N3551 escaped an attack by four Bf 110s on 28 May, diving to ground level. Pilot Officer Robinson was attacked by eleven Bf 109s on 31 May and R3733 badly damaged.

Escorting Blenheims to St Omer on 27 May, Hurricanes of No.605 Squadron engaged Do 17s, Flying Officer N. Forbes Hurricane I L2119 was shot down, last seen over Poperinge and taken prisoner. Flying Officer P.J. Danielson, Hurricane I P3581, was shot down by an Me 109 and killed. On the evening of 28 May 1940, the evacuation of Dunkirk (Operation Dynamo) commenced. No.825 Squadron FAA, operating from Manston, was deployed on 29 May 1940 to Hawkinge, suffering from the effects of losing five Swordfish earlier that day, the remaining aircraft of the squadron arrived at the airfield at 1700hrs. Their mission, to attack an enemy battery shelling the mole at Dunkirk, SW of Bergues. Swordfish arrived over the area at 1855hrs, circled but could not locate the target. The CO Lieutenant Comm. J.B. Buckley DSC, was shot down and taken prisoner.

No.825 FAA Squadron attacked an enemy battery, Swordfish I L2828 was damaged by Bf 109s of 3/JG 54 crashing near Bollezeele, shot down by Oblt. Schmoller-Haldy (Staffelkapitain). Sub-Lieutenant C.S.F Hogg missing, LAC L.P. Gardner killed, Lieutenant R.H.G. Grey captured, aircraft G5-C written-off. Swordfish I P4022 was shot down by Bf 109s of 3/JG 54, overturned on landing, claimed by Lieutenant Kitzinger. Lieutenant Commander J.B. Buckley CO No.825 Squadron, and LA F.G. Rumsey were captured. Swordfish I L2756, was shot down by Bf 109s of

RAF HAWKINGE GOES TO WAR 1940

3/JG 54 by Lieutenant Kitzinger, the pilot rescued unhurt but LAC H.K. Murrin was reported missing. Swordfish I P3997 was shot down by Bf 109s of 3/JG 54 and crash-landed, possibly that claimed by Uffz. Strohauer. Sub Lieutenant J.T. Nicholson and LA V.S.A. Moore captured. One Swordfish I returned to Hawkinge damaged by Bf 109s of 3/JG 54 during the same sortie to attack enemy battery. Pilot and Air Gunner were wounded, the fate of the aircraft unknown.

No.245 Squadron operating from Hawkinge were patrolling Dunkirk, encountered a Do 17 of 1/KG 3 and Me 109s. Flight Lieutenant J.A. Thomson's Hurricane was hit by return fire from the Do 17, his windscreen was shattered, slightly wounded in the thigh he managed to land at Hawkinge. Hurricane N2496 forced landed in bad weather following aborted patrol over Dunkirk, Sergeant P. Banks unhurt. Hurricane 1 N2597 and Hurricane N2709 forced landed in bad weather, Pilot Officer Marshland and Pilot Officer R.A. West unhurt. On 28 May No.605 Squadron, who had lost several pilots during their brief stay at Hawkinge, were relieved by No.245 Squadron. Pilot Officer A.S. Deni (NZ) taking off in Hurricane I L2117 'UP-R' from Hawkinge was barely airborne when his aircraft, a few feet above the road, turned over on its back and dived, crashing near Folkestone killing the pilot, who had been overcome by glycol fumes.

No.111 Squadron operating from Hawkinge patrolled Dunkirk. Hurricane I P2884 landed at Manston, damaged by He 111s of KG 27 engaged over Dunkirk. Sergeant W.L. Dymond unhurt. Hurricane L1973 landed at Manston damaged during attack on He 111s of KG 27. Sergeant J. Robinson wounded in ankle. Hurricane P2902 No.245 Squadron landed badly damaged by Lieutenant Ulenberg 2/JG 26 in combat near Dunkirk. Pilot Officer K.B. McGlashan wounded in thigh, aircraft DX-R abandoned. This aircraft was excavated in 1988 and returned to the UK where it was registered G-ROBT, restored during 1994–2017 and returned to flying condition as DX-R. By the end of May 1940 No.3 GCS attached to Hawkinge, responsible for the repair of airfield surfaces, it would not be long before their expertise would be needed.

No.111 Squadron at Croydon flew to Manston on 5 June and were ordered to Hawkinge. On 6 June Sergeant R.J.W. Brown was shot down by an Me 109, escorting Blenheims near Abbeville. Injured, he baled out of Hurricane I P2885, was picked up by soldiers and taken to a field hospital, Brown was put on a train, later returning to Hawkinge where he continued operations with No.111 Squadron. On 8 June 1940, Hurricane Is of No.245 Squadron arrived at Hawkinge, for operational duties. Following their short stay at Hawkinge, the main party of the Pilotless Aircraft Section left and No.416 Flight, attached to Hawkinge, returned to Cosford. No.699 General Construction Company RE, were replaced by No.655 GCR on 27 June, adding to the overcrowding at Hawkinge.

Flight Lieutenant R.H. Hillary's connection with Hawkinge goes back to 1939 when he flew with the Oxford University Air Squadron (UAS) attending Summer Camp. Many pilots who had joined UAS in the 1930s were recruited into the RAF during the Battle of Britain. Although this was held at Lympne, the ground base was Hawkinge and attended by UAS members travelling by rail and arriving at Hawkinge on 9 June 1939, and using tents as barracks. These were camouflaged with paint, which cut all the light out from inside, everyone soon got used to this. A Hawker Audax, Hawker Hinds and Avro Tutors arrived on 17 June from Abingdon. Instructional flying took place, the weather was poor, Hillary and others were ferried to Rochester for a tour of Short Brothers aircraft factory. In September 1940 Hillary was shot down and severely burnt. During a long and painful recovery, he wrote *The Last Enemy,* about his flying and the accident which changed his life. Hillary rejoined the RAF, crashing in Blenheim V BA194 No.56 OTU on 8 January 1943, killing him and Sergeant K.W. Fison.

On 21 July 1939, Pilot Officer D.C. Lewis RAFVR was killed flying Hawker Hind K5418, during a map-reading flight between Dover and Dymchurch. DH Gypsy Moth G-ABJZ flown by the Chief Instructor K.K. Brown of the Kent Flying Club who had been CFI with the Cinque Ports Flying Club, struck the Hind from astern; both crashed at Beeches Wood, Tilmanstone, killing K.K. Brown and D.W.A. Pragnal. No.245 Squadron, completed their operational duties and returned on 1 July to Turnhouse. No.79 Squadron arrived from Biggin Hill with Hurricane Is and was soon joined by ground staff. No.610 (County of Chester) Squadron RAuxAF began using Hawkinge for operations and refuelling before returning to Biggin Hill. In adopting Hawkinge as the forward base, it would save fuel, and other squadrons would follow this tactic.

That week No.64 Squadron, based at Kenley were flying Reconnaissance Patrols over France, equipped with Spitfire Is. Flying Officer D.K. Milne was shot down in Spitfire I P9507 by an Me 109 of JG 51 near Rouen and Sub Lieutenant Dawson Paul in Spitfire I P9450 was attacked and damaged by an Me 109, but landed safely at Hawkinge. Protecting convoys in the Channel, during a sortie on 7 July, Squadron Leader J.D.C Joslin

No.79 Squadron, went missing. Hurricane I, P2756 was found at Chilverton Elms, Joslin was killed. Next day, Pilot Officer J.E.R. Wood reported shot down, baled out of Hurricane I N2384, his body was found by a RN patrol; he died of severe burns, attacked by Me 109s. Hurricane I P3461 flown by Flying Officer E.W. Mitchell, shot down by RAF fighters was found in the burnt-out wreckage at Temple Ewell, identified by serial numbers of his aircraft's guns. Pilot Officer W.H Willington destroyed an Me 109 over Dover on 9 July. Returning to Hawkinge, No.79 Squadron proceeded to Turnhouse, at Hawkinge for ten days, the squadron had lost four pilots.

Chapter 6

The Battle of Britain 1940
Hawkinge Frontline Airfield

10 July – 7 August 1940

The Battle of Britain is usually recorded in four phases. The first being the Channel Battles, testing Britain's defences while the German government hoped Britain might sue for peace following the fall of France. The second phase, attacks on Fighter Command's airfields, was an attempt by Göring to destroy the RAF's ability to fight prior to invasion by Germany, Operation Lowen (Operation Lion). The third commenced when German bombers were ordered to attack London following Bomber Command's raid on Berlin. The fourth came as the summer began and bombers were withdrawn, being replaced by fighter-bomber attacks. The year ended with the final months of the tumultuous air battles fought in the skies over Southern England.

On 10 July 1940, Wing Commander W.L. Payne, who had become CO on 1 May that year, handed over command of Hawkinge to Squadron Leader H.B. Hurley. The funeral of Pilot Officer J.E. Wood of No.79 Squadron, killed on 8 July, took place at Hawkinge Cemetery. It was also the day when No.79 Squadron moved to Turnhouse. Following combat off Folkestone on 10 July with Me 109s, Sergeant R. Carnall No.111 Squadron based Croydon, crash landed at Hawkinge. Hurricane I, P3663 sustained damage to the wing, the pilot was not injured. Shortly after, Squadron Leader A.T. Smith of No.610 Squadron, crash landed on the airfield, Spitfire I, L1000, hit by gunfire from an Me 109.

Squadron Leader Thompson left Croydon on 10 July for Hawkinge with Flying Officer Ferris DFC, Flying Officer D.P.K. Higgs, Flying Officer A. Fisher, Pilot Officer B. Fisher, Pilot Officer Mackenzie and Sergeants Dymond, Craig and Carnall, and intercepted bombers attacking a convoy off Folkestone. Two Do 17s of 3/KG 2 were destroyed, Flying Officer Higgs rammed Hurricane I P3671 into a Do 17. Although he managed to bale out, he landed in the sea and drowned. Flying Officer Ferris shot down an Me 109, was attacked by three Me 109s, damaging his aileron controls; Sergeant Carnall crashed at Croydon. Flying Officer Ferris returned to Croydon then returned to Hawkinge. No.111 Squadron operated throughout July/August between Croydon and Hawkinge unscathed, until 11 August when four pilots were killed. Pilot Officer J.H.H. Copeman P3105; Pilot Officer J.W. McKenzie P3922; Pilot Officer R.R. Wilson P3595; and Sergeant R.B. Sim P3942 were shot down off Margate. Another pilot, Sergeant H.S. Newton, P3548, crash landed near Boyton, Oxford when his aircraft ran out of fuel; he survived.

On 18 July, HRH Duke of Kent arrived by air to inspect the airfield's defences and No.610 Squadron. HRH was able to witness the squadron scramble, as twelve Spitfire Is took off, led by Flight Lieutenant E.B.B. Smith. During the engagement with 5/JG 51, Pilot Officer P. Litchfield was shot down and killed by Hptm. Horts 'Jakob' Tietzen, Staffelfuhrer of the German unit. Spitfire I P9452 crashed in the sea, Litchfield was not confirmed dead until seven months later.

No.141 Squadron based at West Malling used Hawkinge as a forward base, flying the Boulton Paul Defiant I, having previously been equipped with Blenheim IFs. Shortly after 0900hrs on 19 July 1940, twelve aircraft were operating from Hawkinge on convoy patrols. The Defiant was crewed by the pilot and an air gunner, the problem was that the Defiant's gun turret was rear facing, little defence if attacked by the superior Bf 109. No.141 Squadron, having taken off on 19 July, were pounced by Bf 109s of Bf 109s of III/JG 51. Pilot Officer J.R. Kemp was shot down in Defiant I L6974, both he and Sergeant R. Crombie were never seen again. Pilot Officer R. Kidson and Sergeant F.P.J. Atkins were also lost with Defiant I L7015. The Defiant I L7001, of Flight Lieutenant Loudon and his gunner, Pilot Officer Farnes, was badly damaged. Loudon ordered Pilot Officer Farnes to bale out, he was rescued from the sea. Pilot Officer Farnes became the second airman ever to have saved his life by using the 'X' Type static line parachute manufactured by the GQ Parachute Company. As such he was awarded a commemorative gold lapel badge inscribed: 'Pilot Officer E. Farnes July 19, 1940.' Forty years later that badge was discovered by a man digging in his garden at Headington, Oxford. Loudon crashed near Hawkinge, and was admitted to Canterbury Hospital with an arm wound. F.N. MacDougall and Sergeant J.F. Wise, Defiant I, L6983, were shot up, MacDougall ordered his gunner to bale out; he was never found. MacDougal flew to West Malling.

RAF HAWKINGE

Pilot Officer D.M. Slatter with Pilot Officer J.R. Gardner in Defiant I L7016, was one of the four rear aircraft immediately shot down. Unlike the other three victims their aircraft did not catch fire and Gardner landed on the sea off Dover. The Defiant sank, the pilot climbed out, Slatter was never seen again. Flying Officer H.N. Tamblyn and his gunner Sergeant S.W.M. Powell returned to base, they destroyed a Bf 109 on 8 August 1940 and were awarded the DFC. Total losses for No.141 Squadron on 19 July, were four pilots killed, or missing, six air gunners missing. The squadron was released from operations for a short period. The same day, Flight Sergeant C. Turner No.32 Squadron was badly burnt in combat with an Me 109, he baled out, Hurricane P3144, crashed at Hougham, Dover.

The following day seven new Defiants were delivered to Biggin Hill, replacements for those lost, all soon air tested and transferred to No.141 Squadron, new pilots arrived, apprehensive about their future. Squadron Leader J. Worrall serving with No.32 Squadron at Hawkinge, destroyed an Me 109 on the 19 July, the following day he attacked and damaged three Ju 87s. The engine and gravity tank of his Hurricane, N2532 GZ-U, were badly damaged in the combat, attacked by Obfw. Illner of II/JG 51 forced landing near Hawkinge; the aircraft burned out, Worrall was uninjured. Sub Lieutenant G.G. Bulmer was shot down in Hurricane N2670 by an Me 109 of II/JG 51in the sea off Dover and killed.

Pilot Officer G. Keighly No.610 Squadron was shot down on 31 May 1940 and baled out again on 20 July 1940, his tail was shot away by Obfw. Schmid 1/JG 51 in combat over Hawkinge, slightly wounded his Spitfire 1 N3201 crashed at Wootton. Flight Lieutenant A.T. Smith No.610 Squadron took command when the CO Squadron Leader L.A. Franks was killed. Smith was killed on 25 July 1940, when he stalled attempting to land at Hawkinge after an action with Bf 109s. Spitfire I R6693 'DW-A' crashed and burnt out in a disused testing shed. The same day, on convoy patrol, Pilot Officer F.T, Gardiner, Spitfire I R6595 'DW-O', was wounded in the arm by an Me 109, but managed to return to base where he landed safely.

Following combat on 25 July, Sergeant P. Else No.610 Squadron was circling over Hawkinge airfield, when he thought he saw two Me 109s. In fact, a Hurricane was chasing an Me 109, and Else joined the attack, the other Hurricane broke away, the Me 109 dived into the sea. No.501 Squadron moved to Gravesend on 25 July, forming part of the Biggin Hill Sector of

THE BATTLE OF BRITAIN 1940

During July/August 1940 Hawkinge was visited by the press. Pilots of No.610 (County of Chester) Squadron RAuxAF relax, in the background is a Spitfire of the squadron. This and others like it became the iconic images depicting the summer of 1940 on a forward Fighter Command airfield.

No.11 Group. The following afternoon they were scrambled and engaged an enemy formation of Bf 109s over Dover. During the combat, Pilot Officer 'Pan' Cox flying Hurricane I P3808, was reported missing. It is believed that Cox was shot down by an AA unit at Dover, due to poor aircraft identification. From then on No.501 Squadron's CO 'A' Flight, was extremely careful when operating off Dover.

During this period, pilots of No.257 Squadron often flew from Tangmere or Hawkinge, returning to Northolt in the evening. On 28 July, eleven Hurricane Is, set off for Hawkinge arriving at 1315hrs. Sergeant R.V. Forward's Hurricane I P3622 was damaged on 28 July during Convoy Patrol. They had been intercepted by Me 109s of JG 26 off the coast of Dover, Sergeant Forward returned to Hawkinge and crash-landed Hurricane P3622. Pilot Officer G.H. Moffatt, also operating from Hawkinge with Sergeant Forward during the squadron's short stay at Hawkinge, was killed on 31 August. That day he was flying

RAF HAWKINGE

Hurricane I P3175, recovered near Walton-on-the-Naze, Essex during the summer of 1972; today it is on display at the RAF Museum, Hendon. No.501 Squadron were airborne on 29 July, attacking Bf 109s and Ju87Bs over Dover Harbour, destroying six, damaging others. Pilot Officer R. Don and Pilot Officer G. Parkin took off that evening to return to Gravesend after Operating from Hawkinge, both were seriously injured in flying accidents. Don baled out of his blazing Hurricane I P3646, crashing at Lydden Marshes. Pilot Officer G. Parkin flew Hurricane I P3349 and crashed inverted at Gravesend, hanging upside-down in the cockpit, before passing out and waking up in hospital, with a bandaged head. By 25 July No.501 Squadron was at Gravesend, using Hawkinge as a forward landing ground. Aircraft were parked at dispersal points at Killing Wood, where the fuel bowsers, starter batteries on trolleys, belts of ammunition and oxygen bottles were stored. At the time the airfield was also shared with the 6th Battalion the Buffs Regiment, their HQ being Reinden House, located in Reinden Wood. A few tents were scattered around the airfield at dispersal points, pilots waited to be scrambled, trying not to show the tension, waiting for the phone to ring.

Many Luftwaffe aircraft which crashed during the hectic days of July-September 1940, were taken by RAF Salvage Units depots, such as this at Elham not far from Hawkinge.

THE BATTLE OF BRITAIN 1940

Pilot Officer K.N.T. 'Hawkeye' Lee, later Wing Commander K.N.T. Lee DFC would 'christen' his aircraft's tail wheel when the call came, for good luck.

During the afternoon of 27 July, Stukas attacked Dover, knowing that the Balloon Barrage was not operational due to a thunderstorm. No.501 Squadron were airborne again, defending Channel shipping, engaged in combat with three Bf 109s and a Ju 87. Flight Lieutenant P.A.N. Cox, Hurricane I P3815, was reported missing. He was shot down by Feldwebel Fernsebner III/JG 52, crashing in the sea, lost without trace. Sergeant E. Howarth, despite being damaged by return fire, landed safely at Hawkinge.

The contribution of the WAAFs (Women's Auxiliary Air Force) cannot be underestimated, their memories are often overlooked. LAC Rosemary Horstmann (WAAF) served as a wireless operator with 'Y' Service

Pilots of No.610 (County of Chester) Sqdn. RAuxAF, Hawkinge 29 July 1940. (Standing L-R) Flying Officer S. Norris, Sergeant H. Chandler, Squadron Leader J. Ellis, Sergeant N. Ramsay Flight Lieutenant W. Warner, Sergeant R. Hamlyn, Pilot Officer F. Gardiner. (Seated L-R) Flight Lieutenant E.B.B. Smith, Pilot Officer J. 'Joe' Pegge, Sergeant C. Parsons, Sergeant D. Corfe.

RAF HAWKINGE

(a network of British signals intelligence collection sites) at Hawkinge during the Battle of Britain. Operators were located away from the airfield:

> One day, a notice was put on our Orderly Room notice board, asking anybody who could speak German to report to the adjutant. Although my German wasn't good, I went along and said I could speak German. The adjutant turned out to be a very good German speaker and he shamed me by putting me through a very searching interview at the end of which he said, 'But you told me you could speak fluent German!' There were a dozen WAAFs who took it in turns to sit in a little bungalow off the perimeter track of Hawkinge aerodrome and listen to the radio conversations of the German fighter and bomber pilots. We were writing down what the German pilots were saying, and they were saying things like, 'I've got him!', 'He's gone down!' and you would hear people screaming.
>
> *The Battle of Britain*
Osprey/IWM

An incident occurred on 1August 1940, involving Avro 504N AX871, attached to the Hawkinge Station Flight. Avro 504N G-ADBM originally K1055, flew with the Central Flying School (CFS). In June 1940 it was

Avro 504N G-ADBM originally AX871 was assigned to Hawkinge Station Flight, which hit the watch hut taking off from RAF Hawkinge on 1 August 1940.

impressed into RAF and allotted serial AX871. Its career was cut short when it hit the watch hut while taking off from Hawkinge.

No.1 Coast Artillery Cooperation Unit, with HQ at Detling, Kent, in May 1940, worked with established defences at Medway and the Thames, the unit cooperated with those at Dover and was on standby from dawn to dusk at short notice. In August, two Avro Ansons were detached from Detling to Hawkinge to cooperate with the Royal Marine Siege Regiment at Dover. Their role was spotting for the Royal Marines at Dover, whose 14inch (35cm) guns bombarded the French coast. In August and September, they flew ten sorties, observing the fall of shot on the targets in the Cape Gris Nez and Calais Harbour area. German aircraft harassed them; the final operation resulted in both Ansons landing near Dover. An air gunner was killed, the remaining crew injured, the pilot was awarded the DFC.

8 August – 6 September 1940

On 8 August Sergeant N.H.D. Ramsay flying as 'weaver', protecting the rear of twelve Spitfires of No.610 Squadron, patrolled at 20,000ft (6,096metres) over Dungeness. Ramsay, flying Spitfire 1 DW-T R6765, was attacked by an Me 109. The Spitfire suffered damage to the cooling system. Ramsay headed for Hawkinge, despite being wounded in the leg; landing, he was sent to hospital, returning six days later. Spitfire 1, L1045 flown by Sergeant W.J. Neville, was fired on by an Me 109 of JG 51, crash landing at Wittersham, overturning, Neville got out uninjured. Pilot Officer C.J.D Andreae flying Spitfire I R6639 No.64 Squadron was damaged by return fire from Bf 109s on 9 August, landing at Hawkinge uninjured. Both these pilots were again shot down, Donahue on 12 August in Spitfire I, X4018, crashing at Sellindge wounded. Andreae was killed in Spitfire I, R6990 patrolling Dungeness on 15 August.

Because of its proximity to the coast and France, pilots were grateful for the use of Hawkinge while in combat over the Channel, as was Pilot Officer J.A. McClintok No.615 Squadron (County of Surrey), on 11 August 1940. Hurricane I N2328 was damaged by Bf109s, he decided to try for Hawkinge. Coming into land he misjudged his height, hitting a fence and overturning the aircraft but walking away uninjured. At 0830hrs on 5 August, six Spitfires of No.64 Squadron from Kenley, relieved No.615 Squadron Hurricanes patrolling the Dover Beachy Head area. They were immediately attacked by Me 109s of JG 54, Sergeant L.R Issac was shot down in Spitfire I L1029, which crashed in the sea off Folkestone, killing the pilot. Pilot Officer A.G. Donahue's Spitfire I K9991 was damaged, landed at Hawkinge. On 11 August 1940, Flight Sergeant J.H. Tanner and Sergeant W.J. Neville No.610 Squadron attacked a Heinkel He 59, a twin-engine float biplane. Tanner was flying Spitfire 1 DW-D R6918, Neville Spitfire I DW-X R6630 when attacked by Me 109s of JG 52, both were shot down and killed. The He 59 was shot down into the Channel, the German crew missing presumed killed, were trying to rescue crew of a Blenheim shot down by Hptm. Wiggers of 1/JG 51. Two pilots of No.610 Squadron crash landed at Hawkinge on 12 August, Sergeant S.J. Arnefield Spitfire I P9495 and Sergeant P.H. Willocks Spitfire I R6621, both were uninjured.

Pilot Officer A.R.H. Barton No.32 Squadron claimed a Bf 109 on 11 August and was shot down on 12 August flying Hurricane I N2596 during combat with III/JG 54, crashing near Hawkinge. Flying Officer J.A.A .Gibson destroyed a Ju 87 followed by a Bf 109, landing Hurricane I P2986 at Hawkinge he nosed over due to runway damage. Hawkinge prepared for an inspection by the Inspector General of the RAF, Sir E.A. Ludlow-Hewitt GCE, KCB, CMG, DSO, MC. No.32 Squadron arrived at midday, from their base at Biggin Hill. They relaxed, waiting for their Hurricanes to be refuelled, knowing that they would soon be scrambled; exhausted, they would replace No.610 Squadron who had been on patrol, following attacks on five RDF Stations, which were damaged earlier that day. Then came the call, No.32 Squadron took off to patrol off Margate area. Hawkinge was attacked by fifteen Ju 88s of II/KG 76, which formed up over France, approaching Dungeness at 5,000ft (1,524mtrs.) they split into two groups, heading for Hawkinge and Lympne. This attack lasted ten minutes, both No.3 and No.6 hangars were damaged and No.5 partially wrecked.

The doors of No.3 hangar collapsed, equipment store and two married quarters were damaged. Slit trenches were full of people, including WAAFs and civilians, watching as airmen evacuated a workshop, the first wave of bombs damaged the runway, others hitting the technical site. Ju 88s dropped bombs and incendiaries. Many attempted to put out fires, looking for victims. Five were killed, seven badly injured. The Watch Tower survived, and Hurricanes of No.32 Squadron preparing to land, low on fuel avoiding the many craters. Five aircraft landed without incident; four Hurricanes were damaged. One crater measured 72ft x 76ft x 28ft deep (22 x 23 x 8.5 metres), the runway was repaired, it took two days to clear the debris.

THE BATTLE OF BRITAIN 1940

Flying Officer D. Grice DFC No.32 Squadron was advised over the RT:

> I flew to Hawkinge where there were considerable signs of bomb damage the airfield seemed to have molehills on it. Seeing a path between them, I landed and taxied between them to where I'd taken off from. A flight sergeant came up and said, 'You'd better take off again very quickly, sir!' 'Why?' 'You see all those molehills? They're unexploded bombs!' I found the same avenue between them, took off and flew to Biggin Hill.
>
> *Hawkinge Airfield 1912–1961*
> R.S. Humphreys

The Chain Home Defence Radar Station at Rye was attacked early on the 12 August, as part of the German all-out air assault on the southeast; another attack came that evening. Chain Home stations comprised of transmission and receiver blocks, four 240ft (73 metres) timber receiver aerial towers, four 350ft (107 metres) steel transmitter aerial towers that concrete pads. Other buildings dispersed, accommodation huts, guard huts and standby set houses (essential component of radar stations, providing an emergency power supply). From 1940, defences were installed at radar stations, including Light AA guns, pill boxes, roadblocks, and shelters. Other sites attacked were Pevensey CH, Dunkirk CH (near Canterbury), Dover. Both Pevensey and Rye were out of action but were repaired and returned to operation within six hours. Although known as RDF stations, the official name for such sites was AMES or Air Ministry Experimental Station.

An Me 110 flown by Wilhelm Rossiger of Erprobungsgruppe 210 dropped bombs on the camp which exploded on huts, just missing the Telegraph/Radio buildings. A soldier from the Sussex Regiment was killed and six injured, Private Les Bailey who was serving at Rye wrote:

> I arrived at Rye in August 1940; seven pylons were up, not all in use. The three tall ones (steel) were brought into use after the bombing on 12 August 1940. The old 'R' and 'T' blocks were damaged in the raids, and when they started up, they were only off air for a few hours, the new blocks were used. The wooden towers were constructed before the war in 1938 and early 1939, the three taller ones, which were 360ft high, started after the war began in 1939. I was in the RAF and my unit was PAC. It was a defence outfit and it consisted of lines of

boxes which contained parachutes attached to wires and they were set out in lines and attached to a control box. There were either nine or ten and the idea was to fire at low flying aircraft below 500ft all the time I was at Rye – August 1940 to May 1942, we didn't fire a single salvo. Jerry must have known we were waiting for them so stayed away. My first year was spent billeted with Mrs Apps at Pear Tree Cottage in the High Street a few doors away from the bake house in Brookland. Although there were eight planes shot down in a radius of two miles during one day of the Battle of Britain, I only went to the scene of two of them. One Jerry was brought down between the Pylons and Camber, and the other on what we used to call the back road going towards Fairfield Court and Beckes Barn, it was in a field beside the road and I was detailed with others to go along with spades and sacks to dig the pilot out, he was in a terrible mess, the only way he could be identified was by the buttons on his jacket. He was a Canadian.

L. Bailey letter

RAF Rye (barracks and camp) was situated at Brookland, not far from the RDF Station, home to RAF personnel, this photo shows No.2 Barrack block. There were also workshops on the site. In 1958 equipment was auctioned, but several of the buildings can be seen today.

THE BATTLE OF BRITAIN 1940

Recruited into the WRAFs for Special Duties was Daphne Carne, who later wrote a vivid account of the attacks at the RDF Station Rye:

> We went on the 'ration run' to Hawkinge, for rations and equipment one of the drivers went over at least twice a week, in the morning. The road to Folkestone follows the coast for most of the way and we had to steer a course through concrete tank traps and roadblocks. Between us and the sea the barbed wire entanglements were anything up to twenty feet wide and concrete 'pill boxes' lined the route. Climbing the hill out of Folkestone, we could see shipping going in and out of Dover Harbour, many flying a barrage balloon. We watched as those 'monsters' succumbed to machine gun fire. While the lorry was loaded at Hawkinge we walked to the edge of the perimeter track. We stood there gazing at aircraft lined up on the airfield, we felt we really belonged in the RAF. Part of the attraction of the trip to Hawkinge was our stop on the way home at a little roadside cafe at Hythe, we had bacon and eggs waiting for us.
>
> *The Eyes of the Few*
> Daphne Carne

The RDF station situated near Rye, Sussex, at the time of the Battle of Britain, along with other such sites as Pevensey, Dunkirk (Canterbury) which played a vital role in Britain's defence during the Second World War. (D. Carne)

RAF HAWKINGE

On 13 August, 'Adler Tag' or 'Eagle Day', Göring promised the ADGB would crumble, Hawkinge airfield was operational, despite the threat of unexploded bombs. Although caught off-guard, ground defences managed to fire two Hispano guns. Mr Brisley and Mr Caister, civilian contractors for the Works Directorate, were killed. Corporal McColl, LAC Symes and LAC Langdon based at Hawkinge also died. Six injured airmen were sent to Kent & Canterbury Hospital. At the time of the attack all were in No.3 hangar, two Spitfires under repair were badly damaged, two others showered with splinters. Also, other non-operational aircraft were damaged but later repaired.

On 14 August Pilot Officer A.R.H. Barton landed at Hawkinge in Hurricane I P3146, damaged in combat. Eighty Stukas of II/StG1 and IV/LGI attacking Dover and Hawkinge, escorted by a hundred Me 109s of JG 26, No.32 and No.615 Squadrons scrambled to intercept. Pilot Officer R.F. Smythe No.32 Squadron shot down Feldwebel G. Kemen I/JG 26, who was captured. The Ju 87s did not attack Hawkinge but destroyed the Goodwin Sands lightship and eight barrage balloons at Dover. Flying Officer J.A.A. Gibson attacked another Ju87 on 15 August and was hit by return fire, he steered Hurricane I P3582 away from Folkestone, at 1,000ft (305 metres) successfully baling out. An attack commenced on 15 August at Hawkinge and Lympne, No.32 Squadron led by Squadron Leader H. Hogan scrambled to intercept were accompanied by No.54 Squadron. Sixteen Ju 87 Stukas of 1V/LG I were part of the force, Sergeant D.A.S McKay No.501 Squadron shot down a Stuka of 10/LG 1 which crashed into power cables at More Hall, Folkestone, debris scattered among houses at Shorncliffe Crescent. Uffz. Franz-Heinrich Kraus the Radio operator baled out landing outside 81 Harcourt Road, he died in hospital.

The pilot Uffzr. Herman Weber was found mutilated among the debris of his Ju 87, scattered among houses. Staffel Hptm. Rolf Munchenhagen who led the attack, crashed in the sea, badly wounded, his Radio Operator Fw. Herbert Heise killed. The Stuka crashed near the South Folkestone Gate Light Vessel, sunk the previous day, Heise remained a PoW for the rest of the war. No.5 (Handley Page) hangar was destroyed by a direct hit from a 1,100lb (500kg) bomb, a barrack block used by sergeant pilots badly damaged. Later that afternoon, Hawkinge was attacked by HeIIIs of KG 1 and Do 17s of KG 2, little damage was caused with no fatalities or casualties. Flight Lieutenant A.R. Putt, Hurricane I P3040, was shot down, baled out, landed in the sea, was rescued uninjured. Flying Officer Grice No.32 Squadron was shot down on 15 August by an Me 109s near Harwich,

THE BATTLE OF BRITAIN 1940

On 15 August 1940, Ju 87B of 10/LG 1 struck wires at Shorncliffe during a raid on Hawkinge, crashing on houses at Shorncliffe Crescent, Folkestone. The crew Uffz. H. Weber and Uffz. F.H. Kraus were buried at the new Folkestone cemetery, Hawkinge.

baling out of Hurricane I N2459, landing in the sea, rescued, and taken to the RN Hospital, HMS *Ganges*, Shotley to treat his burns.

While RAF personnel and civilians cleared and repaired the airfield buildings, Royal Engineers worked on the runway and hangars. The Rt Hon. Anthony Eden, Secretary of State for War, arrived at Hawkinge on 18 August to inspect damage. During his visit, air raid warnings continued; unperturbed, the VIP and those with him talked informally to many pilots, RAF and Army personnel and civilians, before leaving Hawkinge. The Luftwaffe returned with six Do 17Zs escorted by Bf 109s, flying low over the village, they opened fire causing little damage. Ground defences fired back, none of the attackers were destroyed. No.151 Squadron scrambled from Rochford on 15 August, ran into seventy Me 109s protecting Do 17s heading inland between Dover and Folkestone. Pilot Officer M.T. Ellacombe and Pilot Officer M. Rozwadowski shot down two Me 109s, but later Pilot Officer M. Rozwadowski, Hurricane I V7410, and Pilot Officer

RAF HAWKINGE

Pilot Officer J. Ellacombe No.151 Squadron who on 21 August 1940 attended the funeral of Pilot Officer J.T. Johnston at Hawkinge cemetery, during which Ju 87s attacked the airfield.

J.T. Johnston, Hurricane I P3941, were shot down and killed. Pilot Officer J.T. Johnston crashed off Dymchurch, his body recovered from the sea. A third pilot, Sub Lieutenant H.W. Beggs, Hurricane I P3065, was shot down, crashing at Shorncliffe.

Pilot Officer A.G. McIntyre, Hurricane I P3595, No.111 Squadron, was injured during combat with Me 109s escorting Do 215s, landing at Hawkinge, his aircraft was written off. Flying Officer M.B. Fisher P3944 was shot down over Selsey Bill by a Ju 88 and killed. The following day Flight Lieutenant H.M. Ferris, Hurricane I R4193, collided with a Do 17 of KG 76 over Marden during a head on attack, killed instantly. Sergeant R. Carnall P3029 was shot down near Paddock Wood, slightly injured, his aircraft a write off.

By 18 August No.111 Squadron were exhausted. Flight Lieutenant S.D.P. Connors was killed when Hurricane I R4187 was hit by AA fire attacking a Do 17 near Wallington, London. Sergeant H.S Newton P3943 and Sergeant H.A. Deacon N2340 were shot down attacking Do 17s, Deacon crashed at Oxted, Kent, both survived. No.111 Squadron moved on 19 August to Debden for much needed 'rest and recuperation'.

THE BATTLE OF BRITAIN 1940

Pilots of No.111 Squadron – Left to Right: Sergeant R. Carnall, Sergeant R.J.W. Brown, Flying Officer P.J. Bruce, Flying Officer P.J. Simpson during August 1940. Note the Luftwaffe officer's cap. (R. Carnall)

Pilots of No.64 Squadron during a brief respite from fighter operations. On 16 August 1940, Squadron Leader A.R.D. MacDonnell (3rd from left) was shot down uninjured. Spitfire I P3554 returning to RAF Kenley from Hawkinge crashed at Black Boy, Uckfield.

RAF HAWKINGE

On 18 August, 'The Hardest Day' as it became known, Squadron Leader A.R.D. MacDonnell, No.64 Squadron Spitfire I R6623, based at Kenley detached to Hawkinge shot down Me 110C4 'U8+BB' of 1/ZG 26 which crashed at Dering Farm, Lydd. Spitfires of No.64 Squadron led by Squadron Leader MacDonnell made a scything attack on the Me 110 hitting both engines, wounding Bordfunker (Radio Operator) Uffz. Hans Mobius. The pilot Oblt. R. Proske, opened both throttles, he took his hands and feet off the controls, allowing the heavy aircraft to go into a violent spin. A risky manoeuvre but it worked, throwing off British fighters who were convinced the Me 110 was finished. Proske's comrades witnessed his dive, equally convinced, giving him up for dead. Spinning through 6,000ft (1,829 metres) before regaining control, Proske then set course for home. Both engines were smoking but running; crossing the coast at Dungeness, both engines stopped, catching fire.

Mobius, badly wounded in the legs could not move; Proske decided against ditching in the Channel, turned inland to put down. Proske cleared

Squadron Leader A.R.D. MacDonnell No.64 Squadron Spitfire I R6623, shot down Me 110C4 'U8+BB' of 1/ZG 26 on 18 August 1940, crashing at Dering Farm, Lydd. Oblt. R. Proske and Bordfunker (Radio Operator) Uffz. H. Mobius were both captured.

THE BATTLE OF BRITAIN 1940

HT cables before belly-landing at Dering Farm, Lydd. The heavy landing cost him a few teeth; releasing his seat harness, he pulled Mobius out of the cockpit, dragged him away from the aircraft. They slid down into a ditch but were found by troops based at an AA site. Six pilots of No.501 Squadron were shot down on 18 August: Pilot Officer K.N.T. Lee, Hurricane I P3059 'SD-N'; Flying Officer R.C. Daffron R4219; Pilot Officer K. Kozlowski P3815; Sergeant D.A.S. McKay N2617 survived. Sadly, Pilot Officer J.W. Bland P3208 'SD-T' and Flight Lieutenant G.E.B. Stoney P2549 were both killed.

Pilot Officer J. Ellacombe No.151 Squadron left Rochford and flew via Abingdon to Hawkinge for the funeral of Pilot Officer J.T. Johnston on 21 August:

> I took along Johnnie Comar, a Canadian, who had trained with me. We flew to Hawkinge, locals had laid on a padre and a firing squad of six airmen. At the end of the service, we heard a scream,

Hurricane I P3059 'SD-N' No.501 (County of Gloucester) Squadron RAuxAF, and P3208 'SD-T', lift off from Hawkinge in early August 1940. Note the camouflaged hangars in the background.

looking up we saw Junkers 87s heading our way, dropping bombs as they dived. The airmen disappeared in a flash. I told the padre to run like hell and Johnnie Comar and I jumped into the grave on top of Jim's coffin, giving us four or five feet of trench. When it was quiet, we climbed out we couldn't see the padre or the airmen. Even the gravediggers had disappeared, horrifying, saying goodbye to a friend during a raid.

Five of the Few
Steve Darlow

Patrolling Folkestone at 15,000ft (4.57km) on 22 August, No.610 Squadron were attacked by twenty Me 109s, from above and out of the sun. Sergeant D. Corfe was hit, and tried to land at Hawkinge, but crashed, leaping from Spitfire 1 R6695 which burst into flames, before it exploded. Flying Officer P.G. Lamb was shot down, forced landed at Hawkinge, wounded. During this engagement four Me 109s and a Do 215 were destroyed, another Me 109 probable. Pilot Officer J.P. Pfeiffer crashed Hurricane I P3205 No.32 Squadron at Hawkinge. The following day No.32 Squadron intercepted Bf 109s. Hurricane I P2795 was hit, crashing at Hawkinge on one wheel. Pilot Officer J. Rose No.32 Squadron Hurricane P3900 landed at Hawkinge, the reason unknown.

Some aircraft were shot down by local AA gun crews, often the culprit was never identified. In the heat of aerial combat, some such incidents by coastal defences or even RAF aircraft were often never reported. Pilot Officer J. Lockhart No.85 Squadron was on patrol over the Dover area on 24 August, when Hurricane I L1933 was hit by AA. Wounded, he headed for Hawkinge, over-running the runway due to flap damage. Cursing, he climbed from his Hurricane, another victim of 'friendly fire' rather than that of the Luftwaffe.

On 25 August Pilot Officer J. Rose Hurricane I V6547 shot down over the Channel by Me 109s, was rescued uninjured, by ASR that evening. Sergeant W.J. Green joined No.501 Squadron officially on 20 August 1940. Four days later he crashed at Hawkinge, being hit by AA fire during combat with Ju 88s and Bf 109s attacking Manston. Green was again shot down by Bf 109s on 29 August, baling out at 1,000ft (305 metres) he fell to 300ft (91.5 metres) before the parachute opened properly, the pilot chute cords severed by shrapnel. Rescued from the sea off Folkestone, his Hurricane 1 R4223 crashed at Elham Valley.

Sergeant 'Ginger' J.H. Lacey of No.501 Squadron had his first kill of the Battle of Britain on 20 July 1940, when he shot down a Bf 109E of 3/JG 3.

THE BATTLE OF BRITAIN 1940

Pilots of No.501 (County of Gloucester) RAuxAF Hawkinge during July/August 1940. Left to Right: Pilot Officer S. Witorzenc, Pilot Officer R.C. Daffron, Sergeant P.C.P. Farnes, Flight Lieutenant G.E.B. Stoney (KIA 18 August), Flying Officer K.N.T. 'Hawkeye' Lee, Sergeant F. Koziowski, Flight Lieutenant J.A.A. Gibson and Pilot Officer H.C. Adams (KIA 6 September).

The pilot, Oblt. Floerke, was killed, his aircraft burst into flames crashing in the sea. Between 12 August and 29 August, 'Ginger' Lacey destroyed and damaged a Ju 87, Ju 88, two Do 17s, two Bf 109s and an Me 110. Another famous pilot of No.501 Squadron Hawkinge was Pilot Officer Stanislaw Skalski, one of Poland's legendary fighter pilots. He joined the squadron as a replacement pilot, already responsible for the destruction of 6½ aircraft, flying with the Polish Air Force before escaping Poland and joining the RAF.

Based at Biggin Hill, No.32 Squadron continued using Hawkinge as a forward base during August 1940. Pilot Officer Keith Gillman joined No.32 Squadron on 10 May 1940, having previously been at Manby with No.1 Air Armament Course. He flew his first sortie on 7 June, escorting Blenheims attacking Abbeville. On 19 July he claimed an Me 109 destroyed. He often returned to Hawkinge following patrols in July and August, landing there twice on 24 August. At 0825hrs on 25 August Pilot Officer Gillman

RAF HAWKINGE

had taken off from Biggin Hill in Hurricane I P2755, with Squadron Leader Crossley and Flight Lieutenant Brothers, landing at Hawkinge they later returned to Biggin Hill, Pilot Officer Gillman again returned to Hawkinge.

At 1820hrs Pilot Officer Gillman Hurricane I P2433 with seven others were ordered to patrol Dover, and soon engaged Me 109s escorting Do 215s. Pilot Officer J. Rose, Hurricane I P6547, was shot down, baling out and landing in the sea – he was rescued uninjured. It soon became apparent that Pilot Officer Gillman was missing, shot down by Me 109s. Pilot Officer Keith Gillman is remembered, with many other pilots and aircrew, on Runneymede Memorial. A portrait photo him was often used on magazines, even today it has appeared on the cover of such books as *The Battle of Britain – Then and Now* 'published by *After the Battle* magazine.

No.610 (County of Chester) Squadron RAuxAF was scrambled from Hawkinge on 26 August led by Squadron Leader J. Ellis flying Spitfire I R6993, accompanied by ten Spitfire Is, one of these being Sergeant P. Else,

A view across the airfield during July/August 1940. Spitfire Is of No.610 (County of Chester) Squadron RAuxAF are at readiness. Note the starter trolleys (Accumulator trolleys) often found on RAF airfields to assist in starting aircraft engines, although the aircraft could be started from their own batteries.

THE BATTLE OF BRITAIN 1940

flying P9496 DW-L. The flight met Me 109s, Sergeant Else got on the tail of one, opening fire, hitting the target. At that moment he was warned over the RT that an Me 109 was behind him, suddenly his cockpit and instrument panel exploded in flames.

Else tried to open the hood but found it jammed; managing to get his left arm out, he was hit again, his arm falling to his side. At 25,000ft (7,620 metres) he managed to bale out, the Spitfire somersaulting over the Channel. With his injured arm useless, his right hand trapped in the parachute straps, desperately pulling the cord, the parachute finally opened. He was horrified to see an aircraft bearing down on him, fortunately a Spitfire, which began circling. As he drifted towards Folkestone he noticed his Mae West was damaged; he saw Hawkinge where he subsequently landed, 200yds (183 metres) from where he had taken off earlier. Rushed to Kent and County Hospital, Canterbury, he was treated for burns to his hands and face, his arm was amputated below the elbow. Spitfire I P9496 crashed, bursting into flames at Cole Farm, Paddlesworth. After several months, during which Peter Else lost the rest of his arm, he gradually recovered, but

Sergeant Peter Else at Hawkinge with Spitfire I P9496 'DW-L' of No.610 (County of Chester) Squadron RAuxAF in which he crashed at Paddlesworth on 26 August 1940. (P. Else)

always insisted his Spitfire crashed into the sea. Incredibly, after the war Peter joined Marshalls Aerospace at Cambridge as an engineer where he had previously been employed.

No.32 Squadron used Hawkinge as a forward base throughout the Battle of Britain, until 26 August when they moved from Biggin Hill to Acklington. Twelve pilots had been shot down or injured flying from Hawkinge, but none were killed. On 1 September, seven Me 109s, carrying bombs, swept over the airfield causing little damage, the airfield was quickly repaired. The German fighters had detached themselves from a formation of fifty aircraft. Eight bombs were dropped, which hit No.3 hangar already damaged by the raids in August and a small building was destroyed. It was decided to disperse some sections of the airfield, during which a 'Q Site' was completed at Wootton – a decoy site, used to divert attacking aircraft from the main airfield. In addition, a rest camp was under construction at Hockley Sole, known as 'Hawkinge D, as a precaution against air raids. On 4 September the Station HQ moved to Meridian House 2½ miles from the airfield.

A Hurricane of No.32 Squadron at Hawkinge, preparing for a patrol during the height of the Battle of Britain summer 1940.

THE BATTLE OF BRITAIN 1940

No.72 Squadron took off from Croydon at 0745hrs, on 2 September, later destroying three Bf110s and a Do 17, after which five Spitfires landed at Hawkinge joined by Spitfires from Croydon that afternoon. Squadron Leader R.B. Lees was wounded, Spitfire I K9840 was badly damaged and crashed at Hawkinge; the ground crew struggled to rescue him from the cockpit, bullets had struck the canopy, welding the framework.

Spitfires which had taken off from Hawkinge caught sight of AA fire over Chatham, firing at Do 17s, escorted by Bf 110s, and Bf 109s which they attacked. Squadron Leader A.R. Collins Spitfire I X4262 was shot down by a Bf 109 at Marden, and wounded in his knee and hand.

On 4 September, No.72 squadron was back at Croydon. After an early raid by Luftflotte 2, the Luftwaffe introduced new tactics, splitting its forces between the airfields of Fighter Command and factories constructing fighters. No.72 Squadron scrambled, Spitfires sighted an enemy formation over Tenterden and Tunbridge Wells, Junkers Ju 88s escorted by Bf 110s at 15,000 ft. (4,572 metres). Six Bf 110s and three Ju 88s were destroyed, two Bf 110s probables one Bf 110 damaged.

Flying Officer D. Sheen joined up with some Hurricanes only to find they were Me 109s. He immediately spun away out of trouble. Elated with No.72 Squadrons results, Air Chief Marshal Sir Keith R. Park, GCB, KBE, MC & Bar, DFC, AOC 11 Group, wired his congratulations. Flying Officer R. Deacon Elliot remembers: 'That evening several of us went up to London but just could not get going, so we bathed, fed, and tumbled into bed early, feeling rather exhausted. (*Swift to Battle* – Tom Docherty)

Following attacks on aircraft factories on 4 September, No.11Group ordered special cover for them on 5 September. The Luftwaffe concentrated on attacking airfields, the main targets being Biggin Hill, Croydon, Eastchurch, Lympne and North Weald. To counter these attacks No.72 Sqn moved to Hawkinge, after refuelling seven Spitfires patrolled the airfield at 25,000ft (7,620 metres). They engaged two formations of Bf 109s but came off worse, although one Bf 109 was destroyed and another damaged, Pilot Officer D.C. Winter in Spitfire I X4013 was shot down and killed by a Bf 109s at Elham, as were Sergeant M. Gray Spitfire I L1093 and Flying Officer D.F.B. Sheen Spitfire I X4034, shot down near Hawkinge.

As rumours of impending invasion by German forces spread, rifles were issued to non-combatants such as cooks and clerks. In the late afternoon of 6 September, Bf 109E-7/B of 6.II(S)/LG 2, flown by Feldwebel Werner Gottschalk, left his base at St Omer escorting bombers. Flying at 12,000ft

Fw. W. Gottschalk's Bf 109E-7/B following capture was taken to RAE Farnborough for evaluation, a golden opportunity for the RAF and engineers to assess the opposition.

(3,658 metres) near Chatham, his aircraft's fuel tank was hit by AA fire, made a perfect landing, much to the surprise of Flying Control. Under small-arms fire the pilot left the aircraft running for shelter in a hangar; wounded in the process, he was soon captured, and taken prisoner.

The Bf 109E was taken to the Royal Aircraft Establishment (RAE) Farnborough for evaluation and put on display. Captured German aircraft were often flown to RAF bases, enabling pilots and groundcrews to look over the opposition.

7 September – 30 September

Pilot Officer C.A.W. Bodie, Spitfire I LZ-F, No.66 Squadron force-landed at Hawkinge following combat with Bf 109s. Many aircraft shot down during the Battle of Britain survived to fly again. One such, X4321 No.66 Squadron, crash landed near Barnhurst Lane, Hawkinge on 7 September 1940. Flying Officer T.A.F. Elsdon was hit by our own flak, wounded and unable to bail

THE BATTLE OF BRITAIN 1940

out, he crash-landed Spitfire I X4254 near Stapleford, returning the same evening to Croydon.

Barrack Stores were evacuated to 'Chipdean', a house on Canterbury Road, as a precaution, just in time as Hawkinge was attacked by Me 109s armed with 250lb (113kg) bombs. Twelve aircraft dropped bombs straddling the Officers' Mess, the hangar, which had survived previous attacks, and old HQ Office buildings across the north side of the airfield, killing a soldier, injuring six others – two airmen, three civilians and an RAF officer. Unfortunately, six civilians died when a shelter in Hawkinge village received a direct hit.

Despite the Me 109s firing their guns prior to dropping bombs, airfield defences sustained no hits, but managed to open fire on the attackers. Accommodation known as the 'Hostel' was damaged, another destroyed the station HQ. The airfield was cratered around the northern perimeter and the centre of the airfield. However, no aircraft were damaged and Hawkinge remained operational, although pilots had to be careful taking-off and landing. All leave was cancelled and those on leave were immediately recalled to duty on 8 September. The Luftwaffe returned during the afternoon of the following day; their bombs fell harmlessly outside the

Spitfire I X4321 'LF-F' No.66 Squadron flown by Pilot Officer C.A.W. Bodie crash landed near Barnhurst Lane, Hawkinge on 7 September 1940, shot down by Bf 109s. This aircraft returned to service with No.303 (Polish) Squadron.

RAF HAWKINGE

airfield. On 11 September, Pilot Officer T.S. Wade No.92 Squadron arrived over the airfield, Spitfire I P9513 damaged during combat. Checking the condition of the runway, he forced landed without incident.

At Kenley No.501 Squadron was on thirty-minute availability on 14 September. Blue Section moved to Hawkinge, during a patrol a Do 215 was damaged by Sergeant Farnes. The previous day the Luftwaffe badly damaged Manston. They would return with every aircraft they could muster to attack Lympne and Hawkinge, preparing for a major attack on southeast airfields on 15 September, now recognised as the climax of assault on Great Britain and Battle of Britain Day; at Hawkinge, Royal Engineers repaired the runway in difficult circumstances.

Following concerns by Air Vice Marshal Park about defects in the British Defence system, including the lack of precise details of enemy aircraft being provided, the use of spotter techniques was introduced. On 15 September, a Spitfire of No.92 Squadron based at Manston was borrowed for this purpose. Flight Lieutenant A.R. Wright arrived at Hawkinge in Spitfire

NCOs of No.501 (County of Gloucester) Squadron RAuxAF display a fin recovered from a crashed Me 109 – possibly during the Battle of Britain period.

THE BATTLE OF BRITAIN 1940

P7441 to act as 'spotter pilot'. The idea was for the pilot to climb above enemy formations observing which type of aircraft were seen, numbers, direction, height etc. This information would then be passed to operators who would respond accordingly. On Wright's second flight, he was spotted by two Bf 109s but was instructed by control not to engage the enemy and managed to return without being attacked.

On 19 September the London Rifle Brigade tested the airfield defences; Pickett Hamilton turrets sited by the Station CO Wing Commander E.E. Arnold AFC, were at first seen as the answer to the problem of airfield defence. Manned by two men, they were entered by a hatch in the roof, when retracted it was flush with the aerodrome surface and able to bear the weight of a taxiing aircraft.

By June 1941 a total of 335 had been installed on airfields before it was finally realised they were virtually useless. Winston Churchill remarked after viewing Pickett Hamilton turrets: 'I saw these pillboxes for the first time when I visited Langley. This appears to afford an admirable means of anti-parachute defence and it should surely be widely adopted. Let me have a plan.' They could not, however, be used until flying had ceased and the crews would have had to carry ammunition across open ground with no cover. There was a risk of hitting or being hit by airfield defences. Water seepage at many places required continuous pumping. In 1942 it was considered the pillboxes were useless, and installation ended.

On 20 September, sixty-five men were evacuated to 'Hockley Sole', a house which became 'Hawkinge D'. The following evening, despite the threat of raids at Hawkinge, a Spitfire Fundraising Dance took place at Folkestone. Pilot Officer R. Deacon-Elliot No.72 Squadron had good cause to remember that date, he lost his close friend Pilot Officer D.F. 'Dutch' Holland, killed flying Spitfire Ia X4410, shot down over Canterbury.

In late September 1940, ACM Hugh Dowding was faced with two problems. The first was a change in Luftwaffe tactics. Until then the daylight striking force had been German bombers, escorted by fighters. With the shift in phases in the Battle of Britain, bombers concentrated on Channel convoys, then No.11 Group airfields, finally London. Göring's aim was to wear down the RAF squadrons, but instead he saw an unacceptable level of bombers lost. 'Jabos' – the German term for fighter bombers – had been tried by Luftwaffe units such as Erprobungsgruppe 210 during the battle, attacking at low level.

RAF HAWKINGE

Now bombers switched mainly to night attacks, day operations often consisting of Bf 109 sweeps and large numbers of Bf 109 Jabos with escorts intended to force the RAF to engage Luftwaffe fighters, while keeping pressure on the RAF. Jabos could always jettison bombs and revert to being fighters if intercepted. But they were not much of a tactical threat in that, apart from specialists like Erprobungsgruppe 210, they were highly inaccurate dropping bombs; against area targets such as London, however, they could cause significant damage and civilian deaths. It was impossible for Fighter Command Controllers to identify which incoming raids were fighter sweeps, which were escorted Jabo raids, or escorted bomber raids, the last two requiring different tactics to minimise RAF losses and maximise those of the Luftwaffe.

Dowding's second problem was how to hide the information the RAF was gleaning from Ultra, the information from interception of German transmissions encoded with the Enigma machine. Ultra had given the RAF advance warning of major Luftwaffe raids, with radio interceptions from the Y-Stations also providing clues. It was also providing information on German shipping. Dowding did not want the Germans becoming suspicious of how well prepared the British were. Dowding created a special unit of experienced pilots to patrol the Channel during daylight hours, alone or in pairs, identifying which incoming raids were Jabos and which were fighter sweeps, also providing information on German naval activity. Unwittingly, the Germans provided a believable source for the RAF's preparedness, and protected Ultra. This unit was called No.421 Flight, one of the first pilots joining was Pilot Officer James O'Meara, who received the DFC for his service with No.72 Squadron and was posted to Hawkinge on 28 September 1940 to commence training and organising pilots arriving to form No.421 Flight. On 1 October 1940 the flight was allotted six Spitfire IIas from No.66 Squadron. Flight Lieutenant Charles 'Paddy' Green was posted as the commanding officer.

On 23 September, Flying Officer J. MacKenzie, Hurricane R6887, Flying Officer H. Baker P9394 and Sergeant 'Bam' Bamberger R6697 No.41 Squadron, took off from Hornchurch, heading for Hawkinge to provide escort for Avro Anson N4914 of No.1 Coastal Artillery Cooperation Flight (CACF), based at Detling. The Anson was on a reconnaissance flight over Calais, to observe shells fired by the Army in cooperation with the Royal Marine Siege Regiment. The three Hurricanes took off from Hawkinge, the crew of the Anson observed three shells within the target area. They came under fire from AA units, followed by a surprise attack by 4 Me 109s, diving out of cloud cover. Flight Lieutenant R. McConnell immediately

THE BATTLE OF BRITAIN 1940

dived the Anson to sea level, flying hell for leather for the English coast, pursued by the Me 109s. Mackenzie opened fire, smoke poured from one of the Mess, which McConnell witnessed diving into the sea. Bullets entered the cockpit, killing the gunner, injuring the Wireless Operator, Sergeant J H Dowley was killed, the dingy housing and starboard engine caught fire. Shutting down the port engine, McConnell forced landed the Anson at East Langdon. Climbing out, he managed to put out the fire with the aircraft's extinguisher, saving the lives of Flight Lieutenant R H McConnell, Sergeant J McAllister, Leading Aircraftman L A C John who was injured.

No.41 Squadron, based at Hornchurch on 30 September, were engaged in combat with Me 109s over Dungeness, during which Spitfire 1 P9394 flown by Sergeant R. Beardsley, was hit. Heading for Hawkinge he forced landed, coming to a halt, he climbed out uninjured. Later he returned to Hornchurch by rail from London, carrying his parachute. Reaching the base, he was asked, 'where the hell have you been!' Somewhat surprisingly, as he had destroyed a Do 215 over the Channel and shot down an Me 109 shortly before crashing. By the end of September 1940, Hitler's plans for the invasion of Britain lay in ruins, the Luftwaffe defeated by day, a fateful month in the history of Britain. RAF Hawkinge had once again proved its worth, but there were still battles to be fought.

1 October – 31 October 1940

No.303 (Polish) City of Warsaw Squadron based at Northolt in September 1940 was the first Polish fighter squadron to be formed. Flying Officer W. Januszewicz, who joined the squadron on 2 August 1940, had already been involved in many operations. On 5 October 1940, twelve Hurricanes of the squadron joined No.1 (Canadian) Squadron over Rochester, engaging enemy aircraft. Januszewicz, flying Hurricane I P3892 RF-V, was hit by one of the Me 109s escorting Me 110s. The aircraft caught fire, the pilot was trapped inside. The blazing Hurricane was seen over Hawkinge, horrified onlookers watched as it plummeted to the ground, crashing at Stowting, not far from Hawkinge. Januszewicz was the twenty-third Polish pilot killed in the Battle of Britain and was awarded the Silver Cross of Virtutis Militari, the Cross of Valour and two bars.

One of the most famous episodes of this period at Hawkinge took place on 7 October, involving Pilot Officer K.W. 'Mac' Mackenzie DFC, AFC, AE with No.501 Squadron RAuxAF based at Kenley, the squadron using

RAF HAWKINGE

Hawkinge as its forward base. Brought to readiness early that morning, No.501 Squadron was scrambled to intercept a large force, comprising of Ju 88s, Me 110s and Me 109s. In company with No.605 Squadron RAuxAF, patrolling the approaches to Sevenoaks, they were vectored south, heading southeast, and attacking Me 109s. During this encounter Mac was attacked by a Me 109E-4, escaping he followed his CO down chasing another, which he fired at and hit. The German disappeared into cloud, but Mac caught him as he reappeared. In a half roll, closing fast, Mac opened up, hitting the Me 109's radiator, which then crashed into the sea. Lieutenant Erich B.O. Meyer of 2/JG 51 was rescued and taken PoW. 'Mac' Mackenzie, flying Hurricane I V6799, then joined an attack on eight other Me 109s, opening fire on another. He watched as the Me 109's belly was struck by his gunfire, the pilot broke away nearly colliding with Mac's Hurricane. The German dived towards Folkestone, Mac ran out of ammunition, then flew alongside the Me 109, gesticulating him to ditch. The pilot was slumped over the control column. Mac lowered his undercarriage to knock his tail off, but this reduced the Hurricane's speed too much.

He formated on the aircraft's port side and smacked his starboard wing down onto the Me 109s port tail plane. As 'Mac' pulled up, the aircraft plunged into the sea off Sandgate, partially sank without opening the canopy. Pilot Officer Mackenzie pulled up following the collision, crash-landing Hurricane I V6799 SD-X not far from Hawkinge. Unfortunately, he had unstrapped the cockpit harness and smashed his jaw on the gunsight. He was picked up by an Army car and driven to a RN Sick Quarters, Folkestone, his jaw was stitched up. 'Mac' was taken prisoner when shot down off France on 29 September 1941 flying with No.247 Squadron, eventually sent to Stalag Luft III at Sagan. Repatriated in October 1944, returning to the RAF retiring in 1967. Lieutenant Erich B.O. Meyer Me 109E-4 was recovered by Brenzett Aeronautical Museum, Romney Marsh in 1976, later moved to the Kent Battle of Britain Museum, where parts of the aircraft such as the wing are displayed.

A further attack on Hawkinge took place during the late morning of 9 October, during a heavy rainstorm. A formation of Me 109s dropped six bombs around the perimeter of the airfield, only one found its target, with no casualties or serious damage. During the afternoon at 1530hrs, Fw. Fritz Schweser of 7/JG 54 was shot down, and forced landed at Meridian Hut Farm, Hawkinge, his aircraft Me 109E-4 (5327) 6+, was set on fire by Schweser, and was taken prisoner. He had been attacked over Chatham, by Flying Officer E. Thomas in Spitfire I R6685 of No.222 Squadron, based at Hornchurch, at the same time Pilot Officer E. Lock No.41 Squadron, flying

THE BATTLE OF BRITAIN 1940

Me 109E4 of 2/JG 51 flown by Lieutenant E. Meyer, shot down by Squadron Leader H.A.V. Hogan and Pilot Officer K.W. 'Mac' McKenzie No.501 (County of Gloucester) Squadron RAuxAF on 7 October 1940, being recovered off Dymchurch in 1976 by Brenzett Aeronautical Museum, Romney Marsh.

Spitfire I X4017, also attacked Schweser. Pilot Officer Lock had destroyed another Me 109, south of Dungeness, which crashed into the sea.

Three pilots of 'B' Flight No.66 Squadron from Gravesend flew to Hawkinge for an unspecified mission. Pilot Officer R.O.W. Oxspring, Pilot Officer H.R. 'Dizzy' Allen and Pilot Officer J.H.T. 'Pickles' Pickering, had flown patrols from Hawkinge in September 1940, briefed by the CO of Hawkinge Wing Commander E.E. Arnold AFC. Pilot Officer R.O.W. Oxspring wrote:

> Our task was to escort an Avro Anson to Calais to spot the fall of Royal Artillery shells from long-range guns at Dover; one shell to be fired every fifteen minutes over the period of an hour. Orders are orders – we pressed on across the Channel. Our charge and its apprehensive crew extracted every ounce of power from the Cheetah engines. If they hit 120 mph it was

pushing it, at altitude of 10,000ft was nudging the operational ceiling. We tottered over Calais when presumably the first shell arrived from Dover. It was not recorded whether the crew pinpointed the fall, we retreated out to sea, returning fifteen minutes later for another shot. We sighted six German fighters climbing up sun to the south. Not being in radio contact with the Anson we used the prearranged warning signal by rocking our wings. The Anson pilot needed no urging, heading back for Hawkinge as fast possible. It is unbelievable that Fighter Command with a shortage of Spitfires and pilots could hazard its resources on a pointless mission, we would all have been sitting ducks. Shepherding our Anson to Hawkinge we hurried back to Gravesend. A further four operations were to be flown that day; we forced a Heinkel III to crash land at Walland Marsh burning on impact.

Spitfire Command
Group Captain R.O.W. Oxspring DFC, AFC

During the afternoon of 12 October, Flying Officer A.J.S. Pattinson took off with No.92 Squadron from Biggin Hill to patrol the Maidstone area, and soon intercepted Bf 109s. Pattinson's Spitfire I, X4591 was hit and crashed at Bartholomew's Wood, Postling near Hawkinge, killing the pilot as it burnt. Hawkinge was again attacked on 14 October at 1540hrs by an unidentified bomber, flying in clouds at 1,000ft (305 metres), dropping four bombs. One fell on the airfield south of the Signals Section, with no damage. A second fell near No.3 hangar, damaging the water main carrying the supply to the operational side of the airfield. A third demolished the officers' squash court, damaging the Sergeants' Mess, Education Block, and the old Officers' Mess. The fourth landed on a haystack outside the airfield, seriously injuring a soldier of the Buffs who died later. Thirteen airmen were injured, two civilian NAAFI women were cut by flying glass. Airfield defences opened fire but without success, telephone communications were disrupted, damage was repaired but no aircraft on the airfield were damaged. The aircraft strafed both the airfield and Folkestone, before making a hasty retreat. As a further precaution, the Stores Account section moved to 'Holmlea' house at Hawkinge on 15 October Air raid warnings continued during the day.

Raids took place in the southeast area on 27 October; although not comparable to the air battles fought by the squadrons of No.11 Group on 15 August, no less than twelve German aircraft were destroyed. Hawkinge,

THE BATTLE OF BRITAIN 1940

Coltishall, Feltwell, Driffield, Leconfield, Martlesham, and Kirton-in-Lindsey were attacked by KG 1, 3, 4 and KG 76. Hawkinge was attacked at 1715hrs by Me 109s, escorted by another four Me 109s, which remained above the attacking group. Six bombs were dropped, two outside the perimeter of the airfield. One struck the runway, 150ft (46 metres) from the Duty Officer's hut, making a large crater. Another exploded in an existing grater, and the old Officers' Mess, a cabbage patch and the Postal Office were damaged. There were no casualties, aircraft dispersed around the airfield survived the attack, airfield defences fired on the intruders, one reported hit. The last days of October 1940 were fairly peaceful despite continuous air raid warnings, giving everyone at Hawkinge time to take stock and effect repairs unhindered by further attacks. Poor weather helped. The 31 October 1940 officially closed the Battle of Britain, being the quietest month, the war, however, had only just begun; Hawkinge battered and bruised would continue the fight.

Flight Lieutenant R.A.B. Learoyd VC, who was born in Folkestone in 1913, was presented with the Honorary Freedom of his hometown on 2 November 1940. New Romney. A Hampden flew to Blackpool from No.49 Squadron Scampton, from there Learoyd, accompanied by the crew and the ferry pilot, headed for Hawkinge. Prior to that he flew over his home at New Romney; completing three circuits he prepared to land. Lowering the undercarriage as he entered air space at Hawkinge, he came under gunfire from airfield defences, who obviously had a problem with Aircraft Recognition. The co-pilot was hit in the leg by debris from the damaged instrument panel, he immediately raised the undercarriage and headed for Detling; the injured pilot was rushed to hospital where he made a full recovery. Learoyd was loaned a car and driver, and rushed off to New Romney, where he gave a speech about his VC and near demise at the hands of trigger-happy AA units.

An inquiry held at Dover Castle revealed Hampden P1176 had landed safely at Detling with no less than thirty-two bullet holes peppered over the airframe. Such incidents were common during the war; much effort was made to train gun crews in Aircraft Recognition, although in this case it appears that Hawkinge was not fully briefed about Flight Lieutenant Learoyd's flight. Learoyd was fired on by small arms, although the crew were not aware of this. The Colonel in charge of the AA units watched the Hampden's progress from Learoyd's home with his mother, who frantically appealed to him to stop the guns firing on the Hampden! One pilot of No.421 Flight was Pilot Officer J. O'Meara, who had just received the DFC for his service with

RAF HAWKINGE

No.72 Squadron was posted to Hawkinge on 28 September 1940, to train and organise pilots being sent to form No.421 Flight. It was through the determined efforts of their CO, Squadron Leader C.P. Green, that they were re-equipped with Spitfire IIs, best suited for the new role.

No.421 (Reconnaissance) Flight was formed from No.66 Squadron based at Gravesend on express orders of AVM Dowding, initiated by Winston Churchill who wanted a special unit operating over the English Channel to report the build-up of bombers over the southeast coast to Uxbridge. Despite the use of the term 'Reconnaissance' to describe No.421 Flight's operational role, the unit was not involved in Photographic Reconnaissance, but had been formed with Hurricane IIs to meet a requirement for a special unit flying standing patrols over the Kent/Sussex coast. Although enemy activity in the area had diminished, they proved a great asset to the RAF. Following experiments in the use of a spotter aircraft – flying a Spitfire from Hawkinge to observe incoming Luftwaffe aircraft, a new unit, No.421 (Reconnaissance) Flight, was formed at Hawkinge on 15 November 1940 with nine Spitfires IIs; the first Hawkinge based unit formed for many months, which initially flew an assortment of Hurricanes and Spitfires.

Despite the Luftwaffe turning to night attacks, Air Sea Rescue by armed camouflaged Heinkel He 59s continued. As dusk fell on 26 November, Flight Lieutenant O'Meara flying a Hurricane of No.421 Flight, attacked what he thought was an He 60, which in fact was an He59:

> The presence of an He 60 and its fighter escort approaching Dungeness was given to us by the 'Y' service Unit at Capel le Ferne by telephone, instead of going via Biggin Hill. I took off in the nearest aircraft available, arriving in the area plotted by 'Y' service, I found the Heinkel. I didn't know think about the possibility of a fighter escort and went for it from the beam. I watched it fall into the sea and then raced back. I recollect that I had been in the air for only 14 minutes. The He 59 had been searching for Fw. Adolf Rosen of IV/JG 51, shot down by No.66 Squadron. For the Seenotdienst floatplane crews, the Battle over Britain had been a long and bloody campaign.
>
> AIR 50 Combat Report – NA

On 27 November, Sergeant D.A.B. McKay No.421 Flight, shot down an Me 109E, five miles south of Folkestone. Two Me 109s headed towards

Folkestone, one trailing black smoke, he followed both out to sea; closing in; he opened fire on the damaged aircraft, turning over it dived into the sea and disintegrated; McKay had hit the Me 109's fuel tank. McKay was again on patrol on 17 December 1940 off Dungeness, when he shot down a Do 17. Flying Officer K.A. Lawrence (NZ) No.421 (Reconnaissance) Flight damaged a Bf 110 on 23 November; flying alone on an early morning weather recce on 27 November over Ramsgate, he attacked three Bf 109s of II/JG 26, but was attacked by a fourth flown by Oblt. Gustav Sprick Staffelkapitän 8/JG 26.

Lawrence's Spitfire II P7499 lost a wing and he found himself falling in his stockinged feet with his right arm useless but managed to deploy his parachute, landing in the sea; he was picked up by a lifeboat and taken to Ramsgate.

Flying Officer K.A. Lawrence (NZ) No.421 (Reconnaissance) Flight Hawkinge, shot down and wounded flying Spitfire II P7499 on 27 November 1940 by Oblt. G. Sprick Staffelkapitän 8/JG 26. (RNZAF)

Lawrence was admitted to hospital with a fractured right leg, lacerated left leg and dislocated right shoulder later transferring to RAF hospital at Halton, where he was to meet his future wife. On 1 December 1940, Flying Officer P. McDonnell Hartas was on a reconnaissance patrol with Flying Officer D. Parrottt when they spotted two Bf 109s above them. Deciding not to engage they dived away. But Hartas, flying Spitfire IIA P7498, got on the tail of a Bf 109E-4 flown by Oberf B. Seufert 6/JG 53 who crashed into the sea, and was killed. Flying Officer P. McDonnell Hartas joined No.421 Flight at Hawkinge in October 1940 from No.603 Squadron.

December 1940 began well when Pilot Officer J.J. O'Meara No.421 Flight, intercepted a Do 17Z-2 south of Eastchurch, which he damaged. On 5 December, Hawkinge again received the attention of Me 109s, dropping bombs which fell harmlessly on the airfield's perimeter. There were no injuries, damage to aircraft or buildings, Me 109s attacked minesweepers in the Channel. Pilot Officer J.J. O'Meara No.421 Flight took on six Me 109s, destroying one, another probable and damaging a third. Among this turmoil an Autogiro C30.A, flown by Flying Officer G.C. Turner came into view, landing at Hawkinge, engaged on reconnaissance flights. Turner would later be involved with No.529 Squadron on Radar Calibration duties.

Flight Sergeant J. Gillies No.421 Flight crash-landed his Hurricane on 17 October following combat with Bf109s and was injured. During 7 December, he and another pilot chased a Dornier to the French coast. Low on fuel, he crashed No.421 Flight's special blue Spitfire, so camouflaged for high altitude flying, just short of Hawkinge. Sergeant D.H. Forest posted to No.421 Flight shared the destruction on 8 December 1940 of a Do 17 off Dover. Sergeant D.A.S. McKay moved to No.421 Flight Hawkinge on 22 October 1940. McKay claimed a Bf 109 on 27 November 1940 and a Ju 88 on 17 December; he was awarded the DFM on 07 January 1941.

Sergeant M.A.W. Lee was posted from No.72 Squadron on 3 October 1940 to No.421 Flight Hawkinge. Lee was wounded, his Spitfire P7444 damaged by Bf 109s and crashed attempting a forced landing at Blackman's Farm, Broadoak, Canterbury on 12 December. Later that day, with weather deteriorating, unable to return to Hawkinge, he wrecked his Spitfire trying to make an emergency landing at Lingfield. Taking off on 22 December to find Wellingtons which were lost, he escorted two over the Sussex Coast. One crashed, killing the crew, the other forced landed. Low on fuel, Lee had to glide down through dense cloud, belly-landed. Lee was killed on 31 December 1940, crashing near Biggin Hill in bad weather, attempting to land, the aircraft burnt out.

Flying Officer D.T. Parrott was posted to No.421 Flight at Hawkinge in October; wounded on 19 October, he force-landed at Clement Street, Old Swanley in Hurricane Z2352, the cause unknown. Sergeant A.W. Spears arrived at No.421 Flight Hawkinge on 4 October 1940, remaining with the flight when it became No.91 Squadron on 11 January 1941. Spears was shot down by Adolf Galland over Kent on 4 April 1941, his 58th victory. Flying Officer Parrott was admitted to Deal Hospital with splinters in the right arm and bullets in the leg. Spears lost his flying category and was attached to Redhill in September 1941, as a duty pilot on flying control, a week later posted to Croydon control tower. Flying Officer Parrott was killed on 22 June 1941 with No.29 Squadron and buried at Maidstone Cemetery.

Chapter 7

A Year of Change 1941
'Jim Crow' and Air Sea Rescue

The CO of No.91 Squadron Flight Lieutenant C.P. 'Paddy' Green DFC, who had also been the CO of No.421 (Reconnaissance) Flight, hosted a party on New Year's Eve 1940, for those who could be spared operational duties. Despite appalling weather, flying continued that day with Spitfires of No.91 Squadron taking off in pairs. No.421 Flight was later expanded to full squadron strength and renumbered as No.91 Squadron on 11 January 1941. Its role led to pilots being nicknamed 'Jim Crows'. At least eight pilots who joined No.421 Flight, were or later became fighter aces, a reflection of the level of experience and ability and why the squadron had a reputation as a 'crack' unit, Hawkinge being the ideal location for the squadron's operations.

Squadron Leader C.P. 'Paddy' Green DFC No.91 (Nigeria) Squadron at Hawkinge who took over command from Squadron Leader F.C. Hopcroft on 18 January 1941 until 11 June 1941. A popular leader, seen here on News Year Day 1941 with his pet 'Husky'. (RAF Museum Hendon)

RAF HAWKINGE

Flight Lieutenant B. Drake DFC and Flying Officer J.J. O'Meara DFC of No.421 Flight, took off from Hawkinge on the morning of 7 January 1941, patrolling Dover. They intercepted and damaged a Ju 88, shortly after Drake claimed another Ju 88 in the vicinity of Hawkinge. Three Me 109s found Hawkinge again on the evening of 12 January; diving, they dropped bombs just outside the airfield, there were no casualties, damage to buildings or parked aircraft. At the beginning of 1941, there was a distinct lack of accommodation for RAF personnel at Hawkinge. To alleviate the problem the Air Ministry requisitioned six houses in the village and the local primary school, which became available on 20 January, providing much needed living quarters, also reducing the casualties during further air attacks, a constant threat.

Flying Officer J.J. O'Meara DFC flying Spitfire II P7601 No.421 Flight was returning from a routine patrol on 2 February. Coming into land he struck soft mud, the Spitfire's brakes did not operate properly and it crashed on the airfield. O'Meara climbed out, unscathed. He had been patrolling over the straights of Dover with Flight Lieutenant Lee Knight when they intercepted a Do 17 off Calais, which was damaged by Flying Officer J.J. O'Meara. Flight Lieutenant B. Drake DFC No.91 Squadron

Mechanics swarm over Spitfire IIa DL-N at RAF Hawkinge, the squadron was formed from No.421 Flight, initially flying a mixture of the Spitfire IIa and Vb, operating from RAF Hawkinge from 9 January 1941. (RAF Museum)

A YEAR OF CHANGE 1941

forced landed at Hawkinge following a patrol on special duty at 36,000ft (10972 metres) over France when his Spitfires engine seized. Near Le Crotoy, about seventy miles from base, Drake managed to glide his Spitfire home, landing with only 25yds (23 metres) of runway to spare.

On 4 February 1941, Bf 109s dived out of cloud, dropping a bomb close to No.91 Squadron's 'B' Flight dispersal. Spitfire II P7735 was struck by an incendiary cannon shell, bursting into flames. This aircraft flown by Flight Sergeant D.A.S. McKay's pride and joy, and he got his revenge when he took off in Squadron Leader C.P. 'Paddy' Green's Spitfire IIA P7307, intercepting two Me 109s flying near Deal, firing two quick bursts of gunfire he saw one of the fighters explode, and damaged the second. Later that day Pilot Officer Beake, injured, forced landed at West Cut Farm, out of fuel, following a prolonged patrol. Squadron Leader A.G. 'Sailor' Malan DFC, DSO had to put down at Hawkinge on 5 February, while attached to No.74 Squadron. Taking off from Biggin Hill in Spitfire II P7623 XP-A he forced landed at Hawkinge due to a Glycol leak, following combat.

The same day between two aircraft of No.615 Squadron based at Kenley collided. Hurricane I V7598 KW-S flown by Pilot Officer S.J. Czternastek (Polish) RAFVR, returning from escort duties, collided with Hurricane I V6618, Pilot Officer B. Wydrowski baled out injured. Czternastek was killed and his Hurricane crashed at Appleton Manor Farm, Dover; he was later buried at Hawkinge. Two days later Pilot Officer W. Watling was killed when Spitfire II R6924 No.92 Squadron, flew into high ground at Woodhill Cops, Deal, having left Manston in poor weather.

Two Bf 109s 5/LG 2, based at Calais-Marck, attacked Hawkinge. AA units opened fire, hitting Lieutenant Werner Schlathe Bf 109E-7 (6410) 'Black T' crashed at Arpinge Farm, Newington, Kent, killing its pilot. Identified by its distinctive red nose and yellow tail, he tried to dodge the gunfire with an impressive aerobatic display. But the gunners were on target, and as it stall-turned, the port wing started to fall, its undercarriage dropped; out of control, it spun into a field. The other German pilot watched in horror as his colleague died as the aircraft disintegrated on impact. The remains of the aircraft and its pilot were found by personnel from Hawkinge at a depth of 12ft. (3.65 metres). The other Bf 109E-4 was hit but escaped out to sea. This crash site was excavated by Brenzett Aeronautical Museum (now Romney Marsh Wartime Collection) in 1973, today these remains can be found at the Kent Battle of Britain Museum, Hawkinge. Spitfire II P7615 was burned out, but no casualties, another P7598 damaged by machine gun fire, both No.91 Squadron.

RAF HAWKINGE

On 10 February Flying Officer Peter McDonnell Hartas flew Spitfire IIA P7888 No.421 Flight flew into the Downs near Hawkinge in low cloud, he later died in hospital of his injuries. The same day Warrant Officer Rudolf Ptacek (Czech) based with No.615 Squadron Kenley, forced landed Hurricane I P3811 at Dungeness, due to lack of fuel. This Hurricane was transported to No.3257 Maintenance Unit and converted to a Hurricane II during repair – renumbered DG644. On 12 February, three Me 109s swooped down on Hawkinge from a height of 5,000ft (1,524 metres) dropping bombs. Airfield defences failed to hit any of the intruders, there was no damage or injuries reported.

At 1300hrs on 13 February Sergeant McKay was scrambled to patrol the Dover area when he intercepted an Me 109, immediately opening fire, causing some damage, the German headed for cloud cover. McKay arrived just in time as the Me 109 had destroyed no less than three barrage balloons at Dover. The funeral of Flying Officer Peter McDonnell Hartas No.91 Squadron took place at Hawkinge on 14 February. The CO Squadron Leader C.P. Green with other members of the squadron, many airmen, officers and WAAFs serving at Hawkinge attended the service. The same day Spitfire II P7351, flown by Pilot Officer Gage, crash landed at the airfield, its wheels having dug into soft ground. Another P7751 crashed due to enemy action, came down at Longage Farm, the pilot Pilot Officer Lawson was uninjured.

On 16 February as No.421 Flight reformed as No.91 Squadron, the Archbishop of Canterbury W.C.G. Lang, 1st Baron Lang of Lambeth, GCVO, PC, arrived and gave a service in the village of Hawkinge. Lang had been responsible for drafting King George V's silver jubilee broadcast message in 1935, and the King's last two Christmas messages.

Casualties on 20 February 1941 included Sergeant Pilot J. McAdam of No.41 Squadron operating from Hornchurch, who with Sergeant R. Angus were shot down by Oberlt. Werner Molders JG 51. McAdam's Spitfire IIA P7302, was seen diving towards the sea, the pilot baled out of the aircraft which burst into flames, landing in the sea. An ASR launch arrived looking for McAdam and Angus, who had also crashed in the sea. The body of McAdam was found ten miles northeast of Dover. Angus was never found. The search had been joined by a Lysander flown from Hawkinge.

Two days later, Spitfire IIA P7816 No.41 Squadron Hornchurch, was returning from a sweep when it dived into the ground at Chilham near Canterbury. The pilot, Sergeant J. Gilders, did not bale out of his aircraft, which buried itself into the ground at a depth of 20ft (6 metres), the crater quickly filled with water. It was thought Gilders suffered from lack of oxygen, causing him to pass-out. An eyewitness suggested the aircraft was a Hurricane, this was proved false, as no Hurricane was reported missing that day.

No.49 Maintenance Unit attended the crash site, and found some aircraft remains, it was assumed the pilot was buried with his aircraft. In 1993 the Air Ministry refused permission to excavate the site as requested by Aircraft Archaeologist Mark Kirby on behalf of the Gilders family. The excavation took place against the Air Ministry ruling, the pilot and Spitfire IIA P7816 were recovered on 11 May 1995. Sergeant J. Gilders was buried at Brookwood Cemetery, he had proposed to his girlfriend on Valentine's Day 1941, and she attended his funeral in 1995.

At Hawkinge in February 1941, the weather reduced flying, in fact the mists that rolled in over Hawkinge were nicknamed the 'Hawkinge Horror', often preventing patrols. Lympne suffered the same problem, although pilots who flew from both airfields would have been grateful for a temporary pause in operations. Returning from operations over the Channel on 22 February, badly shot up with shrapnel, Spitfire IIA P7738 crashed at Rye. Pilot Officer Winskill, miraculously, climbed out of his beat-up aircraft, with no serious injuries.

During the night of 24 February, Spitfire IIA P7675 crashed due to an error by Sergeant J. 'Jack' Gillies No.41 Squadron. Flying from Tangmere on 26 February, Spitfire IIA P7691 No.610 Squadron, forced landed due to enemy action. Pilot Officer J.E.I. Grey, shot down over Rye harbour, was slightly injured. Sergeant N. Morrison RAFVR No.74 Squadron, failed to return from a routine ASR (Air Sea Rescue) flight on 24 February 1941; his body was recovered off Lydd-on-Sea on 7 April. Killed while flying in Spitfire II, P7618 of No 74 Squadron, he was buried in Glasgow (Eastwood) Cemetery. During the Battle of Britain, he had served with No.54 Squadron until moving to No.72 Squadron. Sergeant N. Morrison destroyed an Me 109 on 29 October, another over the Channel between Dover and Calais on 1 November and shared the destruction of a Me 109 on 2 December 1940 with Squadron Leader A.G. 'Sailor' Malan.

On 27 February, Sergeant P.M.A. McSherry No.609 Squadron was shot down over Dungeness by an Me 109 of I/LG 2. Spitfire IIA P7785 crashed near Hawkinge at St Martin's Plain, killing the pilot. The following day, 'Whitegate House' in Old Hawkinge was taken over as the dispersed Officers' Mess, situated on Coach Road between Acrise and Densole. which survives today, listed on 29 December 1966 as a building of historic importance.

RAF HAWKINGE

An attack took place on 10 March 1941, when two Me 109s flew over the airfield dropping four bombs. There were some slight casualties when a bomb fell outside the Officers' Mess breaking windows, another struck the wall around the Gas Centre. Shortly after, Squadron Leader Z.K. Henneberg KW and Bar No.303 Squadron, approached Hawkinge in Spitfire IIA P7821 following a patrol over Calais. On landing, the aircraft tipped-up, Henneberg climbed out uninjured. Sergeant M. Popek also of No.303 Squadron, followed him in Spitfire IIa P8040, damaging his aircraft.

On 12 March, Sergeant Jack Mann DFM forced landed Spitfire IIA P7693 near Newington, not far from Hawkinge. Hit by gunfire during combat with Bf 109s he was relieved to have landed safely. No.91 Squadron had engaged aircraft of Stab/JG 51 over Dungeness, and were joined in the fight by No.74 Squadron, who lost Sergeant J.N. Glendenning during the same operation when Spitfire IIa P7506 crashed not far from Brenzett. The same day, an Avro Rota or Cierva C30A (Autogyro) of No.74 (Signals) Wing, Duxford, Cambridgeshire had a taxiing accident at Hawkinge. This was one of four Rotas on charge, with another thirteen civil Rotas impressed into RAF service and used for the slow, precise flying needed to calibrate the aerial arrays of coastal defence Chain Home radar installations. They usually operated autogyros on individual detachment, flying from an airfield close to the radar station to which they were assigned for calibration. The Rotas flew out into the English Channel and back. Fighter escorts were provided, usually Gladiators, Skuas later Hurricanes, as they were occasionally needed in areas where enemy aircraft might be encountered. One such encounter, which occurred in 1943, will be related later. Autogyros of No.74 Wing later became No.1448 (Radar Calibration) Flight, based at Halton, Buckinghamshire. On detachment each machine worked with a designated radar station, in the case of Hawkinge, Rye the staff consisting of pilot, fitter, and rigger. The Luftwaffe seemed to relish attacking Hawkinge, returning on 13 March during breakfast. Bf 109s of II/JG 54 on a sweep over Kent, crossed out over Folkestone. Five peeled off, dropping two bombs outside the airfield. No.91 Squadron were scrambled to intercept, Flight Lieutenant R.H. Holland and Sergeant A. Spears claimed two destroyed. Not to be left out, the AA at Hawkinge claimed a third damaged.

The morning of 4 April 1941 began peacefully at Hawkinge, but during late afternoon No.91 Squadron was scrambled searching for raiders reported over the Channel. A Ju 88 of II/KG 76 was spotted near Deal and attacked by Pilot Officer Cage, bullets striking the Ju 88, killing one of the crew and injuring two others. Oberlt. Kroner escaped, making his way to Amiens.

A YEAR OF CHANGE 1941

Moving southeast, two Stab/Bf 109s of JG 26 were seen by Sergeant A.W. Spears and Sergeant J. Mann who were seeking another Ju 88. Major Adolf Galland and Oberlt. R. Menge were flying a transfer flight to Brest, Galland attacked, hitting Spitfire IIA P7565. Sergeant Spears baled out wounded, his aircraft crashed at Reinden Wood, Hawkinge. Sergeant Jack Mann was shot down by Menge, crash-landing his blazing Spitfire IIA P7783 at Little Mongeham, Hawkinge and leaping out just in time, as the fuel tanks exploded. Badly burnt, he eventually recovered; in later life he enjoyed a successful career in civil aviation, retiring in Beirut, only to become one of the unfortunate hostages, held prisoner for several years.

Hawkinge was visited on 7 April by Archibald Sinclair, Secretary of State for Air, who regularly visited RAF establishments. On arrival he was shown around No.91 Squadron's dispersals and chatted to pilots. By coincidence he witnessed the destruction of a barrage balloon, which had broken loose from Dover heading southwest at 6,000ft (1,829 metres), before it was finally shot down. A regular occurrence, these renegade balloons were sometimes destroyed by ground-fire or aircraft. During the day it was announced that Squadron Leader C.P. Green had been awarded the DFC; he led many patrols and was popular with all ranks he commanded for this reason.

Five Hurricanes of No.302 Squadron landed on 10 April to refuel; they were on a mission to locate the CO of No.303 Squadron. Returning from a mission against French airfields on 12 April 1941, Squadron Leader Henneberg's Spitfire IIA P8029 was damaged by enemy fire, crashing in the sea 10/13 miles (16/21km) off Dungeness; it was not found, and he was presumed to have drowned. Early in the morning of 13 April, four Spitfires of No.303 Squadron landed at Hawkinge to refuel, they were airborne again at 0910hrs, they had been on an Air Sea Rescue patrol. Two of these returned to Hawkinge landing at 1030hrs having been in action. One of these was Spitfire IIA P7567 flown by Flight Lieutenant W. Lapkawski, who was attacked by an Me 109 off Le Touquet, he was injured in the head, but managed to bring his damaged Spitfire in to land; assisted out of the cockpit by staff, he was taken to Folkestone Hospital for treatment.

Sergeant W. Morgan served with No.541 Flight, part of No.1 (PRU) Squadron a Photo Reconnaissance Unit based at Benson. On 14 April 1941 he undertook a reconnaissance mission to Northern Italy that lasted seven hours and ten minutes. He landed his Spitfire I (PR) Type D serial P9552 at Hawkinge with only two gallons of fuel left; for this extraordinary flight, Morgan was later awarded the DFM. Many of the PRU Spitfires were painted blue or even pink, ideal camouflage for PRU missions at high altitude, these Spitfires were not armed. Spitfire I P9552 was lost on 10 May 1941on a PR mission to Stettin and Swinemunde, the pilot Sergeant P.A. Mills believed killed.

At 1745hrs on 15 April, No.65 Squadron joined forces with No.266 and No.402 Squadrons, to fly a 'sweep' via Dungeness round Boulogne, returning via Hornchurch and Dover. At 1758hrs, Sergeant Foulger was shot up and crash landed at Hawkinge, the tail section of Spitfire IIA P8179 was severely damaged, later repaired. Also shot down during this operation, crash landing at Hawkinge, was Sergeant R.T.G. Whewell of No.266 Squadron in Spitfire IIA P8014; he fell to the guns of Adolf Galland JG 26. Group Captain T.N. McEvoy No.601 Squadron CO, was also shot down by an Me 109 of JG 51, crash-landing at Lydd. A Miles Mentor of the Station Flight, Northolt, arrived to return McEvoy to his squadron. During the early months of 1941, Fighter Command allied with the Royal Navy for Operation *Channel Stop*. Its purpose, to deny enemy shipping access to Channel Ports, and prevent the Germans attacking British ships and rescue vessels duration evacuation the of Dunkirk. Two Hurricane squadrons were based at Manston, supported by Spitfires of No.91 Squadron.

On 18 April, Spitfire IIa P7351 piloted by Sergeant E.E. Sykes No.91 Squadron hit the sea off Sandgate following combat with an Me 109. Suffering from shock and slightly injured, Sykes climbed out, swimming ashore, watched by passers-by who had seen the Spitfire approaching the coast. An Me 109 flew over the airfield on 24 April, but did not attack, none of the ground defences opened fire. Another aircraft, this time luckily a Blenheim, performed a mock attack on Hawkinge, for Gun Sighting purposes; another exercise took place two days later, this time a Defiant assisted by a Blenheim, acting as aggressors. A Barrage balloon tethered in the Dover area broke away on the night of 5 May. Still in the vicinity the following day, it was destroyed. Also on 5 May, when Dover was being shelled, Hawkinge was attacked by a lone Bf109, Spitfire IIA P7294 a Presentation Spitfire christened 'Derrick' of No.91 Squadron, caught fire, fortunately ground crew were not servicing the aircraft. Flight Sergeant A. Smitton Darling in Spitfire IIA P7615 of No.91 Squadron was shot down and killed by Bf 109s on 26 April 1941. The aircraft crashed at Reinden Wood, near Hawkinge.

An unusual event took place on 6 May 1941, recorded in the Hawkinge Operations Book; four Dutchman stole a German seaplane, flying it back to England. Lieutenant G. Steen, Corporal E.W. Boomsma, both Dutch

A YEAR OF CHANGE 1941

Army Aviation Brigade, Fokker aircraft technician W.J. Lindeman (former Dutch Army), and Lieutenant Jan Beelaerts van Blokland swam out to a Luftwaffe Fokker T. VIIw (TD+CL) seaplane moored on the Minerva Haven, Amsterdam. At dawn they took-off. Steen had never flown the type, but evading British AA fire they landed at Broadstairs. Jan Hof, a Dutchman, recorded this amazing story in his book *Niet Schieten. We are Dutch!* Lieutenant van Blokland and Lindeman joined the Princess Irene Brigade, with van Blokland becoming its CO during operations in Normandy. Leiutenant T. Steen joined No.129 (Mysore) Squadron, flying seventy-nine sorties before being shot down and killed on 5 June 1942.

RAF Tangmere on the coast of Sussex was home to the Tangmere Wing, No.145 Squadron, No.610 (County of Chester) and No.616 (South Yorkshire) RAuxAF Squadrons, commanded by Group Captain Douglas Bader DSO, DFC who, with AVM Trafford Leigh-Mallory, was responsible for the introduction of the 'Big Wing'. Douglas Bader, who had flown in Air Vice-Marshal Keith Park's Big Wings over Dunkirk in 1940 covering the French beaches against air attack, was convinced that large formations were essential. Bader practised his new tactics leading No.616 Squadron, all three squadrons flying the Spitfire II. No.616 lead the wing, No.610 flying top cover, No.145 on a flank between them. On 7 May 1941, Flying Officer J. Dundas No.616 Squadron, Squadron Leader H. Woodhouse, CO No.610 Squadron and Sergeant Mains led by Group Captain Bader, took-off to practise 'Finger Four', a formation comprising of a wingman 50 yards (46 metres) apart and four aircraft disposed in relation to each other as the fingers of an outstretched hand, staggered in height.

Flying Officer J.C. Dundas spotted Bf 109s over the French coast, the Germans saw them and attacked. Bader told his pilots to wait for the command 'Break', he broke left, Dundas followed in a tight turn, losing sight of Mains and Woodhouse, who broke right. Losing contact with the Bf 109s, Dundas flying Spitfire II P7827 'QJ-K' 'Cock of the North', was badly hit. Trailing smoke, losing height fast, the engine died approaching Hawkinge. Too high and too fast he belly-landed, P7827 bounced onto a scrapyard, just missing a line of Spitfires recently delivered for No.91 Squadron. Sergeant Mains' aircraft was damaged but had made off to land safely at another airfield. Squadron Leader C.P. Green DFC, unimpressed, tore a strip off Dundas. Not surprising as Hawkinge was losing too many aircraft due to frequent strafings; only a month before, Czech pilots landed on the airfield all at the same time. Dundas was reprimanded by Bader on his return to Tangmere.

RAF HAWKINGE

Aircraft of No.1 CACU (Coast Artillery Co-operation Unit) based at Detling were often called upon to operate from other airfields. On 7 May 1941 a Blenheim and a Defiant were flying from Hawkinge when the Blenheim was attacked by fighters. Flying Officer Hicks Blenheim Z5758, was missing believed killed, his aircraft shot down into the sea. Other crew, Sergeant J.M. Macdonald, Sergeant C.V.R. Scott and Sergeant R.C. Livings, were killed. On 8 May, three Me 109s swept over the airfield firing as they went, causing no damage or casualties. Spitfire IIa P7753 flown by Flying Officer L.H Casson, based at Tangmere, crash landed at Hawkinge, climbing out he inspected the damage. Six Me 109s attacked crash-boats, six miles south of Folkestone, one caught fire. Flying Officer N.M. Dunn No.238 Squadron, Kenley, forced landed near Dungeness Signal Station at the same time as the Me 109s were in the vicinity.

On 11 May 1941 there was an incident involving No.74 (Trinidad) 'Tiger' Squadron, operating from West Malling. Flying Officer Roger Boulding was on detachment and flying Spitfire IIA P8380 'ZP-Q' 'Black Velvet', a Presentation Spitfire. Flying in the company of Squadron Leader Mungo-Park DFC, Flight Lieutenant John Freeborn DFC, Pilot Officer Bob Poulton and Sergeant Tony Mould in the vicinity of London at night-time, he attacked a Heinkel He 111H-5. Night fighting was still in its infancy, the glow from the two rows of exhausts of the Merlin, impaired the pilot's vision.

On Hurricane night fighters, a horizontal metal plate was fitted just in front and below the cockpit which obscured the glow. Heinkel of 5/KG 53 A1+JN, was flown by Hptmn. A. Hufenreuther, Fw. R. Futhrthmann, Uffz. K. Gerhardt, Uffz. J. Berbach and Gefr. E. Weber. By chance, Flying Officer Boulding intercepted the German intruder, as 'Knockout 17', he was known to the controller that night. Descending in an easterly direction, he noticed a twin-engine bomber at the same height. Approaching the Heinkel, he opened fire at close range. Caught in a hail of bullets, the pilot, Huefenruether, decided to fly nearer the ground.

The bomber crash-landed at Kennington, Ashford, in a recreation field behind houses in Church Road, its crew were all taken PoW. Huefenruether, a retired teacher, returned to Kennington in 1978, to find the site of the crash. The Heinkel belly-landed behind his house, at the rear of Church Road. It is interesting to note that the radio mast of the He 111 is displayed at the Kent Battle of Britain Museum, Hawkinge, and other items are in private collections. This incident took place on what became known as 'The Worst Raid' of the London Blitz, the night of 10/11 May 1941. Meanwhile

A YEAR OF CHANGE 1941

at Hawkinge, seven bombs were dropped, only one exploded causing little damage; there were no casualties.

An Me 109 shot down a Barrage balloon at Dover on 26 May, two more were destroyed by thunderstorms, an impressive sight, seen for miles around the Dover area. The following day another was hit by an Me 109. A bomb dropped on Folkestone on 29 May, extinguishing all lights, including those of Hawkinge. Six Hawker Hurricane Is of No.303 (Polish) Squadron, arrived for an Operational Flight. Much to the pilots' frustration, this was cancelled; refuelling, they returned to Northolt on 4 June. That evening, an aircraft was reported ditched in the Channel off Dover, this being Spitfire Vb W3186 No.609 Squadron, Gravesend, shot down by an Me 109, Flight Lieutenant W.K. Burgon was killed. An ASR mission, searching for Flight Lieutenant Gribble DFC Spitfire V, V7275, was attacked by an Me 109 of II/JG 53, Gribble baled out off the coast, his body never recovered.

An Air Sea Rescue Flight (ASR) was established at Hawkinge on 4 June 1941, the newly formed unit was equipped with Westland Lysander IIIA aircraft ideal for the task, an aircraft which had already been flying at Hawkinge with No.2, 4 and 16 Squadrons. ASR's first flight at Hawkinge took place on 4 June; Flying Officer Fairhurst and Sergeant Jones flew Lysander IIIA V9407 on three operational flights. Also equipped with two Supermarine

Flight Lieutenant 'Drip' Driscoll pilot, Pilot Officer J. Winfield, Warrant Officer Air Gunner E.H. Cartwright and Sergeant J. Lawrence No.277 Squadron, one of several successful crews based at RAF Hawkinge, who flew the Walrus on ASR operations. (E.H. Cartwright)

RAF HAWKINGE

Walrus amphibian biplanes, operating from Hawkinge and Shoreham, the Walrus was able to put down in the sea to rescue crew or pilots, without assistance of the RAF's High Speed Launches, although this depended on sea conditions. Rescues were undertaken as quickly as possible, as they were sitting targets. Walrus W2736 often flew from Hawkinge, but crashed on take-off at Worthing on 21 July 1942; practising take-offs and landings, it broke a float and nosed under, the crew climbed into their dinghy. Walrus L2315, operating between Hawkinge/Shoreham joined the search with Defiant N3443 No.277 Squadron, but the crew were rescued by the Royal Navy.

Hawkinge was attacked on 9 June, when eight Me 109s flew over the airfield, Spitfires of No.91 Squadron scrambled to intercept, ground defences opened fire. Flying Officer P.P.C. Barthropp intercepted and shot down a Me 109F over Dover, which crashed in the sea. Sergeant J.E. Cooper chased another away from Hawkinge to the coast, opening fire over Hythe, the Me 109F heading for safety, trailing smoke. Flying Officer P.P.C. Barthropp joined No.91 Squadron at Hawkinge. At about this time Barthropp acquired a two-litre Lagonda in exchange for a large quantity of aviation fuel. Groundcrew fitted a fuel tank under the car's back seat. One evening he collided with a London taxi, on another occasion he and a colleague were fined £1 for assaulting the proprietor of the Red Lion Hotel, Hounslow. after they were refused entry to a dance. Barthropp called the magistrate a 'silly old bastard' and the fine was doubled. Shot down in May 1942, he went to Stalag Luft III. Following the war he supported the Battle of Britain Fighter Association, and for many years he fought to get ex-PoWs their back pay.

The CO of No.91 Squadron, Squadron Leader C.P. 'Paddy' Green DFC, who had commanded the squadron since its formation as No.421 Flight, left Hawkinge to join HQ Fighter Command. He was replaced by Squadron Leader J.N. Watts Farmer DFC, Squadron Leader C.D. Goodcliffe had completed a tour of thirty-three operations with Bomber Command and Flying Instructor courses on Lancaster bombers, when he was posted to Hawkinge on an unusual assignment. Given command of thirty airmen including Sergeant Billingham, who by coincidence lived in Folkestone, was responsible for 'care and maintenance' of equipment gathered from Fighter Command stations closed on the escalation of the war. The unit categorised, equipment at Hawkinge and since there were three Spitfires which were unserviceable, a team of fitters was recruited from Manston to prepare them for service. An item which the CO could not categorise was a Spitfire's 'spinner' or nose cone, retrieved from a damaged Spitfire. It was thought to be from a Spitfire flown by Squadron Leader A.G. 'Sailor'

A YEAR OF CHANGE 1941

Malan CO of No.74 Squadron, which crashed at Hawkinge during the Battle of Britain. This is disputed, as the 'spinner' was possibly taken from a Spitfire V of No.74 Squadron flown by Squadron Leader J.N. Mungo-Park who took over as CO from 'Sailor' Malan on 10 March 1941. On 16 June 1941 three aircraft of No.74 Squadron, took off from Hawkinge, Pilot Officer Sandman Spitfire V W3212, Pilot Officer Poulton W3172 and Squadron Leader Mungo-Park Spitfire V W3170. They were soon engaged by Bf 109s. Squadron Leader Mungo-Park shot down two, but during the combat his Spitfire V was damaged. The engine seized as he crossed the coast but he managed to stay airborne, and glided back to Hawkinge. For this display of skill, as well as his continued leadership and growing tally of kills, he was awarded a Bar to his DFC. Squadron Leader C.D. Goodcliffe remembered that the 'spinner' had been mounted on a wooden stand made by an RAF 'chippy' at Hawkinge, this served as a font for the christening of Squadron Leader Mungo-Park's ground crew's sergeant's first child. It must be added that Squadron Leader A.G. 'Sailor' Malan did make a hasty landing at Hawkinge on 17 May 1941, following combat with Bf 109s, the engine of his Spitfire vibrating so badly, he had to put down quickly. Unable to fly back to Biggin Hill, he returned to base in a Miles Magister. Squadron Leader J.C. Mungo-Park DFC & Bar was killed on 27 June 1941 when Spitfire V X4668 ZP-E No.74 Squadron, based at Gravesend, was shot down. The 'Spitfire Spinner' christening font changed hands in 1945 when Hawkinge was closing and acquired by Squadron Leader C.D. Goodliffe, who donated the font to an RAF Benevolent Fund auction in 1990.

The first successful ASR flight took place on 21 June, when Flying Officer Fairhurst and Sergeant Glew flying Lysander V9483 No.277 Squadron located a pilot in the sea, an ASR launch picked up the airman, grateful for the dinghy the Lysander dropped. Nearly every day in June, Lysanders of the ASR Flight, Hawkinge patrolled coastal waters helping to rescue many RAF crew. This embryo flight remained at Hawkinge until being reformed as a detachment flight of the newly formed unit on 26 November 1941, that being No.277 (ASR) Squadron.

Prior to the Second World War, there was still no fully functional coordinated British air-sea rescue organisation for rescuing aircrew from the sea. The aircrew relied on the High-Speed Launches (HSL) established at flying boat bases. On 14 January 1941, the first Air Sea Rescue was set up (the Directorate of Air Sea Rescue Services). The aircraft flown were diverse, Westland Lysanders were used for scouting the coastlines, while the Supermarine Walrus was planned for long-term use. By June 1941 rescue from the seas had increased to 35 per cent.

RAF HAWKINGE

The Supermarine Walrus which played a critical role serving with No.277 (ASR) Squadron 'B' Flight, detached to RAF Hawkinge from 1941 until November 1944. The squadron had an exemplary record saving the lives of many pilots and aircrew from the English Channel.

The Air Ministry decided the service could do better. It was merged with another Directorate, Aircraft Safety.

Escorting an ASR Lysander from Hawkinge on 16 June 1941, 'A' Flight No.91 Squadron ran into a flight of Me 109s escorting a Heinkel He 59 floatplane, eight miles south of Folkestone. Sergeant Connolly damaged at

Flight Lieutenant J.S. Anderson joined No.91 Squadron at Hawkinge in July 1941, seen here seated in Spitfire Vb W3405 DL-N *Monmouth Chepstow and Forest of Dean Spitfire.*

A YEAR OF CHANGE 1941

least one of the Me 109s, Pilot Officer D.H. Gage, leading 'A' Flight failed to return, Spitfire IIA W3126 shot down in the sea during the combat. 'Top cover' was flown by No.1 Squadron, they dived on the He 59B-2 and four of the escorting Me 109s. The He 59 B-2 was painted white with Red Cross markings, it was claimed that these aircraft were being used for reconnaissance, therefore a legitimate target, particularly as it was flying in the same air space as the Me 109s. Following the capture of the He 59 crew downed off Deal, it was found the pilot had noted the position and direction of a British convoy in his logbook. The Air Ministry issued Bulletin 1254 indicating that all enemy air-sea rescue aircraft were to be destroyed. Winston Churchill cast doubt on his own government's claims and wrote: 'We did not recognise this means of rescuing enemy pilots who had been shot down in action, in order that they might come and bomb our civil population again.'

To pass the time between operations pilots at Hawkinge often took up various pastimes, in this case two pilots of No.91 Squadron try their skills at archery on 23 July 1941.

RAF HAWKINGE

Germany protested, quoting the Geneva Convention agreement stipulating that both sides of the conflict must respect 'mobile sanitary formations', including field ambulances and hospital ships. Churchill claimed rescue aircraft were not anticipated by the treaty therefore not covered. As RAF attacks on He 59s continued, the German *Seenotflugkommando 1*, the German equivalent of our own RAF Search and Rescue units, ordered the rescue aircraft armed and camouflaged. The use of civil registration and red cross markings was abandoned. In July 1941 a *Seenotflugkommando* gunner later shot down an attacking Hurricane of No.43 Squadron, and rescue flights were ordered to be protected by fighters when possible.

During a daytime sweep over Boulogne/St Omer/Dunkirk by No.19 Squadron on 27 June 1941, Pilot Officer Andrews' Spitfire II P7379 was hit. Attacked from above by Me 109s, Pilot Officer Andrews managed to damage one, which dived away in flames. Andrews nursed his Spitfire over the Channel, before baling out. Shortly after he crashed, two Army officers arrived and said they had seen his Spitfire appear out of the mist, trailing smoke, then disappearing behind trees. Helped by soldiers in an Army truck he was taken to the Officers' Mess at Lympne, unusual for a sergeant, and given whisky. Following a phone call to Hawkinge, transport arrived and took him to the airfield Sick Quarters, where he was given eggs and bacon. The following morning No.91 Squadron flew him back to Fowlmere in their Avro Tutor where he was welcomed back by No.91 Squadron, the CO Squadron Leader Lawson DFC gaving him two days leave.

Wing Commander J.R.A. Peel DFC CO Kenley Wing, was flying Hurricane II of No.312 (Czech.) Squadron on 9 July 1941. The wing was airborne in support of a formation of Stirling bombers attacking Mazingarbe, France. On the return flight twenty Me 109s were encountered; shot down, Peel baled out over the Channel, successfully boarding his dinghy. A Lysander crewed by Sergeants Hurst and Glew scrambled from Hawkinge, soon spotted Peel waving a flag and called up a RN patrol, which picked him up.

Marshal of the RAF Lord Trenchard GCB, OM, GCVO, DSO, arrived at Hawkinge on 11 July 1941. His visit was good for morale, at a time when many pilots had been lost or killed flying from Hawkinge. During his visit, a report was received that Pilot Officer J. Dougall of No.92 Squadron flying Spitfire V W3120 was seen by Sergeant Lloyd under attack by an Me 109, during which his Spitfire burst into flames and crashed into the sea, he was picked up by a German patrol and taken PoW.

On 9 August, four Spitfires of No.616 and No.452 Squadrons landed following an offensive patrol. Later six Spitfires of No.616 Squadron,

A YEAR OF CHANGE 1941

The Luftwaffe had carried out many aerial reconnaissance flights over Great Britain, and taken detailed photographs of many airfields, this image is dated July 1941 and gives some details of buildings at RAF Hawkinge.

led by Flight Lieutenant J.C. Dundas were detailed to search for Wing Commander D.R.S. Bader DSO, DFC. It was later revealed he had been shot down in Spitfire I W3185 coded 'DB'. During the same combat Flight Lieutenant L.H. Casson DFC Spitfire Vb W3458 No.616 Squadron, was shot down by JG 26. Both he and Bader, minus one of his artificial legs,

RAF HAWKINGE

Pilot Officer William R. 'Bill' Dunn, an American pilot. flew with No.71 (Eagle) Squadron seated in Spitfire IIA P7308 'XR-D' in which he crash landed at Hawkinge on 27 August 1941.

crashed in France, and were captured. Many years later, detailed research revealed that Bader was indeed the victim of crossfire from a Spitfire, but he always insisted that he fell victim to the guns of JG 26.

Pilot Officer William R. 'Bill' Dunn, an American pilot, was serving with No.71 Squadron, North Weald in 1941. With Nos.121 and 133 Squadrons, they formed an American fighter wing, known as the 'Eagle Squadrons'. By 27 August 1941, No.71 Squadron was equipped with Spitfire IIAs, which replaced their Hurricane IIAs, much to the joy of the American pilots. On 29 September 1942, they were absorbed into the 8th USAAF as the 334th, 335th and 336th Fighter Squadrons.

On that day No.71 Squadron escorted nine Blenheims bombing steel works at Lille, Pilot Officer W.R Dunn Spitfire IIA P7308 'XR-D' took off heading for France. Nos.121 and 133 Squadron provided close support to the Blenheims which they met over North Foreland. Pilot Officer Dunn experienced oxygen problems, dropping to a safer height, was attacked from behind by an Me 109F. The German overshot the Spitfire in a dive; raising the nose of P7308, Dunn opened fire, the Me 109F poured smoke and the pilot baled. Another attacked, Dunn opened fire, the Me 109F burst

A YEAR OF CHANGE 1941

into flames and crashed to the ground. A third attacked, cannon fire struck P7308 behind the cockpit damaging the RT and wounding Dunn in the foot. The German pilot turned away before Pilot Officer Dunn could return fire. Passing over the Channel, other Spitfires joined him as they approached Hawkinge, waggling their wings to let him know his undercarriage was down. Despite the damage he sent a May Day call; landing at Hawkinge, an ambulance already waited to take the injured pilot to the Royal Victoria Hospital, Folkestone, for treatment. Spitfire IIA P7308 had holes in the port wing, the instrument panel had been hit by a 20mm shell. It was the last time Dunn flew P7308, which was repaired. Pilot Officer Dunn was told he would remain in hospital for two weeks before transferring to a hospital in Torquay. While at Folkestone Dunn was befriended by Pilot Officer 'Tommy' Tomlinson who had broken his leg in a parachute jump. It transpired that one of the Me 109F pilots shot down by Pilot Officer Dunn was Major Gerhardt Weiss. Dunn became the first American Ace of the Second World War.

Sergeant J.E. Cooper was killed on 9 September 1941 while escorting an ASR Walrus during a routine practice. Spitfire IA R7296 was seen to dive into the sea out of a low cloud, there were no enemy aircraft in the vicinity of the exercise. Heavy raids took place on Italy on 11 September 1941, a HP Halifax was reported lost over Kent. Flying Officer Le Roux No.91 Squadron

Flying Officer Chris Le Roux DFC & Bar No.91 Squadron with his Spitfire Vb at Hawkinge, note the artwork below the cockpit. During his service with the squadron, he claimed thirteen enemy aircraft, he was killed in a flying accident on 19 September 1944.

was scrambled to locate the aircraft, which he did over Tunbridge Wells, escorting the Halifax to Manston, which landed without incident.

On 17 September a Lysander of No.277 Squadron reported a pilot downed off Folkestone, and an ASR launch was guided to the area. Pilot Officer B. Bartholomew No.92 Squadron was killed, shot down in Spitfire Vb AB915. Pilot Officer G.E. Brettell in Spitfire Vb W3709 was wounded, landing at Hawkinge, he reported seeing Bartholomew baling out over the Channel. That evening, a Lysander spotted Pilot Officer Atkinson of No.609 Squadron, who, with other pilots, escorted six Hampdens raiding Marquise; Atkinson was shot down by an Me 109 crossing Boulogne and his engine failed. Seeing flames beneath the cowling he baled out and was rescued by the Royal Navy.

An Armstrong Whitley V remains undisturbed, 4,921ft (1,500 metres) distant from Dymchurch Redoubt, close to the location of the Me 109 shot down by Pilot Officer K.W. 'Mac' MacKenzie. The aircraft was found by members of the Folkestone & Hythe Diving Club but thought to be a Handley Page Hampden. Further research suggests it is Whitley V Z9213 of No.78 Squadron, the incident is recorded in the Operational Records of Hawkinge as having taken place on 14 October 1941, but incorrectly reported as crashing on Hythe Cricket Ground. That night Whitley Vs of 78 Squadron took off from Middleton St George, Yorkshire, as part of No.4 Group, the mission being to bomb Nuremberg. The primary target attacked, Whitley Z9213 dropped its bombs and they turned for home:

> As Observer I remember we flew in cloud all night it was a long run for Whitleys and the constant use of de-icers meant the aircraft used up so much fuel that we ran out just as we approached the English coast. Despite our Mayday call to put down a local airfield, we received no response, so I was told to open the hatch and prepare to bale out. The second pilot in the forward turret had to come back to the hatch – he baled out first. I was next – on landing I relaxed the lower part of my body. Still dark I couldn't see where I was and landed astride a fence. Thankfully not a spiked fence! It was painful but I could still walk. I gathered up my chute, and found a house, so that I could call for help. But before I could get to the door, I was surrounded by the Home Guard with fixed bayonets who thought I was a German parachutist! I convinced them I wasn't, and the occupant drove me Hawkinge.
>
> L.C. Jupp letter

A YEAR OF CHANGE 1941

Local fishermen proudly display an oil tank recovered from the wreck of AW Whitley V Z9213 following its ditching in the sea off Dymchurch on 14 October 1941. (Tart Family)

Apart from the unfortunate Sergeant Jupp, the crew were uninjured. Pilot Officer D.S. King (pilot), Pilot Officer N. Pruden (pilot), Sergeant N.P. Norman (waist air gunner), Sergeant C.R. Campbell (air gunner) and Sergeant Lyndon (waist air gunner) were taken to Hawkinge.

On the night of 14/15 October 1941, Squadron Leader A.J. 'Jimmy' Heyworth and crew took off from Binbrook flying Wellington W5571 with others of No.12 Squadron, to attack Nuremberg. Shortly after dropping their bombs, the starboard engine failed. Flying over enemy territory on one engine, the crew debated heading for Switzerland, but with his wedding only two weeks away, Heyworth decided to head for base. Despite full power on the port engine the bomber steadily lost height. Disposable items, guns, and ammunition were jettisoned. To hold the aircraft straight, Heyworth had to apply full rudder, but after a few hours the strain began to tell, so the crew lashed the pedal to the airframe, giving his leg some respite. Crossing the French coast too low to bale out, parachutes were jettisoned. Reaching the Kent coast at dawn, W5571 crashed on Romney Marsh. The uninjured crew were confronted by a farmer with a shotgun. Heyworth convinced him that they were not Germans; he was later awarded the DFC.

On 8 November 1941, a hectic day at Hawkinge, no less than twenty-nine aircraft landed there, returning from France. Spitfires of Nos.72, 401 (RCAF), 609, 607, 316 (Polish), 315 (Polish), 452 (RAAF), 412 (RCAF), 602, 317 (Polish), 306 (Polish), 412 (RCAF), 485 (NZ) including two Curtis Tomahawks of No.239 Squadron based at Gatwick littered the airfield, refuelling before returning to base, some damaged, a few pilots with injuries.

Air Vice Marshal T.L. Mallory AOC 11 Group arrived on 19 November to present Flight Lieutenant Jean-Francois Demozay No.91 Squadron with a DFC, following which a march past took place. Demozay a Frenchman, destroyed or damaged sixteen aircraft, including two Hs 126s. Prior to joining No.91 Squadron, he served with No.1 and No.245 Squadrons, destroying or damaging six enemy aircraft. In 1942, flying with No.91 Squadron, he claimed four destroyed with one damaged. Descending on Hawkinge in fine weather on 23 November 1941, twenty Blenheim IVs of 'B' Flight No.614 (City of Manchester) RAuxAF, took part in Operation *Binge*, involving ground training and aerial photography.

No.277 (ASR) Squadron was formed at Stapleford Tawney on the 22 December 1941, following a communication from 11 Group HQ to Tangmere, Biggin Hill, Northolt, Kenley, Debden and North Weald. ASR Flights, previously stationed at Martlesham Heath, Hawkinge, Friston and Tangmere would be formed as No.277 Squadron, its HQ at Stapleford Tawney. The squadron comprised of three detached Flights based at Shoreham, Hawkinge and Martlesham Heath. Aircraft had to be checked and examined at Stapleford Tawney. Pilots were given practice in searching, dinghy dropping, vectors and fixes, fighter affiliation, dusk landings, photography, firing and sea landings for those who completed the Walrus course. The existing ASR Flight based at Hawkinge since 4 June 1941, became part of No.277 Squadron 'B' Flight. The CO Flight Lieutenant W.P. Green had previously flown with No.240 Squadron, and had experience flying the Short Stranraer I Seaplane. The flight at Hawkinge now comprised of twenty-nine airmen, including Air Gunners/Wireless Operators, Armourers, Fitters, Mechanics, Instrument Fitters and a Radio Telephony Operator.

Chapter 8

Hawkinge During 1942
Flying for their Lives

On 24 February 1942, Sergeant T. Omdahl (RAAF) and Sergeant Beaumont No.91 Squadron were scrambled to Dover and Dungeness. A German fighter was reported in the area off Gris Nez, seeing nothing they headed for Hawkinge, but were jumped by an Fw 190 of 9th Staffel JG 26, flown by Oberf. Erwin. Both aircraft were damaged, Sergeant Omdahl Spitfire Vb W3175, crash landed at Hawkinge, Sergeant Beaumont landed safely, both uninjured. On 8 March 1942, three Spitfire Vbs No.401 (RCAF) Squadron Biggin Hill, were caught by searchlights. Spitfire Vb BL538 Sergeant A.D. Blakey, broke away from the other two. Suddenly its port wing broke off and, catching fire, the Spitfire crashed at Fairfield on the Kent/Sussex border. It is thought that BL538 suffered structural failure and was not hit by gunfire.

During a reconnaissance flight over the Channel on 13 March, pilots reported seeing small balloons, with what looked like boxes attached to them. These balloons, inflated with hydrogen, trailed wires or incendiary devices to cause fires and short circuit over-head power cables. The incendiary type would cause forest fires and set fire to heathland in German occupied territory. A surplus of weather balloons was employed for the task, Operation *Outward*, with some success.

In March 1942 No.320 (Dutch) Squadron based at Bircham Newton, equipped with Douglas Mitchell II twin-engine bombers, attacked a Special Construction Works at Gorenflos. Mitchell FR177 'NO-M' was hit by flak with others after leaving the target, two ditched in the sea, one being FR177. H.J. Voorspuij, J. Vink, R.F. van Nouhuis and M. Engelman not seriously injured were rescued by a Walrus and flown to Hawkinge. The crew of Mitchell II FR188, were picked up by a Sea Otter, transferred to an ASR launch, and eventually taken to Hawkinge. It was reported that the aircraft had exploded, but this turned out to be bombs jettisoned by B17s.

Early on 16 April Flight Sergeant Waddington and Flight Lieutenant Faune inspected camouflage, recently applied to Lysander I V9843, then

Spitfire Vb AB248 DL-D, 'Katsina Province' allocated to No.91 (Nigeria) Squadron on 14 March 1942, flown by Flight Lieutenant F.H. Silk CO of 'B' Flight following promotion. (IWM CH5445)

took off for an Army Coop flight. Later that day V9843 was flown by Flight Sergeant G.W. Jones and Flight Sergeant Hartwell on estuary mine patrol. The engine cut out and the Lysander crashed at Foxholt Farm, Swingfield Minis near Hawkinge. Flight Sergeant Jones was seriously injured, and Flight Sergeant Hartwell was unhurt. Short of serviceable Lysanders,

HAWKINGE DURING 1942

V9431 was ferried from Kenley to Hawkinge by Sergeant Coddy. Flight Sergeant Knowlton in Lysander V9547, delivered much needed dinghies and supplies.

Hawkinge Station Flight operated various aircraft available for authorised to pilots fly. Miles Magister L5962 was used by No.91 Squadron for spotting, cooperation, and communications flights. Coming into land at Lympne on 24 April 1942, the wing tip of L5962, hit the ground and the Magister flew into trees, badly damaging the aircraft. No.401 (RCAF) Squadron based at Biggin Hill, patrolled St Omer on 28 April, four pilots were killed, another taken PoW. Pilot Officer G.B. Whitney, an American, flying Spitfire Vb AB917, tried to make for Hawkinge but crashed and exploded at Napchester Road, Whitfield near Dover. This Spitfire was gifted by the 'Wolverhampton Express and Star Fund', named 'The Inspirer'. Pilot Officer Whitney in Spitfire Vb W3452 'Midnight Sun', was shot down at Sandwich, Kent on 27 October 1941 by an Me 109 of JG 26. Pilot Officer Whitney bailed out but survived uninjured.

In heavy cloud and rain on 26 May, Spitfires of No.91 Squadron escorted two Lysanders of No.277 Squadron, searching for Group Captain R.L.R. 'Batchy' Atcherley, Spitfire Vb BM235 reported to have ditched off Dover. 'Batchy' was recovered from the sea by a trawler and taken to Union Road Hospital, Dover. Baling out, wounded in the left arm and hand, the attaching strap broke and he had to swim to the dinghy. The trawler's crew watched him as he glided down to the sea. Taking off from Kenley, where he was CO, on a reconnaissance flight, he was spotted by three Fw 190s and was immediately attacked and hit, Spitfire BM235 went into a spin, and Atcherley was lucky to get out of the aircraft.

No.56 Squadron operating from Manston on 1 June 1942, reported that two Hawker Typhoon Ibs were missing on operations. They were shot down by Spitfires off Dover, whose pilots mistook them for Fw 190s. Referred to as 'blue on blue', such incidents occurred frequently in the heat of combat. Flying Officer Spence No.277 Squadron was dispatched in a Walrus, accompanied by two Spitfires of 'A' Flight No.91 Squadron to locate the pilots. Pilot Officer R.H. Deugo was found in the sea off Dover, Flying Officer Spence guided ASR boats to pick him up. Deugo's Typhoon I R7678 crashed in the sea after he baled out, as did Typhoon Ib R8199 US-E, the pilot, Sergeant K.M Stuart-Turner was never found. Flying Officer Deugo was admitted to Union Road Hospital, burnt and wounded. The Typhoons were silhouetted by the sun, the Canadian pilots were Flight Sergeant Morrison Spitfire BM372 and Flight Sergeant Murray

RAF HAWKINGE

Spitfire Vcs of No.91 (Nigeria) Squadron 'B' Flight at Hawkinge in May 1942. The nearest being 'DL-Z' AB216 'Nigeria Oyo Province', flown by the CO Squadron Leader R. Oxspring standing in front of his aircraft. (IWM CH5429)

Spitfire BL268 'A' Flight No.401 Squadron based at Gravesend. Both were patrolling the Hastings/Dover area. No.91 Squadron were scrambled from Hawkinge on Offensive Patrols and No.277 Squadron was continually airborne for 'spotter' and ASR patrols in the Dover Straits, North Sea and Channel. On 15 June 1942, No.91 Squadron lost Sergeant E.E. Sykes, a Canadian who had taken off from Lympne on a Reconnaissance Flight over Dieppe. 'A' Flight No.91 Squadron were on detachment from Hawkinge, Spitfire Vb AR370 disappeared, 'A' Flight moved back to Hawkinge.

Flight Lieutenant Tom Fletcher moved from No.43 Squadron to No.91 Squadron during 1942, to fly Spitfires escorting Air Sea Rescue operations. Transferring No.277 (ASR) Squadron 'B' Flight, flying the Lysander and Walrus, both slow aircraft, a far cry from Spitfires which he had flown with No.43 Squadron. On one patrol he spotted several men in the sea and directed RAF launches to pick them up, saving their lives. On 2 October 1942 Sergeant M.H.F. Cooper Spitfire VI BR159 No.616 Squadron, baled

HAWKINGE DURING 1942

No.91 (Nigeria) Squadron at dispersal in June 1942, behind them Hawkinge village. On the wings of Spitfire VB 'DL-H' – left to right: Sergeant 'Shag' O' Shaughnessy, Flying Officer Bishop (Intelligence. Officer), Sergeant I.W. 'Scotty' Downer, Sergeant J. Down, Pilot Officer C.G.C. Pannell, unknown, Sergeant R.M. 'Ronny' Ingram, Flight Lieutenant M.D. 'Sammy' Hall, unknown. Seated on the cowling, Flight Lieutenant J. 'Chris' Le Roux, under the propeller stands Squadron Leader J.E.F. 'Moses' Demozay. CO. (R.S Humphreys)

out, landing among mines off the French coast. Spitfires circled above the dinghy reporting his location, but the Royal Navy at Dover decided it was too dangerous to send a launch. Sergeant Tom Fletcher set off in a Walrus, escorted by Spitfires. Approaching the area, other Spitfires were in combat with German fighters. Spotting the pilot, Tom settled on the sea not far from Sergeant Cooper who struggled to grasp a boathook offered to him, and fell out of the dinghy. Trying again, Cooper was pulled out of the rough sea, made worse by strong winds. Navigating the Walrus through the minefield, Tom took off under fire by German gun batteries.

Sergeant Fletcher was recommended by the CO of No.11 Group for the Victoria Cross: In the event Tom was awarded a DFM, the next-highest award available for non-commissioned officers. On the evening of 14 December 1942, patrolling Dover Tom spotted six men on a raft, despite high seas, he managed to land. Picking up a few of them and another in the sea, he turned into the wind, leaving reluctantly as the light faded, taxiing towards Dover. The Walrus was taking in water, after nearly two hours

Having landed close to a pilot in his dinghy, the crew of a Walrus I No.277 Squadron prepare to pick-up the airman. Most attempts were successful but if the sea was rough, it could cause problems for the ASR crews. (Air Comm. G. Pitchfork MBE)

arriving at Dover, where he was reprimanded by the harbour master for not having permission taxi into his harbour! Those rescued were German seamen, Tom was awarded a bar to his DFM.

For the first time since the Women's Auxiliary Air Force (WAAF) was formed in June 1939 when war seemed imminent, WAAFs came under the administration of the RAF. These women did not serve in individual female units, as with Army and ATS, but as individual members of RAF Commands. So, when WAAFs arrived at Hawkinge on 24 June 1942, they created much interest, the first females on the base since the war began. On the evening of 25 June a dance was held in the Officers' Mess, attended by many of the officers based at Hawkinge and serving with the various squadrons using the airfield.

No.91 Squadron received the first two Spitfire VIs, flight tested by Flight Lieutenant R. Spurdle, Later Squadron Leader R. Spurdle DFC who wrote in his book *The Blue Arena*: 'They sent us two Spitfire VIs, they had pressure cabins and could stagger around at over 42,000ft – what earthly use were they to us? The hoods couldn't slide back but were clamped down over us on rubber seals; again, no cameras so we didn't use them.' Squadron Leader R. Spurdle DFC flew with 'A' Flight commanded by Flight Lieutenant G. Pannell with Squadron Leader R. Oxspring squadron CO. Spurdle transferred to the Merchant Ship Fighter Unit in 1941. Serving earlier with No.91 Squadron, he was pleased to be back at Hawkinge.

From Great Sampford, No.65 Squadron moved to Hawkinge for an indefinite period on 30 June 1942. Sixty ground personnel, Engineer Officer, and Intelligence Officer and twenty-one Spitfire Vbs were expected, groundcrew arrived in two HP Harrows. No operational flying took place, the squadron having periods of readiness upon alternate days. Groundcrew painted their Spitfires in a new camouflage pattern (the 'A' Scheme of dark green and medium sea grey) and with only a minimum of flying permitted on 7 July 1942 moved back to Great Sampford.

Half of No.41 Squadron's personnel moved to Hawkinge on 30 June, others remained at Martlesham Heath. They were told No.65 Squadron had been taken off operations and Nos.71, 111, and 350 (Belgian) Squadrons were moving to Gravesend, they realised some important operation was about to take place. No.41 Squadron moved to Debden on 8 July, detailed to prepare for overseas duties, they were brought together at Debden as a Fighter Wing. Due to the loss of ships on Convoy PQ17 not going overseas, No.41 Squadron returned to Hawkinge until 12 April 1943, re-equipped Spitfire XIIs replacing the Vb.

Cloud covered Hawkinge on 1 July 1942 at ground level, dubbed by everyone as 'The Hawkinge Horror', preventing flying until late morning. That evening No.91 Squadron scrambled from Hawkinge searching for Group Captain P.R. Barwell DFC, CO of Biggin Hill. During a sortie Barwell was attacked and shot down by Spitfires from Tangmere. Spitfire AB806 assigned to No.72 Squadron, was joined by the CO of No.91 Squadron Hawkinge, Squadron Leader R.W. Oxspring, on patrol from Biggin Hill. Assisting in the search before darkness, Squadron Leader Demozay found nothing. Biggin Hill control warned of unidentified aircraft in the area, which proved to be two Spitfires from Tangmere. Barwell, apparently oblivious to the warning, was attacked by one and shot down into the sea. Although Oxspring saw him trying to open his hood, Barwell did not bale out, his body later washed up on the French coast and was buried at Calais.

Following early morning recce flights on 15 July 1942, two Spitfire Vbs of No.91 Squadron left Hawkinge as 'spotters' over Hastings. Flight Sergeant F.Y. Campbell (RCAF) Spitfire Vb BL662 and Sergeant A.J. Clayton

RAF HAWKINGE

(RAAF) arrived in the area. Jumped by three Fw 190s, they had no warning of them being in the vicinity. Sergeant Clayton's Spitfire was badly hit and went into a spin; managing to bale out, Clayton landed in the sea and got into his dinghy. Later seen by Flight Lieutenant Hall and Flight Sergeant Downer, Clayton was picked up by an ASR launch. Returning to Hawkinge he said he did not see Flight Sergeant Campbell after the attack, who was not found. That day thirty-six operational hours were flown by the 'Jim Crow' squadron. Squadron Leader R.W. Oxspring DFC & Bar CO since 28 December 1941, was posted to command No.72 Squadron, replaced by Squadron Leader J.E.F. Demozay DSO, DFC & Bar who was nicknamed 'Moses', because of his impressive black moustache. An episode for which 'Moses' would be remembered, took place at Hawkinge. Coming into land he was obstructed by a field-mower; in a fit of rage – French style – he opened fire, the earth exploding around the tractor. The terrified driver leapt from his machine and ran off to seek shelter, thinking he was under attack from German fighters. Onlookers witnessed the event, and were highly amused to see the tractor, now out of control, gracefully wandering off until it hit earthworks and stalled.

The CO of RAF Hawkinge at this time was Wing Commander R.W. Bungey DFC, who suffered a breakdown and was often seen running around the airfield at dusk. It was said that if the guards didn't challenge him, he would put them on a charge, if they did, they suffered verbal abuse for not recognising their CO. Squadron Leader Oxspring tried to protect his men, but without success, things got so bad that a psychiatrist was called, and the unfortunate Wing Commander was shipped home to Brighton, Australia. On 10 June 1943, he shot himself on Bondi Beach; he was found wrapped in a Union Jack, a brave pilot who had won the DFC and served his country well. On 25 September 1942, Wing Commander D.G Jones DSO, DFC the newly appointed CO of Hawkinge arrived.

Tragedy struck again for No.91 Squadron on 22 July 1942, the CO of 'B' Flight Flight Lieutenant W.B. Orr Spitfire Vb BL816 flying near Cap Grez Nez area, went missing. A 'Mayday' call was received, Orr was shot down by flak during a shipping patrol. Flight Lieutenant R.L. Spurdle OC 'A' Flight was airborne during early afternoon with Flying Officer Clarkson on 'spotter' patrols. Off the coast off Dungeness, they met four Fw 190s and became involved in a dogfight, lasting five minutes. Spurdle damaged one as did Clarkson, another shot down by Spurdle crashed in the sea. Lieutenant H. 'Benno' Kruger flying Fw 190A-2 of 5/JG 2, baled out; rescued from the sea, he had broken an ankle and was taken to Dover hospital.

HAWKINGE DURING 1942

Hearing of his survival Spurdle and Clarkson visited Kruger, a pilot awarded the Iron Cross 1st/2nd Class. When searched some letters were found and a packet of condoms and eleven photos of himself. He was a *Schwarme* commander in JG 2, the famous 'Richthofen' squadron. On meeting the two pilots, he congratulated them on their success, following some discussion both returned to Hawkinge to a hero's welcome. It was later revealed that Kruger had valuable documents on him, of great interest to the Intelligence Service. That night at Biggin Hill, the 900th kill was celebrated, much to the annoyance of Flight Lieutenant Spurdle the invite did not extend to No.91 Squadron, but at least the capture of Kruger was celebrated in the mess at Hawkinge in great style. The celebrations for shooting down Kruger were short lived, when Spurdle and Clayton found out that the German pilot claimed he had shot down both Flight Sergeant J.E. Walker (RCAF) and Sergeant A.J. Clayton (RAAF) on 15 July 1942. Kruger stated he witnessed both pilots bale out. Flight Lieutenant R.L. Spurdle was particularly upset as the ASR search did not last very long, and as it was now known that both pilots landed in the sea alive, they may have been saved. Spurdle remarked on hearing the news: 'God damm it! I wish I had killed the bastard!' On 1August 1942, Flight Lieutenant Spurdle and Flight Sergeant Prytherch received notification they had been awarded the DFC. That night a dance was held in the Officers' Mess, guests included officers from the Royal Navy, the Army and other airfields and squadrons of the RAF.

August opened with the loss of Flying Officer R.K.J. Wildish 'B' Flight, on a routine reconnaissance flight. He had taken off in the afternoon in Spitfire Vb BL283, last seen south of Boulogne by Flight Sergeant Omdahl, but could not be contacted due to his radio not working. Next day Pilot Officer G. Sydel No.350 (Belgian) Squadron baled out of Spitfire Vb AD322 in the Bray Dunnes area was seen by Pilot Officer Edwards and Sergeant Down in his dinghy off Ramsgate; although picked up by ASR, two Fw 190s tried to attack, but were fired on and chased off by Pilot Officer Edwards.

There was some excitement on 8 August when two Fw 190s appeared over Dover and destroyed a barrage balloon. Spitfires of No.91 Squadron were scrambled flown by Pilot Officer Gillitt and Pilot Officer Mathew, both airborne within thirty seconds, they chased off the fighters in the direction of Hastings, following them to Boulogne before they could do any more damage. Shortly after Pilot Officer Le Maire and Pilot Officer Batten No.91 Squadron were on a defensive patrol. Spotting a Ju88, they immediately attacked, causing some damage; the Ju 88 jettisoned its bombs off Dungeness heading for home.

RAF HAWKINGE

That night a Heinkel III appeared over the airfield, fired on by the AA guns and chased away by a Beaufighter. There were no casualties reported, although a dud shell fell on a building, causing some damage. On 9 August Hawkinge was visited by members of No.131 AA Battery, and shown several aircraft, an opportunity to improve their skills in recognition. No.71 (AA) Regiment RE, arrived on 10 August to liaise with No.91 Squadron over three days, and were joined by No.46 Reconnaissance Corps. Fourteen Spitfires VIs of No.416 (RCAF) and No.616 Squadron arrived at Hawkinge and took over dispersals in preparation for a reinforcement exercise. Groundcrew arrived in Bristol Bombays, a large twin-engine aircraft. On arrival Flight Sergeant J.A. Wilson (RCAF) was unable to bring down the undercarriage of his Spitfire but managed to perform an impressive 'belly-landing'. No.616 Squadron flew convoy patrols, as well as carrying out cine gun practice and dogfighting, in preparation for the special operation, due to take place on 19 August. No.401 (RCAF) and No.133 (Eagle) Squadron were to join in this exercise, based at Lympne. During the afternoon of the following day, six Fw 190s were seen, and bombed Folkestone, causing some damage. These 'hit and run' raids would become a familiar experience for the inhabitants of the south and south-east coast.

The raid on Dieppe, initially codenamed Operation *Rutter* and planned at Combined Operations Headquarters, was to take place at the end of June 1942. Due to the unsuccessful exercise and poor weather, this was abandoned on 7 July. The idea was to land a force of troops at Dieppe, comprised mostly of Canadians, supported by commandos on the flanks to knock-out gun emplacements overlooking the Dieppe beaches. There would be no initial air attack or naval bombardment or paratroopers, but those landed would be given support from Churchill tanks. The RAF's role would be to protect the landings from aerial bombardment. A full-scale invasion of the French coast was not possible at the time, but a determined landing and attack would keep the Germans guessing. By 27 July a new plan was agreed by the Chiefs of Staff, this would be known as Operation *Jubilee* and take place on 27 July 1942. The RAF was given assigned attacks to take place on 19 August 1942, involving forty-eight squadrons, mainly Spitfires. Four of the squadrons had the new Spitfire IX, two Spitfire VIs, the remainder flew the Spitfire Vb and Vc. Apart from essential ground cover they would escort B17 Flying Fortresses and light bombers of the USAAF. They were supported by Hurricane IIs with 20mm cannon which would attack light and heavy guns behind Dieppe, while the Spitfires would protect shipping. Hawkinge was already host to many of these aircraft, being a forward base, took part in Operation *Jubilee*, an important test for planning the invasion of Europe in June 1944, and other operations at North Africa and Sicily.

Two days previously, on 17 August, B17s bombed Rouen, escorted by Spitfires, some from Hawkinge, No.91 Squadron worked with No.277 (ASR) Squadron. But it was not until the evening of 18 August that Hawkinge was notified that the raid on Dieppe was to take place early the following day. No.416, and No.616 Squadrons were briefed by Wing Commander R.M.B.D. 'Duke' Woolley DFC, who in June 1942 had been made Wing Leader of the Debden Wing. No.91 and No.277 were briefed by Squadron Leader Demozay, crews were confined to base, telephone wires connecting the airfields telephone boxes to the GPO (General Post Office) were cut and other security measures taken. For once most of the staff at Hawkinge were in their beds soon after dusk in preparation for the early start at 0430hrs and Operation *Jubilee*.

On the morning of 19 August, the weather was fine with some heavy cloud. From dawn onwards pilots at Hawkinge were at constant readiness. Until dusk there was a continuous stream of aircraft departing and returning from Dieppe. Led by Squadron Leader Brown and Squadron Leader Chadburn, No.416 (RCAF) and No.616 Squadrons took part in four sorties to Dieppe. The area was an inferno, with great fires and a pall of smoke over the town, drifting several miles out to sea. RN ships, transports and landing craft formed a great semi-circle around the harbour. These were protected by between three to six squadrons, many engaged in combat.

Twelve Spitfires VIs of No.616 Squadron took off from Hawkinge at 1045hrs on 19 August, arriving over Dieppe at 1120hrs acting as high escort. No less than fifty Fw 190s were seen, some escorting Do 217s attacking shipping. Flight Lieutenant F.A.W. 'Tony' Gaze DFC, destroyed a Do 217 and damaged an Fw 190; four other Fw 190s were damaged in the attack. Sergeant N.W.J. Coldrey (Rhodesia) was killed, shot down by Fw 190s and Sergeant Welch hit by return fire, he managed to return to Hawkinge, and belly-landed. Flight Lieutenant J.S. Fifield was shot down, baled out and was picked up by a RN minelayer and taken to Newhaven. No.616 Squadron ended their last patrol during Operation *Jubilee* with six Fw 190s damaged, one Do 217 destroyed for the loss of one pilot, flying seventy-five operational hours. During the day, cooperation between No.616 Squadron personnel and those at Hawkinge was reported as excellent. There was one accident, caused by severe fatigue. While taxiing Spitfire VI, Sergeant J.K. Rodger struck a crash tender, catching the wing tip of his aircraft. With the Dieppe raid over, the squadron returned to Great Sampford on 20 August.

RAF HAWKINGE

No.277 Squadron 'B' Flight led by Flight Lieutenant Spence, operated Defiants and Lysanders throughout the day without escort. By the end of 19 August Fighter Command had destroyed ninety-two enemy aircraft (including bombers), probably destroyed thirty-eight and damaged 141. The RAF lost ninety-eight aircraft with thirty of the pilots being rescued. No.416 (RCAF) suffered no losses but destroyed a Ju 88, damaged five other Ju 88s, an Me 110 and an Fw 190. Sergeant C.H. Evans (Canadian) No.91 Squadron was flying a 'Jim Crow' sortie, when Spitfire Vb YQ-A suffered engine failure, Evans baled out and was rescued from the sea off South Foreland, the only aircraft lost by No.91 Squadron on 19 August. Hawkinge ground staff worked steadily all day, refuelling Spitfires of Nos.64, 332, and 165 Squadrons and No.602 Squadron. The Dieppe raid was hailed as a great success for Fighter Command. The RAF lost thirty-two pilots killed, several injured or taken prisoner. But thanks to aircrew and pilots of No.277 (ASR) and No.91 Squadron many were rescued. During the morning of 20 August No.416 (RCAF) Squadron prepared to leave for Martlesham Heath, as did No.616 who were based at Great Sampford. But before they left Hawkinge, a BBC unit arrived, and Canadian pilots of No.416 Squadron made records, and interviews took place with pilots of No.91 Squadron and No.277 (ASR) Squadron. For No.91 and No.277 Squadrons, there was no rest: between 1230 and 1345hrs, they were operating singly, searching between Beachy Head and Dieppe for ships' crew and pilots reported missing during Operation *Jubilee*.

Lieutenant J.R. Heap 'A' Flight, flying Spitfire Vb DL-B No.91 Squadron intercepted a Dornier Do 24, a flying boat looking for downed airmen or suitable ships to attack as it carried bombs fitted under the aircraft's wings. He approached the formidable target, which was flying at sea level, opening fire he saw the rear gunner jump out, the Dornier turned over and crashed in flames. Pilot Officer Eddie Tonge in Spitfire Vb BM558 DL-L was reported missing, he was flying in the vicinity of German fighters, shot down and killed by JG 2. Flying Officer A. Le Maire and Sergeant E.C. Sutton No.91 Squadron were scrambled the following day from Hawkinge and spotted two Fw 190s flying away from Hythe, heading for France. Le Maire dived on them, two Fw 190s appeared and attacked him. Badly damaged he flew his Spitfire back towards Folkestone, but the engine failed. Sergeant Sutton crash landed slightly injured, the aircraft was a write-off. The next few days were more peaceful, and a Variety Show was put on by ENSA in the station's gymnasium.

HAWKINGE DURING 1942

Pilot Officer H.J.M. de Molenes took off on a ASR sortie early on the evening of 27 August, flying Spitfire Vb B230, last seen by Flight Sergeant Younge, who had dropped his own dinghy for a pilot in the sea, circling over him. This pilot was picked up by an ASR launch which then spotted a body floating in the sea off Hastings, this turned out to be Pilot Officer de Molenes. It was thought he baled out of his Spitfire Vb due to lack of fuel, striking the tailplane. Rushed to Dover he died of his injuries. Flight Lieutenant R. 'Spud' Spurdle 'B' Flight Commander No.91 Squadron, was particularly upset as he had been sharing quarters with the Free French pilot, who he named the 'Count'. Flight Lieutenant Bob Spurdle, Pilot Officer J.R. 'Heapo' Heap and Flying Officer E.F. 'Knobby' Clarkson, set off for an evening drinking session to drown their sorrows. During the night they met three WAAFs, and took them back to Reindene Mess, something that was strictly forbidden. The incident was blown up out of proportion, and the three pilots were reprimanded by the Station Commander at Hawkinge.

Flight Lieutenant A.G. Donahue, who had forced landed at Hawkinge in August 1940 while with No.64 Squadron, was serving with No.91 Squadron in September 1942. Donahue had taken off from Hawkinge on 11 September to patrol Flushing and Gris Nez in Spitfire Vb BL511 then disappeared. A faint distress signal was picked up by Radio Telecommunications, shortly after a Wireless Transmission was intercepted off the Dutch Coast from a Ju 88: 'One of my engines is on fire my rear gunner been killed. I am trying to get to Brussels.' It was assumed that this was an aircraft attacked by Flight Lieutenant Donahue. No.91 Squadron took off searching the Straits and North Sea, but no trace of him was ever found.

No.99 (Folkestone) Squadron Air Training Corps (ATC), based locally at Malvern House, Folkestone, were lucky to be close to Hawkinge. On 13 September 1942 some thirty cadets arrived. They were supervised by Flight Lieutenant Clark, who was given the responsibility of escorting the cadets around certain locations at Hawkinge. During war, cadets considered it a privilege to be in what was a 'Restricted Area', surrounded as they were in the Folkestone area by military authority. Even in wartime some cadets were given the opportunity to see the aircraft parked at Hawkinge and in the hangars, a lucky few even had the opportunity to fly. During the morning and afternoon of 18 September, Hawkinge was visited by several journalists of Kent newspapers, who under the supervision of Flight Lieutenant Tomlinson, No.11 Group Public Relations, were there to see No.91 and No.277 (ASR) Squadrons in action. They were also able to talk

RAF HAWKINGE

ATC Cadets taking a keen interest in a Walrus of No.277 (ASR) Squadron during 1943, aided by RAF personnel. Even in wartime RAF airfields were visited by the ATC, a few lucky cadets had a chance to fly, many went on to join the RAF. (Model & Allied Pub. Ltd)

to pilots and airmen at Hawkinge and enjoyed an informal lunch in the Officers' Mess before leaving the airfield later that day.

Squadron Leader Jean-Francois Demozay DSO, DFC & Bar celebrated his nineteenth enemy aircraft destroyed on 23 September. When he was attacked by two Fw 190s, he managed to return fire, hitting one which flipped over and dived into the sea. Demozay had thirteen victories during his service with No.91 Squadron based at Hawkinge. Pilot Officer J.B. Edwards had been shot down in Spitfire Vb EN844 off Griz Nez that morning by Lieutenant Beese of the 1st Staffel JG 26. Edwards had reported over the RT that he was being chased by two Fw 190s, then silence, his body never found.

The next day, three Typhoon Ibs of No.609 Squadron landed at Hawkinge from Biggin Hill led by Squadron Leader Richey. They were

HAWKINGE DURING 1942

assigned to Hawkinge to support No.91 Squadron on 'scramble' duty for a period until further notice. Two pilots of No.609 Squadron Flying Officer C.C.A Ortmans and Squadron Leader P.H.M. Richey had been touring the airfields at Gravesend, Lympne and Hawkinge to assess their suitability for operating Typhoons, Hawkinge was chosen. A move much appreciated by the overworked pilots at Hawkinge, particularly as that day twenty Fw 190s bombed Hastings and St Leonards, fifteen others appeared off the coast to cover them. All operational Spitfires of No.91 Squadron were airborne, with sirens wailing at Hawkinge and controllers 'flapping'. Wing Commander E.G. Jones DSO, DFC took over as CO RAF Hawkinge, arriving on 24 September. Wing Commander Aitken was posted to Bradwell Bay as the new CO, before leaving a party took place in the Officers' Mess.

Pilot Officer F.N. Gillitt 'B' Flight No.91 Squadron intercepted a Ju 88, damaging the aircraft which dropped its bombs in the sea. It was reported flying through the Dover barrage balloons with both engines on fire. Unfortunately, Spitfire Vb EN771 flown by Pilot Officer Gillit, was hit by return fire from the Ju 88s, and forced landed his aircraft near Dover, tearing a wing off and overturning. Gillitt climbed out of his Spitfire slightly injured. On 30 September Flight Lieutenant A.J. 'Andy' Andrews DFC 'B' Flight No.91 Squadron took off from Hawkinge in poor weather. He intercepted a Ju 88 off the French coast and watched as the stricken aircraft crashed onto the beach at Gris Nez, in flames. Later that morning Andrews and Flight Lieutenant Le Roux 'A' Flight CO, flew over the Straits and could see the Ju 88 still burning, smoke could be seen from Folkestone. Andrews was flying a Spitfire VI the high-altitude variant with pointed wingtips and a pressurised cockpit. He had been making notes on the Ju 88's camouflage and armament before he shot it down. Returning to Hawkinge Andrews was followed by an Fw 190, but a fellow pilot came to his aid. Flight Lieutenant Le Roux who had taken off on an air test, intercepted an Fw 190 flying high above Hawkinge, opened fire immediately damaging the aircraft, shortly after he intercepted two other Fw 190s, firing on one which he claimed as damaged.

No.91 Squadron moved to Lympne on 2 October 1942, where they were to continue operations for a few days. Spitfire VIs of No.616 and No.124 Squadrons arrived at Hawkinge to refuel later that evening, returning from escorting B17 Flying Fortresses. Sergeant M.H.F. Cooper No.616 Squadron was missing, Pilot Officer Large took off from Hawkinge without rearming, his Spitfire VI damaged to try and locate Cooper who baled out of Spitfire VI BR159 over the sea. A Walrus of No.277 Squadron, located the pilot off Blanc Nez, he was sitting in his dinghy waving a flag.

RAF HAWKINGE

No.277 (ASR) Squadron 'B' Flight rescued Sergeant M.H.F. Cooper No.616 Squadron from the Channel on 2 October 1942. Sergeant Tom Fletcher, 2nd left, was awarded the DFM for his gallant attempt to rescue the Spitfire pilot. (Air Comm. G. Pitchfork MBE)

Sergeant Fletcher put down his Walrus, by now under fire from German flak and coastal batteries. Flight Sergeant Roberts and Sergeant Healey managed to haul Cooper into the Walrus, taking off for Hawkinge. After they landed twelve Spitfires of No.402 Squadron, who acted as high cover for the rescue arrived guided in by a flarepath.

Hawkinge was busy on 8 October, when No.10 Group Wing arrived for a joint operation, which included Spitfire Vics of No.501 Squadron from Middle Wallop, No.66 Squadron and No.118 Squadron based at Zeals, Wiltshire. Six Spitfires of No.1 CACU Flight, Detling, also arrived at Hawkinge to help No.91 Squadron. The weather was so bad, the operation was cancelled, the squadrons returned to their bases on 9 October. Hawkinge was covered with Spitfires, but by the time No.91 Squadron returned from Lympne, No.10 Group were gone. An American B17 crew were rescued off North Foreland. Three P38 Lightnings of No.94 FS 9th USAAF based

HAWKINGE DURING 1942

at Ibsley arrived, flown by Captain Rimke, Lieutenant Starbuck, and Lieutenant McWherter. Hot on their heels was a Spitfire of No.334 FS, flown by Captain Coen DFC and two Spitfires of No.616 Squadron based at Tangmere, flown by Flight Lieutenant Fifield and Sergeant King. The next day the weather was poor, little flying took place, the ten aircrew of the B17 rescued from North Foreland arrived at Hawkinge. In the early afternoon, following lunch, they were picked up by a Lockheed Electra to fly them back to their base. Air Cadets of No.99 (Folkestone) Squadron arrived and were given an introduction on the Link Trainer, an early type of flight simulator, which provided a cheaper alternative for training pilots in instrument flying than flying actual aircraft.

For No.91 Squadron October 1942 was an extremely hectic period, continuously flying defensive patrols and supporting Air Sea Rescue. On 12 October during a defensive patrol, Pilot Officer Batten and Sergeant K. Hawkins (RCAF) engaged four Fw 190s, over the Deal, Dover area at 1045hrs. They claimed two Fw 190s destroyed but Sergeant Hawkins was hit and went down, Spitfire Vb AD548 crashed into the sea, Hawkins baled

SGT. D.H 'Ace' Davy No.91 Squadron seated in his Spitfire adorned with an image of 'Jane', the cartoon character which appeared in the *Daily Mirror* newspaper during the Second World War.

RAF HAWKINGE

out and was seriously injured, he was picked up by ASR Launch. Following a successful attack on a Ju88 on 18 October, which crashed in the sea in flames, Sergeant Davy returned safely to Hawkinge.

Flight Lieutenant A. Andrews CO of 'B' Flight No.91 Squadron was extremely lucky on 26 October, when attacked from astern by Fw 190s. The cockpit hood of his Spitfire Vb R7292 DL-T 'Newbury II Carol' was damaged. Flight Lieutenant Andrews was not hit, but it was a near miss, landing back at Hawkinge. Spitfire Vb R7292 was repaired at Hawkinge where it remained with No.91 Squadron moving on to No.306 (Polish) Squadron and No.345 Squadron. Flight Lieutenant Andrews would be credited as being the first pilot of No.91 Squadron to attack what he thought was a U-Boat but turned out to be a porpoise!

A Westland Whirlwind of No.137 Squadron, based at Manston was reported missing on 31 October while attacking military camps in France when hit by ground fire. Although initially wreckage of his aircraft was seen by pilots of No.91 Squadron, it was not until Pilot Officer 'Johnny' Round was returning from a shipping patrol that he spotted an airman in a dinghy off Griz-Nez. Pilot Officer Hilton (RAAF) No.277 Squadron found

No.277 (ASR) Squadron 'B' Flight on detachment to RAF Hawkinge, distinguished themselves during their time serving on the airfield.

the pilot floating between two rows of a German minefields. Landing, he managed to pull the pilot from the dinghy aided by Flight Sergeant Seales. Preparing to take-off, Hilton saw a mine directly ahead, but managed to bounce the Walrus over the mine. Flight Sergeant Seales was injured in the process; the pilot of Whirlwind I P7064, Flight Lieutenant J.E. Van Shaick DFM was unhurt. Returning to Hawkinge that evening, there was an attack on Canterbury by Me 109s and Fw 190s. No.91 Squadron were scrambled, intercepting forty to fifty fighters, seen over the Straits of Dover, destroying five Fw 190s, damaging four others. Flying Officer R.G.V. Gibbs' Spitfire Vb AD458 was last seen being attacked by an Fw 190.

Back at Hawkinge, two of No.609 Squadron's Typhoon Ibs, flown by Pilot Officer H.D.F. Amor and Pilot Officer R.H. Payne, took off to patrol off Deal. AA defences, most probably seeing the two aircraft, mistook them for Fw190s of the JG 26 formation. Typhoon Ib R7708 was hit, catching fire, Pilot Officer Payne baled out. As his parachute opened, he watched his aircraft plough into Pegwell Bay, hitting the water he released his parachute, wading ashore unhurt. Pilot Officer Amor was also hit, and limped back to Hawkinge. Attempts to prevent such incidents occurring were made, one was painting the nose of Typhoons white, to identify them from the radial engines of the Fw 190s. AA Defences were instructed to fire on any aircraft approaching the coast flying at less than 1,000ft (305 metres) but these measures were not always successful. In a phone call to the Duty Gunnery Officer, North Foreland, complaining about the regularity of this problem, the officer said: 'Could you ask Pilot Officer R.H. Payne, very tactfully – whether we got anywhere near them'.

During the afternoon of 31 October, Hawkinge 'Rugger' XV beat No.560 Coast Regiment by 14-0, and a party was held in the Officers' Mess which the Naval officers attended, celebrating Halloween and the day's successful rescues by No.277 Squadron and No.91 Squadron's operation against JG 26. The main event of the evening was a 'ducking-for-apples' contest held in the anteroom. Attacks on Canterbury continued during the evening and night, thirty-five aircraft bombed the city, AA defences in the Hawkinge and Lympne area opened fire. A local 'Q' site, or decoy airfield, located at Wootton near Lydden, attracted the attention of the bombers, and it was near this site that a Dornier Do 17 crashed in flames, killing all the crew when its bombs exploded, shot down by AA defences. Records suggest this aircraft could have been one of five Do 217E-4s of KG 2 which were destroyed during the attack on Canterbury on the night of 31 October/1 November 1942.

RAF HAWKINGE

ASR patrols continued on 1 November, No.277 and No.91 Squadron were searching for Flying Officer G.G. Galway an Australian No.453 (RAAF) Squadron, missing on operation. In a fight with Fw 190s, Flying Officer Galway was shot down in Spitfire Vb EN786, baling out he realised he was too low, his parachute opened seconds later after he had hit the sea. Cutting himself free he climbed into his dinghy, despite losing a paddle he survived on rations provided. Seeing a light he paddled towards it, the current was strong, but he finally reached a buoy, tying the dinghy to it he tried to signal by covering the light intermittently. When daylight arrived, he was rescued by an ASR launch, given dry clothes and hot drink and later returning to Hawkinge. Galway telephoned his base at Hornchurch and was later picked up, his only complaint being the relentless noise from a foghorn!

Flight Lieutenant A.J. Andrews DFC Spitfire Vb AB378 and Flying Officer J.P. Maridor DFC No.91 Squadron were searching on 2 November for downed Spitfire pilots when they ran into Fw 190s. Fw. Adolf Glunz 4/JG 26 shot down Andrews off Berck sur Mer, Andrews yelling over the RT 'They got me.' Flying Officer Maridor retaliating, destroyed an Fw 190 before returning to base. Flgr. Kornelius Ott's body was recovered from the sea, thought to be one of the crew of Do 217E-4 3/KG 2, shot down by No.91 Squadron on 31 October 1942, but was in fact one of the crew of a Dornier Do 217E-4 of 3/KG 2, destroyed off Folkestone on 1 November 1942. A Beaufighter IF of No.29 Squadron, based at West Malling, flown by Flying Officer G. Pepper DFC and Pilot Officer J.H. Toone DFM, intercepted the Do 217E-4. Uffz. W. Kunn, Obgefr. H. Kohl and Gefr. W. Ahrens were lost. Folkestone AA shot down a Dornier Do 217E-4 of 8/KG 2 on 5 November at Beachborough Park, killing the crew, Gefr. H. Kuhlmann, Gefr. Stresemann, Uffz. K. Knorr, and Obergefr.V. Breier, and taken to Hawkinge for burial. Parts of their aircraft are on display at the Kent Battle of Britain Museum, Hawkinge. Heavy rain flooded the airfield, which was out of action during 6/7 November, only emergency landings were permitted.

Pilot Officer G.C. Griffin No.165 Squadron, died when Spitfire Vb EP381 was shot down by Fw 190s, escorting B17s attacking targets in France. No.91 Squadron efforts gained them recognition when the following day, they were presented the squadron crest by AM Leigh Mallory OBE, DSO Air Officer Commander No.11 Group. A parade and ceremony took place at 'B' Flight's dispersal when the crest was handed to the CO Squadron Leader J.E.F. Demozay. That afternoon there was a concentrated attack on Le Harve, No.611 Squadron escorted twelve Bostons. Flight Sergeant

HAWKINGE DURING 1942

T. Whitfield crash landed Spitfire IX BR629 at Hawkinge with no flaps, narrowly missing the Control Office. Hit by enemy action during a sweep over France, he climbed out of his aircraft. Whitfield was followed by Flight Sergeant R. Harris Spitfire IX BR978, who had also been hit, landed at Hawkinge, wounded over his left eye.

The morning of 10 November, Flight Sergeant 'Scotty' Downer No.91 Squadron, took off on a RDF Calibration test. South of Dungeness he saw two Fw 190s, at sea level which he attacked, destroying one of JG 26 based at Abbeville. Known as the 'Abbeville Boys', they were the main adversaries of No.91 Squadron, and many other squadrons. 'Scotty' landed safely, his windscreen covered in oil. During the night of 11 November, heavy gunfire was heard at Hawkinge from the guns on the French coast, one shell hit the AA site at Folkestone Golf Course, killing four soldiers. Flight Sergeant Glew of No.277 (ASR) Squadron attended Buckingham Palace to receive his DFM from King George VI; on his return to Hawkinge there was a party held in the Officers' Mess to celebrate his success in rescuing several airmen from the sea.

The next few days were peaceful due to fog, an opportunity for football and rugby, the RAF played against the Coastal Batteries, the stations

Sergeant Tom Fletcher 2nd left, joined No.277 (ASR) Squadron at Hawkinge to fly the Lysander IIIA and Walrus I. Sergeant Fletcher had flown with No.91 Squadron, remaining in the RAF until retiring in 1964.

RAF HAWKINGE

teams beat the visitors. On 15 November, twenty cadets of No.354 (Dover) Squadron ATC arrived, just in time to see Spitfires of 'B' Flight No.91 Squadron take off for Lympne, remaining there for a few days due to fog; they were soon joined by 'A' Flight.

During late 1942, JG 26 were given a new task by Adolf Hitler, who decreed that fighter units were to commence Terrorangriffe (terror attacks – these became known as hit & run raids) on Southern England. The first of these involved two Fw 190A-4s of 5/KG 26, officially known as Storangriffe or harassment raids. In early 1943 RAF Regiments were redeployed from several airfields to coastal towns between Ramsgate and Exmouth. Increasing the AA defences, armoured car flights (each comprising of six Beaverettes armed with twin Vickers 'K' machine guns, operated by gas) withdrew from twenty-nine RAF squadrons in Fighter Command for coastal defences. A bizarre incident occurred on 27 November at Lydd, Romney Marsh. Two Fw 190A-4s of 5/KG 26, noticing a train from Lydd approaching the Caldicott Crossing en route to Brookland, attacked head on. Cannon fire from Fw 190 'Black 5' hit the engine, the boiler exploded. The following Fw 190, flown by Obfw. Heinrich Bierworth collided with the steam dome; caught in the explosion and uprush of steam, he was flung from the disintegrating aircraft, drowning in a dyke, later buried at Hawkinge. The driver of the train Charlie Gilbert and his fireman Dan Hill were both scalded, surviving as did passengers. The engine South Coast Railway 'D3' class 0-4-4T No.2365 was restored to working condition, returning to work during 1943.

No.277 (ASR) Squadron and aircraft of No.91 Squadron took off on the morning of 29 November in search of a Stirling bomber, reported in the sea off Dymchurch. The dead members of the crew were brought back to Hawkinge. On the night of 28/29 November, Stirling I BF372 'OJ-H' No.149 Squadron, based at Lakenheath, was part of a force attacking the Fiat works in Turin, and the city. During the raid the Australian pilot Flight Sergeant R.H. Middleton made three runs across the city; his aircraft was hit by light anti-aircraft fire, with a shell exploding in the cockpit. The pilots and wireless operator were wounded, Flight Sergeant Middleton was rendered unconscious and lost an eye, the co-pilot, Flight Sergeant L.A. Hyder, keeping control, released the bombs, turning for home. The aircraft received further damage over Boulogne. Reaching the coast, Middleton decided there was little chance of landing safely, being short of petrol and because of damage to the aircraft and the injuries of both pilots. Middleton, very weak, could hardly see or speak. Turning parallel with the coast he

HAWKINGE DURING 1942

The Gunner/Observer being helped into the rear cockpit of Lysander IIIA V9547 'BA-F' of 'B' Flight No.277 (ASR) Squadron, complete with dinghy pack.

ordered the crew to bale out. Five men survived but Middleton and two other men were still in the Stirling when it crashed into the sea. Flight Sergeant Middleton was posthumously awarded the VC, Flight Sergeant L.A. Hyder the DFM and four other members of the crew were decorated. Middleton's body was washed up on the Kent coast and buried at Mildenhall near his home at Lakenheath. Sergeant J.W. Jeffreys Flight Engineer, Flight Sergeant J. Mackie Air Gunner were killed, both washed ashore on 29 November shortly after the crash, and were brought to Hawkinge. Flight Sergeant Middleton's body was recovered on 1 February 1943 at Shakespeare Beach, Dover. Flying Officer G.R. Royde DFC Air/Bomber was killed, Pilot Officer N.E. Skinner DFC Air Gunner, Pilot Officer D. Cameron DFM Air Gunner, and Sergeant H.W. Gough DFM were injured.

A hockey match took place on the afternoon of 29 November between Hawkinge Hockey XI and the Dover Balloon Barrage team. As the game progressed, there was an unscheduled interval when two Fw 190s of JG 26, swept over the playing field. Everyone immediately dived onto the ground, but there were no casualties, and once recovered the game continued, and

RAF HAWKINGE

Hawkinge lost 6–2. On 30 November Flight Lieutenant A.J. Andrews DFC, killed on 2 November, was posthumously awarded a Bar to his DFC. No.2826 RAF Regiment (AA) was originally formed as No.826 Squadron at Cambridge in July 1941. Moving to Hawkinge on 1 December 1942, they took part in intensive training exercises, commanded by Flight Lieutenant Griggs and Squadron Leader P.A. Palmer VC, MM. The squadron converted to the Light Anti-Aircraft role in May 1943 and joined 2nd Tactical Air Force in April 1944. It converted to the Rifle role in December 1944 and back to the Light Anti-Aircraft role in January 1945. It moved to the continent in February 1945, initially being deployed to Courtrai and later Lubeck and Flensburg, where it disbanded in December 1945. One member of the squadron was mentioned in despatches.

Flight Sergeant D.R. Hartwell and Flight Sergeant L. Butler No.277 Squadron took off from Hawkinge at 0825hrs. in a Lysander searching for Wellington IC DVB19 No.1474 Wireless Interception Flight based at Gransden. Flying in the Frankfurt area the aircraft was intercepted by a night fighter. At 0645hrs. the aircraft crossed the coast at about 10 miles (16 km) NE of Dunkirk, searchlights tried to pick it out, but these were dodged by evasive action, coming down low over the sea. When the searchlights were switched off, the pilot managed to gain height. The Wireless Operator sent an SOS and a message to the effect that they had been attacked by an enemy aircraft. He again transmitted the coded message in case it had not been received the first time. At 0720 hrs the English coast was reached. The pilot tested the landing light to see if he could ditch using it, but this was impossible. He decided to wait for daylight before ditching and asked the crew if anyone preferred to bale out rather than ditch. The aircraft ditched off Deal. Their dinghy inflated but was damaged by gunfire, the crew got out of the dinghy and climbed onto the aircraft. Soon a rowing boat approached, taking them ashore. Apart from Flight Sergeant H.G. Jordan (S/Op. RAFVR) who was injured, the crew of Wellington IC DV819 were RCAF: Sergeant E.A .Paulton (Pilot), Flight Sergeant W.A.R. Barry (Navigator) were not injured, Flight Sergeant W.W. Bigoray (WO/AG), Flight Sergeant F.P. Gram (AG), and Flight Sergeant E.T. Vachon (AG), were all injured. They later received a telegram from Marshal of the RAF Sir Charles Portal KG, GCB, OM, DSO & Bar, MC with his congratulations, several of the crew received awards for their bravery and actions.

Two pilots of No.91 Squadron failed to return to Hawkinge on 6 December 1942, from a reconnaissance flight to Dieppe. Engaged in combat with Fw 190s of JG 26, Flying Officer G.H Dean Spitfire Vb AB982, Flight Sergeant

HAWKINGE DURING 1942

M.K Eldrid Spitfire Vb BL994, were shot down and killed. The following morning Flying Officer 'Jackie' J.P. Lux, alias Flying Officer J.P. Coudray, a French pilot, died when Spitfire Vb BL853 was hit by gunfire from a Fw 190. Leaving Lympne, he crashed in Pas de Calais area. A party took place in the Officers' Mess on 8 December in honour of Squadron Leader J.E.F. Demozay AOL, CG, DSO, DFC & Bar who was leaving No.91 Squadron to take up Air Liaison Officer duties with the Dover Naval base as Wing Commander. Sergeant pilots and air gunners of No.277 Squadron were also invited to the 'binge'. Demozay had been CO since 11 July 1942 and was replaced by Squadron Leader R.H. Harries DSO & Bar, DFC & Bar.

An order was received that all Spitfire Vbs of No.91 Squadron were to have their wing tips removed. The clipped wing was used by several Spitfire variants, the standard wing tips were replaced by wooden fairing reducing the span by 3ft 6in (1.07m). Following the Battle of Britain in 1940, the Germans introduced improved fighters such as the Me 109-E and Fw 190. Early reports of a new Luftwaffe fighter were not really considered, but losses soon began to mount, leading to the realisation that this latest adversary had an advantage with its incredible rate of roll and manoeuvrability. The 'clipped-wing' increased the roll rate of the Spitfire Vb and improved its combat qualities, the wingspan needed to be made shorter for these reasons. One drawback was that it made the Spitfires look like the Me 109-E or 'Emil' as it was named by the Luftwaffe, which could be a problem for both pilots and ground defences.

Four Fw 190s of JG 26, swept in over the coast on 11 December, two attacked Lympne. Two Spitfire Vbs of No.91 Squadron were parked at the airfield, which were hit, there were no casualties. Other Fw 190s beat up the airfield and headed towards Dungeness. Flight Lieutenant J.A. Spence and Sergeant H.W. Brunckhurst had taken off in a Defiant I AA312 of No.277 Squadron, to carry out air to sea firing off Dungeness. Heading back to Hawkinge, control was unable to contact them, to warn them that Fw 190s were in the area. Brunckhurst had cleared a gun stoppage, when they were hit by an Fw 190 who dived out of the sun. They managed to get back to Hawkinge, both lower guns had been smashed and the Defiant's fin, starboard flap, wing and one tyre were damaged. Spence landed safely, both pilot and air gunner uninjured. The Defiant's rear gun turret was no match for the new German fighters. Dutch pilot Second Lieutenant O.R. Malm No.331 (Dutch) Squadron based at North Weald was shot down on 12 December by Fw 190s operating in the Somme area. Baling out of Spitfire IX BS389 he crashed in the sea. He was later rescued by an English trawler and taken to Rye Memorial Hospital. The following morning four Spitfire IXs of No.331 Squadron landed, reporting seeing several airmen in a dinghy off Le Touquet. The sea was extremely rough and perhaps unusually the Germans were contacted and asked to rescue the crew!

On 14 December six men were reported seen on a raft off Dover. Sergeant Fletcher DFM, Flight Sergeant R.C. Glew and Sergeant Healey No.277 Squadron were sent off in Walrus X9521.Three were rescued in extremely dangerous conditions and failing light. The remaining three men were lost, one killed when the Walrus was swept onto the raft by heavy sea. The Walrus had shipped a lot of water and could not take-off, Sergeant Fletcher taxied the aircraft back to Dover, having been led into the harbour by a tugboat using its searchlight, and tied up. Following the German rescue of the British bomber crew, the previous day, Fletcher rescued German sailors whose ship had been sunk by a Royal Navy destroyer. Flying Officer Morrison, Sergeant Fletcher, Sergeant Healey and five ground staff arrived at Dover to inspect the damage to Walrus X952, and decided the aircraft would have to be landed before being picked up by No.86 (MU) Maintenance Unit. Flight Lieutenant Fletcher taxied his Walrus into the submarine base, up against a wall. It was lifted out of the water by a crane, lowered on to dry land and the wings folded back. Certain important equipment was also removed from the Walrus.

The problem of identification of Spitfire Vbs with clipped wings was highlighted on 17 December. Flight Sergeant P.C. Standen and Flight Sergeant J. Snell took off in a Walrus to search for Sergeant J.C. Chittick No.91 Squadron, shot down off Deal. Two Typhoon Is of No.609 Squadron based at Manston on patrol were advised of German fighters in the vicinity. Accompanied by Sergeant O'Shaughnessy, he and Sergeant Chittick recognised the two Typhoons. Unfortunately, the Typhoon pilots thought the Spitfires of No.91 Squadron were Me 109-Es. Sergeant Chittick was shot down in flames in Spitfire Vb EP508, Sergeant O'Shaughnessy returned, proof of the 'clipped wing' saga.

With Christmas just around the corner, news arrived that Wing Commander G. Jones DSO, DFC was leaving Hawkinge to join the RAF Staff College. He had been CO since 29 February 1942. A party was held in the Officers' Mess, Wing Commander L.L.A. Strange DSO, DFC & Bar, MC joined the party; he would later took up his new post as CO at Hawkinge on 22 December 1943. An Air Ministry photographer arrived on 23 December to take photographs of No.277 Squadron's Spitfires in formation, but this was cancelled as German fighters were reported in the area. That afternoon

HAWKINGE DURING 1942

they tried again, a Walrus took off, flown by Flight Lieutenant J.A. Spence and Flying Officer Forward, the Air Ministry photographer took some excellent photos. On Christmas Eve, Flight Lieutenant J.A. Spence and Sergeant H.W. Brunckhurst had taken off in a Lysander I, for an Army Cooperation Flight over the Tenterden. Reaching the required height, they received orders to land at Biggin Hill due to poor weather. Landing, they left their aircraft at the airfield, returning to Hawkinge by train. On 25 December they returned to Biggin Hill in a Walrus flown by Flying Officer R.A. Morrison to collect their aircraft. Christmas Day 1942 was celebrated in the usual way at Hawkinge. It was an RAF tradition that Senior NCOs waited on airmen during their Christmas lunch. Officers celebrated in their mess, with their newly appointed CO Wing Comm. L.L.A. Strange DSO, DFC, MC presiding. There was a toast for King George VI and all 'Absent Friends' lost during 1942 or taken PoW. The party continued with the officers waiting on the staff, celebrations continued with a dance held in the camp theatre.

Pilot Officer I.W. 'Scotty' Downer (RNZAF) was the first victim of No.91 Squadron following Christmas Festivities. Patrolling off Beachy Head during 29 December, attacked by a lone Fw 190, Spitfire Vb EN782 dived into the sea. Despite a search by ASR patrols, nothing was found of him or his Spitfire. Pilot Officer Downer was the fourth pilot to be lost in December 1942; he had married a girl from Folkestone only a few months before his death, a tragic episode. Following the terrible news that 'Scotty' had been killed, the first snow of the winter brought 1942 to a close. Pilot Officer Mart attacked the Fw190 of JG 26 which shot down Pilot Officer I.W. 'Scotty' Downer, which made a hasty retreat. Despite a search by the Walrus and Pilot Officer Mart, nothing was seen of Pilot Officer Downer or his Spitfire. That night extra guards were placed on aircraft as a message had been received that a few Italian PoWs had escaped from a local camp. This did not deter RAF staff at Hawkinge from enjoying the party and dance held on the last day of December 1942. As the snow crept over the airfield, freezing on the ground, everyone was thinking what 1943 would bring.

Chapter 9

Taking the War to the Enemy 1943
Rescue and Patrols

The New Year got off to a slow start, the weather being atrocious. Low cloud, heavy rainstorms and high winds battered the hangars at Hawkinge. The decision to continue to harass Luftwaffe over Holland and Northern France was made, and the only force capable of applying such pressure was the RAF. With attacks on Europe by the 8th and 9th USAAF, both fighter aircraft of the RAF and the USAAF fighter groups did not have the range, even with drop tanks, to escort the bombers deep into Europe. Their role was mainly defensive. RAF spitfires continued to escort RAF and USAAF light bombers with Typhoons as a formidable ground attack aircraft. The introduction of the P51 Mustang gave the Americans the ability to penetrate deep into Germany by the end of 1943. As RAF squadrons were gradually being re-equipped with the Spitfire XI, there were still many who had to continue operations from Hawkinge and other airfields flying Spitfire Vb and Vcs. As for Air Sea Rescue operations, these continued unabated, their role vitally important in the quest to save aircrew from the sea or being captured by the enemy.

The weather on 1 January was poor, with low cloud and fog; there had been no flying between Hawkinge and Lympne. A Fairy Fulmar I of No.790 Squadron FAA had been trying to locate Lympne, and crash landed near the airfield. Sub Lieutenant D'Arcy and his Observer were both uninjured. During the afternoon of 3 January, Flight Lieutenant G. Turner arrived at Hawkinge in an Cierva C.30A Auto-Giro from West Malling, possibly of No.1448 (Rota) Flight No.74 (Signals) Wing Duxford, later reformed as No.529 Squadron. Previously posted to Hawkinge in 1940/1941, he was flying calibration tests from Hawkinge for a period of a week.

The weather was improving, and many patrols took place on 2/3 February. Even the Luftwaffe sent four Fw 190s to attack Canterbury, and Folkestone, by then 'hit & run' raids were a common feature. The Fw 190 was able to carry bombs – a highly formidable aircraft, respected by the RAF and nicknamed 'Butcher Bird'. Flight Lieutenant I. Mathew No.91 Squadron was on patrol and tried to intercept them, but he had a problem when AA Defences at Dungeness fired at him, fortunately not shooting him down; he landed safely back at Hawkinge. That afternoon No.91 Squadron flew several sweeps over the Pas de Calais and No.277 Squadron flew patrols searching for eight missing pilots. A pilot was seen on the Goodwin Sands frantically waving his arms, his Spitfire close by. Flying Officer J. Rainville (RCAF) flying Spitfire IX EN907 No.416 (RCAF) Squadron based Redhill, had been shot down by Fw 190s, wounded in the leg and rescued by an HSL returning to Dover and taken to hospital. Flying Officer Rainville fell victim to Hptm. W.F. Galland, the Luftwaffe Ace CO of 11/JG 26. Four other pilots of No.416 Squadron had been shot down, one dead, one PoW, two missing.

During 4 January two Fw 190-A4s of 10/JG 26 flew over the coast attacking Rye, dropping bombs. Leaving the scene, the wing of one of the attackers struck overhead cables and immediately disintegrated over Castle Farm, Winchelsea. Fw. Herbert Muller was killed instantly; his body was taken to Rye Mortuary, and later brought to Hawkinge. This aircraft was one of four which were flying 'hit and run' missions. That evening Dornier 217E-4 (F8+BM), laying mines, flying low, flew straight into Furze Hill, Fairlight, near Hastings, all crew were killed. Flight Lieutenant Johns Engineer Officer based at Hawkinge, had attended the crash site of the Fw 190-A4 at Rye, arrived on the scene the next day. As he approached, he saw remains of the Dornier's crew scattered among a wreckage. The Dornier had crashed into a bungalow, unoccupied at the time. Later that day No.277 Squadron were re-equipped with Spitfire IIs, modified to carry a dinghy and smoke floats. Pilots assigned to fly them flew in turn to Gravesend, from Hawkinge and Shoreham, to be trained and test-fly the new Spitfires, which reduced the time downed-aircrew spent in the sea, as dinghies could be dropped for their survival, prior to rescue. The crew of the Dornier 217 which crashed at Fairlight, were buried on 6 January at Hawkinge. Gefr. R. Fischer, Uffz. K. Tomcyzk, Gefr. E. Kern and Fw. H. Euker were given a military burial. Fw. Herbert Muller pilot of the Fw 190 which crashed at Winchelsea was buried the same day.

AVM H.W.L Saunders, the newly appointed AOC No.11 Group, arrived at Hawkinge on 7 January, to inspect the airfield, accompanied by the station CO Wing Commander L.L.A Strange and Wing Commander Demozay ALO at Dover. 'B' Flight No.91 Squadron, temporarily based at Lympne, moved back to Hawkinge. No.91 Squadron carried out reconnaissance and 'spotter' patrols in connection with the increasing air offensive against targets at Abbeville and over Holland. 'A' Flight's move from Lympne back to Hawkinge was delayed due to weather conditions. Although Hawkinge airfield was partly waterlogged by 13 January, 'A' Flight No.91 Squadron had moved back just in time; reunited with 'B' Flight, operations continued.

An Army Exercise took place on 14 January, the main road through Hawkinge airfield was packed with troops. Captain Riding and Courtney No.653 (AOP) Air Observation Post, arrived from Penshurst, Kent in two Auster aircraft. Two days later three more of the squadron arrived, all taking part in Army manoeuvres. An Escape Exercise 'King O' was organised and took place on 19 January. Two sides comprised of aircrew and personnel of the RAF Regiment. Eight aircrew from a total of eighteen evaded capture by the regiment and police patrols, entering the camp undetected, even the RAF padre joined in – but was not captured. Folkestone and Dover came under attack from Ju 87s and bombers, AA defences returned fire. No.4107 Light AA Flight part of No.2882 (Light Anti-Aircraft) Squadron RAF Regiment formed at Kingscliffe from No.4029, 4107 and 4108 (AA) Flights, then moved to other airfields including Hawkinge, Eastchurch, Drem and Llanbedr. They arrived at Hawkinge on 17 January from the Isle of Man, commanded by Flight Lieutenant Morren, to strengthen the airfield's defences. Hawkinge received a report on 20 January, that thirty fighter bombers were heading towards London, escorted by fifty fighters over the Channel and Coastal area – a *'Vergeltungsangriff'*, 'revenge attack' by the Luftwaffe. No.91 Squadron scrambled twelve Spitfires.

Squadron Leader R.H. Harries DFC & Bar the CO of No.91 Squadron Hawkinge, informed of the impending raid took off, heading for Beachy Head. Not far from the coast he saw four Me 109Fs, heading for France. He attacked one on the port side, which crashed in the sea. He fired at a second and it caught fire, but he did not see it crash. He was then attacked by four Fw 190s and took evasive action, opening fire on the rear Fw 190 which he damaged. Feeling rather pleased with his efforts, he set off for Hawkinge, but was attacked by Spitfires, fortunately escaping. Harries was granted one destroyed another damaged.

Patrolling the same area, Flight Lieutenant R.S. Easby Spitfire Vb BM541 and Pilot Officer B. Fey Spitfire Vb BL333 No.91 Squadron, were informed of aircraft over Deal, climbing towards the sun, they became separated. Pilot Officer Fey lost control of his aircraft, which had been attacked. Baling out, it was twenty minutes before he plunged into the sea, landing between rescue launches, soon being picked up uninjured. Pilot Officer Fey had been attacked by an Fw 190 flown by Hptm. Mietusch 7/JG 26, who also claimed another. Squadron Leader Harries had shot down Obfw. P. Kierstein 2/JG 26, killed when his Fw 190A-4 hit the sea. Rainstorms and gales had raged since 28 January, and continued to ravage the airfield on 1 February 1943. Some weather reconnaissance patrols were flown by No.91 Squadron. The following day the weather had improved, and several patrols took place, during which a pilot was seen on the Goodwin Sands, eventually rescued by the HSL based at Ramsgate.

Flying Officer Ron Batten took off from Hawkinge in poor weather on 9 February, to intercept a Dornier Do 217 which had bombed Hastings. He was heard to say on his RT that he had destroyed the Dornier, but was going to bale out of Spitfire LF Vb AD261 due to engine failure. Four Spitfires and three Lysanders took off to search for him, but nothing was seen. Batten realised he was near the French coast, and eventually landed in France, only to be taken prisoner for the remainder of the war.

Spitfires of No.91 Squadron escorted a Walrus No.277 Squadron on ASR patrol looking for a missing pilot on 10 February. Sergeant R.K. Watne No.332 (Dutch) Squadron based at Woodvale, was found off Ramsgate, Spitfire IX BS176 had mechanical problems; baling out, Watne was killed. On 11 February Flight Lieutenant Parnell DFC and CO of 'A' Flight No.91 Squadron, was awarded the French Croix de Guerre. Wing Commander L.L.A. Strange DSO, DFC, MC, the Station CO, was being posted, replaced by Wing Commander F.F. Barret CO of Redhill. Wing Commander Strange had been CO of Hawkinge since 20 December 1942, that evening a party was held. Flying Officer Naysmith also celebrated his first year at Hawkinge as No.91 Squadron's Engineer Officer.

That week Spitfires of No.91 Squadron had spotted the Armed Raider MS *Togo* in Boulogne Harbour. The *Togo* was a German merchant ship employed in a minesweeping role as a *Sperrbrecher* (Pathmaker), clearing a safe lane through a minefield. Bostons, with fighter escort, attacked the *Togo* and flak ships in the harbour on 13 February. The ship was photographed by Sergeant O'Shaughnessy and Pilot Officer Mart off Boulogne, they took aerial shots of the ship at some considerable risk. Both Spitfires came under fire from Boulogne defences but were undamaged. Photographs revealed that the ships had not been damaged. Early on 14 February, the MS *Togo* slipped out of Boulogne, under fire from Channel guns. Spitfires of No.91 Squadron were scrambled to search for the ship, but mistakenly thought it was moored at Monitors Quay, Dunkirk. MS *Togo* a German

RAF HAWKINGE

merchant ship, was employed in a minesweeping role as a *Sperrbrecher* (Pathmaker), clearing a safe lane through a minefield.

Aircraft of No.277 Squadron and No.91 Squadron patrolled off Ramsgate the following day locating a B-24 Liberator of the 44th Bomb Group 67th BS 8th USAAF, which crash landed on Sandwich flats. Walrus W3402 was involved in the search flown by Pilot Officer T.M. Hilton and Flight Sergeant J. Snell, accompanied by Lysander V9431 flown by Flight Lieutenant J.A. Spence and Flight Sergeant H. Brunckhurst V3402, V9487. The B24 Liberator was part of a force on a mission attacking the MS *Togo*, located earlier. Seventeen aircraft of the 44th BG 67th BS based at Shipham, Norfolk were soon airborne. They rendezvoused with aircraft of the 329 BS, 93rd BG, led by the 67th BS's Captain Cullen and the CO of the 67th BS, Major D.W. MacDonald being the formation's Command Pilot. Two aircraft were lost, a third B-24D-H 41-23794 'Railway Express' crash landed at Sandwich Bay. The crew of the B24 which crashed on Sandwich Flats on 15 February 1943 all perished, and were as follows: First Lieutenant R. A Oliphant (Pilot), Second Lieutenant C.E. Wilkes (Co-pilot), First Lieutenant C.B. Franklin (Nav.), Second Lieutenant C. W Bryant (Bombardier), Technical Sergeant C. Littell, (Eng.), Technical Sergeant H.B. Burns, (Radio Operator), Staff Sergeant W.E. Douthit (Gunner), Staff Sergeant R.E. Frye (Gunner), Staff Sergeant C.D. Goddard (Eng.), Staff Sergeant A.L .Boutin (Gunner) and Sergeant W. Lawley (Gunner), whose body was spotted by a Walrus of No.277 Sqdn. searching for any survivors.

No.91 Squadron were notified they were to move to Honily to be re-equipped with the Spitfire XII; they would be replaced by No.41 Squadron No.9 Group, Llanbedr, the move scheduled for 12 April. Flying Officer Slack and Flying Officer Hogarth of No.41 Squadron arrived at Hawkinge for a few days to act as under-study with No.91 Squadron. Other pilots of No.41 Squadron would then take over, with this rotation of pilots they would become familiar with 'Jim Crow' operations at Hawkinge. The weather prevented flying on 21/22 February, an escape exercise was organised. Escapers consisted of twenty-seven pilots of No.91 Squadron and aircrew of No.277 Squadron and a few other officers from Hawkinge. Transported to Elham area they had to find their way to Hawkinge. Personnel of the RAF Regiment were sent off to find the escapers, most were apprehended and only seven got through to Hawkinge.

Squadron Leader Harries showed initiative when he stole an Army officer's uniform in Elham and returned without being stopped. Pilot Officer Hartwell and Warrant Officer Waddington borrowed a milk waggon, disguising themselves with the help of some Land Army Girls dungarees and other items of clothing, made it back to Hawkinge, through the security by pretending to deliver eggs to the mess. In the evening No.91 Squadron attended at the Majestic Hotel, Folkestone, organised by the Home Defence Unit. The following day the weather was so bad that no flying took place, so a party was arranged at 'The Plough', Hougham, near Dover. Even the Station Band arrived, and it turned out to be a riotous evening.

Pilot Officer J.D. Edwards of No.403 (RCAF) Squadron had taken off from Kenley on a routine training flight with two other pilots on 25 February. During a mock dogfight, Spitfire IX BS287 went into a steep dive and crashed at Stone Green Farm, Mersham, near Ashford. Edward's body was found in the burnt-out wreck; the cause of the accident remains a mystery. MS *Togo* was again attacked at Dunkirk, early on 26 February 1943; the raider slipped out of harbour, heading north, slightly damaged. A report confirmed that Flying Officer Ron Batten No.91 Squadron, who failed to return on 9 February, had survived but had been taken prisoner.

No.91 Squadron continued ASR patrols. On the last day of February Flying Officer Nash and Flying Officer Seydel spotted a dinghy with a pilot off Dungeness, circling until Walrus W3024 No.277 Squadron arrived, flown by Flight Sergeant J.A. Spence with Flight Sergeant W. Butler and Sergeant P. Graham. Landing close to the dinghy, they picked up the pilot, returning to Hawkinge escorted by the Spitfires. Flight Sergeant R.W. Lamont No.416 (RCAF) Squadron Kenley was flying Spitfire Vb AD560 when he struck the sea following a low-level offensive, near Le Treport. Climbing out of the Walrus he thanked Flying Officer Spence and his crew, and spent the night at the station sick quarters. Sergeant Shouldice No.416 Squadron, landed shortly after the Walrus, his Spitfire had also struck the sea, damaging the propeller. Hawkinge took part in a successful gas exercise on the airfield, organised by Pilot Officer Chamberlain. A non-lethal gas was released throughout the camp. In the event of a real gas attack, it was essential all staff at Hawkinge were prepared and trained properly.

Brigadier Sadler of the 71st AA Division accompanied by Brigadier D.A. Learmont, arrived at Hawkinge on 1 March 1943, Learmont was taking over command of the division. To familiarise him with the coastal area and gun sites, Flying Officer Pullen and Pilot Officer Omdahl No.91 Squadron flew the Brigadiers around the coast in DH Tiger Moths. NAAFI officials led by General Cave-Brown arrived on a tour of inspection accompanied by the station CO Wing Commander F.F. Barret, to review the NAAFI accommodation at Hawkinge and Lympne. Flight Lieutenant Lord David

Flight Lieutenant R. Nash No.91 Squadron inspecting the brakes of his car at 'A' Flight dispersal Hawkinge, he served with the squadron from 16 September 1942 until 21 November 1944. (No.91 Squadron Diary – NA)

Douglas-Hamilton landed, en route to Swingate RDF Control, he had flown with No.91 Squadron during the summer of 1941. When Germany's Deputy-Führer Rudolf Hess landed in Scotland in May 1941 in an Me 110, he claimed he knew Hamilton, who denied this, although the two were believed to have met at the Berlin Olympics in 1936. Hamilton was cleared by Parliament of any breach of national security.

TAKING THE WAR TO THE ENEMY 1943

During the morning of 4 March, Squadron Leader R.R. Harries and Flying Officer R.S. Nash, intercepted an Fw 190 over Dover Straits. The pilot dived steeply, the Spitfires followed, pulling out with difficulty and unable to get closer. But the German did not pull-out, crashing in a massive explosion near Calais. Four days later, Pilot Officer J.G. Johnson (RAAF) 'A' Flight No.91 Squadron failed to return from patrol near Flushing. Spitfire Vb AB984 was last plotted NE of Ostend, an SOS was broadcast by No.11 Group, but he and his aircraft were lost.

No.7 Squadron based at Oakington were equipped with the Stirling III bomber, on 8/9 March they were part of a force of 335 aircraft attacking targets at Nuremberg. BK610 MG-V took off from Oakington, formatting with nine other Stirlings of No.7 Squadron. Reaching the target area, BK610 dropped 144 incendiary bombs and Sergeant L.L.V. Toupin headed for home. During the return flight the aircraft was damaged by flak and the crew were ordered to bale out. They had almost made it home, but the Stirling crashed in the sea off Dungeness. Sergeant D.R. Spanton Engineer/Mid-Upper Gunner, did not hear the order to bale out and was last to leave the Stirling, landing uninjured near Lympne, he was taken to Hawkinge and flown back to Oakington. The remaining crew: Sergeant J. Goddard Navigator, Sergeant H. Kilvington Wireless Operator, Sergeant R.G. Thorne Front Gunner, Sergeant W.W. Freeland Rear Gunner, Sergeant G. Bell Engineer all perished. Sergeant Kilvington was the only one recovered, he was found in the sea off Newhaven. No.277 Squadron searched the Channel on the morning of 9 March for Lysanders V9431 Flight Lieutenant J.A. Spence, Flight Sergeant R. Glew, V9402 Sergeant A. Gooch, Flight Sergeant J. Rose, and V9431 Sergeant H. Kipping and Flight Sergeant J. Small. They searched until wreckage was found, but no crew members were seen. On the same day two Fw 190s flew southwards over Hawkinge airfield, but did not attack, however, one of them jettisoned a large petrol tank which landed in a field north-east of the airfield's perimeter track, which was recovered and passed on to No.86 Maintenance Unit (MU).

Three AA Defence Flights equipped with 20mm Hispano guns arrived at Hawkinge on 11 March, increasing the airfield's defences: Flight Lieutenant Renshaw No.1 Flight sited at Hythe and administered by Hawkinge, Pilot Officer Wybrew No.2 Flight sited at Sandwich and administered by Manston, and Flight Lieutenant Edwards No.3 Flight sited at Hastings, administered at Eastbourne. The following morning, aircraft of No.91 Squadron were scrambled when twenty-four Fw 190s were reported over the Thames Estuary, attacking northeast London, but did not engage the enemy. However, because of increased enemy activity, a standing order was issued by the CO, to ensure that all officers at Hawkinge were ready for immediate action and prepared for dawn attacks by the Luftwaffe on Hawkinge. Spitfire IXs of No.403 Squadron (RCAF), flown by Flight Lieutenant Hagwood, Flight Lieutenant Godefroy and Sergeant McGarrigle had been escorting B17s to Amiens, were attacked by Fw 190s, undamaged all returned to Hawkinge. Flying Officer Aitken and Sergeant Morrow belly-landed in the Rye area after running short of fuel, neither were injured.

Flight Lieutenant J.A. Spence CO of 'B' Flight No.277 Squadron, was awarded the DFC in recognition of nearly two years work in the ASR service. Spence from Ontario joined the squadron in June 1941, and flew seventy-three sorties in Lysanders and Defiants, locating downed crews, dropping emergency supplies, and assisting in the rescue of seven men. Several fighter sweeps took place on 14 March in the Abbeville area, as dusk approached Hawkinge was notified by Biggin Hill that two senior officers, who had taken part in the operation, were missing. Wing Commander R.M. Milne DFC, Biggin Hill Wing Leader, Spitfire Vb BS240 was attacked by Fw 190s of JG 26 had baled out slightly injured, and had been taken prisoner. Squadron Leader J.H. Slater AFC No.611 Squadron, also shot down by Fw 190s of JG 26, was killed when Spitfire IX EN133 crashed. Both were shot down by the Gruppe commanded by Adolf Galland's brother, Hptm. Wilhelm-Ferdinand 'Wurz' Galland.

There was some good news at Hawkinge that month, the marriage of Pilot Officer J.K. Down No.91 Squadron, which took place at Holy Trinity Church, Folkestone on 22 March. The groom's bride was Miss P. Sheridan, a sergeant in the WAAF based at Capel HDU (Home Defence Unit) located between Folkestone and Dover. Wing Commander Barret, Squadron Leader Harries DFC and officers of the squadron attended the service. Flight Lieutenant J.A. Spence, who had recently been posted as temporary CO of No.277 Squadron, Gravesend, arrived back at Hawkinge in a Spitfire XII. By 24 March the squadron had received four of the new Spitfire XIIs, one being test flown by Squadron Leader Harries DFC. By the end of March 1943, all pilots of No.91 Squadron had flown their new Spitfires XII.

During a routine convoy patrol on 24 March, Flying Officer J.A. Anstie and Flying Officer R.G.H. de Hasse No.91 Squadron, were bounced by Fw 190s JG 26. Spitfire Vb BL410 Flying Officer Anstie was hit, heading for Lympne where he crashed near the airfield, and was taken to Canterbury Hospital with head injuries. Flying Officer de Hasse (Belgium) Spitfire Vb W3425 crashed in the sea off Dungeness killing the pilot, on his first operation with the squadron. Despite an ASR search nothing was found. Squadron Leader R.H. Harries DFC accompanied by Pilot Officer A. O'Shaughnessy were also scrambled and attacked the Fw 190s diving out of the sun, saving Flying Officer Anstie from certain death. Harries destroyed one Fw 190, the other was damaged by O'Shaughnessy. Fw 190s and Me 109s attacked Ashford in a 'hit and run' raid the same morning, too late for Spitfires of No.91 Squadron to help, but one of the attackers blew up in mid-air hit by AA fire.

Obit. Paul Keller Staffelkapitan known as 'Bomben Keller' 10/JG 54 flying Fw 190A-5 (2587) Black 7, killed during a raid on Ashford on 24 March 1943 and buried at Hawkinge.

RAF HAWKINGE

Obit. Paul Keller Staffelkapitan known as 'Bomben Keller' 10/JG 54 flying Fw 190A-5 (2587) Black 7 was killed leading a formation attacking Ashford, exploding over Stanhay's Agricultural Engineers, Godington Road. After bombs were dropped (main target was the railway junction), Keller's aircraft, flying in a wide climbing turn to starboard, received a direct hit – its bomb exploding. The propeller was seen flying away by itself, after the explosion. A small part of the aircraft's engine went through the roof of Ashford Hospital. This raid resulted in the counties greatest number of civilian casualties in an air attack for the whole of the war: fifty-one killed, seventy-six badly wounded and seventy-eight suffering from less serious wounds. Many casualties occurred around the Godington Road area when Keller's aircraft exploded. The main part of his aircraft fell in allotments, but Keller's body was thrown from the wreckage and landed in the recreation field at Barrow Hill, he was buried at Hawkinge cemetery. Many roads were hit by bombs and the primary school in Beaver Road was flattened, fortunately all the children were in the shelters. The CO of Hawkinge Wing Commander F.F. Barrett with Flying Officer Naysmith, drove over to Ashford to inspect the wreckage of the aircraft.

The following day, during 'Wings for Victory Week', a national fund-raising event to raise money for the RAF, Flight Lieutenant Maclean volunteered to attend a special exhibition in Rye. A selection of items recovered from downed German aircraft, kept in the Intelligence Office at Hawkinge, were displayed, generating much interest and helped to boost the morale of local people. Flight Lieutenant T.W.P.L. Chaloner, 2nd Baron Gisborough of Cleveland, Yorkshire, Intelligence Officer of No.41 Squadron (who had flown in the First World War and was taken PoW) arrived on 30 March to prepare the squadron's return. The squadron had been operating from High Ercall since 25 February 1942 and were due to return to Hawkinge on 12 April 1943. Flying Officer R.N. Hoare had been attached to Hawkinge prior to the squadron's move since 28 March, to familiarise himself with the squadron's new role.

During a shipping patrol on 1April off Nieuport, Flying Officer Hoare and Flying Officer Todd No.91 Squadron flew across the Channel heading for France in pouring rain. Descending to ground level, Todd saw Hoare forming up on him emerging from rain clouds. Spitfire Vb BL423 flown by Hoare was hit by flak, baled out and was taken PoW, though it was not until 8 May this was confirmed. A German aircraft recovery unit had gone to Leffinge, Belgium, to the crash site of Spitfire Vb BL423, which was buried

TAKING THE WAR TO THE ENEMY 1943

in marshy ground. No.198 Squadron based at Manston reported on 1 April that Sergeant E.J.R. Ansell was missing. No.277 Squadron found nothing; later, Flight Sergeant Uptigrove and Flight Sergeant Rose spotted oil on the sea off Dover. The pilot's body was found by an HSL and recovered, but there was no trace of Typhoon Ib DN299, which had sunk below the waves. The same day a search for a Liberator off North Foreland was abandoned by Flying Officer Morrison and Pilot Officer Wilson who could find no trace of the American bomber. A Ceremonial Parade took place at Hawkinge to celebrate the 25th Anniversary of the RAF, formed on 1 April 1918. In the early afternoon, airmen and WAAFs were served dinner by officers and sergeants, that evening a concert was held by the Entertainments National Service Association (ENSA).

On 3 April twelve Fw 190s were reported off Eastbourne, Spitfires of No.91 Squadron were scrambled but recalled. Disappointed, the day improved when two Spitfire XIIs of No.41 Squadron based at High Ercall arrived at Hawkinge in the evening. It was a good opportunity for the pilots of No.91 Squadron to inspect these new aircraft, which they would be flying later that month. The following day No.312 (City of Canterbury), 354 (Dover) and 99 (Folkestone) Air Training Corps visited Hawkinge. Despite No.277 Squadron's usual patrol duties, they gave five lucky cadets flights in Lysanders. They were joined for the duration of their visit by Squadron Leader Morrison the Area Inspecting Officer for Kent ATC. Apart from seeing first hand activities at Hawkinge, the cadets also witnessed Hawkinge hockey team losing 1–0 to a team from HMS *Wasp*, Dover. If they had been at the airfield on 5 April the cadets would have been delighted to see seventy B17s Flying Fortresses flying over Hawkinge, heading off for another raid on Europe.

An embarrassing incident took place when Sergeant D.P. Fisher No.41 Squadron, returning from a flight over Dieppe, overshot the runway Spitfire XII EN610 and turned over. Fisher was helped from the cockpit but was uninjured – except for his pride. On 9 April Folkestone was attacked by Me 109s armed with bombs. Three were dropped, causing damage and some casualties. An Me 109 was hit by ground-fire and crashed into the sea off Dungeness. Four Spitfires of No.91 Squadron took off to intercept, but nothing was seen. Much to the surprise of the pilots, they were fired on by a German launch, but before the Spitfires could respond, it had disappeared in a thick haze.

RAF Bomber Command massed a raid on Frankfurt which took place on 10/11 April 1943, involving 500 aircraft. One of the units was

RAF HAWKINGE

No.102 Squadron based at Pocklington. Many of these were seen returning early on 11 April, when a Halifax appeared over Hawkinge, obviously with the intention of landing. Halifax II W7912 developed low pressure in one of its four engines twenty-five minutes before reaching the target. The pilot Sergeant W.G.J. Happold, decided to drop the aircraft's pay-load on the designated target. After landing, it taxied clear of any aircraft and came to a standstill. The crew disembarked, exhausted but relieved to have made it back untouched by flak or night fighters, they were given a warm welcome at Hawkinge and were well looked after until the engine of the Halifax was repaired.

The weather on 12 April started fine, but low cloud developed covering the airfield. An advance party of No.41 Squadron arriving from High Ercall, Spitfires and the main party were delayed due to the weather. Next day, nineteen Spitfire XIIs of No.41 Squadron and two Spitfire Vbs arrived, two Handley Page Harrows later landed with ground crew,

Pilots relaxing between operations outside the bungalow, used for No.91 Squadron 'A' Flight dispersal during 1943, note three of pilots are on readiness. (No.91 Squadron Diary – NA)

TAKING THE WAR TO THE ENEMY 1943

commanded by Squadron Leader T.F. Neil DFC. The squadron replaced No.91 Squadron temporarily, who were moving to Honiley to re-equip with Spitfire XIIs.

Flying Officer Johnson and Sergeant Watlington patrolling on 13 April spotted a dinghy off Gravelines. Circling, they alerted ASR Launches and lead them to the area, the pilot was Lieutenant Colonel J.L. Dickman USAAC, Deputy Group CO 78th FG Duxford, who crashed his Thunderbolt during a sweep in the Pas de Calais area; fortunately he was rescued. Dickman, on his first combat mission, experienced engine trouble and baled out, dislocating his right arm, following an offensive sweep by Spitfires and P47 Thunderbolts. Flight Lieutenant Mathew and Flying Officer Johnson No.91 Squadron patrolling off North Foreland on 15 April, spotted a pilot in a dinghy. Sending an SOS to Hawkinge, Walrus I W3024 flown by Warrant Officer A. Saunders, Sergeant R. Glew DFM and Flight Sergeant F. Gash, was escorted to the area by Spitfires.

Lieutenant Colonel C.G. Peterson DSO, DFC & Bar CO of 78th FG at Debden, crashed his P47 in the sea, rescued by Warrant Officer A. Saunders (Pilot) Flight Sergeant R. Glew DFM and Flight Sergeant F. Gash in a Walrus I W3024 of No.277 (ASR) Squadron 'B' Flight on 15 April 1943. (American Air Museum)

RAF HAWKINGE

Landing on the sea close by to the occupant was Lieutenant Col. C.G. Peterson DSO, DFC & Bar USAAF who had been CO of No.71 (Eagle) Squadron, now CO of 78th FG at Debden. The dinghy hooked by Flight Sergeant Glew was fouling the undercarriage of the Walrus, as Warrant Officer Saunders had lowered it to hold the aircraft in position as the sea was choppy. Peterson was lifted into the Walrus through the front hatch, wrapped in blankets and flown to Martlesham Heath, from there taken back to Debden. Peterson's P47 was shot down by Fw 190s of JG 26, suffering from facial injuries he was taken to the station sick quarters at Hawkinge. On 19 September 1940, No.71 Squadron was reformed at Church Fenton as the first 'Eagle' Squadron to be manned by American personnel. The Squadron received Hurricanes in November and became operational on defensive duties on 5 February 1941. No.71 converted to Spitfires in August and took part in sweeps over northern France. On 29 September 1942, the Squadron transferred to the 4th Pursuit Group, 8th US Army Air Force as the 334th Pursuit Squadron and ceased to be an RAF unit.

At dawn on 16 April, No.41 Squadron took over 'Jim Crow' operations from No.91 Squadron, flying several sorties. Ground crews and other personnel were finding their feet, settling into a new routine. No.91 Squadron had moved to Honiley, where they would re-equip with the Spitfire XII. The following morning, enemy aircraft were reported in the area, local AA defences opened fire unsuccessfully. The Halifax of No.102 Squadron, which had landed at Hawkinge on 11 April, returned to Hawkinge – with ten minutes worth of fuel left. On this occasion, returning from a raid on the Skoda factory at Pilsen, it was flown by a different crew; they refuelled and headed for home.

Over Ostend, Flying Officer R. Hogarth No.41 Squadron, Spitfire XII EN235 spotted a Ju 88, dived to attack, opening fire hitting the aircraft's tail and rear fuselage, which started to break up. Renewing his attack on the port side of the fuselage, the Ju 88 glided down and crash landed on the beach at Bredene. It is interesting to note that this combat was filmed on an 8mm gun camera, fitted to the new Spitfire XII, the first time the Spitfire XII had seen action. Hogarth's Spitfire was damaged by return fire from the Ju 88, hit in the starboard wing. Having spotted a coaster off Dunkirk, accompanied by a flak ship, Flying Officer Birbeck Spitfire XII EN604 No.41 Squadron attacked. Strikes were seen, but his aircraft was hit by return fire. Turning for home he caught sight of a red Verey (flare) light, fired from a dinghy not far from Berck-sur-mer. A second was fired, he took a closer look, seeing airmen in the dinghy. Birbeck reported their

TAKING THE WAR TO THE ENEMY 1943

location, and four men were rescued by the RN. Flying without an airspeed indicator, which had been damaged in the attack, he radioed Hawkinge for assistance, and Flight Lieutenant D. Hone Spitfire XII EN234 guided him in just as darkness fell.

There was time for a double celebration that evening, for No.41 Squadron's success and for No.91 Squadron leaving Hawkinge, as for the first time in two years the squadron was released for twenty-four hours. A supper and dance was held in Folkestone, attended by all ranks with guests from No.277 Squadron. Another safe return was celebrated, Walrus I W2773 'C' Flight Shoreham had been shot down by Me 109s of JG 27 on 14 April. The crew Pilot Officer J.L. Barber DFM and Flying Officer I.R. Healey were recovered from the sea. Guests that night also included pilots of No.1 Squadron now based at Lympne, equipped with Typhoon Ibs.

On 18 April 1943 aircraft of No.41 Squadron and No.277 Squadron, assisted Typhoons of No.181 Squadron No.83 Group based at New

On 17 March 1942 Pilot Officer Crozier No.91 Squadron baled out of Spitfire Vb R7338 *'Papyrus'* 'DL-F'. His radio failed and lost in fog, R7338 crashed at Park Farm, Smeeth near Ashford. (No.91 Squadron Diary – NA)

RAF HAWKINGE

Romney Advanced Landing Ground (ALG) operating from Lympne. Eight Typhoons flew offensive patrols over France, one against Poix airfield used by the Luftwaffe. During the evening two HP Harrows landed at Hawkinge, flying No.91 Squadron personnel to Honiley the following day.

By the afternoon of 19 April, the weather had cleared, it was time for those of No.91 Squadron still at Hawkinge to leave. Climbing into the two waiting Harrows, many gathered along the perimeter to watch them take off, accompanied by nineteen Spitfire Vbs and a DH Tiger Moth. It was thought they would return to Hawkinge, once they had replaced the Spitfire Vbs for the much needed Spitfire XII. Shortly after leaving Hawkinge the weather got worse, they landed at West Malling, remaining overnight. A force of German bombers was seen on 20 April, heading for Northolt and Richmond where they dropped bombs. The intruders jettisoned auxiliary petrol tanks at Stelling Minis, these were recovered by No.86 (MU) Maintenance Unit. Spitfires Vbs of No.91 Squadron finally continued their flight to Honiley. Flying Officer O'Shaughnessy 'B' Flight made a hasty wheels-up landing near Redhill due to a glycol leak, was picked up by an Airspeed Oxford, heading for Honiley.

Three days later, Walrus I W3024 of 'B' Flight was damaged during practice landings off Folkestone. Sergeant G. Brown, Sergeant R. Kippling and Flight Sergeant W. Butler damaged a German float plane taking off in rough sea, an (HSL) High Speed Launch arrived to assist. Having secured a line to the launch they towed the Walrus towards shore for beaching, a wing dipped in the sea and W3024 sank. An hour later Flight Lieutenant T.R. Poynton CO 'A' Flight No.41 Squadron operating over Dieppe, was reported missing. Although given a course for Hawkinge, contact was lost. Poynton, flying Spitfire XII EN601, was advised there were Fw 190s in the vicinity, but was shot down and killed by Obfw. P. Fritsch 5/JG 26, claiming it was a Mustang. Heavy seas and bad weather hindered attempts to find him. Spitfires of No.41 Squadron took off to search the Dieppe area, but were forced to turn back. The squadron lost another pilot on 24 April when Sergeant D. Fisher Spitfire XII EN607 in company with Spitfire XII EN601 was returning from an uneventful operation over Ostend/Flushing. Coming into land, turning on approach, Spitfire XII EN610 lost speed and stalled, dropping to the ground. Flight Lieutenant Poynton crashed in a field close to The White Horse Inn on the Canterbury Road, close to the end of the runway at Hawkinge. The Air Investigation Branch were called in, as it was not thought the accident was caused by pilot error. Initially the AIB, suspected that five big ends had gone into the engine. Rolls-Royce engineers

TAKING THE WAR TO THE ENEMY 1943

examined the engine at Derby, concluding that it was in fact a broken oil pipe, or connection in the installation causing oil starvation or excessive oil aeration. The young pilot's father was devastated as he had recently lost his wife. Flight Lieutenant Poynton was buried at his hometown of Glamorgan.

Although pilots at Hawkinge were aware of the new P47 Republic Thunderbolt, they had not seen one at close quarters. So, on 26 April, eyes turned to the sky when a new sound filled the air. Captain M.L. Stepp No.78 FG 8th USAAF arrived from Debden and taxied to dispersal, an opportunity for pilots to inspect the P47. Stepp, an American from San Jose CA, joined No.121 (Eagle) Squadron, one of three squadrons, the other two being No.71 and No.133 Squadrons which formed the famous Tangmere Wing, the first American units to be formed. Later, No.121 was reformed as the 335th FS, No.71 as 344th FS and No.133 as the 336th FS No.4 Fighter Group Debden 8th USAAF.

Some 240 pilots came to England from the USA, some flying in the Battle of Britain in 1940, many becoming RAF Aces. Later they joined squadrons

Captain M.L. Stepp No.78 FG 8th USAAF who had served with No.41 Squadron in June 1942, visited Hawkinge on 26 April 1943 in his P47 Thunderbolt. (American Air Museum)

of USAAF. In the case of Captain Stepp, joining No.41 on 23 May 1942 as Acting Lieutenant and CO of 'A' Flight Merston, then Martlesham Heath. The squadron moved to Hawkinge on 30 June 1942, where he damaged an Fw 190 on 19 August. Stepp transferred to the 336th FS USAAF Debden on 26 September 1942; on 26 April he flew to Hawkinge in P47 41-6541 to show it to friends of No.41 Squadron. Stepp was killed on 30 September 1943 when P47 Thunderbolt 42-7872 from Atcham, crashed on high ground at Cats Tor, Cheshire.

No.41 Squadron's first victory took place on 27 April; Flying Officer Haywood and Flying Officer Birbeck were ordered off for a weather reconnaissance flight over Calais and the Somme. Completing the task both headed for home, seeing two Fw 190s approaching them. Haywood's engine cut out, Spitfire XII EN607 was badly hit from above and astern. With as much speed as he could muster, he headed for Hawkinge when the engine packed up; he made a wheels-up landing at Littlestone, Romney Marsh. Shaken, he climbed out with a splinter wound in his foot. Haywood was taken to Canterbury Hospital returning to Sick Quarters at Hawkinge.

Flying Officer Birbeck attacked an Fw 190s, giving it a second burst; flames spewed from its port side as it headed off for the French coast. He was then attacked by three Fw 190s but managed to evade them, landing back at Hawkinge with his Spitfire slightly damaged. An intercepted R/T message confirmed that the first Fw 190 had been shot down, opening No.41 Squadron's score book. Two days later Flying Officer Davies was flying a shipping reconnaissance flight when Channel defences opened fire. His Spitfire was hit by shrapnel, one fragment passed through the cockpit canopy, missing his head by inches. Davies returned to Hawkinge but was again airborne with Flying Officer Birbeck, who had been ordered to search for a new minefield which the RN suspected had been laid off Le Touquet under cover of darkness. The location was reported, and steps were taken to eliminate the threat.

There was good news for No.41 Squadron: Flying Officer R.M. Hoare had survived, his mother had a letter from the PoW camp at Dulag Luft, the Luftwaffe's interrogation centre. Flight Lieutenant Lord Gisborough had written to his mother. She replied, thanking him, expressing her relief that he had not died. On the morning of 3 May, No.41 Squadron lost another pilot, Sergeant W.R. East who with Flight Lieutenant Parry (Rhodesia) CO of 'A' Flight was intercepted by Fw 190s when returning to Hawkinge from shipping reconnaissance near Dieppe. Parry engaged one of these, observing strikes on the Fw 190's cowling, it jettisoned its extra fuel tank.

Parry was pursued by three others, escaping by flying at sea level, losing radio contact. An R/T message was intercepted, stating that Sergeant East had been shot down by Lieutenant Radener 4/JG 26. Despite an intensive search, no trace of Sergeant East or Spitfire XII EN612 was found.

The following day fighters of the RAF and the 8th USAAF took part in several offensive sorties. This involved ASR patrols by No.277 and No.41 Squadrons, a pilot was reported ditched in the sea but despite extensive searches was not found. During the evening, Hawkinge was visited by various officers, one being Squadron Leader R.P. Beamont DSO, DFC & Bar in a Typhoon IB of No.609 Squadron, based at Manston. Another search for a German minefield west of Le Touquet and WNW of the Somme took place, involving four Spitfire XIIs of No.41 Squadron, flown by Flight Lieutenant Hone, Flying Officer Birbeck, Flying Officer Hogarth and Flying Officer Davies, to protect Channel shipping and requested by RN Operations at Dover Castle. At 0300hrs the following morning, ground crews had a rude awakening when fire broke out in a hut at No.41 Squadron's 'B' Flight Dispersal, which was destroyed. The cause was unknown, but an investigation took place. If that wasn't enough, the Fw 190 claimed destroyed on 27 April by Flying Officer Birbeck, was reduced to a 'probable' by Fighter Command.

Miss Beatrice 'Tilly' Shilling OBE, PhD, MSc, CEng., and Group Captain Scroggs, Ministry of Aircraft Production, landed at Hawkinge on 5 May in Miles Proctor III LZ727 Station Flight Farnborough, to see the Station's Engineering Officer. 'Tilly', a brilliant Aeronautical Engineer, studied engineering at the University of Manchester in 1929. In 1934 she raced motorbikes at Brooklands. Later Scientific Officer at the RAE Farnborough, fore moving to the Carburettor Section under W.C. Clothier, testing RAF carburettors. She solved a fuel problem with the carburettors of the RR Merlin in Hurricanes and Spitfires during the Battle of Britain. When diving, the negative 'g-force' would flood the carburettors, stalling the engine. German fighters with fuel injection engines did not have this problem and could easily evade RAF fighters by flying a negative g-force manoeuvre, giving the Luftwaffe a huge advantage. Beatrice's solution was simple: the installation of a RAE restrictor, basically a small washer, placed into the carburettor to prevent flooding, and Known as 'Miss Shilling's orifice', or the 'Tilly orifice'. Miss Shilling visited airfields where aircraft had RR Merlin engines, offering advice on several engineering problems.

A heavy gale prevented flying for two days; on 10 May No.4107 AA Flight RAF Regiment, moved from Hawkinge to Thetford, replaced by No.4187 AA Flight commanded by Flying Officer J. Orrell based at Kemble. On 12 May, a DH Tiger Moth landed at Hawkinge with Sergeant Shawyer, the pilot – who flew over from Lympne – had a special passenger, Flying Officer Oliver Wakefield, a British actor/comedian during the 1930s and often billed as 'The Voice of Inexperience'; known for his satirical monologues, he appeared in British Pathé newsreels of the 1930s. Booked to open at the Rainbow Room in New York City shortly after the outbreak of war, he remained in England to serve with the RAF, becoming the Intelligence Officer for No.1 Squadron at Lympne. Marshal of the RAF Lord Trenchard GCB, OM, GCVO, DSO arrived at Hawkinge on 14 May in a Lockheed 12. An important day as Trenchard, once a pilot, was known as the 'Father of the RAF', was given a tour of the airfield by the CO and Squadron Leader Neil. During his brief stay he talked to pilots at dispersal before tea in the Officers' Mess before leaving for his headquarters.

No.122 Wing (No.83 Group) Nos.19 Squadron based at Eastchurch, Nos. 132 and 602 (City of Glasgow) Squadron RAuxAF based at Fairlop in May 1943, arrived at Hawkinge on 15 May, under the command of Wing Commander H. Bird-Wilson DFC & Bar. During the afternoon they refuelled, in preparation for duties escorting aircraft attacking Poix, France. No.122 Wing did not lose any pilots, but Pilot Officer E.S. Opie of No.19 Squadron was shot down in Spitfire Vb BL544 by an Me 109 of JG 2. This Spitfire crashed near Poix; Pilot Officer Opie was taken prisoner. Spitfires of No.122 Wing, unaware of what happened to Pilot Officer Opie, flew onto Eastchurch. Pilot Officer N.L. Smith Spitfire Vb BL655 of No.132 Squadron, landed at Newchurch ALG uninjured, and was picked up later by Sergeant T. Swindlehurst in a DH Tiger Moth and flown to Eastchurch. Squadron Leader Clouston landed at Hawkinge in a Miles Martinet from Biggin Hill, with news that because of the operations that day, Biggin Hill Wing had destroyed three aircraft, making the total now 1,000, a score to which Hawkinge had contributed.

Lancaster I R5688 'PH-G' No.12 Squadron based at Wickenby, was one of thirteen Lancasters on an operation to attack Bochum on 13/14 May. Over Holland they were hit by flak; unable to continue on to Bochum, they headed for home. Sergeant G.V. Scott told his crew, Sergeant G.H. Russell (Nav.), Sergeant G.D. Mitchell (W/T), Sergeant R.F. Rees (B/A), Sergeant H.T. Redford (F/E), Pilot Officer P.H. Phillips (MU), Sergeant L.F. Range (RG), to prepare for ditching. Landing, the crew climbed into their dinghy, during which they lost some of their supplies. Aircraft from Hawkinge searched for wreckage or a dinghy but were recalled, finding nothing.

TAKING THE WAR TO THE ENEMY 1943

Fourteen tins of water were stored away in the dinghy with enough rations to last twenty-four hours. The crew found 'Verey' pistol cartridges in the dinghy, but the pistol was missing. They drifted aimlessly until seen by a minesweeper, despite a six-day ordeal they survived. Following medical checks, they later returned to Wickenby.

Lympne hosted a party at Hawkinge on 15 May for funds raised during 'Wings for Victory Week', amounting to £1,050. Presentation Aircraft were donated and intended to bear the donor's name. 'Wings for Victory' aircraft were paid for by savings to be repaid by the Government in the future. The National Savings Committee encouraged towns, cities, and villages to raise money through the Local Saving Committee, during a series of 'Wings for Victory Weeks', between 5 March and 3 July 1943. The committees had to select a target amount for the chosen week, and within that period an amount not less than that raised in a similar way during 'Warship Week'. Aircraft were chosen from an official list: Flying boats (Sunderland) £50,000; Bombers (Stirling, Lancaster, Halifax, Liberator, Fortress £40,000; Twin-engine bombers (Wellington, Mosquito, Boston, Whitley) £20,000; Twin-engine Flying boats (Catalina), £20,000; Twin-engine fighters (Beaufighter, Whirlwind), £8,000; Fighters (Spitfire, Hurricane, Typhoon, Tomahawk) £5,000; Reconnaissance aircraft (Hudson, Mustang) £4,500; Training aircraft (Anson, Oxford, Master, Harvard, Proctor) £2,500; Troop-carrying gliders (Hotspur), £2,500; Air Sea Rescue aircraft £2,500; Ambulance aircraft £5,000. Hawkinge increased their sum to £3,125.

On 18 May, Spitfires of No.277 and No.41 Squadrons were scrambled to search for five Typhoon Ibs of No.3 Squadron based at West Malling. They had taken off to raid Cayeux and were attacked by Me 109s of JG 27. The crews were Sergeant F.K. Whitall Typhoon Ib DN246, Flying Officer L.G. Gill Typhoon Ib R8835, Sergeant V. Bailey Typhoon Ib R8879, Pilot Officer R. Inwood Typhoon DN598 and Flying Officer D.R. Hall DFC Typhoon Ib R8979. All were shot down and killed, Flying Officer Hall being hit by AA fire; a disaster for No.609 (West Riding) Squadron RAuxAF then based at Manston.

No.91 Squadron, now flying Spitfire XIIs, returned to Hawkinge on 21 May to resume 'Jim Crow' duties. No.41 Squadron returned to Biggin Hill. The experience gained cooperating with No.277 Squadron and other units was invaluable. From April 1943 the Typhoons on patrol were often joined by Griffon engine Spitfire XIIs of No.41 Squadron operating from Hawkinge. The performance of the Spitfire XII was substantially slower than the Typhoon at sea level, and marginally slower than the Fw 190.

RAF HAWKINGE

No.91 (Nigeria) Squadron was the second unit to be equipped with the Spitfire XII powered by the new Griffon III/IV engine. Left to right: Flying Officer Van de Velde, Prince de Merode and Flying Officer J.A. Anstie standing on the left, date June 1943. (No.91 Squadron Diary – NA)

On 25 May, no less than fifteen Fw 190s fighter-bombers flew over the Kent coast at low level, to attack Folkestone. No.91 Squadron, led by the CO, Squadron Leader Harries DFC, scrambled to intercept before they could reach Folkestone. Two of the Fw 190s were shot down by Squadron Leader Harries, a third by Flying Officer Maridor CdeG, DFC and two more destroyed by Pilot Officer Round and Pilot Officer Davy. The Deputy Chief Constable R.C. Morton Jenkins, OBE, KPM, OSJ, Folkestone telephoned to congratulate the CO for what might have been a disastrous attack on Folkestone with many casualties.

On the last day of May a dinghy was reported by Flight Lieutenant Matthew and Flying Officer Bond, 'B' Flight No.91 Squadron off North Foreland. This time a German pilot was rescued by a Walrus of No.277 Sqdn. 'A' Flight Martlesham Heath. Sergeant Waterson and Sergeant Ettles in Spitfire XIIs No.91 Squadron, accompanied by Warrant Officer Waddington and Sergeant Roffe in Spitfire II of No.277 Squadron, had taken off from Hawkinge to replace Flight Lieutenant Bond and Flight Lieutenant Matthew. Spotting another dinghy, they circled the occupant until the HSL from Ramsgate arrived. Flying Officer J.G. Torney a Canadian of No.402 (RCAF) Squadron, had been shot down in Spitfire Vc AB371 by Fw 190s of JG 1, and slightly wounded.

Work on Kent's Advanced Landing Grounds, of which there would be twelve, commenced as early as 1942. One of these was constructed at Swingfield, being completed by 6 June 1943. There had been flying there during the First World War, when No.50 (Home Defence) Squadron occasionally used fields in the vicinity of Swingfield between 1917 and 1919. In 1943 it would be used by No.819 Squadron FAA and No.119 Squadron RAF No.157 (General Reconnaissance) Wing, flying Swordfish and Albacore biplanes. On 6 June Colonel Hancock, the officer in charge of the ALGs completion, arrived at Hawkinge and was flown to the site by Flight Lieutenant J. Spence DFC No.277 Squadron 'B' Flight in Walrus IIa L2289, the first aircraft to land at the temporary airfield. Two pilots of No.65 Squadron, Flying Officer J.R. Heap Spitfire Vb BL830 and Flying Officer R. Stillwell Spitfire Vb BL735 based at Selsey, arrived at Hawkinge, later flying on to Swingfield ALG to practise landings on Sommerfeld Tracking, metal matting pegged down on ALGs.

No.65 Squadron moved to the ALG at Kingsnorth near Ashford on 1 July 1943, then to Ashford, Great Chart ALG on 5 October 1943, re-equipped with the Spitfire IX. On 16 June Flying Officer Stenberg and Sergeant Fraser were searching for a Typhoon pilot reported to be in a dinghy near Cap Grez Nez. Sergeant E.K. Ticklepenny of No.3 Squadron had been shot down by German E-Boats; Typhoon Ib DN948 crashed in the sea off Calais. A Walrus flown by Flight Lieutenant J. Spence DFC took off from Hawkinge to rescue the pilot.

Flight Lieutenant Spence was escorted by Flying Officer Nash, Flying Officer Seydel and Sergeant W. Mitchell No.91 Squadron. There were no German fighters reported in the area, so they were surprised to see 20 Fw 190s approaching. To protect the Walrus, they immediately engaged, Flying Officer Nash destroyed one and damaged another, Flying Officer Seydel in Spitfire XII EN627 destroyed a second, but was himself shot down and injured, rescued by an HSL. He had fallen victim to Hptm. W.F Galland II/JG 26. Sergeant W. Mitchell was shot down and killed in Spitfire XII MB835 by Obfw. Glunz of 4/JG 26.

Sergeant Humphreys dropped a smoke float, as he manoeuvred towards the Typhoon. Six attempts were made to get the pilot onto the Walrus, who fell out of his dinghy twice due to rough seas. Humphreys moved

RAF HAWKINGE

Flight Lieutenant J.A. Spence CO of 'B' Flight No.277 Squadron, who was awarded the DFC in recognition of nearly two years' work in the Air Sea Rescue service.

to the back of the Walrus, then taxied close to the pilot. Spence left the controls, trying to grab the pilot but missed. Humphreys managed to seize the pilot, with the help of Spence dragging Sergeant Ticklepenny onboard. Flying Officer Spence, unable to take off in the rough seas, was eventually met by two ASR launches who towed the Walrus into Dover harbour, during which the wings were damaged.

No.501 Squadron which had been based at Hawkinge during the Battle of Britain, returned on 21 June to replace No.91 Squadron, on their 'Jim Crow' operations. Only four days after their arrival at Hawkinge, Flight Lieutenant Lenton attacked an Fw 190 which disappeared behind trees, later claimed as a probable. Flight Lieutenant Peter Parrott who joined No.501 Squadron at the end of May 1943, claimed seven enemy aircraft during the Battle of Britain while serving with Nos.145 and 605 Squadrons, remembers flying from Hawkinge:

> At the time we were flying cropped blower Spitfire Vbs, (clipped, cropped and clapped!), which were fast below 10,000 ft and hopeless above that height. They were very suitable for the two tasks we had at Hawkinge, 'scrambles' to intercept the low-flying 109s and 190s which were raiding the Kentish coastal towns, and shipping recces along the enemy Channel coast and harbours. For the shipping recces two pairs would go across the Channel at low level, one pair turning north to inspect Calais, Dunkirk and Ostend, and the other going south to cover Boulogne, Le Touquet and Dieppe, plus Cherbourg sometimes. Radio silence was kept by us, and in the event of a sighting

TAKING THE WAR TO THE ENEMY 1943

the report was not made until we returned to Hawkinge, when it was passed to Fighter Command, and the rocket-equipped Typhoons would be despatched to deal with the target.

Fear Nothing
David Watkins

The 56th Fighter Group 61st Fighter Squadron 8th USAAF based Horsham-St. Faith, operating from Manston on 26 June on a mission to Villecoublay, were attacked by Fw 190s of JG 26. Four P-47s were shot down and ten more damaged, one of these being P47C 41-6620 flown by Second Lieutenant Justus Foster. Severely damaged, he put the P47C into a series of spins, fighting to recover control. Approaching the English coast, he made for Hawkinge, and belly-landed. The 'Flying Jug', the P47's nickname, slithered to a halt without somersaulting or crashing, the rather shaken pilot was helped from the cockpit uninjured. Foster's aircraft was claimed destroyed with nine other P47s by JG 26 that day.

Severely damaged on 26 June 1943, P47C 41-6620 flown by Second Lieutenant J. Foster 56th Fighter Group 61st Fighter Squadron 8th USAAF based Horsham – St Faith, crash landed at Hawkinge following combat with an Fw 190.

RAF HAWKINGE

Lancaster III ED369 AR-A No.460 Squadron based at Binbrook 1943, crash landed at Hawkinge on 9 July 1943, returning from raid on Cologne. Flight Sergeant J. Goulevitch, the pilot had an undertaker's top hat which he wore prior to take off. When taking off he would religiously dip his hat to the control tower as his bomber passed by. Over enemy territory, if he was forced to take any sort of evasive action, he invariably had one hand on his hat to stop it from falling off, using the other one for what he regarded as the less important task of flying the bomber.

Six shells hit the Lancaster, penetrating the fuselage, and cutting control lines for the trim tabs on the ailerons. Flying below the level at which the flak shells were set to explode, the flak shells pierced the aircraft without exploding. A propeller was shot off, another engine was hit, which seized. A third engine was over-revving and could only be run for ten minutes at a time to prevent overheating. This left one engine out of four, which could only be used for short durations. A shell hit close to the pilot, while another

Flight Sergeant John Goulevitch, far right with top hat, the pilot of Lancaster I ED369 No.460 (RAAF) Squadron, which crash landed at Hawkinge on 8 July 1943. (P. Dunn)

passed close where the Flight Engineer would normally be standing. Due to the combination of the loss of three engines and damaged aileron trim tabs, the aircraft became difficult to fly. Flight Sergeant J. Goulevitch pushing on the control column, had the Flight Engineer practically sitting on his back forcing the control column forward. He had to have the column rotated almost fully in one direction and one of his rudder pedals pushed in to maintain a reasonable flying attitude.

The Lancaster had been hit over Paris, Goulevitch told the crew to get ready to bale out, but they wanted to stay with the aircraft. All unnecessary equipment was thrown out, including parachutes. While crossing the French coast the Lancaster was attacked by an ack-ack barrage. The Wireless Operator fired the colours of the day, enough to confuse the German gunners and allow them to get out of harm's way. Crossing the English coastline between Dover and Folkstone, Flight Sergeant J. Goulevitch called 'Darkie' over his radio, the equivalent of today's 'Mayday', a system whereby pilots unsure of their position while flying over the UK would transmit on a designated frequency. Airfields maintained a listening watch on this frequency and receiving such a call they would activate the airfield 'Pundit light', searchlight or runway lights for a limited period, enabling a crew to have a visual reference to the airfield. Goulevitch established contact with a WAAF wireless operator at Hawkinge and located the red beacon marking the airstrip's location.

When he told the WAAF that he was in a Lancaster, she directed him to a larger airfield, as Hawkinge was too small. Flight Sergeant J. Goulevitch said he could not go any further and the WAAF pleaded with him to go on to the next strip. At 0400hrs, the light from the Chance light made the field look flat and John did not allow for the dip. Lowering the undercarriage he restarted the engine; unable to use flaps, he hit the ground hard and bounced into a potato field, ripping off both wings. Before the aircraft stopped, fire hoses appeared in the open hatches and a doctor peered in. Flight Sergeant J. Goulevitch's only injuries were to his knees and a bump on his head. The Flight Engineer hit the roof on sudden impact, they had bounced over the top of some fuel tanks at the end of the airfield. The crew quickly scrambled out of the wrecked Lancaster in case it exploded, but after running some distance they remembered their passenger, 'a carrier pigeon'. Flight Sergeant P.L. Jones returned and retrieved their feathered friend, less shaken than any of them. The crew did not get an opportunity to have a look at the aircraft in daylight as it was placed under close guard.

Flight Lieutenant Norman Hill was attached to No.1448 Flight Halton in 1943, equipped with the C.30A Rota and the Blenheim IV, the unit also flew

RAF HAWKINGE

Avro Rota (Cierva Autogyro) K4232 allocated to No.529 Squadron on 15 June 1943, the type flown by Flight Lieutenant Hill who was 'buzzed' by an Fw 190 in July 1943.

a DH Hornet Moth, DH Tiger Moth and an Auster aircraft. They were tasked with extremely accurate course flying to enable scientists at radar stations who listened to the echoes to make alterations to aerial arrays, enhancing their performance and increasing the accuracy of the range of approaching aircraft, German or Allied. Flight Lieutenant Hill had flown the Autogyro before the war, his experience was invaluable. On 14 July 1943, operating from Hawkinge, he took off on his first calibration flight in perfect weather, for an operation in conjunction with the Chain Home Radar station or RDF Station situated at Rye. At first he had to orbit several markers dropped at sea for a period of three to six minutes, at various altitudes. This exercise was repeated over markers on land, while special signals were transmitted to Radar Stations. Such exercises were carried out from the nearest RAF airfield, in this case Hawkinge.

Towards evening, having completed the fourth and final trial, he was contacted over the R/T, thanking him for his assistance. Flying near Dungeness, it was not long before he was over the village of Ivychurch, near Brenzett. The Autogyro entered turbulent air, this coincided with the sighting of a German Fw 190. Seeing the C.30, the fighter climbed vertically, looping in front of Flight Lieutenant Hill, who realised he would soon be hit. Using his skill, making the most of the C.30's unusual ability, he tried to outmanoeuvre the Fw 190, making a dash for Hawkinge. Biding his time until the German came closer, Hill pulled up, lifting the nose of the C.30. The Fw 190 was now overhead, he pushed the control stick hard to port, until the C.30 dived straight for the ground, gaining speed increasing to 100mph (161kmh), the maximum safe speed for these Rotas being about 85mph (137kmh). The C.30 shook violently and could have broken up; Hill tried to dive, but the controls were not responding. Looking behind, there were now two Fw 190s, Hill considered throwing out the self-blocking oscillator (electronic equipment) at the Fw 190s or firing the 'Verey' pistol at them. The nose of the C.30A began to respond, one of the Fw 190s lined up to open fire, but instead it dived towards the ground, perhaps thinking they would collide. Low on fuel, Pilot Officer Hill realised there was only one Fw 190; seeing Hawkinge, he made a fast and straight descent, landing next to a hangar. The Fw 190 pilot had not opened fire, Hill had been spared by the pilot of JG 26. The C.30A was AP507 (G-ACWP) which he flew regularly, and is on display at the Science Museum, London.

Spitfire Vbs of No.411(RCAF) and No.412 (RCAF) Squadrons based at Redhill were dispatched on 27 July to take part in a sortie to Poix, France. Returning Spitfire Vb BL773, flown by the CO of No.412 Squadron Leader D.C. Keefer DFC reported a glycol leak, which seized the engine. 'B' Flight No.277 Squadron were scrambled to search, Walrus I HD908 'BA-D' flown by Flight Sergeant Brodie, Flying Officer Wilson and Sergeant Mallinson and escorted by Spitfires of No.501 Squadron, led by Squadron Leader 'Bats' Barthold, they were unable to locate Squadron Leader Keefer so returned to Hawkinge. Later, two Spitfire Vbs of No.412 Squadron located the pilot off Cayeux, France. Walrus HB908, escorted by Spitfires of No.412 and No.501 Squadrons led by Squadron Leader E. Barthold reached the area and spotted the CO in his dinghy. This activity attracted the attention of six Bf 109s flying near the French coast. No.501 Squadron intercepted them just in time and dived on them, Flight Lieutenant J. Grottick shot one down. A second Walrus was dispatched, Squadron Leader Grace circled over the Dungeness area just in case Brodie needed assistance. Keefer was picked up by Flight Sergeant Brodie who returned to Hawkinge. On 28 July, Squadron Leader Grace rescued Squadron Leader R.W. 'Buck' McNair DFC the CO of No.421 (RCAF) Squadron Kenley. Squadron Leader MacNair's Spitfire IX MA586 developed engine trouble when off the coast. Pilot Officer Parks escorted him, but McNair lost height off the French coast, and at Dunkirk the engine caught fire; losing control, the Spitfire aircraft dived for the sea and McNair baled out, his parachute opening just in time. Pilot Officer Parks sent a Mayday call and orbited for approximately 1½ hours, relieved by No.411 (RCAF) Squadron. Hearing of Squadron Leader McNair's difficulty they landed at Manston, refuelled and took off again, escorting the Walrus to Hawkinge. Squadron Leader MacNair received treatment for facial burns, after resting for a few days he returned to duties at Kenley.

For 8th USAAF Bomber groups attacking Oschersleben on 28 July 1943, the operation turned into a disaster when high cloud caused several formations to become separated. Ideal conditions for Luftwaffe Fw 190s to exploit, particularly now a few were armed with rockets. One B17, based at Thurleigh, was 42-3076 (GY-H) of the 306BG – 367BS, had been hit by Fw 190s and flak near Kassel. The pilot, First Lieutenant W. Thomas, aided by co-pilot Second Lieutenant J.G. Parks, limped back over the Channel; unable to make Thurleigh, they crash-landed at Hawkinge. The B17 'The Queen of the Skies' caught fire and burnt out. With the help of station staff at Hawkinge, all crew escaped. First Lieutenant H. McCaleb, Navigator; First Lieutenant J.W. Lukens, Bombardier; Staff Sergeant A. Heybourne, Flight Engineer/Top turret Gunner; Second Lieutenant F. Palmer, Radio Operator; Staff Sergeant E. DeByer, Ball turret gunner; Staff Sergeant E. Henderson, Waist Gunner; Staff Sergeant M. St Louis, Waist gunner; Staff Sergeant J. Harris, Tail gunner.

No.313 Squadron was one of three Czechoslovak Fighter Squadrons, the other two being No.310 and No.312 Squadron. Since 28 June 1943 No.313 Squadron had been based at Peterhead, commanded by Squadron Leader J. Himr. On 21 August 1943, they transferred to Hawkinge to provide escort cover for bombing operations over France. Being re-equipped with Spitfire VIs in June that year was an improvement on the Vb and Vc. Eighteen Spitfires had left Peterhead, landing at Church Fenton for the night, then flying on to Hawkinge. A train party of personnel arrived at Folkestone and were met by RAF vehicles. Spitfires arrived at Hawkinge by 0845hrs, the unit's DH Tiger Moth arrived at 1730hrs, everyone was delighted when a message was received from the AOC No.13 Group, congratulating them on moving so many serviceable aircraft on time.

No.313 Squadron flew sector reconnaissance flights and practised formation flying until 24 August, when they escorted thirty-six B17s over the North Sea; the following day they escorted thirty-six Marauders, bombing Tricqueville airfield, and again on 27 August they escorted thirty-six Marauders attacking Poix airfield. Squadron Leader J. Himr shot down an Fw 190A-4 near Merville, flown by Uffz. H. Krieg 5/JG 26, who was killed. No.313 Squadron had been operating with No.64 Squadron protecting B17s in the St Omer area. Returning to Hawkinge, Flight Lieutenant A. Motycka, unable to release the undercarriage of Spitfire Vc AD191, belly-landed and came to a halt. Motycka climbed out injured, and his aircraft was airborne again later that evening.

Early on the morning of 31 August they escorted twelve Bostons to Merville, but the bombers failed to rendezvous with the fighters, who returned to base. Later No.313 Squadron escorted eighteen Lockheed Venturas to Hesdin (Forest), St Pol, an Arms Dump; due to heavy cloud over France they returned to Hawkinge. On 12 September, a day with no operational flying, Flight Sergeant J.E. Green No.313 Squadron, on a routine flight from Hawkinge, flew into high ground in fog at Wormshill, Kent, and was killed. The following day No.313 Squadron took off in poor weather for Abbeville, Flight Lieutenant S. Rejthar crash landed during take-off, but was uninjured.

No.501 Squadron, which had been based at Hawkinge since 21 June 1943, was involved in ASR searches and 'Jim Crow' operations. Following an unsuccessful sortie on 13 September, four Spitfire Is No.501 Squadron were airborne and spotted a dinghy off Ostend. Sergeant G. A. 'Lefty' Whitman (an American but serving with the RCAF) flying Typhoon Ib JP678 of No.3 Squadron, detached to Manston had been shot down, ditching off Zeebrugge. He was picked up by Squadron Leader A. Grace, pilot, Warrant Officer J. Rose, and Second Lieutenant Hall in a Walrus of No.277 Squadron and taken to Dover.

Returning from Romilly on 15 September, B17F 42-5910 'Ruthie', 326th Bomber Squadron 92nd Bomber Group, tried to land at Hawkinge. Damaged by fighters during the operation, the B17 had taken off from its base at Alconbury. Landing, the B17 swerved off the airfield at Hawkinge and crashed. This aircraft was also known as 'Hell Cat', and following the crash at Hawkinge, it was renamed 'Homesick Angel', when it flew with the 94BG.

The CO of Hawkinge Wing Commander M.N. Crossley DFC, witnessed this event and wrote:

> Hawkinge was hardly suitable for gigantic four engine bombers even when they are in the capable hands of the pilot, let alone the navigator, as this one turned out to be. The pilot and co-pilot both having been killed during the raid. It was soon evident that the man in charge could not, or did not know how to, get his remaining throttles right back as the poor old B17 came sailing across the grass at about ten feet and just

RAF HAWKINGE

On 15 September 1943 B17F 42-5910 'Hell Cat' 326th Bomber Squadron 92nd Bomber Group, based at Alconbury, crash landed at Hawkinge.

>about thirty miles an hour above the stalling speed. When he saw he couldn't make it he slammed open the throttles, and with a ghastly sort of yawing swoop, just missed the Flying Control Office with his wing tips and then disappeared below the immediate horizon of trees.
>
>*Hawkinge Airfield 1912–1961*
>R.S Humphreys

An ASR Spitfire of No.277 Squadron had found the B17, trailing smoke over the Channel. Fortress and Spitfire arrived at Hawkinge when airmen were having a NAAFI break. A dozen or so cycling airmen, bunched together and fooling around, were on the perimeter track when the B17 appeared. Clearing the boundary fence it flopped onto the grass, bouncing with such force that one of the oleo legs collapsed. The careering machine covered half of the airfield getting perilously near to Hawkinge village. A wing dug into the ground, turning the aircraft round into the airfield extension.

No.313 Squadron departed from Hawkinge on 18 September 1943 moving to Ibsley as part of No.10 Group Fighter Command. Flight Sergeant Brodie No.277 Squadron rescued Flying Officer J.W. Fiander No.401(RCAF) Squadron, whose Spitfire Vb BM199 had been damaged, causing glycol to leak; Fiander baled out near Dieppe. With the rescued pilot onboard, Flight

TAKING THE WAR TO THE ENEMY 1943

Sergeant Brodie could not take off due to heavy seas, he taxied the Walrus back to Dover arriving at 2400hrs. No.501 Squadron scrambled to cover the rescue attempt, circling above the Walrus until safely docked. Flight Sergeant Brodie rescued another pilot next day, in similar circumstances. Sergeant J. Krzysztopinski Spitfire Vb W3631 No.302 (Polish) Squadron was shot down by an Fw 190 near Bethune. The Walrus plucked him from his dinghy and taxied back to Dover under the watchful eye of No.501 Squadron. During 20/21 September sixty-three sorties, including thirty-eight by No.609, were flown before Pilot Officer T.S. Turek was rescued off the French coast after a night in a water-logged dinghy; his saviour was a Walrus flown by Squadron Leader Brown and Flying Officer Wilson. Five days later Pilot Officer C.J.G. de Moulin flying Typhoon Ib JP543 No.609 Squadron owed his life to Flight Lieutenant G. Martin (RAAF), who called up for a dinghy to be dropped after Pilot Officer de Moulin had lost his own.

Being a permanent base, Hawkinge provided rations for Advanced Landing Grounds in the area. On one occasion in September 1943, fish and sausages issued by Hawkinge were all returned as they were considered by an RAF Medical Officer to be 'unfit for human consumption'. These were replaced by cheese and a few tins of salmon, so RAF personnel ate reasonably well, though they had been looking forward to having 'bangers & mash'. On another occasion No.3206 Service Echelon arrived at Woodchurch ALG, only to be told that they were not expected, so of course no rations had been allocated to them either; an RAF truck was despatched to Hawkinge to collect food. More importantly, Hawkinge was responsible for the 'pay roll' of men based on ALGs, fortunately, their collection went ahead successfully.

Pilot Officer P. Standen, Pilot Officer J. Snell and Warrant Officer J. Rose, the crew of Walrus II K9526 No.277 Squadron 'B' Flight, left early on 26 September 1943, escorted by Squadron Leader A. Grace in Spitfire Vb W7490. They were vectored to an area off Dungeness to search for a pilot of No.401 (RCAF) Squadron based at Staplehurst ALG. Flight Lieutenant I.C. Ormston DFC Spitfire Vb BM627 recalled:

> Eventually the boys pulled me on board a Walrus, my logbook says we taxied for 2½ hours – heavy seas. After repeated attempt to take off, always striking a wave and falling back, the pilot taxied on. I was told at the time that we were in a minefield and that an ASR boat was waiting outside to which I was transferred and taken to Dover.
>
> *411 City of North York Squadron*
> John McClenaghan

RAF HAWKINGE

Pilots of No.350 (Belgium) Squadron at Hawkinge during October 1943, standing 1st left 3rd row is Flight Lieutenant Paul Leva who successfully destroyed a V1 by wing tipping. (P. Leva/Family)

No.350 (Belgium) Squadron, led by Squadron Leader A.L.T.J. Bousa, arrived at Hawkinge on 1 October 1943, where they would remain until further notice. They were equipped with the Spitfire Vcs, which they flew until re-equipping with the Spitfire IX in 1944. Officers were housed at 'Whitegates', the Sergeants' Mess at Reindene. They took over the 'B' Flight dispersal area allocated to No.501 Squadron who moved to 'A' Flight dispersal. During a routine patrol Captain Bernard Fuchs (Free French) attacked a coaster off Ostend, causing some damage and terrifying the crew. Another pilot was reported in a dinghy on 3 October by Flying Officer Hartwell and Flight Sergeant Loader No.277 Squadron; he was rescued by Squadron Leader A. Grace and Flight Sergeant N.E. Frehner of No.485 (RNZAF) Squadron based at Biggin Hill. The engine of Spitfire IX MH351 had developed engine trouble, so the pilot had baled out near Dungeness. On 7 October Captain Fuchs was flying a weather reconnaissance flight and tangled with four Fw 190s, destroying one. No.501 Squadron's CO, Squadron Leader M.G. Barnett, arrived from No.234 Squadron, taking over command from Squadron Leader E. Barthold. No.609 Squadron celebrated its 200th victory at Folkestone on 20 October, many officers serving at Hawkinge were invited to the party, which turned into a great evening. Hawkinge airfield became crowded, with many squadrons operating from

TAKING THE WAR TO THE ENEMY 1943

the airfield. On one such occasion no less than nineteen Spitfires of No.402 (RCAF) and No.416 (RCAF) arrived commanded by Wing Commander Chadburn DSO, DFC to take part in an offensive patrol on 25 October. This was cancelled due to the terrible weather, so they waited until the 'Hawkinge Horror' cleared, remaining at Hawkinge until the end of October.

Captain B. Fuchs and Pilot Officer Lilburn No.501 Squadron, attacked and damaged two locomotives and a gun post in the Le Touquet area of France on 1 November 1943. A workforce of forty to fifty men, seeing the Spitfires diving, soon scattered. During the early afternoon, Squadron Leader Barnett was leading a 'Jim Crow' flight, when Me 109s were seen flying near Calais. A fight ensued and Barnett damaged one Me 109 before returning to Hawkinge.

Next day, the Coast Guard at Rye contacted Hawkinge, reporting that a German airman had been found dead, washed ashore at Lade, Rye. Uffz. Freidrich Freiberger, was a crew member of the Ju 88S-1 of 8/KG 6 shot down on 30/31 October by Mosquito 'YV-G' of No.85 Squadron flown by Flying Officer R.C.J Bray and Flying Officer R.L.T. Robb based West Malling. Oberlt. K. Selck and Uffz. H. Keppler were missing, their

Free French AF Captain B. Fuchs of No.501 (County of Gloucester) Squadron seated in Spitfire Vb BL688 SD-H 'Annette II' at Hawkinge during June 1943. Note the Free French emblem below the cockpit; this aircraft crashed on 25 May 1943 while with No.58 OTU (Operational Training Unit), Hawarden.

bodies were never found. They crashed into the Channel off Rye, where their aircraft sank. Freiberger was buried at Hawkinge cemetery. No.350 (Belgium) Squadron lost two pilots on 13 November, Flight Sergeant F.E.L. Boute Spitfire Vb EP240 and Sergeant M.A.R.M. de Hepcee Spitfire Vb BM652 failed to return from a mission over Belgium.

A Walrus No.277 Squadron and four Spitfires left Hawkinge during late afternoon of 18 November, searching for a pilot in the sea off Dungeness. No.403 (RCAF) squadron took part in a sweep at Bethune, led by Wing Commander H. Godefroy until his radio failed, Squadron Leader Magwood took over. Two pilots were hit by flak near St Omer, one returned. Flight Lieutenant S.W. Matthews, Spitfire IX MH361 emitting smoke and flames west of Boulogne, intended to glide down and bale out. No more was heard from him, but his position coincided with a pilot seen without a dinghy off Dungeness; before the Walrus could reach him, he had disappeared.

Two Typhoon Ibs of No.181 Squadron landed at Hawkinge to refuel. Shortly after, twenty-two Typhoon Ibs of No.121 Wing, Westhampnett, Sussex, comprising of No.245 Squadron, No.175 Squadron led and No.174 Squadron descended on Hawkinge. They were returning from an attack on the village of Audinghen near Cape Gris-Nez, France, which formed part of the German Atlantic Wall defences. It was here that the 'Batterie Todt', a 380mm gun, was based and therefore a suitable target for Typhoons which delivered two 1,000lb. (454 kg) bombs – hence the name 'Bombphoon'. The weather deteriorated to such an extent that the wing could not return to Westhampnett or Tangmere; Hawkinge was the obvious airfield on which to land. The following day Squadron Leader M.R. Ingle-Finch managed to fly back to his base, the Typhoon Wing remained at a now very crowded Hawkinge.

In May 1943 Squadron Leader C. 'Hoppy' Hodgkinson was posted to No.501 Squadron as 'A' Deputy Flight Commander. However, he joined No.611 (West Lancashire) Squadron at Biggin Hill in June 1943, but returned to No.501 Squadron in October. Squadron Leader Hodgkinson had lost a leg when a DH Tiger Moth he was flying from Rochester collided with another, at the time he was serving with the Fleet Air Arm.

On 23 November 'Hoppy' had taken off from Hawkinge on a high-level weather reconnaissance flight in the vicinity of Amiens, prior to escorting USAAF bombers to attack V1 installations in the Pas de Calais. 'Hoppy' was flying Spitfire IX MJ117 when the oxygen system failed; almost losing consciousness, he decided to force-land once fuel had run out. Diving through cloud, German guns opened fire and Spitfire MJ117 crashed at Audincthun. 'Hoppy' was pulled from the burning aircraft by

TAKING THE WAR TO THE ENEMY 1943

Pilots, NCOs, and aircrew of No.277 (ASR) Squadron 'B' Flight at Hawkinge, behind them one of the few Supermarine Sea Otters operated by the unit between November 1943 until April 1944. Seated front row, 4th from left is Wing Commander M.N. Crossley DSO, DFC who commanded RAF Hawkinge from 1 January 1945 until 3 September 1945.

Sea Otter JM959 served with No.277 (ASR) Squadron at Hawkinge and survived the war, restored it flew with Britavia as G-AJFV, seen here at Blackbushe Airport during May 1949.

French workers, and taken to a farmhouse. German soldiers turned up at the farmhouse, and took him to a military hospital, where his burns were treated; he remained unconscious for three days. His injuries included a fractured upper jaw, internal lacerations and facial injuries. Squadron Leader C.G.S. Hodgkinson was repatriated to Britain via Sweden in September 1944, and received plastic surgery at East Grinstead, returning to flying in December 1944 with No.53 Ferry Unit, retiring from the RAF in 1946.

No.88 Squadron based at Hartford Bridge with No.180, No.320 and No.98 Squadrons were assigned to attack the village of Audinghen, the location of the HQ for Organisation Todt (OT), a civil and military engineering organisation in Nazi Germany founded by Fritz Todt, an engineer and senior Nazi. Following previous attempts, two more raids were arranged for 25 November. No.88 Squadron flew Boston IIIs on a morning raid and suffered badly from the flak. Boston III BL317, flown by Pilot Officer D.J.N. Gibson (RNZAF) who was hit by flak and wounded in the left collarbone and face, with his crew: Flight Sergeant I.I. Gass, Flight Sergeant W.G. Davies and Flight Sergeant H.D. Parker, managed to limp home. The Boston was met by Spitfires of No.501 Squadron, having scrambled from Hawkinge to escort Gibson into Hawkinge. Struggling to maintain control of the Boston, which went into a dive, Gibson ordered his crew to bale out. Pulling out of the dive he saw Hawkinge and put down, almost passing out; the Boston came to a halt with the crew uninjured, they returned to Hartford Bridge that afternoon; Gibson was taken to Canterbury hospital for treatment. Audinghen had been hit hard, and the following day the 9th USAAF completely destroyed the site.

Tangmere Wing arrived on 26 November, which proved to be a hectic day; Heston Wing failed to arrive due to bad weather. They were replaced by No.122 Wing Gravesend comprising of Nos.19, 65 and 122 Squadrons, to use Hawkinge as a forward base, joined for the operation by No.350 Squadron based at Friston ALG. The mission was to fly close support for seventy-two Marauders to attack Rosieres-en-Santerre. During the day there were 108 operational aircraft at Hawkinge as well as those permanently based at the airfield.

Both 'A' and 'B' Sections of No.3210 Servicing Commando moved to Hawkinge from Hawarden 1 December 1943 to service aircraft and engines. Engineers and fitters attended instructional courses at DH Aircraft Co., Burtonwood Repair Depot and Plessey Ltd., DeNapier Aircraft Engines. The unit would remain at Hawkinge throughout December 1943. The same day, aircraft of Nos. 350, 501, 65, 41 and 91 Squadrons, escorted seventy-

TAKING THE WAR TO THE ENEMY 1943

Flight Lieutenant Paul Leva escaped Belgium during occupation and made his way to England, joining the RAF in February 1941, flying from Hawkinge and Lympne airfields. (P. Leva/Family)

two Marauders, attacking Cambrai/Epinary airfields. Nos. 350, 501 and 277 Squadron were airborne searching for B17s returning from a raid on Solingen, Germany. Pilot Officer A. Gooch and Flight Sergeant J. King flying Spitfires Vb R8030 and R8479 located a B17 in the sea off Ramsgate, the crew were rescued by an RN vessel. The B17G that crashed in Pegwell Bay was 42-31243 of the 427th BS 303rd Bomber Group 'Hells Angels', based at Molesworth. The pilot, Second Lieutenant A. Eckhart, and crew all survived with minor injuries.

During 1999 remains of 42-31243 were recovered from the sea at low tide by a group of enthusiasts from Brenzett Aeronautical Museum and Elliott Smock and his team. This aircraft was originally thought to be B24D Liberator 41-23800 'The Captain and His Kids', but turned out to be the B17G described. Today, items recovered – under licence from the Ministry of Defence – are displayed at Romney Marsh Wartime Collection, Brenzett. The museum was later visited by two crew members and their families to view the exhibits, and they were able to assist with details of their mission to the Leverkusen Industrial area of Solingen.

A third B17 crashed off Manston, all crew were rescued by ASR and Spitfires of No.501 Squadron found another B17 in the sea off Tangmere. On 4 December, Squadron Leader A.D. Grace DFC 'B' Flight CO No.277 Squadron found two dinghies off Ramsgate. High Speed Launches (HSL) were directed to the area, locating five USAAF airmen; two had died.

With Christmas a few days away, No.501 Squadron were still in the thick of it, escorting bombers to targets in France, airborne on 21 December to rendezvous with Marauders of the 9th USSAF over Abbeville. Contact with the Americans had been lost, the Marauders were nowhere to be seen. Suddenly, four P47 Thunderbolts appeared, circling the Spitfires. Without warning they dived, opening fire, hitting Spitfire IX EP559 flown by Pilot Officer A.A Griffiths, who was last seen diving away, trailing smoke. Flight Lieutenant D. Davies in Spitfire 1X BL965 was also hit, but made it back to Hawkinge and crash landed uninjured, Pilot Officer A.A. Griffiths survived his crash but was taken PoW.

Everyone complained about the incident, some choice words were used to describe the Americans. Their voices were heard, and it was not long before Air Chief Marshal Sir H.W.L. Saunders, GCB, KBE, MC, DFC & Bar, MM, visited the squadron at Hawkinge AOC No.11 Group. Very sympathetic, he promised that everything would be done to prevent such incidents happening again. But of course they did, usually due to the lack of aircraft identification training. It was pointed out that roundels displayed on RAF aircraft were a clue to their identity.

Although the V1 or Doodlebug campaign did not begin until 13 June 1944, their sites were targets for attack by the RAF. On 28 December, five Spitfire Vbs of No.350 (Belgium) Squadron were ordered to a V1 site in France. Following some success, they were attacked by Fw 190s. Flight Sergeant G.L.M.G. Dancot in Spitfire Vb BM468, burst into flames over Gueschart, crashing near Abbeville; Dancot was buried at Evere. On the 29 December No.322 (Dutch) Squadron prepared to move from Woodvale to Hawkinge, Spitfire IXs took off from on 30 December bound for their new base, the consolation being that they were closer to their homeland, Holland.

During the evening of 30 December, a Walrus of No.277 Squadron, accompanied by Spitfires was directed to a parachute and body of an airman reported in the sea. Flying Officer F.H. Dennison No.164 Squadron had been returning from a raid on a V1 site when he was hit by flak, his Hurricane IV KX540 crashed in the sea. Two other pilots were found in the sea that day by Spitfires of No.277 Squadron. Warrant Officer R.P.A. McKillop Typhoon Ib JP593 No.245 Squadron and Flying Officer R.A. Peters Typhoon Ib JP532 No.486 Squadron, both had ditched due to engine failure and died.

No.245 Squadron based at Westhampnett was briefed to attack targets in the Beauvoir area on 23 December. Nine Typhoon Ibs returned to base, but Flying Officer W.F. Freshwater was hit by flak over the target and flew Typhoon JP801 home with the undercarriage down. Short of petrol, Flying Officer Freshwater crash landed near Hythe not far from Hawkinge, climbing out of his wrecked aircraft uninjured.

Chapter 10

Air Sea Rescue 1944
The V1 and the Fleet Air Arm Arrive

No.3210 Servicing Commando had various tasks to perform. When there were no visiting aircraft requiring maintenance, they assisted other servicing units on the airfield, attached to various squadrons. On one occasion their Motor Transport (MT) unit practised the use of mock-up landing ramps with No.41 Army Division. No.3210 SC was equipped with Bedford FWD 3-ton tenders, Thornycroft FWD 3-ton fenders, Comer vans and two Royal Enfield motorcycles from N0.99 Maintenance Unit. Throughout January the unit received training at Halton, Rolls Royce Ltd., Guncliffe Owen Ltd., De Napier & Sons Ltd., Bristol Aircraft Co. Ltd., Dowty Equipment Ltd., and instructional use of the Coffman starter with Plessey Ltd., and courses on Aircraft Recognition were attended.

No.501 (County of Gloucester) Squadron began the new year flying weather reconnaissance flights and photographing shipping in Boulogne harbour. They attacked a train at Ligres, France, carrying flak guns and damaged a large crane. There was little operational flying for No.322 (Dutch) Squadron, who by 2 January flew air tests and reconnaissance flights. Allocated a hut which had no furniture, the Adjutant and Orderly Room staff acquired what was needed, how or from where is not recorded.

No.322 Squadron were ready for action, their first operation was on 4 January, over enemy territory escorting Mitchell bombers to targets in Northern France, in company with No.501 Squadron. On their return, Flying Officer J. Van Arkell, No.322 Squadron, couldn't lower his Spitfire Vb's undercarriage, and had to belly-land, hitting a starter trolley. Pilot Officer L.M. Meijers also hit a starter trolley, on take-off, badly damaging his Spitfire Vb. During the escort mission, two Spitfires of No.501 Squadron detached to photograph the target. They were attacked by Fw 190s of JG 26, over Crecy Forest. Flight Sergeant L.R. Knight Spitfire Vb AA733 was shot down near Abbeville and killed. Flight

Sergeant R.E. Farrow Spitfire Vb AB186 reported he was going to land, which he did near Abbeville; his engine was shot up. No.277 Squadron searching on 7 January for a pilot shot down by Fw 190s, crashing in the sea off Dover. Flight Sergeant C.H. Jenkins No.602 Squadron was found before nightfall, rescued by ASR launches and taken to Dover, Spitfire IX MH722 sank below the waves.

In early 1944 No.157 Squadron were based at Predannack, Cornwall. On 7 January they were patrolling the coast and intercepted a flight of Ju 88s. Mosquito II HJ660, flown by Flying Officer P.E. Hukin and Flight Sergeant R.H. Graham shot down a Ju 88 of ZG 1, sending it crashing into the sea. But the Mosquito had also been hit by return fire; Flying Officer Hukin radioed that he was going to ditch as both engines had failed, landing in the sea south-west of Brest. The wreckage was not found until 14 January, when aircraft of No.501 Squadron and a Walrus of No.277 Squadron were searching for the aircraft. They noticed a dinghy close by with both crew members obviously alive.

One of the most well-known COs of Hawkinge was Wing Commander D.J. Scott DSO, DFC who became CO on 9 January 1944. Scott was previously CO of No.486 (NZ) Squadron in 1943 based at Tangmere. Shortly before receiving his new appointment, 'Scottie' bought an old Austin 7 for the sum of £40. With his dog 'Kim' sitting in the passenger seat, they left Tangmere for Hawkinge. One of his first duties at Hawkinge, was to provide a funeral party for an RAF pilot killed in a flying accident with his crew. The coffin, along with the family, were to be collected from Folkestone railway station. The officer in charge received a call from the Bomber Command station where the pilot had been killed – they had sent the wrong coffin; the coffin that should have arrived at Folkestone had been sent to a base in Scotland. Wing Commander Scott insisted that both be returned to their rightful bases.

Dogfighting with other squadrons was frowned on, as it put valuable pilots and aircraft in jeopardy, despite it being a good way to improve a pilot's combat skills. On 16 January this was highlighted when Flying Officer C.P. De Neve, although perhaps on an authorised flight at the time, had taken off from Hawkinge during the afternoon and had got into a dogfight with Typhoons, possibly of No.1 Squadron at Lympne. Spitfire Vb AD428 dived into the ground near Dover, killing De Neve. This popular pilot, who left behind a young wife, was buried at Hawkinge Cemetery on 20 January. Flight Lieutenant Chiswell oversaw the cortege which included the CO Major K.C. Kuhlmann DFC, fellow members of the squadron and officers representing HM Queen Wilhelmina of the Netherlands. Flying Officer C.P. De Neve was afforded a full military funeral with the Dutch flag draped over his coffin. From 20 January 1944 until the end of the month, No.501 Squadron moved to No.17 Armament Practice camp at Southend, returning to Hawkinge on 4 February.

During the night of 21/22 January 1944, the Luftwaffe launched an attack on England, known as the 'Little Blitz', the largest raid since Birmingham in July 1942. Ten German aircraft were lost, the raiders dropped incendiary bombs on Hawkinge during the afternoon. A few huts were burnt to the ground, but there were no serious injuries apart from a few burns; five aircraft were shot down by night fighters: Do 217M-1 1/KG 2 off Dungeness; an Me410A-1 of Stab V/KG 2 at Lydd Ranges; another at Lower Chantry Lane, Canterbury; a Ju 88A-4 of 3/KG 76; and a He 177A-3 of 2/KG 40, shot down by a Mosquito of No.85 Squadron West Malling, which crashed off Hastings. A Ju 88 of 6/KG 54, was brought down at Horton Priory, Sellindge a few miles from Hawkinge by a Mosquito of No.488 (RNZAF) Squadron based at Bradwell Bay. Three of the German crew died, their bodies were recovered and buried at Hawkinge cemetery.

Major K.C. Kuhlmann DFC CO of No.322 Squadron, was married on 22 January, a reception was held at the Grand Hotel, Folkestone. He was presented with a silver cigarette box by No.322 Squadron, later engraved by all the pilots. Six Spitfire Vbs of No.322 Squadron were scrambled on defensive patrol and hit by flak over the French coast. On 24 January a Walrus of No.277 Squadron located a pilot near Boulogne. Spitfires of No.401 (RCAF) Squadron were attacking sites in France when Flight Lieutenant J. Sheppard reported engine failure. Spitfire IX MJ145 ditched. The Walrus directed an HSL to the dinghy, where a Canadian pilot was recovered uninjured.

On 28 January Spitfire Vb R8072 flown by Flight Sergeant F.A. Blower, No.277 Squadron searched for a P38 Lightning pilot, but found nothing. Flight Lieutenant D.G. McKay No.412 (RCAF) Squadron, also suffered engine failure, Spitfire IX MJ302 dived into the sea, the pilot was rescued by a Walrus of No.277 Squadron and brought back to Hawkinge. No.322 Squadron were not so lucky, Flying Officer Baron E.J. Van Nagell had taken off in Spitfire Vb AB818 on defensive patrol, accompanied by Pilot Officer Walters. Flying near Calais he was hit by flak, crashing to his death; he was buried at Merville, where French locals and some German soldiers attended the funeral.

RAF HAWKINGE

P-47D 42-8500 HO+P 'Cripes A' Mighty', flown by Captain George E. Preddy 487th Fighter Squadron 352nd Fighter Group based Bodney in 1944, was rescued by a Walrus of No.277 Squadron flown by Pilot Officer P.C. Standen on 29 January. Finding Preddy in his dinghy, two P47s were circling over their section leader, off North Foreland. The Walrus damaged a float taking off and taxied to Ramsgate, arriving early evening. Captain Preddy was killed by 'friendly fire' on Christmas Day 1944 while leading a formation of P-51 Mustangs.

On 30 January 1944 the new CO at Hawkinge, Wing Commander D.J. Scott DSO, DFC, having decided to leave his office for a stroll, witnessed a Spitfire IX MH476 approaching with a dead propeller. The pilot made a wheels-up landing, but crashed short of the airfield. Before the fire tender arrived, Scott tried to rescue the pilot from the blaze. By then foam had been sprayed on the aircraft, and the pilot was badly burnt. Fire crews could not get closer, so Scott pulled the pilot clear; the pilot's lower body was smashed. Flying Officer J.J. Geraud No.350 (Belgium) Squadron died before being placed in the waiting ambulance. Following this accident LAC Warren No.3210 Servicing Commando was commended for his courageous attempt helping to rescue Flying Officer Geraud.

For No.322 Squadron, January ended with lectures by the Intelligence officer on Anti-Fog devices being installed on airfields, such as Manston's FIDO, to disperse the fog using fire. Lectures also included MI9 (the British Directorate of Military Intelligence Section 9), information on the importance of photographs, bogus German evasion organisations, useful knowledge if shot down in occupied Europe and the introduction of pilots being allowed to carry £2 on operational flights. The first week of February 1944, twelve Spitfire Vbs of No.322 Squadron escorted forty-two Marauders attacking German installations in Northern France. Due to the poor weather the operation was uneventful, the Spitfires returned to Hawkinge without loss. The new CO of No.322 Squadron, Squadron Leader H.F. O'Neill DFC, realised that several of the Staff Officers at Hawkinge had been there too long and so had some posted away. These were replaced by officers with more appropriate experience for a front-line fighter base.

Early afternoon of 3 February 1944, Mosquito VI LR381 of No.21 Squadron landed at Hawkinge, flown by Flight Lieutenant H.C.V. Webb and Flight Lieutenant J. Sercombe, returning from attacking a target at Beaumont-le-Harong. Flight Lieutenant Webb's aircraft had been hit in the port engine. Seven Mosquitos, led by Wing Commander I.G. Dale, had taken off from Thorney Island. Shortly after landing, HRH Prince Bernard of the Netherlands, Air Commodore F. Beaumont Director of Allied Air Co-operation and Foreign Liaison (DAFL), and Lieutenant Colonel De Brockent, Head of Air Department Netherlands MOD arrived. Following a parade, HRH Prince Bernard presented medals to Dutch officers and airmen of No.322 Squadron. During this ceremony, sirens sounded when a Spitfire crashed on its belly, skidding through the boundary fence into a gully, breaking its back. Disciplinary action was taken when No.322 Squadron had several taxiing accidents and warned that if further incidents happened, they would be taken off operations and posted from Hawkinge for 'corrective training'. Two weeks after this warning a Spitfire of No.322 Squadron taxied into the back of a 3-ton truck at Hawkinge. Orders swiftly came from AOC H.W.L. 'Ding' Saunders 11 Group, that No.322 Squadron should be posted out of No.11 Group on a course with No.14 (APC) Armament Practice Camp at Ayr, Scotland on 25 February 1944.

The Dutch squadron, with pilots of No.501 Squadron, continued escorting Marauders attacking targets in Northern France. Returning from the airfield at Gilze Rijen on 22 February, Pilot Officer S.H. Cheeseman lost control of Spitfire Vb BL31. He released the fuel drop tank, which collided with the tail section; baling out near Walcheren, he was rescued by an HSL. Following a photographic flight over Boulogne harbour, No.501 Squadron returned to Hawkinge, and taxied to dispersal. Just then a Marauder of the 9th USAAF appeared over Hawkinge, but crash landed; the crew climbed out uninjured.

On 3 March 1944, Lieutenant R.W. Foy of the 363rd FS 357th FG based at Lieston, Suffolk, and Major A.K. Abler were rescued from the Channel by No.277 Squadron. Lieutenant Foy ditched off Deal due to engine problems. Flying Officer A.E. Gooch and Flight Sergeant A.M. Rollo accompanied Walrus K3289, flown by Flying Officer D.R. Hartwell, as it searched for the pilot. Hartwell saw an HSL close by, but did not land; Lieutenant Foy was rescued by the launch and taken to Ramsgate where he was treated for shock. Major A.K Abler was rescued in similar circumstances.

On 1 March 1944, Wing Commander R.F. Watts arrived from Air Defence of Great Britain (ADGB), to take over command of Hawkinge from Wing Commander D.J. Scott DSO, DFC who was posted to Manston. The same day No.322 (Belgium) Squadron returned to Hawkinge from Ayr. They were to escort USAAF bombers attacking sites in Europe. No.322 Squadron later moved from Hawkinge to Acklington on 10 March,

Major A.K. Abler 363rd FS 357th FG 8th USAAF, rescued from the Channel by Flying Officer D.R. Hartwell and crew in Walrus I K3289 No.277 Squadron on 3 March 1944. (American Air Museum)

where they converted to the Spitfire XIV, the first squadron in the Allied Air Force to be re-equipped with this type.

WAAF officers at Hawkinge during early 1944 moved from the house known as 'Mimosa', situated away from the airfield, to Officers' married quarters opposite the Officers' Mess. Spitfire IXBs of No.350 (Belgium) Squadron arrived from Hornchurch in transit, this time preparing to move to Peterhead, Scotland on 13/14 March, with No.3012 Service Echelon, returning to Hawkinge later that summer. A conference took place at Hawkinge on 17 March attended by section commanders where new orders were introduced. The siren would only be used if air raids or shelling from France was imminent, and the swimming pool at the Duke of York Military School, near Deal, would be used for dinghy drill. Finally, arrangements would be made for laying white lines, and 'gooseneck' flares sited to assist aircraft taking off and landing during foggy weather.

AIR SEA RESCUE 1944

On 18 March, Mitchell IIs of No.320 (Dutch) Squadron, bombed targets at Gorenflos, France. Mitchell FR177, flown by Flight Lieutenant H.J. Voorspuij, and FR180 flown by Flight Lieutenant J.H. Ot., had to ditch. A Walrus of No.277 Squadron 'B' Flight flown by Squadron Leader R.W. Wallens, located a crew in their dinghy south-west of Berck-sur-Mer and took them to Hawkinge. The second Mitchell crew were rescued by Squadron Leader L.J. Brown in a Sea Otter of 'A' Flight No.277 Squadron, Gravesend, and brought into Dover. The ALG at Brenzett, Romney Marsh, opened on 21 March 1942; a detachment of RAF personnel comprising of a sergeant, two corporals, a cook and a nursing orderly led by Flying Officer Beadle, were sent from Hawkinge to help with preparations. No.133 Wing Air Defence of Great Britain (ADGB), comprising of No.129 (Mysore), No.306 (Toruński) and No.315 (Deblinski) Squadrons with Mustang IIIs arrived at Brenzett on 10 July 1944. Also, in March and for the first time at Hawkinge, WAAFs stationed at the airfield were assigned to Station Fire Watch duties; by this time attacks were infrequent.

March ended with a rescue by Squadron Leader R.W. Wallens, No.277 Squadron patrolling Dungeness in Walrus K2315, saw two DH Mosquitos orbiting the area. Flight Sergeant S.W. Loader and Flight Sergeant J.H. King reported two airmen in a dinghy; the Marauder crew had been in the dinghy for four days prior to rescue, Spitfires searched but found no other survivors. Marauder B26B-25 41-31775 'AN-N' 'Minute Man' of 386th BG 553rd BS, based at Boxted, flying its 140th mission on 25 March 1944, to targets in France, was hit by enemy fire; the crew baled out with the pilot, Second Lieutenant E.S. Betts being the last to jump. The aircraft's rudder and starboard wing were damaged. Sergeant C.D. Powers, Tail Gunner, was injured, Second Lieutenant Betts and co-pilot Second Lieutenant L.R. Burnett landed, their two dinghies were close together. Voices of other crew members could be heard calling for help, but they could not be seen. Four remaining crew members were lost, the pilot and co-pilot were rescued from their dinghies on 28 March 1944. In addition to the men named above, the crew were: Second Lieutenant R.E. Curtiss Nav./Bomb.; Staff Sergeant J. Bowan, Gunner; Master Sergeant W. Milne (1st Grade) role unknown; and Staff Sergeant W. A. Van Damme, Gunner. No.277 Squadron were involved in several searches over the Channel on 13 April, one pilot being Group Captain Donkin, who had taken off from Odiham in Mustang I FD448 No.168 Squadron. Donkin was hit by flak over Ostend and baled out. Following extensive searches by No.277 Squadron and HSL, he was rescued after six days in his dinghy.

RAF HAWKINGE

No.93 Bomb Group 8th USAAF based at Hardwick, Norfolk was equipped with B-24 Liberators, comprising of four bomber squadrons. On 20 April 1944, while attacking targets in the Pas de Calais area, First Lieutenant Hirschel L. Gutman, the pilot of B24D-20-CF 42-63972 'GO-E' 328th BS, was hit by flak and gunfire. 'Flying Cock II' was in trouble; Gutman coaxed his aircraft home, and on reaching the English coast, prepared to crash land at Hawkinge. On his third approach all four engines stopped and the aircraft crashed near the airfield. Of the twelve crew members, six were killed: First Lieutenant Gutman; Second Lieutenant Edgar S. Crouthamel; Staff Sergeant Robert E. Carrier; Staff Sergeant Andrew J. Smilnyek; Staff Sergeant Vail S. Wolfe; and Technical Sergeant Ivan M. Wright.

Returning from a mission to bomb the V1 launch site at Siracourt on 21 April, Captain Louis R. Wade crash landed B26B-30-MA 41-31887 DR-G 'Mary' of the 450BS 322BG at Hawkinge. The 322BG was based at Great Saling, Essex. Airmen approaching the B26 or Marauder counted no less than 100 flak holes in the fuselage.

At the beginning of May 1944, with the invasion of France imminent, the 2nd TAF (Tactical Air Force), as a diversion tactic, hampered German efforts to discover how, when and where such an invasion would come. The RAF attacked radar stations in an attempt to blind the enemy and to keep reconnaissance aircraft away from ports and areas on the southern coast of Britain where preparations were taking place for D-Day. Pilots of ADGB's day and night fighter squadrons took part in these operations using forward bases like Hawkinge. On occasion these operations would overlap, for 2nd TAF and ADGB units could also mount escort for attacks against targets in northern France, and 2nd TAF would be involved in engagements with German aircraft over coastal areas.

B17 42-30849 (NV-F) 'Fart Sack' of the 92BG 325th BS based at Podington, was hit by flak while attacking V1 sites in the Pas de Calais area on 1 May 1944; the B17 crossed the coast trailing smoke, with two of its engines out of action. At Hawkinge, airmen were enjoying a NAAFI break when a B17 came into land, escorted by a Spitfire. Hopping over the boundary fence, the B17 bounced off the ground and its undercarriage legs dropped open. One of its wings dug in, slowing the B17 to a halt, as nearby airmen on bicycles tore off as fast as they could peddle, thinking the mighty bomber would disintegrate. An RAF Regiment AA crew based nearby saw the wing of the B17 hovering over them. The crew survived: Nicholas Wik, Co-pilot; Leroy Kirkpatrick, Navigator; Ralph Andler, Bombardier;

AIR SEA RESCUE 1944

Joaquin Sarasqueta, Flight Engineer/Top turret gunner; Luther Dove, Radio Operator; Wayne Troyer, Ball turret gunner; Bob Wangen, Waist gunner; Bob Wright, Waist gunner; C.W. Huff, Tail gunner; and Beauford Hamilton, gunner, were not seriously injured. B17 'Fart Sack', named after American cartoon character, was salvaged at Hawkinge on 20 May 1944 by a Maintenance & Recovery Unit.

On 9 May No.277 Squadron rescued two crew members of B24H-15-CF Liberator 41-29451 'Helfer College II' of 567th BS 389th BG based at Hethel: Staff Sergeant J. Busch, Waist Gunner and Second Lieutenant George M. Huck, Navigator. The rest of the crew: Staff Sergeant J. Akin, Bombardier; Staff Sergeant J. Busch, Right waist gunner; Staff Sergeant J. Granados Ball, turret gunner; Second Lieutenant Val Kalligeros ,Co-pilot; Staff Sergeant F. Rossignol, Tail Gunner; Staff Sergeant J. Sequin, Left Waist Gunner; Technical Sergeant D. McGhiey, Radio Operator; and Lieutenant J. Sheperd, Pilot, were all killed. On 10 May, Spitfires of No.277 Squadron searched unsuccessfully for a pilot off Dunkirk. Later, Flying Officer A.E. Gooch Spitfire Vb W3640 found the airman in his dinghy north-east of Gravelines. Squadron Leader R.W. Wallens with Second Lieutenant P. Ellis and Sergeant R.N. Smith took off in Walrus L2315, located the pilot and landed at Hawkinge. Lieutenant Sherwin G. Desens, based at Headcorn ALG (Egerton) near Ashford with the 378th FS 362nd FG 9th USAAF, was hit by flak following an attack on marshalling yards at Valenciennes, France, on 10 May 1944. Desens ditched his P47 Thunderbolt in the sea; following his rescue he returned to his unit at Headcorn.

No.149 Airfield moved to Deanland ALG, Sussex on 30 April 1944, becoming No.149 Wing comprising of Nos. 234, 64 and 611 Squadrons, commanded by Wing Commander R.P.R. Powell. The operations were mainly fighter escorts for RAF Bostons, Mitchells from Hartford Bridge and Dunsfold, and B-26 Marauders of the US 9th Air Force. On 12 May the squadron escorted USAAF Bostons attacking 'Nobal' targets (V-1 launching sites) south-west of Abbeville, the following day they escorted Mitchells to Tourcoing to attack the marshalling yards. On 11 May 1944, No.149 Wing arrived at Hawkinge for a briefing and refuelling prior to a fighter escort operation, following a successful day all Spitfires returned unscathed.

Mosquitos of No.418 (RCAF) Squadron based at Holmsley South attacked Laon and Juvincourt, France, on 10 May, led by the CO Wing Commander A. Barker and Flight Lieutenant G. Frederick flying Mosquito VI NT117. The CO was reported missing, but on 11 May Operations

Lieutenant Sherwin G. 'Butch' Desens (on the right) a P47 pilot based at Headcorn (Egerton) ALG, near Ashford of the 378th FS 362nd FG 9th USAAF was rescued by Walrus L2315 flown by Squadron Leader R.W. Wallens and taken to Hawkinge on 10 May 1944. (American Air Museum)

AIR SEA RESCUE 1944

at Holmsley South received news that both had been rescued by No.277 Squadron off Dieppe, and taken to Hawkinge. They were engaged by searchlights and accurate flak over Juvincourt airfield, hit in the fuselage and wings; the Mosquito was difficult to control.

Heading for Biville, France, Barker opened fire on a gun emplacement on the cliff. Flying low over the sea, he was aware of a fighter on his tail; at that moment the propeller blades hit the water and both engines began to vibrate, he decided to ditch. Successfully landing on the sea, both crew members climbed out of the aircraft; the Mosquito remained afloat, sticking out of the water at about a 60-degree angle. Both climbed into separate dinghies, lashing them both together. They were eventually spotted by Flying Officer J.F. Parisse Spitfire Vb BL377 No.277 Squadron 'B' Flight and picked up by Walrus I L2315 flown by Squadron Leader R.W. Wallens. Following take off, four Me 109s chased the Walrus across the Channel, but protected by Flying Officer Parisse, it landed safely back at Hawkinge unscathed.

No.513FS No.406th FG 9th USAAF based at Ashford ALG (Great Chart), reported Captain H.W. Shurlds missing on 21 May. Hit by flak while attacking a train near Malmedy, Belgium, the aircraft's engine was damaged. Other pilots of 513FS remained in R/T contact, encouraging Shurlds to bring his P-47D-10-RE 42-75061 home, reaching Boulogne before baling out. Spitfire Vbs R3647 Flight Lieutenant O.H. Furlong and Warrant Officer K.C. Moir EN849 No.277 Squadron 'B' Flight, took off to search the area. They were then relieved by Flying Officer P. Dechamps Spitfire Vb R3641 and Spitfire Vb BL377 Flight Sergeant S.W. Loader. P47s were seen circling over Shurld's dinghy as Walrus I K3072, flown by Sub Lieutenant R. Mander, arrived on the scene and rescued the pilot. Attempting to take off a float was damaged, turning the Walrus 90 degrees into wind, Sub Lieutenant R. Mander applied full starboard aileron lifting off. Despite the wing also being damaged, the Walrus managed to land safely at Hawkinge. Sadly Captain Shurlds was later killed in action on 19 August 1944 over France.

On 22 May Wing Commander E. Haabjoern DFC, No.124 Wing Hurn crashed Typhoon Ib MN542 in the sea after being hit by flak over Dieppe. Walrus I L2735, flown by Warrant Officer A.D. Grace, picked him up and taxied back to Ramsgate. Flying Officer A.A. Watkins No.440 Squadron (RCAF), also hit by flak, crashed Typhoon Ib MN489 in the Channel. Although safe, he was not rescued until 28 May, following a search by Squadron Leader R.W. Wallens in Walrus I L2315 'B' Flight No.277 Squadron Hawkinge.

RAF HAWKINGE

No.157 General Reconnaissance Wing was formed at Hawkinge on 17 May 1944, comprising Nos.119, No.819, 854 and 855 (Fleet Air Arm) Squadrons. They were tasked to protect operations in local areas of the English Channel and North Sea, during and after the invasion of Europe, under control of No.16 Group RAF Coastal Command.

On 23 May, twenty-four Grumman Avenger IIs (an American aircraft type) of No.854 and No.855 FAA Squadrons arrived at Hawkinge. According to Flying Control, the Avengers came in using a 'carrier approach', with power on. Almost stalling, the Avengers appeared to be hanging in the air on their propellers. The Avenger had no trouble operating out of Hawkinge, although doubts were raised when Midshipman Litherland No.855 Squadron took off armed with 2,000lb (907kg) bombs and lost power, descending gently onto the bomb storage bunkers without serious consequences. As if to prove their flying ability, No.854 Squadron put on a demonstration of three-plane formation take-offs with fully laden aircraft. Nine Avengers had arrived and carried out local familiarisation flights on 25 May. The following day six Avengers of No.855 (FAA) arrived, both squadrons practised bombing and local familiarisation flights.

Fleet Air Arm Grumman Avenger squadrons operated with RAF Coastal Command from Hawkinge, Thorney Island and Perranporth before and after D-Day. Operation *Channel Stop* was planned to prevent enemy ships from interfering with the Operation *Overlord* landings on 6 June 1944. In briefings it became clear that there was a threat from E-boats (German Schnellboot or 'fast boat'), U-boats (submarines) and R-boats (Räumboot German minesweeper), but fortunately these did not appear. Initially daylight patrols of four to five hours were carried out over the eastern part of the Channel, both before and after the D-Day landings. From 1 July No.854 and No.855 Squadrons started night patrols from Ijmuiden to Cap d'Antifer, individual aircraft taking off at thirty-minute intervals.

At 1400hrs on 23 May 1944, a Douglas Dakota came into land at Hawkinge, out of which stepped General Sir Bernard Montgomery, who would be in command of all Allied ground forces during the Battle of Normandy (Operation Overlord), from D-Day on 06 June 1944 until 01 September 1944. It was a brief stay, as he and his entourage soon left Hawkinge for Dover, returning to Hawkinge that evening to depart in his Dakota. Montgomery visited several airfields and countless RN and Army establishments in the build-up to D-Day, including West Malling on 25 May 1944.

AIR SEA RESCUE 1944

No.127 Squadron were based temporarily at Lympne, on 27 May the squadron attacked a V1 site at Le Treport. Pilot Officer W.A. White Spitfire IX MK696 was hit by flak; unable to reach Lympne, he ditched in the sea. Flight Lieutenant J.V.C. Mitchell, Sub Lieutenant E. Hall and Sergeant R.J. Mullins were scrambled from Hawkinge in Walrus I L9563, following his rescue Pilot Officer White returned to Lympne. Later that day two Spitfires flown by Pilot Officer T.M. Ormiston DFC and Flight Sergeant E.G.F. Green spotted two airmen in dinghies, crew members of a Boston, the remaining crew had baled out over France, this was No.277 Squadron's 500th successful rescue. The two Americans were picked up by Pilot Officer T.M. Ormiston DFC, Flight Sergeant E.G. Green and Sub Lieutenant P.F. Mariner –then flying a Sea Otter off Le Treport.

On 29 May, Mosquito NF. XIII MM503 No.604 (RAuxAF) Squadron, flown by Flight Lieutenant C.L. Harris and navigator Sergeant E.B. Hopkinson were shot down by a Beaufighter over Lyme Bay, a tragic mistake – especially as Hopkinson was killed. At the beginning of June 1944, the weather at Hawkinge prevented flying, with a ground mist covering the airfield. As this cleared, the opportunity arose for Squadron Leader R.W. Wallens to get airborne in Spitfire Vb EP435 on an air test, while other Spitfires of 'B' Flight No.277 Squadron remained on a state of thirty-minute readiness.

On 2 June, Flight Lieutenant J.V.C. Mitchell, Warrant Officer K.H. Rodes and Flight Sergeant J.W.N. Lawrence were vectored off Dungeness, where they could see a Mustang circling over a pilot in his dinghy; joining the Walrus, Pilot Officer W.E. Upitgrove and Flight Sergeant K.S. Moore acted as escort. The sea was too rough and landing was difficult, but Mitchell did land and recovered the pilot, he then tried to take off, but after taxiing for at least forty minutes, HSL No.96 arrived and towed the Walrus back to Dover.

That day a new hostel 'Amaya' was opened to accommodate WAAFs based at Hawkinge, due to the increasing numbers of women, and 'Sunnyside' WAAF hostel also opened that week. By now rumours of an impending invasion were rife, Hawkinge would play a major part on 6 June 1944 D-Day. In fact, in the lead up to the invasion of Normandy, Hawkinge had two roles. The first was to convince the Germans that the invasion would be in the Calais area so a great deal of air traffic was seen around Hawkinge. For the actual invasion, fighters from Hawkinge kept air routes open, ensuring that there was no U-boat activity in the Channel, and depth charges were fitted to the Avengers of No.854, 855 (FAA) Squadrons.

RAF HAWKINGE

As if to confirm the rumours of an invasion of Europe, six Spitfire IXs of No.80 Squadron, from Detling landed at Hawkinge. They had been acting as cover for troop carrying gliders from Littlehampton a few miles west of Cabourg. The gliders landed north-east of Caen, Hawkinge was again in the frontline, but unlike the summer of 1940, the Allies were landing on the beaches of Normandy. ASR operations stepped up considerably, with several rescues taking place by the four flights of No.277 Squadrons.

From early 1944 all the efforts of the USAAF and the RAF concentrated on the preparation of Operation *Overlord*, the D-Day landings. The task of coordinating the operations of Bomber Command and the USAAF in Europe was vast, providing round the clock bombing of vital installations factories in Germany. The Luftwaffe was also targeted in an attempt to destroy forward airfields and aircraft. These bombing formations required fighter escorts, both on the outgoing and incoming journeys, especially the USAAF daylight raids whose losses were greater than the British. Despite this, the Luftwaffe put up tremendous resistance to these continuous bombing raids which were particularly successful in March 1944, when only the USAAF Mustang P-51 fighter and its variants were capable of escorting the formations to the industrial heart and cities of Germany. Spitfire squadrons at that time had to leave the formations at the Dutch coast, returning to our own airfield for refuelling and then flying out to meet the returning bombers.

As the invasion preparations progressed, large areas of wooded valley and tree-lined fields around Hawkinge held concentrations of lorries, jeeps, personnel carriers, and tanks. Camouflaged with the Allied invasion insignia, the build-up revealed a massive military target for the occasional German reconnaissance aircraft. It was impossible to conceal the invasion armada, for air, land and sea exercises were in operation along British coasts. Hawkinge and the surrounding areas played host to thousands of troops of all nationalities. Roads leading to the airfield had been blocked and strict security enforced by twelve RAF Regiment squadrons.

The first week of June ADGB and 2nd TAF aircraft were painted with black and white invasion stripes, including amphibians, hastily applied using brushes, even brooms, essential to identify Allied aircraft. Some aircraft that had force landed in Europe were captured and repaired but not painted in German markings. They were then flown by German pilots, joining flights of Allied aircraft and opening fire on unsuspecting targets. RAF fighters maintained a constant patrol line in preparation for the Luftwaffe's response – which was limited, an indication that they were not capable of coping with the overwhelming strength of the Allied Air Forces.

AIR SEA RESCUE 1944

On 5 June all station personnel were confined to camp; late that evening pilots were briefed regarding the Second Front. Early on the morning of 6 June 1944, hundreds of fighters took off to take up their positions for the biggest invasion in the history of warfare. Squadrons designated the task of creating a false warning in the Pas de Calais used Hawkinge as their forward base. An additional Flying Control had been constructed of wood which stood on high ground to the west, personnel tried to cope with increased air traffic to the tune of over 9,000 aircraft. The day everyone had been waiting for had finally arrived, Hawkinge was again playing a vital role in the defence of Great Britain. ASR patrols by No.277 Squadron 'B' Flight, increased and on 6 June, No.91 Squadron awoke to find all their Spitfires had been painted with the invasion stripes. Despite it being D-Day, everyone on the squadron was disappointed, having expected increased activity by the Luftwaffe. They were scrambled to patrol the Solent early at St Omer, but no contact was made. During the evening of the following day, eleven Spitfires took part in a sweep over Rouen, Fecamp area and

On 05 June 1944, Grumman Avenger JZ434 '5L' No.855 (FAA) Squadron crash landed on take-off. Second Lieutenant P. Litherland (Pilot) and Second Lieutenant K. Belch (Observer) rescued Second Lieutenant C. Porter (AG/Bomb-aimer) from their aircraft. (K. Belch)

attacked an armoured car. On another occasion No.91 Squadron patrolling met P-47 Thunderbolts, one or two fired on the Spitfires, some USAAF pilots obviously not recognising invasion stripes.

Warrant Officer R.A.B. 'Red' Blumer (RAAF) re-joined No.91 Squadron on 8 June; he had been missing since 6 November 1943, after being shot down by flak in Spitfire XII EN626, crashing at Evreux, France, later escaping to Switzerland, then Spain, before being flown back to England. Just three days after his return back home, 'Red' turned up at Hawkinge as if nothing had happened. His skills would be needed to combat the V1 menace. When No.91 Squadron had moved to West Malling on 23 April 1944, 'Red' Blumer was still flying with the squadron. On 25 June 1944, he was taking off in Spitfire X1V RM617, when the aircraft spun, and he was killed.

RAF pilots were about to face a new challenge. In June 1944 Hitler began to unleash his vengeance or 'Vergeltungs' weapon, variously known as the Vl, Ram-Jet, Flying Bomb, Doodlebug, Buzz-Bomb, Divers, or 'Witch' as the Polish named them. Within days, faster fighter aircraft Tempests, Mustang IIIs, Mustang P51, Thunderbolt P47, Spitfires, including night fighter Mosquitoes, were being diverted to combat the V1 by day and night. It was no comfort to the pilots to realise that the Vls could explode if the warhead was hit, taking the attacking aircraft with it. The existence of the Vl was known as early as 1943 as a result of photographic reconnaissance flown by both the RAF and USAAF, supported by intelligence from the underground movement in Europe proved beyond doubt when the Polish secret army recovered warheads, and shipped them out on a Dakota through Bari in Italy. By 23 April 1944 it was clear that the V1 was operational. With a view to being able to provide some public early warning the radars at Swingate (Dover), Rye, Pevensey and Poling in No.11 Group RAF area had been modified.

The Army had gun operations rooms at Dover Castle and Chatham. Later, the Chain Home Low radar at South Foreland, Foreness and Whitstable was modified, and Sandwich was given a missile early warning facility. Information from these sources was filtered by No 11 Group HQ. In an effort to delay and reduce V1 launches, offensive strikes began, the majority from Kent airfields. From April No.11 group ensured that at least two fighters were on armed reconnaissance patrols over V1 storage areas and the logistical routes to them. At night sorties were flown by intruder aircraft, three Mosquito IXs were stationed at Manston and three at Hunsdon (Norfolk), on thirty-minute readiness.

V1 sites were such that they could only be attacked using new techniques, taught to pilots at a 'dummy' site in Wales. Both RAF Bomber Command

and the USAAF 8th Air Force heavy bombers made large-scale attacks. Such efforts made it possible to launch the D-Day invasion on 6 June 1944, before a Vl attack could interfere. The first Vl crossed the Channel on 13 June, flying over the Kent coast and was spotted by the Royal Observer Corps based in a Napoleonic War Martello Tower at Dymchurch. The V1 exploded in a wood at Swanscombe, near Gravesend.

Between D-Day and 15 June ASR operations were intense, with little concern for the V1 campaign. On 16 June a conference took place at No.71 AA Brigade to which the CO of No.2826 RAF Regiment Hawkinge was invited. That night V1s made an appearance, during that day Tempests Vs of No.3 and No.486 (NZ) Squadrons based at Newchurch ALG were heavily engaged. By midday, 244 V1s had been launched, forty-five crashing on take-off and falling straight into the Channel. Several passed over Hawkinge at between 500ft (1,524 metres) and 2,000ft (1,828 metres), their speed was estimated at being 180 to 380mph (290 to 612kmh); AA guns opened fire at Hawkinge and the surrounding area. Metrological balloons in the vicinity were a hazard; two Spitfire Vbs of No.91 Squadron narrowly missed colliding with them on patrol over the Dover straights on 17 June.

A B24 Liberator ditched off the coast of Littlestone on 20 June, which had been returning from attacking V1 launch sites in Northern France. B-24-J Liberator, serial number 42-95191 No.491 Bomb Group, was based at Medfield, Suffolk. A shell destroyed its nose section, killing the bombardier and navigator. Flying on one engine, the B24 forced-landed – two crew jumped out before the landing and died. Pilot/Navigator Second Lieutenant G.E. Tweed was trapped by his leg, Squadron Leader D. Duncan Morrell, an RAF doctor, waded out, but unable to reach the B24 due to the strong current, he commandeered an amphibious vehicle, returning to the aircraft. Squadron Leader Morell was awarded the OBE on 22 September 1944. The Co-Pilot, Lieutenant W.J. Holm; Radio Operator Technical Sergeant L.J. Boersma; Right Waist Gunner Staff Sergeant W.O. Trebing; and Tail Gunner Staff Sergeant R.E. Black survived. But First Lieutenant C.W. Stevens; Bombardier W. Weck; Navigator H. Meng; Staff Sergeant Fulbright, and Sergeant E. Peak perished. A Civil Defence Rescue Party led by John J. Frost, arrived on the scene and Army soldiers helped crew members.

On 24 June 1944, B26C-25-MO 41-35242 RJ-T 'Paper Dolly' was hit by flak attacking Noball targets at Prouville, France. The aircraft, flown by First Lieutenant C.M. Nunneley, and was part of a force of the 454th BS 323rd Bomb Group at Earls Colne, Essex, belly-landed at Hawkinge. Frist Lieutenant R.L. Boone was injured; Staff Sergeant G. Ruffun

RAF HAWKINGE

Bombardier/Navigator; Staff Sergeant G.J. Nugent Engineer/Gunner ,and Staff Sergeant R.L. Hypes, Top Gunner escaped uninjured. Coastal defences were increased by RAF regiments arriving at Hawkinge from 29 June, commanded by Lieutenant Colonel Garrick. From Hawkinge they deployed to various sites to defend against the V1. No.2733 remained at Hawkinge, No.2766 went to Brooklands, No.2797 to Littlestone, No.2890 to Rye, No.2891 Harrowbeer to Lydd, No.2892 and No.2889 moved to Rye. Their Bofors 40mm guns were easily transported and proved effective. Plans for the defence of London, Bristol and the Solent called for an Anti-Aircraft force totalling 528 heavy guns, 804 light guns and 400 searchlights. The Regiment's Light Anti-Aircraft (LAA) formed a substantial part of this task.

When the Vl raids began, a gun belt was formed between Folkestone and Beachy Head; thirty-one regiment squadrons were redeployed from airfields in the southeast between 28 June and 3 July 1944. A further twenty-one deployed in the Eastern Diver gun box, defending the Thames estuary. As the threat diminished, the LAA defences thinned out from 11 September onwards, the last squadrons were withdrawn between 4 and 9 October 1944. Two other regiments arrived at Hawkinge, No.2738 from St Eval moved to Eastbourne to defend the area against 'hit & run' raids, No.2740 from Morton-on-the-Marsh remained as a rifle regiment at Hawkinge. Most of these units moved to Europe with the 2nd Tactical Air Force (TAF), and deployed against attacks on airfields captured from the Germans.

No.277 Squadron Hawkinge were credited with the first V1 destroyed by an aircraft. On a routine ASR patrol on 29 June, Flight Sergeant A.M. Rollo Spitfire Vb AD377, accompanied by Flight Lieutenant P.D. O'Sullivan Spitfire Vb W3647, spotted a V1 off Dungeness, Flight Sergeant A.M. Rollo recalls:

> While on patrol I heard on the RT that a Diver was 2,500ft, flying at 300mph. I was then at 3,500ft, so I dived and engaged it from 500yds., closing to 150yds dead astern. First its port wing dropped, then its starboard wing and again the port wing, finally fluttering down to crash and explode in the sea, confirmed by Flight Lieutenant P.D. O'Sullivan.
>
> *Diver! Diver! Diver!*
> Brian Cull & Bruce Lander

Sub Lieutenant D.P. Davies (RNVR) No.854 (FAA) Squadron left Hawkinge on an early morning anti-shipping patrol on 9/10 July. TAG Leading Airman

AIR SEA RESCUE 1944

F. Shirmer saw a V1 flying at 2,000ft (610 metres), opening fire at a range of 700yds (640 metres) the V1 was destroyed. TAG Shirmer was mentioned in dispatches, giving a good reason for celebrations by the FAA.

On the night of 22/23 July 1944 the No.855 squadron lost two Avengers. Temp./Leading Airman Stanley Norman took off on his final mission from RAF Hawkinge in Avenger JZ550 with Sub Lieutenant R.K.H. Johnson (Pilot) and Temp./Sub Lieutenant J.A. Gleeson. The second Avenger JZ543 was flown by Sub Lieutenant J. Murphy, Sub Lieutenant R.W. Millington and Pilot Officer H.C. Selby, during the same attack on E-boats they were all killed, except Sub Lieutenant R.K.H. Johnson.

Brian Sherran was based at Hawkinge with an RAF Airfield Construction Unit, from where they visited Advanced Landing Grounds in the area, on maintenance work. An accomplished artist and illustrator, Brian made sketches of aircraft he saw:

> I was billeted just outside Hawkinge, and it was about 2200hrs when I heard what I thought was a German aircraft, a very deep engine note, and saw a light which I took to be a searchlight, we didn't know it was the engine. This thing came over Hawkinge and may have been 200ft up, straight over my billet and I was just shattered. Nobody tried to attack it, of course it wasn't taking evasive action. It seemed that all through that night they were coming over and it wasn't until morning that we all saw what they were. I remember it was a misty sort of day and these things were coming in low under the cloud base and were leaving the Spitfires and everything else right behind, it was really worrying.
>
> *Buzz Bomb Diary*
> KAHRS

A contingent of No.402 (RCAF) Squadron's Spitfire X1Vs operated from Tangmere on 8 August, returning to Hawkinge their new location. The remainder of the squadron moved to Hawkinge from Merston the same day, landing in four Dakotas with the advance party, others arrived at the airfield who had travelled by road or rail. During the night of 14/15 August the AA guns at Folkestone and Hythe shared in the destruction of sixteen V1s, all crashed in the Channel before reaching the coast. Flight Lieutenant A.F. Voak (RNVR) No.854 (FAA) Squadron sighted aV1 off Dunkirk. Flying Avenger, I FN854, Lieutenant Voak fired his forward guns, and

RAF HAWKINGE

Squadron Leader N.A. Kynsaton DFC & Bar No.91 Squadron, CO from 19 August 1943 until the evening of 15 August 1944. Leading the squadron on a sweep near St Trond in Spitfire IX MK909 was hit by flak he baled out, his body never recovered.

the V1 exploded. The following day Flying Officer E.A.H. Vickers (RCAF) Spitfire XV1 RM731, destroyed the first of three V1s for No.402 Squadron. Unfortunately the V1 crashed close to the squadron's dispersal, breaking windows of the pilots' rest room, causing no injuries but terrifying the residents. Flight Lieutenant D. Sherk Spitfire XIV RM731 and Flying Officer H. Cowan Spitfire XIV RM737 shot down two V1s, both crashed in the sea.

Air Chief Marshal Sir Roderick Hill KCB, MC, AFC & Bar, who commanded the ADGB, visited Hawkinge on 15 August. Respected, not least because he flew his own Tempest V JN786 'RH' when visiting airfields, and flew on sixty-two V1 patrols. During his visit he discussed, and listened to, pilots concerns and suggestions regarding the V1 campaign and aircraft they flew. Early on the morning of 16 August, Flying Officer E.A.H. Vickers (RCAF) No.402 (RCAF) Squadron intercepted a V1 off Cap Gris Nez; he opened fire and the V1 exploded south of the airfield. Shortly after, Flight Lieutenant Don Sherk Spitfire XIV RM731 and Flying Officer Henry Cowan Spitfire XIV RM737 destroyed two V1s which crashed in the sea.

AIR SEA RESCUE 1944

On 17 August Flying Officer D.W. Hastings (RCAF) No.402 Squadron flying Spitfire XIV RM743 while on patrol over Folkestone-Lympne, spotted and chased a V1 near Dymchurch which entered the gun belt. Flying Officer Hastings dived away too late, and was hit by AA fire and injured; he landed safely at Newchurch ALG. Flying Officer W.H. Whittaker No.402 Squadron was also hit by friendly fire; slightly injured, he managed to land at Hawkinge despite thick fog, which prevented any further operations that day.

Flight Sergeant Paul 'Pino' Leva was born on 24 April 1920 in Etterbeek, Belgium. Paul travelled to England to join the RAF, via France and Spain. Unfortunately, he was arrested and imprisoned by the Germans at Figueres on 7 December 1940. During transit to Miranda de Ebro – Lisbon, Portugal, he evaded his captors on 23 December 1940 at Barcelona; trekking across Europe, he finally found passage on the SS *Avocet* bound for Liverpool, arriving on 4 February 1941. Paul met Victor Reynolds who helped people find a safe passage through occupied Europe to England. Reaching England he joined the Army, later admitted to the RAF as an Aircraftman 2nd Class on 7 February 1941, soon promoted to Leading Aircraftman. On 10 May

Squadron Leader L.A. Childs and Flight Lieutenant Sir M. Bruce, RAF Regiment Hawkinge, examine the remains of a VI which crashed near Hawkinge during June/July1944 after being shot down.

No.350 (Belgium) Squadron flew both Spitfire IX and XIV variants. Here airmen rearm the two 20mm Hispano cannons. The IX also had four 0.303inch Browning machine guns, the XIV two 20mm Hispano cannon and four 0.303inch Browning machine guns. (André Bar)

Flying Officer M. Bentine, Intelligence Officer with No.350 (Belgium) Squadron, painting an emblem on the Spitfire IX flown by Squadron Leader M.G.L. Donnet. Michael Bentine CBE, who had lived in Folkestone, became well known as a comedian, actor and author. (André Bar)

he joined the ranks of Flying Personnel (Student). After two years of moving between RAF Depots, on 23 March 1943 he arrived at No.58 OTU at Balado Bridge-Kinross and joined No.350 (Belgian) Squadron, one of two Belgian Fighter Squadrons. By 13 September 1943 they were detached to West Malling, acting as high cover escorts for bombers over France, moving to Digby, then transferring Hawkinge.

No.350 Squadron left Hawkinge on 30 December 1943, to join No.135 Wing at Hornchurch, there they exchanged their Spitfire Vs for Spitfire IX of No.222 (Natal) Squadron who were at rest. Following a move to Peterhead via Hawkinge the squadron joined No.14 Group ADGB in March 1944, exchanging the Spitfire IX for the Spitfire V. Throughout July 1944 they were busy with a variety of operations, ranging from fighter sweeps, attacking shipping, escorting Mitchell bombers and dusk patrols, before moving again to Tangmere, Westhampnett and returning to Hawkinge, having been re-equipped the Spitfire XIV. The V1 Campaign was in full swing and Flight Sergeant Paul Leva was operating within the Fighter Patrol Zone; over the Tonbridge area he encountered a V1. It was market day in Tonbridge, despite the threat posed by the V1s, all seemed quite normal

Paul Leva who 'tipped' over a VI on 20 August 1944 in Spitfire XIV RM701 near Tonbridge, at home in 1973. The wing tip was given to him by groundcrew. Paul's family donated the artefact to Romney Marsh Wartime Collection (ex. Brenzett Museum). (P. Leva/Family)

on 20 August 1944. Opening fire at the V1, several strikes were seen, but the V1 continued flying. In desperation Paul remembered conversations about tipping over V1s using the Spitfire's wingtip, and decided to try this dangerous manoeuvre, described in the following extract from his own account:

> Positioning myself slightly underneath I placed my starboard wing tip under the port wing of the bomb. I came up slowly, made contact with it as softly as I could, and then moved the stick violently back and to the left. This made me enter a steep climbing turn and I lost sight of the bomb. I continued turning fast through 360 degrees, then I saw it well below me, going down steeply, hitting the ground and exploding with a blinding flash. The voice of the controller broke the spell with great urgency; 'turn back, turn back Immediately … the balloons.' Shaken back to imminent realities I made another steep turn. 'All right!' I said, 'I am going home now'. 'Any joy' – 'Yes, I got it, tipped it with my wing' – 'Good show', said the controller, the excited tone of his voice belying the soberness of his words. Soon after, I was landing at Hawkinge, after the ritual victory roll. As I was stepping out of my aircraft, some well-meaning fellow pilot came running from the dispersal. 'What have you done!' he shouted, 'Look at your wing tip', it was drooping sadly – 'You must have touched the ground while you did that roll!' 'Not the ground' – I answered – 'a Buzz Bomb – remember that the Intelligence Officer and his incredible story about upsetting the gyro? Well, it works'. I left him flabbergasted and went to make my report. Squadron mechanics soon removed and replaced the damaged wing tip and gave it to me as a souvenir.
>
> P. Leva – family collection

No.322 Squadron were ordered to fly their Spitfire XIVs from the ALG at Deanland to Hawkinge on 9 August 1944, where they were exchanged for Spitfire IXs. But as a stop-gap measure until the exchange was completed they were to use Spitfire IXs of No.350 Squadron. Spitfire IXs MK520 '3K-K' had a short career with No.322 Squadron; on 12 August Flying Officer Jonker flying MK520, and Flying Officer Burgwal took off to find targets in the British and Canadian operational areas of France and Belgium. Flying

AIR SEA RESCUE 1944

Spitfire XIV 'MN-S' RM693 No.350 (Belgium) Squadron. This aircraft also flew with No.130, 41 and 416 (Canadian) Squadrons. (André Bar)

Officer Jonker landed at Rennes with engine problems, leaving MK520 on the airfield and picked up by an Avon Anson. Wing Commander Tom Neil DFC, AFC, who had served as CO No.41 Squadrons Hawkinge, arrived at Rennes airfield. Seeing MK520 abandoned he made enquiries, no one knew anything about the aircraft, apart from it being an ex-No.322 Squadron aircraft. Unusually the Spitfire IX was found uncamouflaged, in a silver sheen. Tom Neil 'acquired' Spitfire IX MK520 for his own use, which had flown with No.302, 341, 145 and 350 Squadrons before being assigned to No.322 Squadron at Hawkinge.

WO/Air Gunner Ernest Cartwright, No.277 Squadron 'B' Flight based at Hawkinge during the V1 campaign recalls:

> One night, asleep in the Crew Room at Dispersal, I recall hearing an almighty bang. The next morning, we found the tail section of a V1 lying at the dispersal between two of our aircraft. I remember standing outside our crew room one day, watching a V1 approach over Folkestone with a Tempest

RAF HAWKINGE

Spitfire IX MK520 '3W-K' No.322(Dutch) Squadron Hawkinge was often flown by Flying Officer J. Jonker, seated on wing with cap. This aircraft was later abandoned at Rennes on 20 August 1944 and flown by Wing Commander Tom Neil DFC. (Wing Commander T. Neil DFC)

after it. Opening fire, hitting the V1 then flying through the explosion. We fully expected to see the Tempest in trouble, all in a day's work for those boys! My logbook notes that on 24 August 1944 we picked up a pilot of No.91 Squadron, the first to bring down a doodlebug by tipping it with his wing, after running out of ammunition.'

Buzz Bomb Diary
KAHRS

On Wednesday 23 August 1944, Flight Sergeant W.G. Austin No.401 (RCAF) Squadron Spitfire XIV RM686 intercepted a V1 over Ashford. Seeing the target Austin turned his Spitfire and dived. Approaching from behind near Maidstone, firing a five-second burst at the starboard wing, the diver lost height. Suddenly red rockets were fired in front him, braking to starboard he saw a column of black smoke rising from a point on his

Remains of a VI which crashed at Terlingham Manor Farm, Hawkinge during the V1 campaign during the summer of 1944.

starboard side. This interception was filmed by the Spitfire's cine gun, fitted to many Spitfire X1V.

On 24 August 1944, Spitfire XIV RM734 flown by Flying Officer W.S. Harvey (RCAF), shared a V1 destroyed with Flight Lieutenant Griffiths of No.274 Squadron, while Flight Lieutenant J.A.H.G. de Niverville (RCAF) in Spitfire XIV RM727 of No.402 (RCAF) Squadron, scored the Canadian unit's last kill, his combat report states:

> I first saw the diver about one mile east of Folkestone. I dived down on it but was forced to pull up again because of flak. I waited until the diver was clear of the flak and came down on it but was forced to pull up again because of flak. I waited until the diver was clear of the flak and came down again, firing close behind. I saw strikes on the starboard side, another burst and pieces flew off the wing. It wobbled from side to side and

quickly lost altitude. I looked back and saw a pillar of smoke rising into cloud. Green 2, who was slightly above saw the right wing fall off and a few seconds later saw a large chunk of the port wing fly off, the diver then went straight down.

Diver! Diver! Diver!
Brian Cull & Bruce Lander

The V1 fell on Bodsham near Wye, damaging twenty houses, there were no casualties; it was the last V1 destroyed by a squadron based at Hawkinge. On 27 August, pilots of No.350 Squadron escorted bombers to Europe. Spitfire XIV RM751 caught fire during engine start up and Flying Officer P. Pacco fortunately managed to exit his aircraft uninjured. On 1 September a V1 crashed at 'A' Flight dispersal No.350 (Belgium) Squadron, destroying three Spitfire XIVs, one being RM695. One pilot was slightly injured and everyone was shaken, it took several hours to clear the debris. Another crashed about a mile from the dispersal area, the VI appeared to perform a 'Victory' roll, before hitting the ground; the ceiling of the mess collapsed because of the explosion.

A sketch by Sir William Rothenstein of Squadron Leader M.G.L. Donnet DFC No.350 (Belgium) Squadron who was CO of the squadron from March 1944 until October 1944. (Ian Alan)

AIR SEA RESCUE 1944

Wing Commander M.G.L.M. Donnet, a Belgian, had escaped from Belgium with Leon Divoy. In May 1941, they became aware of a Stampe SV 4 biplane, locked in a hangar at a nearby chateau which was used by the Germans as a mess. Donnet and friends worked at night, undiscovered, until finally they had prepared the aircraft for flight by July 1941. They flew it to England, joining the RAF, later posted to No.64 Squadron. In March 1944 Donnet became CO of No.350 (Belgian) Squadron, moving to Hawkinge on 8 July 1944, before moving to Lympne on 29 September. Later, 23 October 1944, he was transferred back to Hawkinge as Wing Commander of No.132 and No.441(RCAF) Squadrons with Spitfire IXs:

> We re-equipped with new Spitfires IX, upon our move to Hawkinge, we could see the French coast in clear weather. We didn't like V1s, new soulless, mechanical menaces. Hawkinge was in the middle of 'Buzz-Bomb Alley', at one time there were about 200 aimed every day. We moved to join No.83 Tactical Group on the mainland of Europe. We moved all right, but only to Lympne. To add insult to injury they took away our Spitfire XIV's leaving us with No.130 Squadron's worn-out machines. I complained to the Belgian Authorities and eventually wrung from them a promise of a certain move to Belgium; and that something would be done about our Spitfires. Then they told me that although the squadron might go I wouldn't! Instead, I was posted to Hawkinge as Wing Commander, I was happy, but sorry to leave my Belgian friends.
>
> *Flight to Freedom*
> Wing Commander M.G.L.M. Donnet

No.2826 RAF Regiment prepared to move to RAF Dunsfold on 1 September. Vehicles were provided by Hawkinge, the following day staff and stores, with six vehicles left Hawkinge. Not long after No.2955 RAF Regiment arrived at Hawkinge from Selsey, and No.2892 RAF Regiment left for Tangmere, No.2813 arriving from Biggin Hill.

In the early morning of 3 September, two Mustang IIs of No.2 Squadron were reported missing during a Tactical Reconnaissance from Beny sur Mer. Flying Officer C.J. Blundell-Hill was thought to have been forced down in enemy territory, during a Tactical Reconnaissance flight, but in fact landed Mustang II FR918 at Hawkinge. His companion, Flying Officer R.C. Williams, crash landed Mustang II FR920 but was uninjured. On 14 September, Spitfire

RAF HAWKINGE

IX NH405 flown by Flight Lieutenant R.G. Sim No.441 (RCAF) Squadron was hit by flak attacking motor transport, but was able to gain altitude and turned for home. However, Williams baled out near Vlissingen, Holland, and was found by two friendly locals who took him in; he eventually made his way back to England. No.441 and No.132 Squadrons remained at Hawkinge, where the weather and the poor conditions at Hawkinge were a problem, as they shared the airfield with No.6402, No.6130 Servicing Echelon and No.2767 RAF Regiment, it was rather crowded.

No.75 (New Zealand) Bomber squadron took in two operations on 17 September 1944, based at Mepal, Cambridgeshire, equipped with Lancaster I and IIIs, the target Boulogne. Lancaster III PB430 was hit by flak, Squadron Leader G. Gunn (NZ) flew his damaged aircraft back over the Channel. He decided to land at Hawkinge, but the Lancaster overshot the short runway and crashed. Squadron Leader Gunn was seriously injured and his navigator was also injured. Flying Officer A. Millar, Bomb Aimer, was seriously injured, and Sergeant J. Bruce Flight Engineer was killed. Flight Lieutenant W. Naismith; Flying Officer C. Robertson, Mid-Upper Gunner; Flying Officer S. Haynes, Rear Gunner, were all injured and taken to Kent & Canterbury Hospital.

No.460 (RAAF) Squadron based East Kirkby were part of an attack on Emmerich on the Dutch coast frontier on 17/18 October. A force of thirty-one Lancasters of No.460 Squadron were scheduled to attack the target. One of these Lancaster PB254 'AR-K', commanded by Flying Officer V.K Gratton (Pilot), was hit by flak, incendiaries had penetrated the fuselage, causing severe damage to the inner engine and starboard flap. Flight Sergeant K.G. Potter, Bomb Aimer; Sergeant D.L. Amos, Flight Engineer; and Warrant Officer N.E. Newton, Navigator, baled out. Priest and Amos were taken PoW, Potter was killed. Flying Officer V. K, Gratton nursed the aircraft home, landing at Hawkinge; Flight Sergeant A.V. Pearson; Sergeant C.W. Priest, Air Gunner; and Flight Sergeant L.C.C. McNaught, Air Gunner, were unhurt. Meanwhile, Walrus I W2766 with Lieutenant R. Mander, Squadron Leader Hall and Sergeant Cartwright left Hawkinge in search of another Lancaster which had ditched in the sea. They were assisted by Flight Lieutenant T.G.V. Roden, Spitfire Vb BL674, and Flight Sergeant K. Moore, Spitfire Vb BL275, who spotted the crew swimming in the sea off Hardelot. Seven airmen were saved by the Walrus and transferred to HSL No.190. Later that day a glider ditched in the sea but was located by Lieutenant R. Mander, Walrus I W2766; four crew who had been sitting on the glider's wing were later transferred to Royal Navy launch ML22 based at Dover.

AIR SEA RESCUE 1944

Flying Officer Roger Hoornaert (with lifejacket) joined No.350 (Belgium) Squadron on 22 June 1944, becoming Flight Commander 'B' Flight. Shot down on 4 April 1945, he crashed near Lingen and was taken PoW. Note blister hangar, photo taken September 1944. (P. Deman)

No.350 (Belgium) Squadron moved to Lympne on 29 September 1944. Although expected, the squadron had to leave their Spitfire XIVes at Hawkinge for No.130 Squadron, also based at Lympne, as part of the ADBG, and No.350 Squadron moved to the 2nd TAF in Holland. The following day No.132 and No.441 (RCAF) Squadrons No.125 Wing arrived from Deurne, Belgium. They were equipped with Spitfire IXbs, having had to leave their Spitfire IXes in France, and would remain at Hawkinge until December 1944.

During the morning of 30 September 1944, six Dakotas landed at Deurne. Not long after, groundcrews started to unload drop-tanks and other equipment. No.125 Wing was due to take off for Hawkinge at 1400hrs, but had to wait for the arrival of the Spitfire XIVs. The Dakota crews were keen to see Antwerp before leaving, so while their aircraft were being loaded, the men were taken into the city. Settling in at Hawkinge everyone began to enjoy the luxury of serving at a permanent base, groundcrews were looking forward to a few days leave.

No.6132 Service Echelon arrived during the afternoon of 1 October, the servicing unit for No.132 Squadron and No.441 Squadrons. Flying was initially for air tests and formation practice, until 5 October when Spitfires escorted twenty-four Bostons to Nijmegen, Holland. On 5/6 October, both squadrons were ordered to escort bombers to oil plants in the Ruhr area. Taking-off the propeller of Flying Officer J.A. McIntosh Spitfire LFIX ML191, struck the ground, Flying Officer R.J Lacerte had to return to Hawkinge when his wing tank failed on Spitfire LFIX MH309. Flight Lieutenant R.G Lake had engine trouble and was escorted back to the airfield by Warrant Officer2 H.G McClinton Spitfire LFIX MJ301.

No.26 (Army Cooperation) Squadron based at Lee-on-Solent were ordered to transfer to Hawkinge on 6 October 1944 for a special assignment, equipped with the Hurricane IIc, armed with four formidable 20mm Hispano cannons. Squadron Leader B.J.A. Fleming the CO the first to arrive at Hawkinge, was taken to Dover for a conference aboard HMS *Erebus*. That afternoon the squadron took off from Lee-on-Solent heading for Hawkinge led by Squadron Leader Roberts. Flight Lieutenant Shepherd's Hurricane's engine cut, but managed to land in a field where several children were working, fortunately without injuring them. Unperturbed, he walked back to the airfield at Lee-on-Solent, climbed into another Hurricane and set off for Hawkinge, where they waited three days. On 10 October the operation was cancelled, No.26 Squadron returned to Tangmere disgruntled.

A section of No.2707 RAF Regiment arrived at Hawkinge from RAF Pett on 7 October 1944, they were directed to Swingfield ALG to prepare the airfield for the main party to arrive on 9 October. They immediately set to work erecting tents; billeted at the ALG they moved to Hawkinge on 18 October to man the AA guns. Other arrangements were made to undertake rifle training and a War Course at the Hythe ranges.

Throughout October 1944 No.441 and No.132 Squadrons escorted bombers heading for targets in Europe. On one day alone they escorted 500 Lancasters and Halifaxs, witnessing the terrible sight of aircraft being hit by flak, before returning to Hawkinge. Pilot Officer R.T. Greer Spitfire LFIX ML345 of No.441 Squadron, returning from escort duties, ground looped his aircraft, when the 'drop tank' partially fell off. There were off days when there was no operational flying, an opportunity for instruction on the Link trainer, or even local flying and sometimes instructional films were shown. No.277 Squadron were notified on 1 October by Squadron Leader Halliwell 11 Group, that the squadron's HQ Maintenance Flight and 'A' Flight would move from Shoreham to Hawkinge. On 5 October, aircraft – including two Walruses – left for Hawkinge. The main party, MT vehicles and other equipment arrived in the evening. His Majesty King Peter of

AIR SEA RESCUE 1944

Yugoslavia arrived at Hawkinge on 19 October and spent time at No.441 and No.132 dispersal areas, chatting casually to the pilots.

Squadron Leader Tom Neil DFC and Bar, AFC, a fighter pilot, often flew a Douglas C53 Skytrooper ferrying passengers between St Dizier and England, returning servicemen for leave. On one occasion in October 1944, he had taken off in bad weather from St Dizier, with his co-pilot Sergeant Smith and twenty-five passengers. Diverting to Amiens he picked up his fiancée – which was against regulations, so it was decided that the young lady should dress as a man and tuck her hair under her cap. The flight was uneventful, but the weather got worse and Neil considered returning to base, nearly flying straight into Beachy Head. Keeping the English coast to his left he flew along to Dungeness, an area he was familiar with. Flying past Folkestone he arrived over Hawkinge unannounced, where he put down – landing heavily. Bouncing along the grass runway the C53 came to a halt and everyone heaved a sigh of relief, the passengers collected their travel warrants and continued onto London, where Squadron Leader Neil and his fiancée spent the night. The following day Neil flew his fiancée from Heston back to Amiens in the C53.

Two pilots of No.441 (RCAF) Squadron were lost on 28 October, escorting Lancasters which were bombing Cologne. Flying Officer A.J. McDonald Spitfire LFIX MK602 and Pilot Officer V.A.G. Brochu Spitfire LFIX MJ301 were last seen descending through cloud, they also reported instruments freezing up. It was later found that the two Spitfires had spun into the ground near Brussels having become lost in cloud; both were buried at Leopoldsburg Cemetery, Brussels. Squadron Leader R.H. Walker CO No.441 Squadron, received a telephone call on 31 October from Flight Lieutenant R.G. Sim, who was also reported missing – he was back in England and in good health!

With the successful outcome of the V1 campaign an exhibition took place in London, two airmen of No.2767 RAF Regiment, Hawkinge, assisted. The event was visited by Squadron Leader Gill No.2767 and members of the London Defence Artillery. In November, Hawkinge was covered in snow, which prevented operational flying. All ranks were involved in clearing the snow. Three sections formed from No.6402 Service Echelon, Special Servicing Flight, Retrieve & Repair Party, No.2767 RAF Regiment, No.6130 Service Echelon, No.277 Squadron, No.4657 Works Flight and Workshop personnel. There was good news though – the CO insisted that cooks would not parade for these duties, ensuring a constant supply of hot food be provided for all concerned.

RAF HAWKINGE

On 16 November No.441 Squadron escorted 418 Lancasters bombing Duren. Flying Officer A.B. Jewett Spitfire IX MJ453, failed to return to Hawkinge. He was last heard over the RT reporting that his engine was faulty. Baling out, the Canadian landed in friendly territory and was assisted by US Army soldiers. Other pilots flying escort on 21 November, led by Wing Commander Donnet, reported seeing three vertical contrails over Soesterburg, Henglo; these were V2 rockets launched against England following the V1 campaign.

No.277 Squadron patrolling on 27 November, found wreckage floating in the Channel, Mosquito NF XVII HK317 No.456 Squadron based at Ford, Sussex had ditched, the crew Warrant Officer J.L. Mulhall and Flying Officer J.D. Jones were killed. They were searching for an He III, a special aircraft which had a V1 mounted under the wing near the fuselage, to be launched from the aircraft but had limited success by the end of the V1 campaign. The number of V1s which fell on Kent, between 13 June and 29 March numbered 1,444, in Sussex 880 and Surrey 295. The total figure, on land, was 5,823 reported by the Civil Defence Authority, 2,242, or 41 per cent, landed on London. Many more crashed into the sea.

By 29 November, accommodation improved at Hawkinge when an additional hostel, 'Linton', was taken over by WAAFs, who redecorated the premises. As well as their normal duties, evening classes were organised, such as cooking, dressmaking and motor mechanics, with an average attendance of twenty airwomen based at Hawkinge. Discussion groups took place, with such subjects as 'The Home Budget' and 'Should married women have a career', in preparation for the time when many WAAFs would leave service.

No.451 (RAAF) Squadron arrived in the UK from Italy on 1 December 1944 and were transported to Hawkinge from Folkestone station. The following morning, the squadron was given twenty-one days' disembarkation leave, ordered to return to Hawkinge on 27 December. No.451 Squadron equipped with the Spitfire IXB, would re-equip with Spitfire XVI during January 1945.

Sergeant Herbert Biggs, a mechanic with No.451 (RAAF) Squadron, appreciated the accommodation at Hawkinge and being quartered in billets rather than tents:

> I had relatives in England. The food was better, the worst aspect was cold. It was a winter, Christmas, when we landed there, and it was freezing. It didn't matter what you did, you

couldn't get warm. They gave us four blankets and even that was cold, I scrounged paper and put it in between each blanket, that stopped the cold a lot. So long as you could get a decent sleep. There would be snow everywhere, you would go to your aircraft and be changing a plug or something like that. The spanner would slip, you wouldn't feel it, but you would see the back off your hand was bleeding. It was that cold.

We Together
Adam Lunney

No.2709 (AA) Squadron RAF Regiment attached to Hunmanby Moor, proceeded by road to Hawkinge on 21 December. By midday on 31 December, the squadron was operational with four guns, and 201 personnel including eight officers and 159 other ranks. Aware their stay at Hawkinge would be brief, they were soon engaged in daily routine and training exercises. No.611 (West Lancashire) Squadron now at Hawkinge, had been based well away from much activity in the Shetlands since 3 October 1944, flying Spitfire VIIs. Nine aircraft of No.611 Squadron landed at Hawkinge on 31 December 1944, commanded by Squadron Leader P.R. McGregor CdG. Their mission was to escort bombers to Europe; at the beginning of January 1945 the weather was poor, and for two days they suffered lectures and inspections.

Chapter 11

The Last Year of War: 1945
Peace Returns to Hawkinge

As Herman Göring, Commander of the Luftwaffe, ordered an onslaught against Allied airfields in Belgium and Holland, No.611 (West Lancashire) Squadron RAuxAF had been rushed to Hawkinge, then across to Ursel in Belgium, to escort the streams of RAF and USAAF daylight bombers flying relentlessly into the heart of the Nazi war industries. The Me262, the new Luftwaffe jet fighter, was sometimes sighted and it was clear to all that the war in Europe must be ended soon if the Allies were to avoid enormous casualties from these and the V2 rockets then being launched.

The wreckage of 'Mary's Sister' B17 42-97528 of the 563rd BG 388th 8th USAAF which crashed at Hawkinge on 1 January 1945.

THE LAST YEAR OF WAR: 1945

On New Year's Day 1945, a B17G of the 563rd BS 388th BG 8th USAAF, crash landed on the airfield, colliding with the building which housed photo equipment. The aircraft was assigned to the 563rd BS based at Knettishall, Suffolk. During a raid on rail and airfields in central Germany, 'Mary's Sister' 42-97528, was hit by a flak over Frankfurt. The pilot, Second Lieutenant J.F. Reuther, assisted by co-pilot, Second Lieutenant R.O. Helminiak, nursed the aircraft home. Eventually reaching the Kent coast without further incident, they tried to put down at Hawkinge. As personnel rushed out of workshops and hangars to see the bomber, it was obvious things would not end well. Rescue teams arrived on the scene where they found a site of devastation; several airmen lay among the wreckage of the B17, obviously dead. The pilot and co-pilot miraculously survived wounded, as did Staff Sergeant Ray Ward R/O, but Second Lieutenant H.W. Swanson, Navigator, with Sergeant F. P. Thielke, Ball Turret Gunner; Sergeant J. Haskett, Top Turret Gunner; Sergeant M. Smith, Waist Gunner; Sergeant A.C Kiss, Waist Gunner; Sergeant V.E. Koon, Tail Gunner were all killed in action. Due to injuries sustained, Second Lieutenant R.O. Helminiak was grounded. Following the rescue attempt, Flying Officer B.A.W. Chamberlain, Station Anti-Gas & Fire Officer, was commended for his bravery.

From 1 January Wing Commander N.N. Crossley DSO, DFC, took command of Hawkinge, posted from Detling, replacing Wing Commander R.F. Watts who proceeded to Air Ministry Unit before being posted overseas. Briefed by Wing Commander M. Donnet DFC on 5 January, Spitfire VIIs of No.611 Squadron finally set off to escort 150 Lancasters returning from a raid on marshalling yards at Ludwigshafen, Germany. Flight Sergeant Mack's Spitfire had engine problems, and he decided to land in Europe.

Lieutenant Knusden forced-landed Spitfire IX MA843 at Charleroi, Belgium on 5 January following engine trouble and was slightly injured. The first operation flown by No.451 (RAAF) Squadron, also took place on 5 January 1945, and was to cover withdrawal for 150 Lancasters bombing Ludwigshafen am Rhine. Six Spitfires had taken part for this operation, and all returned to base. The following day on a similar mission, No.451 Squadron lost one of its pilots when two Spitfires collided over Ostend. Flight Lieutenant J.D. Wallace Spitfire XVI SM333 struck Spitfire XVI SM384 flown by Pilot Officer E.R. Newberry. The tail section broke away from Spitfire SM333, Wallace was killed, Newberry crashed but survived and was taken to hospital in Ostend suffering from shock. By 21 January No.451 Squadron had become non-operational, receiving orders to move from Hawkinge to Manston on 11 February 1945. There was some good news on 6 January, when Flight Sergeant Mack returned to the squadron, having crashed Spitfire IX BS282 at Urzel; he was found and eventually returned to the UK. News was finally received that Lieutenant Knusden was in hospital in Brussels, having suffered a fractured skull and fractured patella.

Snow covered Hawkinge, and pilots received heated clothing, a few had already been issued with this welcome addition to their flying gear. With snow preventing much flying, No.611 Squadron attended lectures on Aircraft Recognition and Squadron Leader Brown CO of No.277 Squadron gave a talk about Air Sea Rescue. With the invasion of Europe underway, Major Englander Intelligence Officer 9th USAAF, lectured aircrew on German methods of interrogating PoWs.

No.611 Squadron were notified they would be re-equipped with the Mustang IV in February 1945; pilots were issued with the relevant pilots' notes. Four Mustang IVs arrived at Hawkinge, Squadron Leader Seaton instructed four pilots of No.611 Squadron regarding these aircraft. On 2 March 1945, the new Mustangs were flown by Flying Officer Smith, Flight Lieutenant Partridge and Flying Officer Beard, returning to Hawkinge; all agreed the Mustang was an excellent aircraft. The weather had improved by 14 January, good news as an operation was due to take place. At 0800hrs Squadron Leader Seaton briefed the pilots, taking off at 0920hrs on a fighter sweep over Munster Rheine, escorting Lancasters bombing Bielefeld and Alt. During the flight a few caught sight of the new twin-engine Me262 jet fighter flying above their formation, but no contact took place. Before returning to Hawkinge, pilots of No.611 Squadron witnessed the incredible sight of a V2 launched north of the Hague as it rose vertically at tremendous speed.

No.278 Squadron moved to Thorney Island from Martlesham Heath on 15 February 1945 'B' Flight moved to Hawkinge on 24 February, assigned to Coastal Command, equipped with the Walrus under command of Squadron Leader Wallens, and tasked to operate ASR flights over the Channel. By 28 February a Walrus was on standby at Hawkinge. The first rescue by 'B' Flight took place on 2 March, when CPO Barley, Warrant Officer W.L. Butler and Flight Sergeant W.J. Propart took off in Walrus I K8554, vectored to a glider still afloat off Beachy Head, with its pilot sitting on its wing, holding his Mae West. Landing close by, the crew of the Walrus prepared to tie a rope to the dinghy when a rescue launch arrived and rescued the pilot. No.504 (County of Nottingham) Squadron RAuxAF

THE LAST YEAR OF WAR: 1945

which had been based at Manston since 13 August 1944, moved to Hawkinge on 25 February 1945. Twelve Spitfire IXEs landed at Hawkinge and were soon joined by No.6504 Service Echelon. During their brief stay, four Spitfires made an uneventful weather reconnaissance flight to the Valenciennes/Eindhoven areas, returning to Hawkinge. The following day the squadron moved to Maldegem in Belgium to escort Lancasters bombing Gelsenkirchen, Germany.

On 3 March, sixteen Spitfires and four Mustang IVs of No.611 Squadron took off and headed for Hunsdon, their new base. The squadron had gradually been converting to the Mustang IV throughout March 1945. No.504 Squadron escorted RAF squadrons bombing sites in Europe, on each of these missions at least twelve Spitfires IX took part, during which there were no losses, ending No.504 Squadron's duties at Hawkinge. At 1210hrs on 8 March, Warrant Officer S.W. Loader and his crew, Flying Officer A.L. Kennedy and Flight Sergeant H.G Humphreys, were scrambled from Hawkinge to investigate a sinking ship and look for survivors south of Beachy Head. Arriving, they could see three lifeboats and two rafts floating among wreckage, survivors had been picked up an RN ship. A Curtis Seagull (a floatplane version of the Seamew), arrived to continue the search and Warrant Officer Loader returned to Hawkinge. The British merchant ship *Lornaston* was torpedoed and sunk by *U-275* in the Channel north-west of Fécamp, HMS *Holmes*, a frigate commanded by Lieutenant Commander P.S. Boyle, RNVR, and the British tug HMS *Palencia* together rescued forty-eight survivors.

No.278 Squadron often witnessed gliders heading for Germany during efforts for the US Army crossing the Rhine. On 24 March Squadron Leader Wallens, Squadron Leader Bowring and Pilot Officer A. Winfield were patrolling Folkestone-Gris-Nez and saw two gliders hit the sea, an HSL was immediately vectored to the scene. Sixteen men were rescued, eight of which were picked up by No.278 Squadron from Hawkinge. Later a B24 Liberator was seen afloat surrounded by empty dinghies; no crew were seen. This turned out to be a B24 of the 448th BG which had been damaged, the crew had baled out over Manston.

No.504 Squadron left Hawkinge on 28 March 1945, for Colerne for conversion training to the new Meteor III jet fighter – a new era was about to begin. By April 1945 No.453 (RAAF) had moved from Matlask to Lympne, but their stay at Lympne was short, moving this time to Hawkinge on 2 May 1945. Their first task the following day was to escort a Dakota taking Queen Wilhelmina of the Netherlands to the Advanced Landing Ground, known by the British as B.77. Arriving safely, the Spitfire XVIs headed back to Hawkinge.

No.124 Squadron had been engaged in dive-bombing attacks on V2 rocket sites – Operation *Big Ben* in the Hague, Netherlands – since 14 February. For two months they continued flying the Spitfire IX HFe in this role from Coltishall. On 7 April they moved to Hawkinge in No.11 Group, escorting bombers to Europe, by now Allied armies had moved north from Arnhem and Nijmegen. From Hawkinge they took part on raids on Hamburg, Bayreuth, Luneburg, Heligoland and the last Wangerooge which took place on 25 April, using the airfields in France B.26 and B.90 Petit Brogel. On 23 April the squadron took part in a display over the MG Motor factory at Abingdon, Oxfordshire, landing at Abingdon for lunch. Their stay at Hawkinge ended on 27 April, when they moved to Hutton Cranswick.

Tuesday 8 May 1945 marked the end of the Second World War in Europe; the only flying undertaken was a training flight by No.278 Squadron. It was the day everyone had dreamed of, there was great excitement at Hawkinge. In the Officers' Mess, airmen, NCOs and WAAFs, all joined in the festivities. At the same time, those who had died during the war years were remembered; many airmen and pilots of the RAF and several of the Luftwaffe had been buried at Hawkinge (cemetery).

That evening the CO of Hawkinge, Wing Commander M.N. Crossley DSO, DFC, gave an unprecedented address on the BBC to King George VI on behalf of the RAF. There was a ceremony the following morning at Hawkinge with the CO taking the parade. That night a party took place, with servicemen and women of all ranks enjoying themselves. At 2400hrs. an effigy of Adolf Hitler was burnt on a massive fire. An Austin Ruby car which had careered off the road at Paddlesworth was retrieved, its occupants had been celebrating in Folkestone. Someone decided it was a good idea to take-off in one of the RAF Hillman vans, it drove around the perimeter of the airfield, with several revellers clinging on, waving certain ladies' garments!

These were later observed flying from various items of RAF property within the airfield. Wing Commander Crossley turned a blind eye to the proceedings but had great difficulty in preventing trees and plants being dug up, which had been planted around the station. Various shows took place in the gymnasium, organised by ENSA; two of the celebrities taking part were 'Stinker' Murdoch and Kenneth Horne, who would become famous for the radio programme *Round the Horne*. The 'Squadronaires Band', formed by the RAF in 1939, gave a fine performance. Other popular entertainments enjoyed at Hawkinge included Ralph Reader's *Gang Show* and the Sky-Rockets Dance Band.

THE LAST YEAR OF WAR: 1945

Following the VE celebrations, Hawkinge gradually returned to some form of normality, everyone's future was uncertain and victory over Japan had yet to happen. In the coming days, aircraft escorted King Peter II of Yugoslavia, who had also been exiled in England in June 1941 with his government, when he returned to his homeland, taking-off from Hawkinge.

There was no further operational flying until 12 May, when Squadron Leader D.G. Andrews DFC led No.453 (RAAF) Squadron, which took off to patrol the Channel Islands of Guernsey and Jersey, protecting troops landing at Guernsey harbour when supplies were being unloaded. On 14 May, No.453 Squadron was notified of a move to Acklington, to take place on 23 May, No.451 Squadron also at Hawkinge would move to Skaebrae, Orkney Islands, on 17 May, both squadrons finally being disbanded in Wunsdorf, Germany, on 21 January 1946. Wing Commander D.F. Willington RAF Regiment, arrived at Hawkinge on 16 May to visit the airfield and Swingate (Radar station) in preparation for the return of No.2707 (AA) Squadron, who had moved from Swingate to the RAF Regiment Gunnery School Hunmanby Moor on 2 May 1945, arriving back at Swingate on 30 May.

No.567 Squadron was formed on 1 December 1943 at Detling, from No.1624 (Anti-Aircraft Cooperation) Flight. The duties of the AACU included target-towing with Miles Martinets, gun-laying and searchlight practice with Airspeed Oxfords and simulated attacks on exercising troops with Hawker Hurricanes. On 13 June 1945, the squadron left Hornchurch for Hawkinge; a convoy of eighteen vehicles with two troop carriers arrived, the unit's aircraft took off for Hawkinge at 1400hrs. Two days later, after groundcrews and pilots had familiarised themselves with their temporary home, all aircraft were ready for operations, the first solo flights took place. Flying Officer Milne took off in Spitfire Vb AR518, on return to Hawkinge he managed to crash land, the aircraft was a write off.

Flight Sergeant Colquhoun crashed when Hurricane IIc LE399 overshot the runway at Hawkinge on 27 June, the pilot climbed out of his aircraft uninjured, the undercarriage had collapsed and the propeller had smashed. Following this incident, the CO of No.567 Squadron, Squadron Leader H.J. Bond, lectured aircrew concerning the problems operating from Hawkinge. Two Vultee Vengeance IV aircraft, serving with No.567 Squadron set off on 2 July for No.3505 Servicing Unit, the same day three Spitfire Vbs arrived and Spitfire XVI, possibly SM278 '14-M'. On 27 July a Vengeance belly-landed, Flying Officer Howes had tried all emergency methods of lowering the undercarriage, but all had failed.

RAF HAWKINGE

All Vengeance aircraft were grounded on 8 August when, during routine maintenance, the fuel tank covers were found to be leaking and had to be replaced. This caused a major problem for No.567 Squadron, who suspended all towing activities until replacement covers arrived and were fitted. As a temporary measure, three Martinets arrived from Bradwell Bay, although they were considered by pilots unsuitable for towing drogues. This may have been why, on the following day, Flying Officer Smith managed to taxi a Martinet into an unmarked gun-pit near the flight dispersal. Rumours that the squadron was to move to Manston persisted, this was confirmed when everyone was informed that they were leaving on 20 August. Problems with the Vengeance continued when an inspection of the flexible hoses used in the fuel system showed them to be faulty and would need replacing, leaving the aircraft unserviceable.

Although there was good news when 'VJ' day was declared (Victory over Japan). This was royally celebrated over a two-day period the 15/16 August 1945. By 21 August the main party of No.567 Squadron left Hawkinge for Manston, leaving behind the Vengeance aircraft. Four Oxford and nine Spitfires set off for Manston, and on 23 August the first serviceable Vengeance joined them, as the fuel hoses had been replaced. Operating on a much-reduced scale during August, No.567 Squadron had reduced the strategic advantage it had over Hawkinge. The Oxfords and Spitfire XVIs and Vbs and two Vengeance aircraft remained with the squadron until disbanded on 15 June 1946 at West Malling.

An officer accompanied by an NCO from the Public Relations section of Overseas HQ (RAAF), arrived at Hawkinge on 16 May to interview pilots of No.453 Squadron, about their experiences of having crashed in Europe. They were in luck as three pilots were available, Flying Officer N. Marsh had been taken PoW, and Flying Officer W. Tonkin who had evaded capture when he crashed in Holland and was befriended by the Dutch until the war ended. Lieutenant W.R. Bennett gave his account of being shot down on 24 December 1944 in Spitfire XVI SM197 following an attack on a V2 target near Hague Harlot, Holland. This mission was an attack on flats where German soldiers operating on V2 sites were billeted. Twelve Spitfires of No.453 Squadron had taken part in this dangerous mission. Returning to the squadron, celebrations were spoilt when they were informed they were moving to Skaebrae, Scotland, not Acklington. Shortly after, a signal was received at Hawkinge to the effect that No.453 Squadron's move to Skaebrae was delayed, for operational reasons, much to their relief. No.453 Squadron moved from Hawkinge to Lasham on 14 June 1945, eventually joining other squadrons of the 2nd Tactical Air Force in Germany, where they were disbanded on 21 January 1946 at Wunsdorf, Germany.

THE LAST YEAR OF WAR: 1945

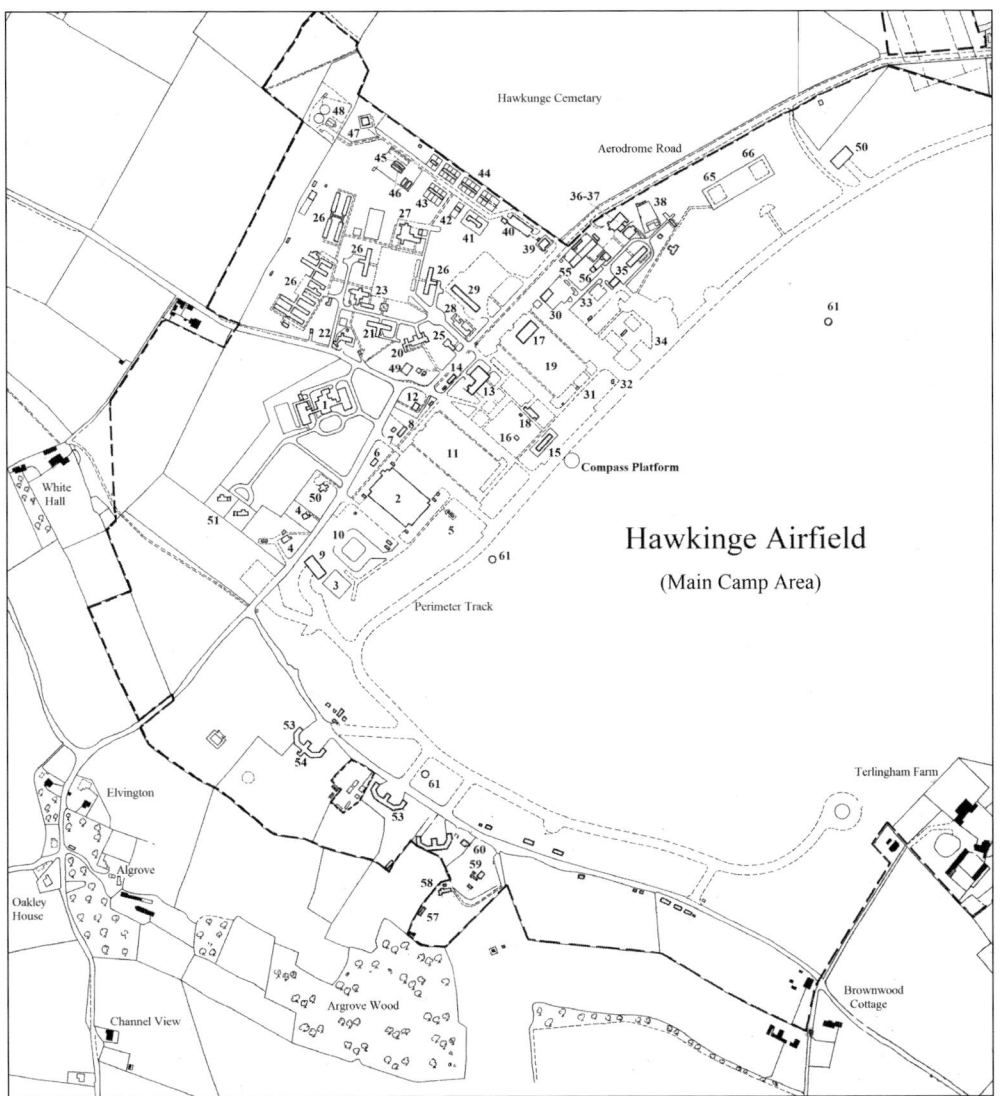

The western side of RAF Hawkinge as it appeared in 1945 detailing the main camp area, many of the buildings remained intact for several years.

No.234 Squadron prepared for a move to Hawkinge from Bentwaters on 22 August 1945, equipped with the Spitfire VIs; they were joining the Armament Practice Camp at Hawkinge they had already spent most of the time on cine gun camera work. On arrival at Hawkinge the squadron spent a few weeks on gunnery and bombing practice. Before leaving Bentwaters, they were supposed to take part in an exercise to intercept a flight of

RAF HAWKINGE

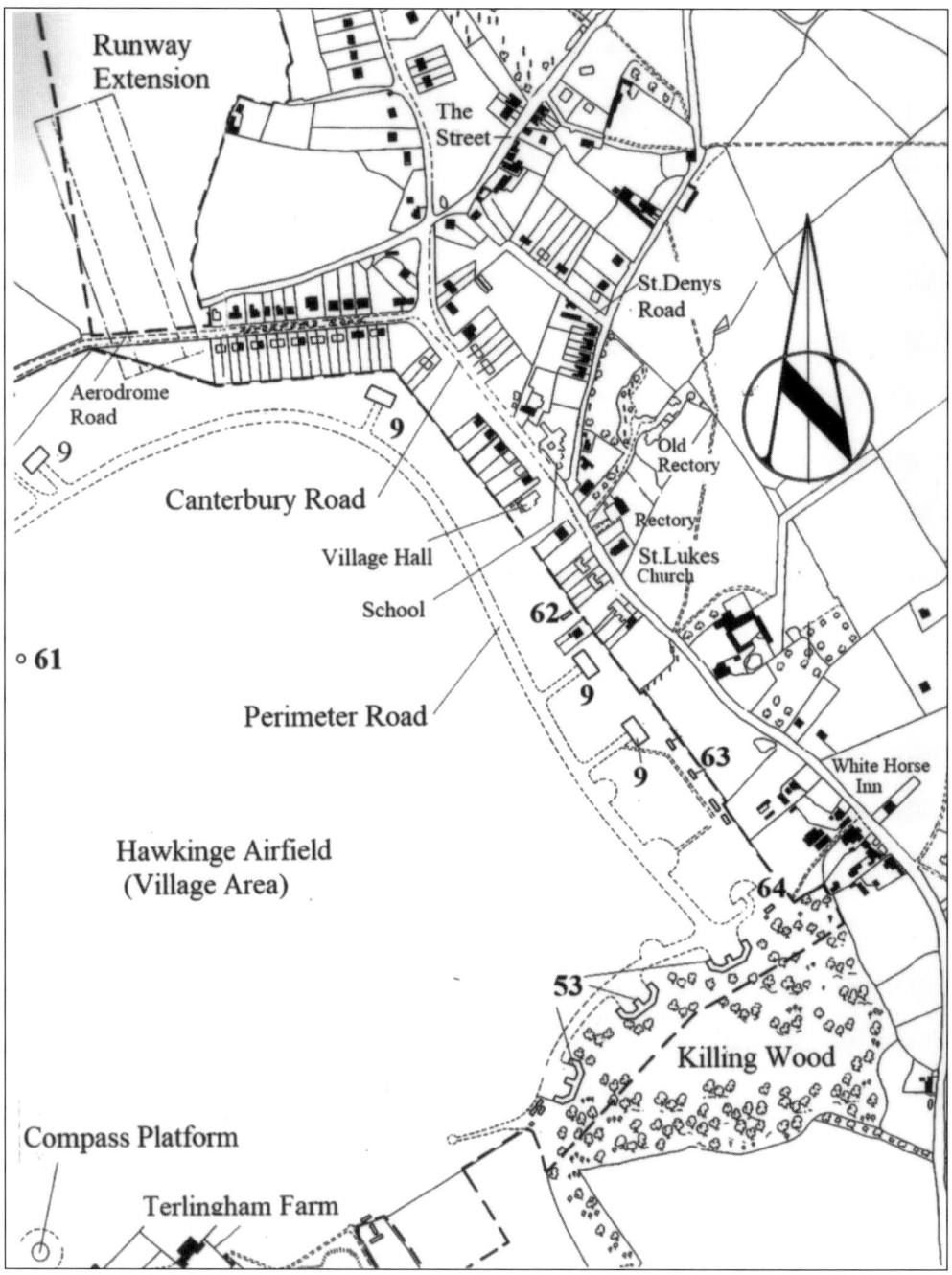

The eastern area RAF Hawkinge in 1945, proposed runway extension which crossed over Aerodrome Road is shown on this drawing.

THE LAST YEAR OF WAR: 1945

RAF Hawkinge - Schedule of buildings.
May 1945.

1. Officers mess & quarters.
2. No.1 Flight shed.
3. Aviation petrol installation.
4. Officers married quarters.
5. Watch hut (temporary.)
6. Store.
7. Inflammable store.
8. Lubricant Store.
9. Blister Hangar.
10. Aviation petrol installation.
11. No.2 Flight shed (war damaged.)
12. 'Bijou' (57th. Eng.
13. Workshops. (ex. Main store.)
14. Parachute store.
15. Operations block.
16. Link trainer.
17. Blister hangar.
18. Armoury.
19. Flight shed. (War damaged.)
20. Sergeants mess.
21. Barrack block. (Single storey.)
22. Sick quarters.
23. Dining room.
24. Barrack block. (War damaged.)
25. Fire party block.
26. Barrack block.
27. Institute.
28. Guard house.
29. Headquarters (ex. Officers Mess.)
30. Blacksmiths & Welders shop.
31. Duty crew room. (Temporary.)
32. Crash party hut.
33. Fuel Store.
34. Test firing butt.
35. ASR HQ. (Photographic block.)
36. Gymnasium.
37. Encroachment dressing room
38. Machine gun range.
39. Power house.
40. Fuel Store.
41. WO married quarters.
42. WO married quarters.
43. OR's quarters.
44. OR's quarters.
45. Stores. (War damaged.)
46. Stores.
47. WT & RT block.
48. Sewage disposal area.
49. Reservoir.
50. Blister hangar.
51. Officers married quarters.
52. Officers married quarters.
53. Aircraft shelter pen.
54. Battle HQ. (LAA.)
55. Air Ministry War Department Office.
56. Small firearms range.
57. 'View de France.' (Requisitioned.)
58. 'Rosemarie.' (Requisitioned.)
59. 'Woodland Dane.' (Requisitioned.)
60. 'Box Cottage'. (Requisitioned.)
61. Pickett Hamilton turret.
62. No.277 Sqdn. 'B' Flight office.
63. No.277 Sqdn. 'B' Flight Crew Room.
64. No.277 Sqdn. 'B' Flight Pilots Room.
65. Pyrotechnic Store.
66. Explosive Store.

RAF Hawkinge 1945 – schedule of buildings and airfield layout May 1945.

Mosquitos, making dummy attacks on Southend and Canterbury; this was cancelled, because of the weather. However, an advance party led by Flight Lieutenant Welch headed for Hawkinge on 24 August; the Spitfire VIs were not flown to the airfield until 27 August, when CO Squadron

RAF HAWKINGE

Leader 'Johnny' Plagis DFC arrived. Following their arrival, they spent the remainder of the day settling in. Initially they attended lectures. By the end of August the weather had improved sufficiently for ground firing and cine gun practice to commence. This involved air to ground firing and firing at a drogue. The following day, 15 September at 0815hrs, the CO's parade took place to commemorate the Battle of Britain. A flypast of nine Spitfire VIs headed for Ashford and gave an excellent flypast. Following what was considered a successful month of gunnery practice, No.234 Squadron prepared to move back to Bentwaters. Having enjoyed the short stay, some commented that they wished the squadron could be based at Hawkinge.

No.1 Squadron, previously based at Lympne in 1943, moved back to Kent, this time Hawkinge, the advance party left Hutton Cranswick on 21 September. Twenty aircraft, including three Spitfire IXs and XXIs took off for Hawkinge; on arrival, they spent the rest of the day settling into their new billets, a house not far from the mess. The remainder of the squadron personnel arrived on 24 September. The following day Wing Commander H.C. Kennard DFC gave an introductory talk. On 26 September eight aircraft took off on a bombing and strafing exercise, five others took part in air-to-air firing. During further bombing sorties on 27 September, Flying Officer T. Glaser Spitfire F.21a LA303, had engine trouble. Stretching the glide, he allowed the Spitfire to stall and crashed near the eastern end of the runway; it burst into flames and was destroyed, killing the pilot. This terrible news was followed by a visit by AVM Sir D. Boyle AFC Air Officer Commanding No.11 Group, who visited No.1 Squadron at their dispersal. Flying commenced on 15 October, Flight Lieutenant 'Jimmy' Adams gave an impromptu display of how to land on one wingtip with both wheels in the air. He skilfully recovered control of his Spitfire, preventing a serious accident. This incident was followed by another on 17 October, involving Flight Lieutenant MacIntosh. Taking off from Hawkinge in Spitfire F.21a LA260 he collided with Sea Otter I JM812 of No.278 Squadron. Despite the propeller being damaged he managed to control the Spitfire, making a crosswind belly-landing. On 14 October, No.278 (ASR) Squadron based at Thorney Island on detachment to Hawkinge was disbanded, and the damaged Sea Otter was abandoned, waiting to be moved to another squadron.

Wing Commander Dyson MBE, DFC No.11 Group presided over a meeting held in the Officers' Mess on 18 October 1945. It was decided

THE LAST YEAR OF WAR: 1945

that a farewell party should be held on 26 October to mark the closure of the Fighter Command at Hawkinge. A course held at Hawkinge by No.3 Armament Practice Squadron which had commenced on 24 September was concluded by 19 October 1945, was attended by No.1 and No.122 Squadrons lectured by instructors of No.3 APS, covering such subjects as the assembly of the 0.303 and 0.5 Browning guns and the 20mm Hispano canons, and belt mechanisms, bomb types, bomb carriers and rocket projectiles, sighting and assessing cinefilm. Pilots were shown instructional films on dive bombing and the gyro gun sight. Air to air firing practice took place at Leysdown and Graveney, and towing lines for air-to-air firing practice were situated off the coast of Herne Bay and Westgate-on-Sea. At Hawkinge pilots viewed the gun camera film footage, taken during practice dive bombing. Tempests, Spitfires, Martinet and Masters flew a total of 310hrs. Spitfire IXes of No.122 Squadron returned to Wick and Spitfire XX1s of No.1 Squadron flew back to Hutton Cranswick. It was rumoured that No.3 APS would move to Charter Hall, becoming an Operational Training Unit.

Sea Otters of No.278 Squadron detached to Hawkinge on 1 March 1945 took off from Hawkinge for the last time, heading for their HQ at Thorney Island, where they were to be disposed of, one of these being JM812. On the last day of October 1945, No.3 APS with twelve Martinets, three Miles Masters, two Tempest Vs and two Spitfires left Hawkinge, followed shortly after by a party of WAAFs travelling by train. While some personnel watched them take off, others were engaged in removing all surplus equipment from offices at Hawkinge, ready for the final move on 5 November 1945. Some forty-three aircraft arrived at Hawkinge in intervals, previously based in Europe. All had to be checked by the Censorship & Customs Section, who set up an office at Flying Control. Passengers had to be cleared by the authorities before being allowed to continue their homeward journeys, some would remain in the RAF, others were pleased to be heading off for civvy street.

Squadron Leader Littler took over command of Hawkinge from Wing Commander H.C. Kennard DFC on 7 November. Kennard left Hawkinge for Charter Hall, later commanding No.74 Squadron. In 1946 he served with the RAuxAF from 1949 to 1952, commanding No.500 (Kent's Own) Squadron RAuxAF flying Gloster Meteors. Retiring from the RAF he was appointed to the RAF Reserve in 1952, relinquishing his commission in 1959. Kennard had a successful career in civil aviation at Lydd, Lympne, Ramsgate and Heston.

RAF HAWKINGE

The Recording Officer at RAF Hawkinge C.B. Seagris and Wing Commander H.C. Kennard DFC wrote:

> RAF Hawkinge has, since the outbreak of hostilities, played a very important part in the Defence of Great Britain and the Empire, is closed down to a Care and Maintenance basis. At no period throughout the six years of war (1939–1945), has the station been non-operational, it can only be hoped that the Air Council in their wisdom, will find it possible to once more use the RAF Station that has achieved immortal fame and earned gratitude of mankind in general.
>
> RAF Hawkinge Operations Book
AIR 28/345 NA

Chapter 12

The WAAFs
An Uncertain Future 1947–1961

On 1 April 1947 the HQ Technical Training Command at Hawkinge was transferred from No.46 Group Transport Command to No.22 Group TTC. Group Officer N. Dinnie (WAAF) took command of RAF Hawkinge on 1 June 1947. Group Officer Dinnie was assisted by six other WAAF officers. Owing to the amount of work required, and the shortage of labour, it was impossible to commence training courses in early 1947. Permanent instructors and staff were organised by Wilmslow with the assistance of No.31 (WAAF) Recruit Centre. The aim of the depot at Hawkinge was to centralise general service and administrative training and holding functions for the WRAF. However, cadets were trained in the old operations block, drilled in a hangar and billeted in tiny study bedrooms in wooden huts with adjoined ablutions for the three months of their course. Here, as on other stations, they were all WRAF trained and did not operate in a totally female world.

The WAAF Administrative and General Service Instructors Course and WAAF Administrative Trades Training Course was due to take place on 11 June 1947, moving from Digby to Hawkinge, thus reopening the WAAF depot. The first intake of WAAF re-entrants to be accepted at Hawkinge took place by 16 June 1947. In a memorandum dated 25 September 1947, the Air Ministry directed that functional control of the WAAF Depot at Hawkinge was to be transferred from the HQ Technical Training School to the Air Ministry with effect from 1 October 1947. Administrative control of the WAAF depot was to be exercised through the Headquarters No.22 Group. A group of Officers and WAAFs were moved to reopen RAF Hawkinge. They refurbished and re-equipped it ready for an Officer Cadet Training Unit (OCTU) to move in. When reopened, the site was in a derelict state, the only building fit for occupation being the Officers' Mess. Much of the airfield's condition was due to previous bomb damage and the basic work undertaken by the Care & Maintenance unit Manston, occupying the airfield

RAF HAWKINGE

for two years. At this time, Hawkinge was commanded by Group Officer A. Stephens MBE, (WAAF), who had taken over from Group Officer N. Dinnie (WAAF) on 15 February 1950.

During 1952, HRH Queen Elizabeth the Queen Mother visited Hawkinge, arriving in Westland Dragonfly XF261 of the Queen's Flight. On arrival HRH was greeted by Group Officer M.H. Barnett, OBE (WRAF), CO at Hawkinge from November 1952. Having been introduced to senior officers, given a tour of the airfield, meeting, and talking to several of the WAAFs, lunch was served in the Officers' Mess.

By now the OCTU had again slightly changed its form. Men and women from civilian life did a preparatory course together, before embarking on the seventeen weeks main course. Women made up about a third of the total numbers at the rate of about eighty to ninety a year, working in mixed flights of about nine cadets, with an RAF or WRAF Flight Commander. The accent was much more on leadership and practical training, with six-day and then eight-day camps in Norfolk being planned and administered by the cadets themselves. It was stimulating and in 1967, according to Lynn Child,

Officer cadets of the WAAF (Women's Auxiliary Air Force) celebrate at RAF Hawkinge during the 1960s.

THE WAAFs

RAF Hawkinge was honoured in 1952 when Queen Elizabeth the Queen Mother visited the airfield. Westland Dragonfly XF261, on loan to The Queen's Flight, Central Flying School (CFS), South Cerney touches down, just visible is the Royal pennant. (MAP)

On the left of the Guard House stand the Water Tower and Booster Pump House and the all-important Fire Block. (D.G. Collyer)

RAF HAWKINGE

'wonderful, hard work but fun'. On 1 November 1952, Air Commandant M.H.B. Barnett OBE (WRAF) was appointed CO of Hawkinge, the only female station commander in the RAF at that time.

In 1953 Spitfire LF IXe MK356 which had been based at Halton since 2 October 1945, was allocated as an 'instructional airframe' and transferred to Hawkinge, where it was displayed in post-war silver colours as M5690 until 1958, when it was camouflaged and given the serial M5690, later changed to MK365. On the closure of Hawkinge on 8 December 1961, the Spitfire was transferred to No.71 MU at Bicester, arriving early the following year, overhauled, and repainted as 2J-, with no individual code letter. Following this restoration, MK356 was dispatched to Locking and displayed on a pole until 1967. It was loaned for use in *The Battle of Britain* film and transported to Henlow, North Weald and Duxford for the duration, with the spurious serials and codes N3328 'AI-R' and N3317 'BO', neither of which existed. The Spitfire designation 'LF', refers to the type being designed for Low Flying.

Re-painted and camouflaged Spitfire LF IXe MK356, the gate guardian at RAF Hawkinge from 1953 until the airfield's closure on 8 December 1961. (MAP)

THE WAAFs

Kirby Cadet TX.3 gliders lined up at Hawkinge during 1956, it was at the airfield that many ATC cadets were given the opportunity to fly gliders with No.1 Home Command Gliding Centre. (*Flight Magazine*)

Air Training Corps gliding, which accounted for 100,000 launches during 1955, had since September 1955 offered continuous courses, as well as normal weekend training. These one-week courses provided the ATC and CCF (Combined Cadet Force) cadets, also offered other gliding training at the Home Command Gliding Centre, a lodger unit at Hawkinge. Until September 1955 gliding instruction for cadets had been provided at forty-three weekend gliding schools throughout Great Britain. For reasons of economy, this was reduced to twenty weekends. The aim being to maintain an annual number of cadets trained at the existing level, accomplished by the setting-up of the Home Command centre at Hawkinge, taking over the functions of the previous Instructors' School at Detling, and the start of one-week courses for cadets not having access to local gliding schools. Some 400 cadets were expected to be trained annually at the centre.

Cadets began their course at Hawkinge with basic training on Slingsby T.21B Sedberghs, this was followed by dual circuit practice on T.31 Tandem Tutors (known in the Service as Cadet TX.3s). After a total of some thirty launches, first solos were made from the front seat of the T.31. Most cadets achieved proficiency certificates equivalent to gliding's international supervisory body, the Fédération Aéronautique Internationale (FAI) 'A' and 'B' certificates, having logged thirty-five to forty launches during the week. Selected cadets received further training and obtained advanced certificates of FAI 'C' standard; gliders were launched by winch. The total number of ATC launches in 1954 was 99,449, the number of proficiency and advanced certificates awarded being 1,585 and 86 respectively.

The Command Gliding Centre at Hawkinge was staffed by regular RAF personnel, plus 'J'–Class civilians required to exercise executive authority or fill a uniformed post in a specified locality (such as ATC Wing Admin. Officers and ATC Regional Commandants). Each of the twenty weekend schools had four RAF Volunteer Reserve Training Branch officers and nine civilian instructors, the CO was Flight Lieutenant R.C. Jones. The training and checking of gliding instructors was the responsibility of the Hawkinge unit. Between thirty-five and forty continuous courses for cadets were organised during school holidays. Instructors who gave basic instruction in primary gliders to school cadets had been trained in gliding techniques. Group Officer J.L.A. Conan-Doyle OBE, (WRAF) – the second daughter of the famous author Sir Arthur Conan-Doyle – took command of Hawkinge on 29 May 1956.

On 13 June 1956 Slingsby T.31B Cadet TX3 XA313 was blown off course landed on the roof of the local hairdresser's shop in the village. (E. Haddow)

THE WAAFs

On 13 June 1956 Slingsby T.31B Cadet TX3 XA313 was blown off course by a gust of wind when taking off at Hawkinge. The glider hit power cables and landed on the roof of a house which was also the village hairdressers. It was taken to 71 MU RAF Bicester and struck off charge. The pilot, an ATC cadet, was uninjured. Hawkinge was the venue for a visit by HRH Duchess of Gloucester in early 1958, the airfield at Lydd (Ferryfield) was to be the diversion airfield should her Transport Command aircraft not be able to land at Hawkinge. HRH had graciously consented to review the Passing Out parade of No.44 WRAF OCTU on Tuesday 18 February 1958. HRH flew from London Airport, landing a Hawkinge at 1200hrs. and was greeted by a Guard of Honour from Uxbridge. Families of all NCOs, airmen and civilian employees at Hawkinge, and those still on duty, were invited to attend the ceremony.

The WRAF Central Band were present as were the Lord Lieutenant of Kent, Colonel W. Stanley Cornwallis, 2nd Baron Cornwallis, AOC

Senior Officers of the WAAF Depot No.22 Technical Training Command, outside the Officers' Mess during 1961. Wing Officer E.M. Benson (WRAF) the last CO of RAF Hawkinge is seated centre front row.

RAF HAWKINGE

No.22 Group RAF and the Director of the WRAF. A gliding display was provided, the day concluded with a service of dedication at the Station Chapel and tea in the Officers' Mess Ante-Room, during which newly commissioned WRAF Officers were presented to HRH Duchess of Kent. Two weeks following the event, the Group Officer J.L.A. Conan Doyle, received a letter of thanks from HRH Duchess of Gloucester, stating how much she had enjoyed the event and was impressed by what she had seen, this was conveyed to everyone at Hawkinge. Group Officer F.B. Hill OBE (WRAF) took over command of Hawkinge on 20 April 1959, eventually replaced by Wing Commander E.M. Benson (WRAF) on 13 May 1960, the last CO of RAF Hawkinge.

By 1961, it was known that Hawkinge would be closing; like so many airfields during this period, it was surplus to requirements, not suitable for the next generation of RAF aircraft or the needs of the newly emerging service in the Cold War. On Monday 27 March 1961, a 'Closing Ceremony Committee' met at Hawkinge, presided over by Squadron Leader R. Dicker Chairman. The date agreed was 8 December 1961, an RAF band would attend, including invited civilians. The RAF ensign on the parade ground would be lowered, the ensign on the parade arena raised at 1300hrs, followed

Loaded onto a Queen Mary aircraft transporter, Spitfire LF IXe MK356 leaves Hawkinge for No.71 (MU) Maintenance Unit RAF Bicester in December 1961 to be restored. (E. Kettle)

THE WAAFs

A barrage balloon post-war used for parachute jumps at Hawkinge, for training purposes. Many of the original hangars and buildings have by now been demolished. (Skyfotos Ltd.)

by the last post by a Tamplin police trumpeter. A final rehearsal took place on 7 December, a new flagpole had to be transported to Hawkinge from Debden. As the following day dawned over RAF Hawkinge it was a time of reflection, the last hours as those still based at the airfield contemplated their future.

The closing ceremony was a sad occasion, but the day went well, ending with celebrations. Several RAF service personnel were retiring or leaving the service, others would continue life in the RAF and WRAF. RAF Hawkinge had played a critical role in the early days of the RAF's formation, its contribution in the Second World War, both in combat and Air Sea Rescue, would go down in the annals of history. Those who sacrificed their lives, or suffered because of injury, will never be forgotten by a grateful nation.

RAF HAWKINGE

A postcard with a view looking towards No.1 Flight Shed (hangar) with No.2 Flight Shed in the background, which sustained war damage. The feature nearest to the camera could be the Aviation Fuel Installation. (Shoesmith & Etheridge)

Slingsby T.31 Cadet TX.3 stalled and crashed at Hawkinge when the launching cable broke on 13 June 1961. Both Instructor and Cadet were not seriously injured, the glider WT876 was struck off charge and scrapped the same day. A month later 25 July 1961, Slingsby T.31 Cadet TX.3 XE787 was written off when landing heavily, the pilot was uninjured. The glider was later allocated for ground instruction at Andover but never flew again.

The story of Hawkinge did not end there, in 1968 a classic film was in production: *Battle of Britain* directed by Guy Hamilton and produced by Harry Saltzman and S. Benjamin Fisz. The script by James Kennaway and Wilfred Greatorex was based on the book *The Narrow Margin* by Derek Wood and Derek Dempster in 1961. Filming took place at many locations, but it was particularly apt that Saltzman and his team of cameramen, technicians, and a cast of many actors, were able to film on the then virtually intact airfield at Hawkinge. To this end, hangars and wooden huts were erected on the site of the original buildings, even bomb craters were dug to simulate the Luftwaffe attacks. At the same time many marks of Spitfires were parked on the airfield, although these were now only static airframes, and the construction of large-scale models took place, although much of the filming used existing Spitfires and Hurricanes.

Replica hangars being erected at Hawkinge airfield by Pinewood Studios during the late 1960s for the filming of *The Battle of Britain*. The intention was to blow the hangar up, but the council prevented this and an original hangar was destroyed at Duxford instead! Replica Spitfires parked close to the structure appear very convincing. (E. Sergison)

Several large-scale models were made for the film, one being this replica HeIII. Behind is the Hiller UH-12E G-ARXV chase helicopter used for filming which was once flown by Plessey Ltd and operated from Southampton Airport. (E. Sergison)

RAF HAWKINGE

A model Hurricane I, perhaps the unsung hero of the real Battle of Britain period. Here technicians prepare the model for filming at Hawkinge. (E. Sergison)

A line up of full-size replica Spitfires at Hawkinge airfield resemble a scene from the Battle of Britain period in 1940. There were several airworthy Spitfires available for filming at the time when the 1968 film was under production.

THE WAAFs

One off several Spitfire models, constructed for filming at Hawkinge. However, the squadron codes painted on the fuselage are purely fictitious. Note the pilot seated in the cockpit awaiting the cockpit canopy to be fitted. (E. Sergison)

The film was notable for its attempt to accurately portray the role of the Germans in the battle, with consultants and advisers including Group Captain T.P. Gleave CBE; Wing Commander R.R. Stanford Tuck DSO, DFC & Two Bars, AFC; Squadron Leader B.H. Drobiński DFC; Group Captain Sir Douglas Bader CBE, DSO & Bar, DFC & Bar, DL, FRAeS; Wing Commander J.H. 'Ginger' Lacey DFM & Bar, Croix de Guerre; and Luftwaffe Gen. Lt. Adolf Galland. Galland had fought against these legendary British pilots, and they were now best friends; their input was of great importance.

Over a period of two years, a total of eighty-two Spitfires, Hurricanes, Me 109s and He 111s were built. Radio-controlled Heinkel He 111 models were flown to depict bombers being destroyed over the English Channel. Churchill's quote from his 20 August 1940 speech was changed when the movie was released on DVD in 2003. Onscreen, instead of 'The Few,' this quote appears as: 'This is not the end. It is not even the beginning of the end. But it is, perhaps, the end of the beginning,' which was a reference to the Second Battle of El Alamein being a turning point in the war. The 2004 Special Edition, however, reverts to the quotation about 'The Few': 'Never in the field of human conflict was so much owed by so many to so few.' Perhaps the most famous speech ever made.

RAF HAWKINGE

A busy day at Hawkinge as work continues during filming, the replica Spitfires are convincing and evoke a similar scene in 1940 during the Battle of Britain period. (E. Sergison)

By 1970 Hawkinge was all but deserted, its future uncertain. At the time this image was taken the airfield was reasonably intact with No.1 Flight Shed (hangar) still standing. Painted on the roof of the hangar is 'Hawkinge' (right), a few surviving buildings would eventually be used to house the Kent Battle of Britain Museum. On the far left of the hangar is the Officers' Mess and Quarters. (Skyfotos Ltd)

THE WAAFs

It is interesting to note that Hawkinge Gate Guardian Spitfire LF IXe MK356 was loaned for use in *The Battle of Britain* film and transported to Henlow, North Weald and Duxford for the duration, with the spurious serials and codes N3328 'AI-R' and N3317 'BO', neither of which existed. The Spitfire designation 'LF', refers to the type being designed for Low Flying. Filming at Hawkinge generated much interest, with many local people watching the proceedings, some taking photographs. The Battle of Britain period of 1940 no doubt contributed later to the new phenomenon of crashed aircraft recovery, which really took hold of enthusiasts' attention in the early 1970s.

In those early days, there was no MOD licence required for such recovery, both German and British aircraft of the Battle of Britain period were being located and recovered, including some with the remains of aircrew and pilots present. For this reason, The Protection of Military Remains Act 1986 was introduced. The Act protected both the pilots from any abuse at the crash site, and also the wishes of their families, but it also ensured the safety of those excavating the sites – particularly where bombs and shells may have been present, which would halt any recovery until made safe by the MOD.

As work progressed to establish Kent Battle of Britain Museum at Hawkinge, a section of wing spar from an Avro 504 was found in the

Close up of Operations Block (Watch Office) and pill box, residential area in the background, shows how close to the action some housing must have been.

RAF HAWKINGE

The Guard Room at Hawkinge as seen during the 1970s, all these buildings have since been demolished.

rafters of the old Watch Office, which could have been from one of several Avro 504s that passed through Hawkinge in earlier times, or even Avro 504 G-ADBM, originally AX871, which struck the building in 1940. Kent Battle of Britain Museum was managed by the late Mike Llewellyn, who established the collection. Today, other surviving buildings, of which there are very few, house many wonderful exhibits of the period. The Kent Battle of Britain Museum Trust, as it is known today, a living memorial to all those who served at Hawkinge. The collection is in the charge of David Brocklehurst MBE, who with a small group of enthusiasts, has created an excellent museum, its origins date back to the 1970s.

A bronze statue of Amy Johnson is too found not far from the pier at Herne Bay, Kent. This impressive figure was sculptured by Stephen Melton. In August 2021 it was announced that he was commissioned to produce seven bronze figures of Battle of Britain pilots of No.32 Squadron at Hawkinge, based on one of the most famous images taken at Hawkinge, which shows pilots of the squadron relaxing by one of their Hurricanes during the summer of 1940. The bronze figures have been completed and are displayed in the same pose as that of the image taken on 29 July 1940 and are located near a Hurricane I replica at the Kent Battle of Britain Museum, Hawkinge. What better tribute to these young pilots who flew from the famous airfield at Hawkinge, both those who lost their lives and those survived, and the airmen and women who served with them.

THE WAAFs

To the left stands the buildings of the MT Section at Hawkinge, far right is the Air Sea Rescue HQ which had previously been the Photographic Block.

The NAAFI and Airmen's Mess which was built in 1929, sadly demolished; how many young airmen passed through its doors – how many lived to tell their stories?

RAF HAWKINGE

The memorial at Hawkinge located outside the old gymnasium, unveiled on 29 April 1978 by Sir William F. Dickson GCB, KBE, DSO, AFC. The inscription, from a speech made by Sir Winston Churchill on 12 November 1940 reads: 'History with its lamp stumbles along the trail of the past, trying to reconstruct its scenes, to revive its echoes, and rekindle with pale gleams the passion of former years.'

The Officers' Mess and Quarters at Hawkinge; like most RAF buildings they were designed to MOD specifications – this one being Barrack Block Type B, which was still used in the 1970s for various functions and meetings.

THE WAAFs

A recent acquisition at Hawkinge and the Kent Battle of Britain Museum, is a Spanish CASA 2.III, used in the filming of the 1968 film *The Battle of Britain*. The museum has also recently acquired the fuselage of a Ju52/3m from the Imperial War Museum, Cosford.

One of the replica Hurricane Is on display at Kent Battle of Britain Museum represents Hurricane I N2532 'GZ-H' No.32 Squadron, which force-landed at Hawkinge on 20 July 1940 and was flown by Squadron Leader J. Worrall CO May–August 1940. (Kent Battle of Britain Museum – Hawkinge)

RAF HAWKINGE

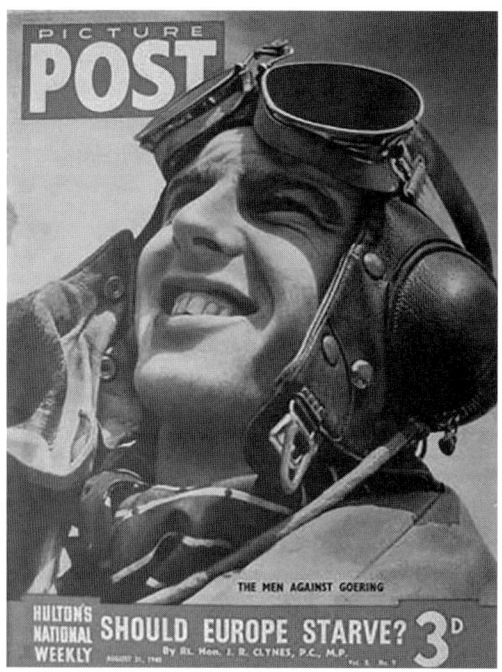

Left: The image of Pilot Officer Keith Gillman No.32 Squadron, shot down operating from Hawkinge on 25 August 1940, appeared on the cover of *Picture Post*.

Below: Pilots of No.32 Squadron relax between operations at Hawkinge in July 1940, from L–R: Pilot Officer R.F. Smythe, Pilot Officer K.R. Gillman, Pilot Officer J.E. Proctor, Flight Lieutenant P.M. Brothers, Pilot Officer D.H. Grice, Pilot Officer P.M. Gardner, and Pilot Officer A.F. Eckford. Apart from Pilot Officer Gillman, all survived the Battle of Britain. Note, the Hurricane I is plugged into the starter, ready for action. This image was used to sculpture the seven bronze figures, depicting those in this photograph.

Bibliography

Air Britain, Historians Ltd, RAF Aircraft, Individual aircraft history series, 1970s –1990s.
Ashworth, Chris, *Action Stations 9: Military airfields of the Central South & Southeast*, Patrick Stephens Ltd, 1985
Bailey, David J., *610 (County of Chester) Squadron RAuxAF 1936–1940*, Fonthill 2019
Boot, Henry & Ray Sturtivant, *Gifts of War*, Air-Britain (Historians) Ltd, 2005
Brew, Steve, *Blood Sweat and Courage, 41 Squadron RAF 1939–1942*, Fonthill Media, 2014
Brew, Steve, *Blood Sweat and Valour, 41 Squadron RAF 1942–1944*, Fonthill Media, 2012
Caldwell, Donald, *The JG26 War Diary Vol.2 1943–1945*, Grub Street 1998
Caygill, Peter, *In All Things First: No.1 Squadron at War 1939–1945*, Pen & Sword Aviation, 2009
Cole, Christopher & E.F. Cheesman, *Air Defence of Great Britain 1914-18*, Putnam, 1984
Collier, David G. *Buzz Bomb Diary*, Kent Aviation Historical Research Society, 1994
Cossey, Bob, *Tigers – The Story of No.74 Squadron RAF*, Arms & Armour Press 1992
Cornwell, Peter, *The story of Gp. Captain J.C 'Johnny' Wells DFC & Bar* Spellmount, 2011
Cull, Brian, *Diver! Diver! Diver! – The V1s over SE England 1944-45* Grubb Street, 2008
Cull, Brian, Lander, Bruce, Weiss, Henrich, *Twelve Days in May*, Grubb Street, 1995
Docherty, Tom, *Swift to Battle – No.72 Fighter Squadron RAF in action*, Pen & Sword, 2009
Donnet, Michael, CVO, DFC, FRAeS, *Flight to Freedom*, Ian Allan Ltd, 1974

Escott, Beryl E. Sqn. Ldr., *The Story of Women in the RAF Since 1918*, PSL Ltd, 1989

Franks, Norman, *Sky Tiger – The Story of Sailor Malan*, William Kimber, 1980

Franks, Norman L.R. *The Greatest Air Battle – Dieppe 4 19 August 1942*, Grub Street, 1992

Franks, Norman L.R. *Sky Tiger – The story of Sailor Malan*, William Kimber, 1980

Franks, Norman L.R. *RAF Fighter Command Losses of WWII*, Vols.1, 2, 3 Midland Publishing 1997, 1998, 2000

Freeman, Roger A., *The Mighty Eighth War Diary*, Arms and Armour, 1990

Graham, Peter, Skypilot, *Memoirs of take-off and landing*, Pentland Books, 2001

Hall, Peter, *No.91 'Nigeria' Squadron*, Osprey Aviation, 2001

Hodgkinson, Colin, *Best Foot Forward, The Autobiography*, Odhams Press Ltd, 1957

Humphreys, Roy, *Hawkinge 1912–1961,* Meresborough Books, 1981

Humphreys, Roy, *RAF Hawkinge in old photographs*, Alan Sutton, 1991

Hunt, Leslie, *Twenty-One Squadrons, The History of the RAuxAF 1925–1957*, Garnstone Press, 1972

Knight, Dennis, *Harvest of Messerschmitts, The Chronicle of a village at War 1940*, Frederick Warne, 1981

Long, Jack, T.C., *Three's Company, Illustrated History of No.3 Fighter Squadron*, Pen & Sword 2005

Lunney, Adam, *We Together – No.451 & No.453 Sqdns at war*, Tempest Books 2020

Mason, Francis K., *Hawks Rising, The Story of 25 Squadron RAF*, Air Britain, 2001

McIntosh, Dave, *High Blue Battle, The War Diary of No.401 Squadron (RCAF),* Spa Books Ltd., 1990

McRoberts, Douglas, *Lions Rampant, The Story of No.602 Squadron*, William Kimber, 1985

Moor, Anthony J., *Lympne Airfield – At War and Peace*, Fonthill Media, 2014

Nicholl, G.W.R., *The Supermarine Walrus, The Story of a Unique Aircraft*, G.T. Foulis, 1966

Nielsen, Tim, *'Jack's Adventures' – The Story of Flight Lieutenant J. Cleland (NZ)*, T. J. Nielsen, 1999

BIBLIOGRAPHY

Onderwater, Hans, *Second to None, The History of No.2 (AC) Squadron*, Airlife, 1992

Rawlings, John, *Fighter Squadrons of the RAF and Their Aircraft*, Macdonald, 1969

Ross, David, Richard Hillary, *The Definitive Biography*, Grubb Street, 2000

Sarker, Dilip, *A Few of the Many – Air War 1939-45*, Ramrod Publications, 1995

Scarth, Richard N., *Echoes from the Sky*, Hythe Civic Society 1999

Scott, Desmond, *Typhoon Pilot, Group Captain D. Scott DSO, OBE, DFC*, Leo Cooper, 1982

Spurdle, Bob, *The Blue Arena*, William Kimber, 1986

Thomas, Nick, *Kenneth 'Hawkeye' Lee DFC*, Pen & Sword 2011

Walpole, Nigel, Group Captain OBE, BA, RAF, *Dragon Rampant, No.234 Squadron, Merlin*, Massara Publishing 2007

Watkins, David, *Fear Nothing, The History of No.501 (County of Gloucester) Squadron* Newton Publishers, 1990

Winston G., *The Battle of Britain Then and Now Mk. IV, After the Battle*, 1987

Index

Airfields/Airports

Abingdon, 74, 93, 242
Acklington, 98, 207, 243, 244
Aldergrove, 18, 50
Amiens, 12, 67–8, 71, 118, 170, 198, 235
Atcham, 180
Ayr, 207

Balado- Bridge, 225
Bekesbourne, 22, 70
Benson, 119
Bentwaters, 245, 248
Bicester, 254
Bickendorf, 19
Biggin Hill, 22, 29, 38, 74, 78, 84, 95–6, 98–9, 108, 110, 112, 115, 125, 134–5, 137, 141, 143, 148, 161, 170, 182, 183, 196, 198, 231
Binbrook, 133, 188
Bircham Newton, 12, 22, 135
Bradwell Bay, 149, 205, 244
Brenzett, 118, 190, 209
Brooklands, 41, 181, 220

Cambridge, 98
Capel-le-Ferne, 9, 26
Charter Hall, 249
Chilverton, 75
Church Fenton, 176, 192
Colerne, 241
Coltishall, 109, 242
Cosford, 74
Croydon, 44, 61, 73, 76–7, 99, 101, 112

Deanland, 211, 226
Debden, 68–9, 90, 134, 141, 145, 176, 179–80, 259
Detling, 104, 109, 122, 150, 216, 239, 243, 255
Deurne, 233
Digby, 225
Drem, 164
Driffield, 109
Dunsfold, 211, 231
Duxford, 118, 175, 254
Dyce, 58

Eastchurch, 22, 46, 51, 58, 99, 111, 164, 182
Earls Colne, 219
East Kirkby, 232

Fairlop, 182
Farnborough, 7, 44, 100
Feltwell, 109
Filton, 35, 46
Ford, 236
Frankfurt, 158
Friston, 200

Gatwick, 134
Gosport, 41
Gransden, 158
Gravesend, 80, 107–108, 110, 123, 125, 138, 141, 149, 163, 200, 209
Great Chart, 185, 213
Great Saling, 210
Great Samford, 141, 145–6

274

INDEX

Halton, 118, 189, 203, 254
Hardwick, 210
Harrowbeer, 220
Hartford Bridge, 200, 211
Hatfield, 51
Hawarden, 200
Headcorn (Egerton), 211
Heligoland, 242
Hendon, 34, 45, 50, 58
Henlow, 66, 254
Heston, 235, 249
Hethel, 211
High Ercall, 172–4
Holmsley South, 211
Honiley, 166, 175–6, 178
Hooton Park, 58
Hornchurch, 29, 71, 104–106, 116, 154, 208, 225, 243
Horsham-St. Faith, 187
Hucknall, 46, 50–1, 58
Hunmanby Moor, 237, 243
Hunsdon, 241
Hurn, 213
Hutton Cranswick, 242, 248–9

Ibsley, 151, 194

Juvincourt, 213

Kemble, 182
Kenley, 20, 29, 66–7, 74, 92, 102, 105, 115–16, 122, 134, 137, 167, 191–2
Kingscliffe, 164
Kingsnorth, 185
Kirton-in-Lindsey, 109
Knettishall, 239

Lakenheath, 156–7
Lasham, 244
Le Bourget, 45
Leconfield, 109
Lee-on-Solent, 234
Liverpool, 50
Llanbedr, 164, 166

London, 257
Lydd (Ferryport), 249
Lympne, 9–12, 16, 18, 34–5, 46, 50, 69, 71, 74, 84, 88, 99, 102, 117, 128, 137–8, 144, 149–50, 153, 156, 159, 162–4, 167, 169–70, 177–8, 182–3, 201, 204, 215, 223, 231, 233, 241, 248–9

Malmedy, 213
Matlask, 241
Manby, 95
Manston, 11, 22, 38, 52, 61, 63, 68, 72–3, 94, 102, 115, 120, 124, 132, 137, 152, 160, 169, 173, 181, 183, 187, 192–3, 201, 207, 218, 240–1, 244, 251
Martlesham Heath, 68, 109, 134, 141, 146, 176, 180, 184, 240
Medfield, 219
Mepal, 232
Merston, 180
Middleton St George, 132
Middle Wallop, 150
Mildenhall, 157
Morton-on-the-Marsh, 220
Montrose, 18–19

Netheravon, 8
Newchurch, 182, 219, 223
New Romney, 178
North Coates, 48
Northolt, 58–9, 79, 105, 120, 123, 134, 178
North Weald, 29, 58, 99, 130, 134, 159, 254, 265

Oakington, 169
Odiham, 209

Perranporth, 214
Peterhead, 192, 208
Pocklington, 174
Poix, 191, 192

Portsmouth, 68
Predannack, 204

Ramsgate, 249
Redhill, 112, 163, 191
Rochester, 74, 198
Rochford, 89, 93

San Stefano, 20, 22
Scampton, 109
Scopwick, 19
Sealand, 63
Selsey Bill, 51, 90
Shipham, 166
Shoreham, 124, 163, 177
Sicily, 145
South Carlton, 19
Speke, 45
Stapleford Tawney, 134
Staplehurst, 195
St Athan, 66
Sumburgh (Shetlands), 237
Swingfield, 185, 234
Tangmere, 29, 40, 79, 117, 121–2, 134, 141, 151, 179, 198, 200–201, 204, 221, 225, 231, 234

Thorney Island, 207, 214, 240, 248
Thurleigh, 192
Tricqueville, 192
Turnhouse, 57, 74, 75

Upavon, 29, 37
Upper Heyford, 51

Watchet, 68
Westhampnett, 198, 202, 225
West Malling, 77, 122, 154, 162, 178, 183, 197, 205, 214, 218, 225, 244
Whitfield, 1
Wick, 69
Wickenby, 182
Woodchurch, 195
Woodvale, 202

Worthing, 124
Wunsdorf, 243–4
Wyton, 12

Places
Abbeville, 73, 95, 155, 164, 170, 193, 202, 204, 211
Acrise, 117
Aldershot, 22
Amiens, 67, 118, 170, 198
Amsterdam, 121
Antwerp, 233
Arnhem, 242
Arras, 69–71
Ashford, 122, 167, 171–2, 185, 211, 213, 228, 248
Audinghen, 198, 200

Barcelona, 223
Bari, 218
Barnhouse Lane, 1–2, 5–7, 11, 101
Barrow Hill, 172
Bartholomew's Wood, 108
Bayenghem-lès-Seningham, 71
Bayreuth, 242
Beachborough Park, 154
Beachy Head, 83, 146, 164, 220, 240–1
Beaumont-le-Harong, 206
Beauvais, 16
Beauvoir, 202
Belgium, 198, 213, 223, 231, 233, 238–9, 241
Beny Sur Mer, 231
Berck sur Mer, 154, 209
Berlin, 76, 168
Bethune, 198
Bielefeld, 240
Birmingham, 205
Biville, 213
Bochum, 182
Bodsham, 230
Boulogne, 34, 69, 120, 128, 132, 143, 156, 165, 186, 198, 207, 213, 232
Brookland, 85

INDEX

Bristol, 220
Broadstairs, 121
Brookland, 156
Brookwood Cemetery, 117
Brunsbüttelkoog, 16
Brussels, 69, 147, 235, 240

Cabourg, 216
Caen, 216
Caesars Camp, 33
Calais, 69, 71–2, 83, 104, 107–108,
    114–15, 141, 159, 163, 169, 175, 180,
    185–6, 198, 210, 215, 217
Camber, 86
Cambrai, 201
Cambridge, 98
Canterbury, 61, 63, 103, 112, 153, 162,
    200, 247
Hospital, 77, 88, 97, 180, 232
Cap d'Antifer, 214
Cap Grez -Nez, 17, 63, 83, 135, 142,
    147–9, 152, 185, 198, 222, 241
Capel le Ferne, 110
Cardington, 15
Cats Tor Cheshire, 180
Cayeux, 183, 191
Chatham, 99, 106, 218
Cherbourg, 186
Chilham, 116
Chilverton, 75
Cologne, 12, 16, 188, 235
Courtrai, 158
Creteway Downs, 32
Cullen, Captain, 166

Dane Farm, 33
Deal, 112, 115, 118, 127, 151, 153, 158,
    160, 164, 187, 207–208
Densole, 117
Derby, 179
Dieppe, 138, 144–6, 158, 173, 178, 180,
    186, 194, 213
Dover, 1, 34, 36, 61, 66, 74–5, 78–81,
    83, 85, 87–9, 94, 96, 107–109,
    112, 114-117, 119–20, 123–4, 135,
    137–40, 143, 147, 149, 151, 153,
    156–7, 159–60, 163, 164, 167,
    169–70, 173, 181, 186, 189, 193, 195,
    204, 209, 214–15, 218–19, 232, 234
    Union Road Hospital, 137, 142
Dungeness, 83–4, 92, 105, 107, 110–11,
    116–22, 135, 142–3, 155, 159, 163,
    167, 169–70, 173, 190, 191, 195–6,
    198, 205, 209, 215, 220, 235
Dunkirk (Canterbury), 85
Dunkirk, 61, 70-73, 120–1, 128, 158,
    165, 167, 176, 186, 192, 211, 221
Dunstable Downs, 34
Dymchurch, 74, 90, 132, 156, 219, 223

Eastbourne, 169, 173, 220
East Grinsted, 200
East Langdon, 105

Eindhoven, 241
Elham Valley, 94
Emmerich, 232
Epinary, 201
Etterbeek, 223
Evere, 202
Evreux, 218
Fairfield, 86, 135
Falmer, 30
Fan Hole, 36
Fecamp, 217, 241
Flensburg, 158
Flushing, 147, 169
Folkestone, 6–11, 20, 22, 26–7, 31–2, 34–7,
    43, 46, 52–3, 57, 63, 67, 73, 76, 84,
    87–9, 94, 97, 103, 106, 108–11, 118–19,
    122–4, 126, 131–2, 144, 146–7, 149,
    151, 154–5, 161–2, 164, 167, 170, 173,
    177–8, 184, 189, 192, 196, 204–205,
    220–1, 223, 227, 229, 235–6, 241–2
    Cemetery (Hawkinge) 63, 76, 172,
        198, 204–205, 242
    Golf Course, 67, 155
    Holy Trinity Church, 170

Racecourse (Westenhanger), 1
Royal Victoria Hospital, 131
Foreness, 218
Frankfurt, 158, 173, 174, 239
Friday Wood, 54

Gelsenkirchen, 241
Gibraltar House, 54
Gilze Rijen, 207
Goodwin Sands, 88, 163, 165
Gorenflos, 135, 209
Gravelines, 211, 175
Graveney, 249
Greatstone, 37–8
Gueschart, 202

Hague, 240, 242, 244
Hamburg, 242
Hastings, 138, 141, 143, 147, 149, 163, 165, 169, 205, 223
Herne Bay, 249
Hougham, 78, 167
Hounslow, 124
Harwich, 88
Haucourt, 70
Headington, 77
Henglo, 236
Herne Bay, 266
Hesdin, 193
Hockley Sole, 98, 103, 296
Holland, 103, 118, 162, 164, 182, 202, 232–4, 238, 244
Hoogstade, 71
Hougham, 78
Hucclecote, 24
Hythe, 37, 87, 124, 132, 146, 169, 202, 221, 234, 297

Isle of Man, 164
Italy, 119, 131, 218, 236
Ivychurch, 190

Jersey, 243
Joss Gap, 36
Juvincourt, 211, 213

Kassel, 192
Killing Wood, 80
Kingsgate, 36

Laon, 211
Le Crotoy, 115
Le Harve, 154
Le Touquet, 119, 160, 180–1, 186, 197
Le Treport, 167, 215
Leverkusen, 201
Leysdown, 58, 249
Ligres, 203
Lingfield, 112
Lisbon, 223
Little Mongeham, 119
Littlehampton, 216
Littlestone, 180, 219–20
Liverpool, 50, 223
London, 15, 51, 164, 169, 220, 235–6
Lubeck, 158
Ludwigshafen, 239
Luneburg, 242
Lydd, 37, 46, 52, 92–3, 117, 120, 156, 220, 249–50, 257
    Ranges, 34, 46, 205
Lydden, 80, 153
Lyme Bay, 215

Maidstone, 63, 108, 112, 228
Maisoncelle, 12
Maldegem, 241
Marden, 90, 99
Marquise, 16, 132
Mazingarbe, 128
Medway, 83
Mersham, 167
Merville, 69, 192–3, 205
Munich, 58, 62
Munster Rheine, 240

Neufchatel-Rethel, 71
Newhaven, 145, 169
Newington, 33, 115, 118
New Romney, 109

INDEX

Nijmegen, 234, 242
Normandy, 121, 214–16
North Foreland, 130, 150, 151, 153, 173, 175, 184, 206
Nunneley, 1st Lt. C.M, 219
Nuremberg, 132, 133, 169

Old Swanley, 112
Ontario, 170
Oostende (Ostend),72, 169, 176, 178, 186, 193, 196, 209, 239
Oschersleben, 192
Oxted, 90

Paddlesworth, 10, 33, 54, 97, 242
Paddock Wood, 90
Paris, 16, 189
Pegwell Bay, 153, 201
Penshurst, 164
Pevensey, 85, 218
Poland, 95
Poling, 218
Poperinge, 71–2
Postling, 33, 108
Prouville, 219

Radnor Park, 53
Ramsgate, 111, 143, 156, 165–6, 185, 201, 206–207, 213, 249
Reindene Wood, 120
Renfrew, 38
Richmond, 178
Rochester, 74, 105
Romilly, 193
Romney Marsh, 35, 106, 115, 133, 156, 180, 201, 209
Rosieres-en-Santerr, 200
Rouen, 70, 74, 145, 217
Rye, 117, 163, 172, 197, 220
    RDF Station, 57, 61, 85–7, 190, 218
    Memorial Hospital,160

Sandgate, 20, 106, 120
Sandwich, 137, 166, 169
Sagan, 106

Scapa, 69
Sellindge, 83, 205
Serny, 18
Sevenoaks, 106
Shorncliffe, 22, 27, 68, 71, 88, 90
Shotley, 89
Siracourt, 210
Soesterburg, 236
Solent, 217, 220, 234
Solingen, 201
Somme, 159, 180–1
Southend, 205, 247
South Foreland, 146, 218
Spain, 218
Stapleford, 101, 134
Stelling Minis, 178
Stettin, 120
St Dizier, 235
St Eval, 220
St Leonards, 149
St Margaret's Bay, 31, 71
St Martin's Plain, 117
St Mary & Eadburg, 20
St Omer, 7–8, 71, 72, 99, 128, 137, 193, 198, 217
St Pol, 71
Sugarloaf Hill, 33, 41, 52
Swanscombe, 219
Sweden, 200
Swinemunde, 120
Swingate,
    RDF Station, 168, 218, 243
Swingfield, 136
Switzerland, 133, 218

Temple Ewell, 75
Tenterden, 99, 161
Terlingham Farm, 1–2, 10, 24, 35
Tetbury, 63
Thetford, 181
Tilmanstone, 74
Tonbridge, 225
Toulouse, 16
Turin, 156
Tunbridge Wells, 99, 132

Uphill, 1, 3
Urzel, 240
Uxbridge, 110, 257

Valenciennes, 211, 241
Vermelles, 70
Villecoublay, 187

Walcheren, 207
Waldershare Park, 34
Walland Marsh, 108
Wallington, 90
Walton-on-the-Naze, 80
Wangerooge, 242
Westenhanger, 2, 11
Whitfield, 1, 137
Whitstable, 51, 218
Winchelsea, 163
Wissant Sands, 17
Wittersham, 83
Woodvale, 165, 220
Wootton, 78, 98, 153
Wormshill, 193
Wye, 230

Zeals, 150
Zeebrugge, 16, 193

People

Abler, Major A.K., 207
Adams, F/Lt. 'Jimmy', 248
Aird, Alfred, 32
Aitken, F/O, 170
Aitken, Wing Comm. R.F., 149
Aitkin MC, AFC, S/Ldr. R.S., 30
Akin, Staff Sgt. J., 211
Aldridge, P/O K.A., 71
Alkin, A/C A., 58
Allen, P/O H.R. 'Dizzy', 107
Allway, F/Lt., 65
Amor, P/O H.D.F., 153
Amos, Sgt. D.L., 232
Anderson, F/Lt. J.S., 126
Andler, Ralph, 210

Andreae, P/O C.J.D., 83
Andrews DFC, F/Lt. A.J. 'Andy', 149, 152, 154, 158
Andrews DFC, S/Ldr. D.G., 243
Andrews, P/O, 128
Ansell, Sgt. E.J.R., 173
Anstie, F/O J.A., 170–1
Arnefield, Sgt. S.J., 84
Arnold AFC, Wing Com. E.E., 103, 107
Ashton, F/O P. Wigram, 52–3
Atcherley, Grp. Capt. 'Batchy' R.L.R., 137
Atkins, Sgt. F.P.J., 77
Atkinson, P/O, 132
Atkinson DFC, AFC, S/Ldr. E.D., 27
Austin, F/O G.W.B., 70
Austin, F/Sgt. W.G., 228

Bader, Grp. Capt. D.R.S., 121, 129–30, 263
Bailey, P/O C.M., 71
Bailey, Private L., 85
Bailey, Sgt. V., 183
Baillie, P/O A.D., 22
Baker, F/O H., 104
Baker, S/Ldr., 46
Bamberger, Sgt. 'Bam' A.C., 104
Barber DFM, P/O J.L., 177
Barker, Wing Comm. A., 211, 213
Barley, CPO, 240
Barlow, Captain, 14
Barnes, C.G., 2
Barnett OBE, Air Commandant Dame M.H.B., 254
Barnett, S/Ldr. M.G., 196–7
Barret, Captain, 12
Barret, Wing Comm. F.F., 165, 167, 170
Barry, F/Sgt. W.A.R., 158
Barthold, S/Ldr. E. 'Bats', 191, 196
Bartholomew, P/O B., 132
Barthropp, F/O P.P.C., 124
Barton, P/O A.R.H., 84, 88
Barwell DFC, Grp. Capt. P.R., 141
Bathurst, S/Ldr. P., 66

INDEX

Batten, P/O R., 143, 151, 165, 167
Beadle, F/O, 209
Beake, P/O, 115
Beamont DFC, DSO & Bar, S/Ldr. R.P., 181
Beard, F/O, 240
Beardsley, Sgt. R., 105
Beaston, F/Lt. C.R., 68
Beaumont, Sgt., 135
Beaumont, Air Comm. F., 207
Beggs, Sub. Lt H.W., 90
Bellamy, A/C L.H., 58
Bennett, Lt. W.R., 244
Bentley, 2nd Lt. A.W., 68
Benson, Wing Comm. E.M., 258
Betts, 2nd Lt. E.S., 209
Bigoray, F/Sgt. W.W., 158
Billingham, Sgt., 124
Birbeck, F/O, 176, 180–1
Black, Staff Sgt. R.E., 219
Blakey, Sgt. A.D., 135
Bland, P/O J.W., 93
Blokland Lt. J.B. van, 121
Blower, F/Sgt. F.A., 205
Blumer, W/O R.A.B. 'Red', 218
Blundell-Hill, F/O C.J., 231
Bodie, P/O C.A.W., 100
Boersma, Sgt. L.J., 219
Bollezeele, 72
Bond, S/Ldr. H.J., 243
Bond, F/O, 184–5
Boomsma, Crpl. E.W., 120
Boone, 1st Lt. R.L., 219
Boulding, F/O R., 122
Bousa, S/Ldr. A.L.T.J., 196
Boute, F/Sgt. F.E.L., 198
Boutin, Sgt. A.L., 166
Bowan, Staff Sgt. J., 209
Bowring, S/Ldr., 241
Boyer, F/O, 66
Boyle AFC, AVM, Sir D., 248
Boyle, Lt. Comm. P.S., 241
Brancker, General Sir Sefton, 15, 33
Bray, F/O R.C.J., 197

Brettell, P/O G.E., 132
Brochu, P/O V.A.G., 235
Brocklehurst MBE, David, 266
Brodie, F/Sgt, 191, 194–5
Brothers, F/Lt. P.M., 96
Brown, F/Lt. A.C., 71
Brown, K.K., 74
Brown, P/O, 72
Brown, Sgt. G., 178
Brown, S/Ldr. 145, 195, 224
Brown, S/Ldr. L.J., 195, 209, 240
Brown, Sgt. R.J.W., 73
Bruce, F/O A.E.T., 24
Bruce, Sgt. J., 232
Brunckhurst, Sgt. H.W., 159, 161, 166
Bryant, 2nd Lt. C.W., 166
Buckley DSC, Lt. Comm. J.B., 72
Bulmer, S/Lt. G.G., 78
Bungey DFC, Wing Comm. R.W., 142
Burgon, F/Lt. W.K., 123
Burgwal, F/O R.F., 226
Burke, F/O, 38
Burnett, 2nd L.R., 209
Burns, Tech. Sgt. H.B., 166
Busch, Staff Sgt. J., 211
Bushell, F/O R., 71
Butler, F/Sgt., 158, 167, 178
Butler, W/O W.L., 240

Cameron DFM, P/O D., 157
Campbell, Sgt., C.R., 133
Campbell, F/Sgt. F.Y., 141–2
Campbell-Orde, F/Lt., 35
Carlow, Lord, 34
Carnall, Sgt. R., 76–7, 90
Carne, Daphne, 87
Carrier, Staff Sgt. Robert E., 210
Carroll, F/Lt., 63
Cartwright, W/O E.H., 123, 227, 232
Casson, F/O L.H., 122, 129
Cave-Brown, General, 167
Chadburn DSO, DFC, Wing Comm., 145, 197
Chamberlain, F/O B.A.W., 239

Chamberlain, Neville, 63
Chanute, Octave, 32
Cheeseman, P/O S.H., 207
Child, Lynn, 252
Chiswell, F/Lt., 204
Chittick J.C, Sgt., 160
Churchill, F/Lt., 67, 127–8, 144
Churchill, Winston, 110, 128
Clark, F/Lt., 147
Clarke, A.R.S. Major, 12
Clarkson, F/O E.F., 142–3, 147
Clayton, Sgt. A.J., 141–2
Clayton, Sgt., 71
Cleaver, Captain, 68
Clothier, W.C., 181
Clouston, F/Lt. A.E., 44–6, 48, 182
Clydesdale, S/Ldr., Marquess, 40
Coddy, Sgt., 137
Cody, Samuel, 5
Coen DFC, Captain, 151
Coldrey, Sgt. N.W.J., 145
Collins, S/Ldr. A.R., 99
Collins, L.C.A., 11
Colquhoun, F/Sgt., 243
Comar, P/O K., 93–4
Conan-Doyle, Sir Arthur, 256
Conan-Doyle OBE, Grp. Officer J.L.A., 256, 258
Connolly, Sgt., 126
Connors, F/Lt. S.D.P., 90
Cooper, Sgt. J.E., 124, 131
Cooper, Sgt. M.H.F., 138–9, 149
Cooper-Slipper, F/Lt. M., 69
Copeman, P/O J.H.H., 77
Corfe, Sgt. D., 94
Cornwallis, Lord Lieutenant of Kent, Colonel W. Stanley, 257
Couchen, A/C, 71
Coudray, F/O J.P., 159
Cowan, F/O H., 222
Cox, P/O P.A.N., 79, 81
Craig, Sgt., 76
Crawley, Sgt., 51
Crerar, S/Ldr. Finlay, 58

Crombie, Sgt. R., 77
Crossley DSO, DFC, S/Ldr. M.N., 96, 193, 239, 242
Crouthamel, 2nd Lt. Edgar S., 210
Courtney, Captain, 164
Cuddon-Davis, Lt. A.W., 22
Currant, F/Lt. C.F. 'Bunny', 69–70
Curtiss, 2nd Lt. R.E., 209
Czernastek (Polish), P/O S., 115

D'Arcy, Sub/Lt., 162
Daffron, F/O R.C., 93
Dancot, Sgt. G.L.M.G., 202
Danielson, F/O P.J., 72
Dainty, F/Lt., 48
Dale, Wing Comm. I.G., 206
Daley, Cpl. A., 71
Darling, F/Sgt. A.S., 120
De Brockent, Lt. Col., 207
De Hasse, F/O R.G.H., 170
De Hepcee, Sgt. M.A.R.M., 198
De Moulin, P/O C.J.G., 195
De Neve, F/O C.P., 204
Desens, Lt. Sherwin G., 211
Davies, Sub Lt. D.P., 220
Davies, LAC J.F., 40
Davies, F/Lt. R., 35
Davies, F/O, 180
Davies, F/Lt. D., 202
Davis, Peter, 34
Davy, F/O B.A., 20
Davy, Sgt. D.H. 'Ace', 151–2
Dawson-Paul (RN), Sub/Lt. F., 74
Deacon, Sgt. H.A., 90
Deacon-Elliot, F/O R., 99, 103
Dean, F/O G.H., 158
DeByer, Staff/Sgt. E., 192
Dechamps, F/O P., 213
De Molenes, P/O H.J.M., 147
Demozay, F/Lt. J.F. 'Moses', 134, 141–2, 145, 148, 154, 159, 163
Dempster, Derek, 260
De Niverville, F/Lt. J.A.H.G., 229
Dennison, F/O F.H., 202

INDEX

Derham, Norman, 32
Desoer S/Ldr. N.L., 52
Deugo, P/O R.H., 137
Dicker, S/Ldr. R., 258
Dickman, Lt. Col. J.L., 175
Dinnie, Grp. Officer N., 251–2
Divoy, Leon, 231
Don, P/O R., 80
Donahue, P/O A.G., 83–4, 147
Donkin, Grp Capt., 209
Donne, F/Lt. M.S., 69
Donnet, Wing Comm. M.G.L.M., 231, 236, 239
Dougall, P/O J., 128
Douglas-Hamilton, F/Lt. Lord D., 168
Douthit, Sgt. W.E., 166
Dove, Luther, 211
Dowding GCB, GCVO, CM, ACM, Sir Hugh C.T., 62, 103–104, 110
Down, P/O., J.K., 143, 170
Downer, P/O I.W., 139, 142, 155, 161
Drake DFC, F/Lt. B., 114–15
Driscoll, F/Lt. 'Drip', 123
Drobiński DFC, S/Ldr. B.H., 263
Dunn, F/O N.M., 122
Dunn, P/O W.R., 130–1
Dundas, F/O J., 121, 128
Dunworth, P/O F.P.R., 41
Dymond, Sgt. W.L., 73, 76
Dyson MBE, DFC, Wing Comm., 248

Easby, F/Lt. R.S., 164
East, Sgt. W.R., 180–1
Eayrs, S/Ldr. D.J., 66, 68
Eckhart, 2nd Lt. A., 201
Eden, Rt. Hon. Sir Anthony, 89
Edinger, Acting P/O P.J., 52, 61
Edmonds, Grp. Capt., 46
Edwards, P/O J.D., 143, 148, 167
Eldrid, F/Sgt. M.K., 159
Ellacombe, P/O M.T., 89–90, 93
Ellis, S/Ldr. J., 96
Ellis, 2nd Lt. P., 211
Elsdon, F/O T.A.F., 101

Else, Sgt. P., 78, 96–7
Emmis, Cpl. Harry, 53
Engelman, 135
Englander, Major, 240
Ettles, Sgt., 184
Evans, Sgt. C.H., 146
Evans, Sgt. W.J.K., 71
Ewen, William Hugh, 6

Fairhurst, F/O,123, 125
Fall, DSO, AFC, F/Lt. J.S.T., 22
Farnes, Sgt. P.C.P., 95, 102
Farnie, F/O Scott, 64–5
Farrow, Sgt. R.E., 204
Faumont, Sgt. A.H., 71
Faune, F/Lt., 135
Ferris DFC, F/O A., 76–7, 90
Fey, P/O B., 164–5
Fiander, F/O J.W., 194
Fifield, F/Lt. J.S., 145, 151
Fischer, Jules, 6
Fisher, F/O A., 76
Fisher, Sgt. D.P., 173, 178
Fisher, P/O M.B., 90
Fison, Sgt. K.W., 74
Fisz, S.B., 260
Fitzmaurice, Lt., 12
Fleming, S/Ldr. B.J.A., 234
Fletcher, F/Lt. 'Tom', 138–9, 150, 160
Forbes, F/O N., 72
Ford, F/Lt. R.J.A., 24, 26
Forest, Sgt. D.H., 112
Forward, Sgt., R.V., 79
Foster, 2nd Lt. J., 187
Foulger, Sgt., 120
Foy, Lt., 207
Frederick, F/Lt. G, 211
Franklin, 1st Lt. C.B., 166
Franks, S/Ldr. L.A., 78
Fraser, Sgt., 185
Frehner, F/Sgt. N.E., 196
Freshwater, F/O W.F., 202
Frye, Sgt. R.E., 166
Freeborn DFC, F/Lt. J., 122

Frost, John J., 219
Fuchs, Captain B., 196–7
Fulbright, Staff Sgt., 219
Furlong, F/Lt. O.H., 213

Gage, P/O D.H., 118, 127
Galway, F/O G.G., 154
Gardiner, P/O F.T., 78
Gardner, LAC L.P., 72
Gardner, P/O J.R., 78
Garrick, Lt. Col., 220
Gash, F/Sgt. F., 175
Gass, F/Sgt. I.I., 200
Gaze DFC, F/Lt. F.A.W., 145
Geddes, F/Lt. A.J.W., 52–4, 59, 61
Geraud, F/O J.J., 206
Gibbs, F/O R.G.V., 153
Gibson, F/O J.A.A., 84, 88
Gibson, P/O D.J.N., 200
Gilbert, Charlie, 156
Gilders, Sgt. J., 116–17
Gill, F/O L.G., 183
Gill, S/Ldr., 235
Gillitt, P/O F.N., 143, 149
Gillies, F/Sgt. J., 112, 117
Gillman, P/O K., 95–6, 270
Gillmore, LAC A.A., 71
Gilmour, Sir John, 24
Gisborough, F/Lt. T.W.P.L.C. The Honourable Lord, 172, 180
Glaser, F/O T., 248
Gleave CBE, Grp. Captain T.P., 263
Gleed, P/O I., 54–5
Gleeson, Temp./Sub Lt. J.A., 221
Glendenning, Sgt. J.N., 118
Glew, Sgt. R.C., 125, 128, 155, 160, 169, 175–6
Goddard, Sgt. C.D., 166
Goddard, Sgt. J., 169
Godefroy, F/Lt. H.C, 170, 198
Gooch, P/O. A.E., 169, 201, 207, 211
Goodcliffe, S/Ldr. C.D., 124–5
Gough DFM, Sgt. H.W., 157
Goulevitch, F/Sgt. J., 188–9

Grace, Cecil, 2
Grace DFC, S/Ldr. A.D., 191, 193, 195–6, 201, 213
Graham, Sgt. P., 167
Graham, F/Sgt. R.H., 204
Gram, F/Sgt. F.P., 158
Granados, Staff Sgt. J., 211
Gratton, F/O V.K., 232
Gray, Sgt. M., 99
Greatorex, Wilfred, 260
Green, F/Sgt. E.G.F., 215
Green, F/Lt. J.E., 193
Green, F/Lt. 'Paddy' C.P., 71, 104, 110, 113, 115–16, 119, 121, 212
Green, Sgt. W.J., 94
Green, Lt. W.P., 134
Greer, P/O R.T., 234
Grey, P/O J.E.I., 117
Grey, Lt. R.H.G., 72
Gribble DFC, F/Lt., 123
Grice, D FC, F/O D., 84–5, 88
Griffin, P/O G.C., 154
Griffiths, P/O A.A., 202, 229
Griggs, F/Lt., 158
Grottick, F/Lt. J., 191
Gunn, S/Ldr. G., 232
Gutman, Lt. H.L., 210

Haabjoern DFC, Wing Comm. E., 213
Hagwood, F/Lt., 170
Halewood, A/C E.V., 58
Hall, F/Lt., 142
Hall DFC, F/O D.R., 183
Hall, Sub Lt. E., 193, 215, 232
Halliwell, S/Ldr. 234
Hamel, Gustav Wilhelm, 6
Hamilton, Beauford, 183, 211
Hamilton, Guy, 260
Hancock, Col., 185
Hanmer, Wing Comm. H.R., 63
Happold, Sgt. W.G.J., 174
Harding, 2
Harries, DFC & Bar, S/Ldr., R.H., 159, 164–6, 169–71, 184

INDEX

Harris, F/Lt. C.L., 215
Harris, Staff Sgt. J., 192
Harris, F/Sgt. R., 155
Harris, P/O, 69
Hartridge, F/Lt., 46
Hartwell, F/Sgt. D.R., 136, 158, 166, 196, 207
Harvey, F/O W.S., 229
Haskett, Sgt. J., 239
Hastings, F/O D.W., 223
Hawkins, Sgt. K., 151
Haygreen, Sgt. A., 71
Haynes, F/O S., 232
Haywood, F/O, 180
Healey, F/O I.R., 150, 160, 177
Heap, Lt. J.R., 146–7, 185
Helminiak, 2nd Lt. R.O., 239
Henderson, Staff Sgt. E., 192
Henneberg (Polish), S/Ldr. Z. K.K.W. and Bar, 118
Herbert, P/O, 70
Hess, Rudolf, 168
Heybourne, Staff Sgt. A., 192
Heyworth, S/Ldr. A.J. 'Jimmy', 133–4
Hicks Peck DSO, AFC, S/Ldr. A., 20
Hicks, F/O, 122
Higgs, F/O D.P.K., 76
Hill, Dan, 156
Hill OBE, Grp. Officer F.B., 258
Hill, F/Lt. N., 189–91
Hill KCB, MC, AFC & Bar, ACM Sir Roderick, 222
Hillary, F/Lt. R.H., 74
Hilton, P/O T.M., 152–3, 166
Himr, S/Ldr. J., 192
Hirschel, F/Lt. L., 210
Hitler, Adolf, 156, 218, 242
HRH Duke of Kent, 77
HRH Duchess of Gloucester, 257–8
HRH King George VI, 116, 155, 242
HM King Peter of Yugoslavia, 234, 243
HRH Prince Bernard of the Netherlands, 207
HRH Queen Elizabeth the Queen Mother, 252
HRH Queen Wilhelmina of the Netherlands, 204, 241
Hoare, F/O R.M., 172, 180
Hodgkinson, S/Ldr. C.G.S. 'Hoppy', 198, 200
Hof, Jan, 121
Holland, P/O 'Dutch' D.F., 103
Holland, F/Lt. R.H., 118
Hogan, S/Ldr. H., 88
Hogarth, F/O, 166, 176, 181
Hogg, Sub/Lt. C.S.F., 72
Holm, Lt. W.J., 219
Holt DSO, Major F.V., 40
Homer Scutt MC, F/Lt. G.H., 22
Hone, F/Lt. D., 177, 181
Hope, F/O, 70
Hopkinson, Sgt. E.B., 215
Horstmann, LAC Rosemary, 81
Howard, Leslie, 70
Howarth, Sgt. E., 81
Howes, F/O, 243
Huck, 2nd Lt. George M., 211
Hucks, Bentfield Charles, 6, 22
Huff, C.W., 211
Hukin, F/O P.E., 204
Hulton-Harrop, P/O O.P de L., 69
Humphreys, F/Sgt. H.G., 185–6, 241
Hunt, Victor, 3
Hurley, S/Ldr. H.B., 76
Hurst, Sgt., 128
Huskinson, A/C R.I., 58
Hutchings, P/O W., 71
Hyder DFM, F/Sgt. L.A., 156–7
Hypes, Staff Sgt. R.L., 220

Ingle-Finch, S/Ldr. M.R., 198
Inwood, P/O R., 183
Issac, Sgt. L.R., 83

Jackson, A/C J.J., 58
Januszewicz (Polish), F/O W., 105
Jeffreys, Sgt. J.W., 157

Jeffrey, LAC, 70
Jenkins, F/Sgt. C.H., 204
Jerrard VC, F/O A., 22
Johns, F/Lt., 163
Johnson, Amy, 266
Johnson, P/O J.G., 169, 175
Johnson, Sub Lt. R.K.H., 221
Johnston, P/O J.T., 90, 93
Jones, Sgt., 123
Jones DSO, DFC, Wing Comm. E.G., 142, 149, 160
Jones, LAC F.R., 59
Jones, F/Sgt. G.W., 136
Jones, F/O J.D., 236
Jones F/Sgt. P.L., 189
Jones, F/Lt. R.C., 256
Jonker, F/O J., 226–7
Jordan, F/Sgt. H.G., 158
Joslin, S/Ldr. J.D.C., 75
Jupp, Sgt. L.C., 132–3

Kalligeros, 2nd Lt. Val, 211
Keefer DFC, S/Ldr. D.C., 191
Keighly, P/O G., 78
Kemp, P/O J.R., 77
Kennard DFC, Wing Comm. H.C., 248–50
Kennaway, James, 260
Kennedy, F/O A.L., 241
Kenny, Colonel H.T.H., 31
Kershaw, LAC 1st Class F., 20
Kettle, Edmund, 1
Kidson, P/O R., 77
Kilvington, Sgt. H., 169
Kitzinger, Lt., 73
King, P/O D.S., 133
King, F/Sgt. J.H., 151, 201, 209
Kippling, Sgt. R., 178
Kipping, Sgt H., 169
Kirby-Green, Mrs. Betty, 44
Kirby, Mark, 117
Kirkpatrick, Leroy, 210
Kiss, Sgt. A.C., 239
Klipsch, Sgt. P.H., 71

Knight, F/Lt. L.R., 114, 203
Knowlton, Sgt. J., 137
Knox, B.W., 36
Knusden, Lt., 239–40
Koon, Sgt. V.E., 239
Kozlowski (Polish), P/O K., 93
Kronfield, Herr, 33
Krzysztopinski (Polish), Sgt. J., 195
Kuhlmann DFC, Major K.C., 204–205

Lacerte, F/O R.J., 234
Lacey, Sgt.'Ginger' J.H., 94–5, 263
Lake, F/Lt. R.G., 234
Lamb, F/O P.G., 94
Lamont, F/Sgt. R.W., 167
Lang, Archbishop of Canterbury W.C.G., 116
Langdon, LAC, 88
Lapkawski (Polish), F/Lt. W., 119
Large, P/O, 149
Lawley, Sgt.W., 166
Lawrence, F/O K.A., 111
Lawrence, F/Sgt. J.W.N., 123, 215
Lawson, P/O, 116
Lawson DFC, S/Ldr., 128
Leacroft MC, S/Ldr. J., 22
Learmond, P/O B.H.G., 71
Learmont, Brigadier D.A., 167
Learoyd VC, F/Lt. R.A.B., 109
Lee, P/O 'Hawkeye' K.N.T., 81, 93
Lee, Sgt. M.A.W., 112
Lees, S/Ldr. R.B., 99
Leeson, F/Lt. P.G., 71
Leigh-Mallory OBE, DSO, AVM Trafford, 121, 154
Le Maire, P/O A., 143, 146
Lennox, Lt. James, 40
Lenton, F/Lt., 186
Le Roux DFC & Bar, F/O C., 131, 149
Leslie, S/Ldr. Sir Norman, 19–20
Leva, F/Sgt. P. 'Pino', 223, 225
Lewis, P/O D.C., 74
Lilburn, P/O, 197
Lindeman, A/C W.J., 121

INDEX

Lines, P/O, 69
Lingard, Sgt. J.C., 59
Litchfield, P/O P., 77
Litherland, Midshipman, 214
Littell, Tech. Sgt. C., 166
Littler, S/Ldr., 249
Livings, Sgt. R.C., 122
Llewellyn, Mike, 266
Lloyd, Sgt., 128
Lloyd, S/Ldr. I.T., 22
Loader, F/Sgt. S.W., 196, 209, 213, 241
Lock, P/O E., 106–107
Lockhart, P/O J., 94
Loudon, F/Lt. M., 77
Lomax, Sgt. E.A., 67
Luck, Sgt. J.A.A., 69
Ludlow-Hewitt ACB, CMG, DSO, MC, Sir E.A., 84
Luke MC, F/Lt. T.C., 22
Lukens, 1st Lt. J.W., 192
Lux, F/O 'Jackie' J.P., 159
Lyndon, Sgt., 133

Macarthur, F/O D.M.I., 20
MacDonald, Major D.W., 166
MacDonald, Sgt. J.J., 122
MacDonnell, S/Ldr. A.R.D., 92
MacDougall, P/O F.N., 77
MacIntosh, F/Lt., 248
Mack, F/Sgt. 240
MacKenzie, F/O J., 104
MacKenzie DFC, AFC, AE, P/O 'Mac' K.W., 105–106, 132
MacKenzie, P/O, 76
Mackie, F/Sgt. J., 157
MacLachlan, P/O, 34
Maclean, F/Lt., 172
Magwood, S/Ldr., 198
Mains, Sgt., 121
Malan DFC, DSO, S/Ldr. A.G. 'Sailor', 115, 117, 124–5
Mallinson, Sgt., 191
Mallory, Air Vice Marshall T.L., 121, 134, 154

Malm, 2/Lt. O.R., 159
Mander, Sub Lt. R., 213, 232
Mann DFM, Sgt, J., 118–19
Manuel, Corporal W.B 'Bill', 32
Maridor DFC, CG, F/O J.P., 154, 184
Mariner, Sub Lt. P.F., 215
Marsh, F/O N., 244
Marshland, P/O, 73
Mart, P/O, 161, 165
Mathew, F/Lt. I., 143, 163, 175, 184–5
Matheson, Private, 65
Matthews, F/Lt. S.W., 198
Maygothling, F/Lt., 34
Maynard, F/O L.E., 26
McAdam, Sgt. J., 116
McCaleb, 1st Lt. H., 192
McClintok, P/O J.A., 83
McClinton, W/O2 H.G., 234
McColl, Cpl., 88
McConnell, F/Lt. R., 105
McDonnell – Hartas, F/Lt. P., 111, 116
McDonald, F/O A.J., 235
McEvoy, Grp. Captain T.N., 120
McGarrigle, Sgt., 170
McGhiey, Tech. Sgt. D., 211
McGlashan, P/O K.B., 73
McGregor Waterston, P/O R. 'Bubble', 58
McGregor CdG, S/Ldr. P.R., 237
McIntosh, F/O J.A., 234
McIntyre, P/O A.G., 90
McIntyre AFC, Wing Comm. D., 40
McKay, Sgt. D.A.S., 88, 93, 110–12, 115–16
McKay, F/Lt. D.G., 205
McKenzie, P/O J.W., 77
McKillop, W/O R.P.A., 202
McLaing, F/Lt. C.T. MC, 22
McNair, Sgt. O.H., 30
McNair DFC, S/Ldr. R.W 'Buck', 191–2
McNaught, FSgt. L.C.C., 232
McRae, Sgt., 71
McSherry, Sgt. P.M.A., 117
McWherter, Lt., 151

Mearns, Sgt. D.B., 7
Med, LAC, 51
Megone, William, B., 2–6
Meijers, P/O L.M, 203
Meng, Navigator H., 219
Meredith, F/O R.V., 69
Mertens, P/O J.A.F., 54
Middleton VC, F/Sgt. R.H., 156–7
Millar, F/O A., 232
Millington, Sub Lt. R.W., 221
Mills, Sgt. P.A., 120
Milne, F/O D.K., 74
Milne DFC, Wing Comm. R.M., 170
Milne, F/O, 243
Milne, Sgt. W., 209
Mitchell, Sgt. G.D., 182
Mitchell, F/O E.W., 75
Mitchell, F/Lt. J.V.C., 215
Mitchell, R.J., 70
Mitchell, Sgt. W., 185
Moffat, Sgt. G.H., 70, 79
Morgan, Sgt. W., 119
Moir, W/O K.C., 213
Moisant, J.B., 2
Montgomery KG, GCB, DSO, PC, DL, Field Marshal Sir Bernard, 214
Moor, LAC (later S/Ldr.) A., 23, 39, 42–3, 50
Moore, F/Sgt. K.S., 215, 232
Moore, L/A V.S.A., 73
Morrell OBE, S/Ldr. D. Duncan, 219
Morren, F/Lt., 164
Morris, Section Officer A.B., 65
Morrison, Sgt. N., 117
Morrison, F/Sgt., 137
Morrison, F/O R.A., 160–1, 173
Morrison, S/Ldr., 173
Morrow, Sgt., 170
Morton-Jenkins OBE, KPM, O/St. John, R.C., 184
Motycka, F/Lt. A., 193
Mould, Sgt. A., 122
Muirhead, F/Lt. I.J. 'Jock', 69, 72
Mulhall, W/O J.L., 236

Mullins, Sgt. R.J., 215
Mungo-Park DFC, S/Ldr., 122, 125
Murphy, Lt., 16
Murphy, Sub Lt. J., 221
Murray, F/Sgt. 137
Murrin, LAC H.K., 73
Naismith, F/Lt. W., 232

Nash, F/O R.S., 167, 185
Naysmith, F/O, 165, 172
Neil DFC, AFC, S/Ldr. T.F., 175, 182, 227, 235
Nelson, F/O, 38
Neville, Sgt. W.J., 83–4
Newberry, LAC, 70
Newberry, P/O E.R., 239
Newton, Sgt. H.S., 77, 90
Newton, W/O N.E., 232
Nicholson, S/Lt. J.T., 73
Niven, David, 70
Noel, Louis, 6
Norman, Temp. L/A S., 221
Norton Newall, Major C.L., 8
Norman, Sgt. N.P., 133
Nugent, Staff Sgt. G.J., 220
Nunneley, 1st Lt. C.M., 219

Oliphant, 1st Lt. R.A., 166
Oliver, Lt., 12
Omdahl, F/Sgt. T., 135, 143, 167
O'Meara, P/O J., 104, 109–12, 114
O'Neill DFC, S/Ldr. H.F., 206
O'Shaughnessy, P/O A., 160, 165, 171, 178
O'Sullivan, F/Lt. P.D., 220
Opie, P/O E.S., 182
Opie, S/Ldr. W.A., 52
Orford, A/C J.E., 58
Ormiston DFC, P/O T.M., 215
Ormston DFC, F/Lt. I.C., 195
Orrell, F/O J., 182
Orr, F/Lt. W.B., 142
Ortmans, F/O C.C.A., 149
Ot, F/Lt. J.H., 209
Oxspring, S/Ldr. R.W., 107, 140–2

INDEX

Pacco, F/O P., 230
Paine, F/O J.T., 22
Palmer, 2nd Lt. F., 192
Palmer VC, S/Ldr. P.A., 158
Pannell, F/Lt. G., 141
Parisse, F/O J.F., 213
Parks, P/O, 191–2
Park GCB, KBE, MC & Bar, DFC, Sir Keith R., 18, 99, 102, 122
Park MC, DFC, S/Ldr. W.H. 'Porky', 27
Parks, P/O, 192
Parks, 2nd Lt. J.G., 192
Parkin, P/O G., 80
Parnell DFC, F/Lt., 165
Parrott, F/O P., 111–12, 186
Parry, F/Lt., 180–1
Partridge, F/Lt., 240
Pattinson, F/O A.J.S., 108
Paulton, Sgt. E.A., 158
Pavey, Sgt., 69
Paxton, S/Ldr. A., 48, 50
Payne, Sgt. A.H., 71
Payne MC, AFC, S/Ldr. L.G.S., 27
Payne, P/O R.H., 153
Payne, Wing Comm. W.L., 63, 76
Peak, Sgt. E., 219
Pearce, Sgt. J.W., 27
Pearce-Gervis, Lt., 16–17
Pearson, F/Sgt. A.V., 232
Peck DSO, MC, S/Ldr. A.H., 27, 50
Pedley, P/O M., 53
Peel DFC, Wing Comm. J.R.A., 128
Pepper DFC, F/O G., 154
Pepys, F/O S.G.L., 71
Peterson DSO, DFC & Bar, Lt. Col. C.G., 176
Peters, F/O R.A., 202
Petrie, P/O R.A.G., 59
Pfeiffer, P/O J.P., 94
Phillips, P/O P.H., 182
Pickering, J.H.T. 'Pickles', 107
Pigdon, A/C C., 58
Pirie, LAC G.R., 70
Plagis DFC, S/Ldr. 'Johnny', 248

Pope, Sgt., 70
Popek (Polish), Sgt. M., 118
Portal KG, GCB, OM, DSO & Bar, MC, Sir Charles, 158
Potter, F/Sgt. K.G., 232
Poulton, P/O R., 122, 125
Powell, Wing Comm. R.P.R., 211
Powell, Sgt. S.W.M., 78
Powers, Sgt. C.D., 209
Poynton, F/Lt. T.R., 178–9
Pragnal, D.W.A., 74
Preddy, Capt. G.E., 206
Priest, Sgt. C.W., 232
Pritchard, Capt. S., 14
Probyn DFC, S/Ldr H.M., 30–1
Prodger, Clifford, 12
Propart, F/Lt. W.J., 240
Pruden P/O N., 133
Prytherch, F/Sgt., 143
Ptacek (Czech), W/O R., 116
Pullen, F/O, 167
Purvis, F/O J.H.C., 24
Putt, F/Lt. A.R., 88

Quinnell DFC, Air Commodore J.C., 58

Radnor KG, KCVO, DL, Lord W. Pleydell-Bouverie, 2, 11
Rainville, F/O J., 163
Ramsay, Sgt. N.H.D., 83
Range, Sgt. L.F., 182
Read, F/O F., 32–3
Redford, Sgt. H.T., 182
Rees, Sgt. R.F., 182
Rejthar, F/Lt. S., 193
Reuther, 2nd Lt. J.F., 239
Reynolds, Victor, 223
Renshaw, F/Lt., 169
Richey, S/Ldr. P.H.M., 148–9
Riding, Capt., 164
Rimke, Capt., 151
Robb, F/O R.L.T., 197
Roberts, F/Sgt., 150
Roberts, LAC, 71

289

Roberts, S/Ldr., 234
Robertson, F/O C., 232
Robinson, S/Ldr., 68
Robinson, P/O, 71
Rochfort, FO, 71
Roden, F/Lt. T.G.V., 232
Rodes, W/O K.H., 215
Rodger, Sgt. J.K., 145
Roffe, Sgt., 184
Rolfe, P/O B.J., 59
Rollo, Sgt. A.M., 207, 220
Rose, P/O J., 94, 96, 169, 173, 193, 195
Ross, F/Lt. R.M.H., 36
Ross, P/O 'Jock', 41
Rossignol, Staff Sgt. F., 211
Rozwadowski (Polish), P/O M., 89
Round, P/O 'Johnny', 152, 184
Royde DFC, F/O G.R., 157
Ruffun, Staff Sgt. G., 219
Rumsey, LAC F.G., 72
Russell, Sgt. G.H., 182
Russel, Wing Comm., 50

Sadler, Brigadier, 167
Salmet, M., 6
Salmond Maitland, ACM, GCB, CMG, CVO, DSO & Bar, Sir J., 27, 46
Salt, John, 34
Saltzman, Harry, 260
Sandman, P/O, 125
Sarasqueta, Joaquin, 211
Sassoon CBE, CMG, MP, Sir Philip, 31, 34, 41, 46
Saunders, W/O A., 175–6
Saunders GCB, KBE, MC, DFC & Bar, MM, Air Vice Marshall Sir H.W.L., 163, 202, 207
Saunders, P/O R.L., 70
Scamp, W/O Sydney, 37
Scott DSO, DFC, Wing Comm. D.J., 204, 206–207
Scott, Sgt. C.V.R., 122, 182
Scott-Taylor, P/O R., 24
Scroggs, Grp. Capt., 181

Seagris, R/O C.B., 250
Seales, F/Sgt., 153
Seaton, S/Ldr., 240
Selby, P/O H.C., 221
Sequin, Staff Sgt. J., 411
Sercombe, F/Lt. J., 206
Seydel, F/O, 167, 185
Shannon, F/O U.Y., 50
Sheen, F/O D.G.B., 99
Shelley, H.J., 53
Sheperd, Lt. J., 211
Shepherd, F/Lt., 234
Sheridan, Miss P., 170
Sherk, F/Lt. D., 222
Sherran, Brian, 221
Shilling OBE, PhD, MSc, CEng., Miss B., 181
Shirmer, TAG F., 221
Sim, F/Lt. R., 77, 232, 235
Simmons, Sgt. S.F., 70
Simpson, LAC J.H., 52–3
Sinclair, Sir Archibald, HM Secretary of State for Air, 119
Skalski (Polish), P/O S., 95
Shawyer, Sgt., 182
Shurlds, Capt. H.W., 213
Skinner DFC, P/O N.E., 157
Slack, F/O, 166
Slatter, P/O D.M., 78
Small, F/Sgt. J., 169
Smilnyek, Staff Sgt. Andrew J., 210
Smith, F/O, 240, 244
Smith, S/Ldr. A.T., 76, 78
Smith, F/Lt. E.B.B., 77
Smith, Sgt., 235
Smith, Sgt. M., 239
Smith, P/O N.L., 182
Smith, Sgt. R.N., 211
Smythe, P/O R.F., 88
Snell, F/Sgt. J., 160, 166, 195
Somerville, P/O H., 58
Spanton, Sgt. D.R., 169
Spear, LAC H., 71
Spears, Sgt. A.W., 112, 118–19

INDEX

Spence, F/O J.A., 137, 146, 159, 161, 166–7, 169–70, 185–6
Spooner, Miss Winifred, 33
Spurdle DFC, F/Lt. R., 140, 141–3, 147
Stacey, LAC H.A.J., 59
Standen, F/Sgt. P.C., 160, 195
Starbuck, Lt., 151
Steen, LT. G., 120–1
Stenberg, F/O, 185
Stephens MBE, Grp. Officer A., 252
Stepp, Capt. M.L., 179–80
Stevens, 1st Lt. C.W., 219
Stevenson, G.H., 34
Stewart, F/Lt. J.C.M., 32
Stillwell, F/O R., 185
St Louis, Staff Sgt. M., 192
Stoney, F/Lt. G.E.B., 93
Strange DSO, DFC & Bar, MC, Wing Comm. L.L.A., 160–1, 163, 165
Struben, F/O H.M., 20
Stuart-Turner, Sgt. K.M., 137
Sucharitkul, Lt. A., 36
Sutton, Sgt. E.C., 146
Swanson, 2nd Lt. H.W., 239
Swindlehurst, Sgt. T., 182
Sydel, P/O G., 143
Sykes, Sgt. E.E., 120, 138
Symes, LAC, 88

Tamblyn, F/O H.N., 78
Tanner, F/Sgt. J.H., 84
Taylor, F/O H.W., 22
Thielke, Sgt. F.P., 239
Thomas, F/O E., 106
Thomas, 1st Lt. W., 192
Thompson, Major, 68
Thompson, S/Ldr., 76
Thomson, F/Lt. J.A., 73
Thynn, S/Ldr., 63
Ticklepenny, Sgt. E.K., 185–6
Todd, F/O, 172
Todt, Fritz, 200
Tomlinson, P/O 'Tommy', 131
Tomlinson, F/Lt., 147

Tomlinson, S/Ldr. G.C., 69
Tonkin, F/O W., 244
Tonge, P/O Eddie 146
Toone DFM, P/O J.H., 154
Torney, F/O J.G, 185
Toupin, Sgt. L.L.V, 169
Trenchard GCB, OM, GCVO, DSO, H.M., Marshall of the RAF, 27, 128, 182
Travers, Herbert, 6
Trebing, Staff Sgt. W.O., 219
Triptree, P/O, 70
Troyer, Wayne, 211
Tuck, Wing Comm. R.R. Stanford, 263
Tucker, Dr. W.S., 38
Turek, P/O T.S., 195
Turner, F/Sgt. C., 78
Turner, F/O G.C., 112, 162
Turner, Major C.M.C., 31
Tweed, 2nd Lt. G.E., 219

Uptigrove, F/Sgt. W.E., 215

Vachon, F/Sgt. E.T., 158
van Arkell, F/O J., 203
van Damme, Staff Sgt. W.A., 209
van Nagell, F/O Baron E.J., 205
van Nouhuis, R.F., 135
van Shaick DFM, F/Lt. J.E., 153
Vaughan-Fowler, P/O Dennis G., 36
Vickers, F/O E.A.H., 222
Villiers-Tuthill, P/O P.F.C., 71
Vink, J., 135
Voak, F/Lt. A.F., 221
Voorspuij, F/Lt. H.J., 135,209
Wade, Capt. Louis R., 210
Wade, P/O T.S.,102
Waddington, W/O, 135, 166, 184
Wakefield, F/O O., 182
Walker, F/Sgt. J.E., 143
Walker MC, AFC, F/O H.E., 20
Walker, S/Ldr. R.H., 235
Wallace, F/Lt. J.D., 239
Wallens, S/Ldr. R.W., 209, 211, 213, 215, 240–1

Walsh, F/O L.A., 26–7
Walters, P/O, 205
Wangen, Bob, 211
Ward, F/O M.V., 22
Ward, Staff Sgt. R., 239
Warren, LAC, 206
Warrington, P/O G.M., 36
Waterson, Sgt., 184
Watkins, F/O A.A., 213
Watlington, Sgt., 175
Watne, Sgt. R.K., 165
Watson, P/O E.J., 26–7
Watten, Lt., 16
Watts, Wing Comm. R.F., 207, 239
Watts-Farmer DFC, S/Ldr. J.N., 124
Webb, F/Lt. H.C.V., 206
Weck, Bombardier W., 219
Weedon, S/Ldr. L.S., 63
Welch, F/Lt., 247
Welch, Sgt., 145
West, P/O R.A., 73
Whewel, Sgt. R.T.G., 120
Whitall, Sgt. F.K., 183
White, P/O W.A., 215
Whitfield, F/Sgt. T., 155
Whitlam, Sgt., 71
Whitman, Sgt. G.A. 'Lefty', 193
Whitney, P/O G.B., 137
Whittaker, P/O R.C., 69
Whittaker, F/O W.H., 223
Wik, Nicholas, 210
Wildish, F/O R.K.J., 143
Wilkes, 2nd Lt. C.E., 166
Wilkinson, Sgt., 67
Wilkinson, 2nd Lt., 68
Williams, F/O R.C., 231–2
Williams, Major G.G.A., 19
Willington, Wing Comm. D.F., 243
Williams, F/O R.C., 231
Williamson, Sgt., 70
Willington, P/O W.H., 75
Willington, Wing Comm. D.F., 243
Willocks, Sgt. P.H., 84
Wilson, F/O, 173, 191

Wilson, F/Sgt. J.A., 144
Wilson, P/O R.R., 77
Wilson, F/O, 191, 195
Wimbush, F/O A.C.G., 54
Winfield, P/O A., 241
Winskill, P/O, 117
Winter, P/O D.C., 99
Wise, Sgt. J.F., 77
Wolfe, Staff Sgt. Vail S., 210
Wood, Derek, 260
Wood, P/O J.E.R., 75–6
Woodhouse, S/Ldr. H., 121
Woolley DFC, Wing Comm. R.M.B.D. 'Duke', 145
Worrall, S/Ldr. J., 78
Worsley, Doctor R.L., 53
Wright, F/Lt. A.R., 103
Wright, F/O G.F.M., 70
Wright, Tech. Sgt. Ivan M., 210
Wright, Bob, 211
Wybrew, P/O, 169
Wydrowski (Polish), P/O B., 115

Young, LAC T.G., 54
Younge, F/Sgt, 147

German Pilots/Crew

Ahrens, Gefr. W., 154

Beese, Lt., 148
Berbach, Uffz. J., 122
Bierworth, Obfw. Heinrich, 156
Breier, Obrgfr. V., 154

Erwin, Obgrf., 135
Euker, Fw. H., 163

Fernsebner, Fw., 81
Fischer, Gefr. R., 163
Floerke, Oblt., 95
Freiberger, Uffz. F., 197–8
Fritsch, Obfw. P., 178
Futhrthmann, Fw. R., 122

INDEX

Galland, Major Adolf, 112, 118–20, 170, 263
Galland, Hptm. W.F., 163, 170, 185
Gerhardt, Uffz. K., 122
Glunz, Obfw. Adolf, 154, 185
Göring, Herman, 76, 88, 103, 238
Gottschalk, Fw W., 99–100
Groth, Hptmn, 71

Heise, Fw. H., 88
Hufenreuther, Hptmn. A., 122

Illner, Obfw., 78

Keller, Oblt. P., 172
Kemen, Fw, 88
Keppler, Uffz. H., 197
Kern, Gefr. E., 163
Kierstein, Obfw. P., 165
Knorr, Uffz. K., 154
Kohl, Obgefr. H., 154
Krafft, Oblt. H., 69
Kraus, Uffz. F.H., 88
Krieg, Uffz. H., 193
Kroner, Oblt., 118
Kruger, Lt. H. 'Benno', 142
Kuhlmann, Gefr. H., 154
Kunn, Uffz. W., 154

Labusga, Obfw., 71

Meyer, Lt. E.B.O., 106
Mietusch, Hptm.,165
Mobius, Uffz. H., 92
Molders, Obelt. Werner, 116
Muller, Fw. Herbert, 163
Munchenhagen, Hptm. R., 88

Ott, Flgr. Kornelius, 154

Proske, Oblt. R., 92
Radener, Lt., 181
Rosen, Fw. Adolf, 110
Rossiger, Oblt. W.M., 85

Schäfer, Oblt. H.C., 69
Scheiter, Uffz., 69
Schlathe, Lt. Werner, 115
Schmid, Obfw., 78
Schmoller-Haldy, Oblt., 72
Schweser, Fw. F., 106–107
Selck, Oberlt. K., 197
Seufert, Obrgf. B., 111
Sprick, Oblt. Gustav, 111
Stresemann, Gefr., 154
Strohauer, Uffz., 73

Terry, Lt., 69
Tietzen, Hptm. Horts 'Jakob', 77
Tomcyzk, Uffz. K., 163

Ulenberg, Lt., 73

Weber, Gefr. E., 122
Weber, Uffzr. H., 88
Weiss, Major Gerhardt, 131
Wiggers, Hptm., 84

Aircraft/Airships/Gliders
Airspeed,
    Oxford I, 64, 178, 183, 244
    AS.30 Queen Wasps, 68
Albatross DIII, 20
Armstrong Whitworth,
    Atlas, 52
    Siskin IIIA, 26–7, 29–31, 36
    Whitley V, 132, 183
Auster – Taylorcroft, 164, 190
Avro,
    504K, 8, 18–20, 46, 82–3, 265–6
    Anson, 66, 104–105, 107–108, 183, 227
    Lancaster, 124, 182–3, 188–9, 232, 234–6, 239–41
    Tutor, 58, 66, 74, 128

BE2c, 7–8
Blackburn,
    Botha, 66
    Dart, 48

293

Blériot, 2, 6
Boeing B17, 135, 144–5, 149–51, 154, 170, 173, 183, 192–4, 201, 210–11, 239
Boulton Paul Defiant I, 77–8, 120, 122, 124, 146, 159, 170
Bristol,
   Beaufighter, 144, 154, 183, 215
   Blenheim I, 55, 57–9, 61, 63, 66, 68–74, 77, 84, 95, 120, 122, 130, 134, 189
   Bombay, 144
   Bulldog, 29, 38

Cierva C.30/C.39 Autogyro, 63, 112, 118, 162, 189, 191
Consolidated B-24 Liberator, 166, 173, 183, 201, 210–211, 219, 241
Curtis,
   Seagull, 241
   Tomahawk, 134, 183

De Havilland,
   Comet Racer, 44
   DH4, 32
   DH9, 12, 14, 16–18, 35–6
   DH10, 12
   DH90 Dragon Fly, 31
   DH Gypsy Moth, 74
   DH Hornet Moth, 190
   DH Leopard Moth, 66
   DH Mosquito, 183, 197, 204–207, 209, 211, 213, 215, 218, 236, 247
   DH Puss Moth, 31
   DH Queen Bee, 66, 68
   DH Queen Wasp, 66, 68
   DH Tiger Moth, 40, 66, 68, 178, 182, 190, 192, 198
Dornier,
   Do 17, 72–3, 76, 88–90, 95, 99, 111–12, 114, 153
   Do 24, 146
   Do 215, 90, 94, 96, 102, 105
   Do 217, 145, 153–4, 163, 165, 205
Douglas,
   Boston, 165, 183, 193, 200, 211, 215, 234
   Dakota, 214, 218, 221, 233, 241
   Douglas C53 Skytrooper, 235
   Mitchell II, 135, 203, 209, 211, 215, 225

F.E.2b, 18–19
F.E3, 4
Fairy,
   Albacore, 185
   Fulmar, 162
   Swordfish, 72–3, 185
Focke Fw 190, 142–6, 148–9, 151–9, 161–5, 169–73, 176, 178, 180–1, 183–7, 191–2, 195–6, 202–204
Fokker T. VIIw, 121

General Aircraft Hotspur, 183
Gloster,
   Gauntlet II, 54–5
   Gladiator II, 55, 57, 61
   Grebe II, 22, 24–7, 50
   Meteor, 241, 249
Gotha Giant, 7
Grumman Avenger IIs, 214, 221

Handley Page,
   Halifax, 131–2, 174, 176, 183, 234
   Hampden, 109, 132
   Harrow, 175, 178
   O/400, 12, 14, 19
   V/1500, 12, 17–19
Hawker,
   Audax I, 52, 54, 74
   Demon, 34, 55, 58
   Fury I, 31, 38, 40–1, 46, 48
   Hart, 35, 38, 51–2, 58
   Hector, 58, 72
   Hind, 74
   Horsley, 46
   Hurricane, 57, 61, 66–76, 78–81, 83–4, 88–90, 93–4, 96, 99, 104–106, 110, 112, 115–20, 122–3, 128, 130, 144, 176, 181, 183, 202, 234, 243, 263, 266
   Tempest, 218–19, 222, 227, 228, 249

INDEX

Typhoon, 137, 148–9, 153, 160, 162, 173, 177–8, 181, 183, 185–7, 193, 195, 198, 202, 204, 213
Woodcock II, 27, 29
Heinkel,
    He 59, 84, 110, 127–8
    He 60, 110
    He 111, 69–70, 73, 88, 109, 122, 144, 236, 263
    He 177A, 205
Henschel Hs 126, 134

Junkers Ju 87 Stuka, 65, 69, 78, 80–1, 84, 88, 94–5, 164
    Ju 88, 84, 90, 98–9, 106, 112, 114, 118–19, 143, 146, 149, 152, 176, 197, 204

Lockheed,
    Electra, 151, 182
    Hudson, 183
    P38 Lightnings, 150, 205
    Ventura, 193

Martin B26 Marauder, 192, 200–201, 206–207, 209–11, 219
Mayfly, 3, 5
    Claude Grahame-White, 4–6
Messerschmitt,
    Me 109/Bf 109, 69–81, 83–4, 88–9, 92, 94–5, 99–101, 103–107, 109–112, 114–15, 118, 120-161, 164, 173, 177, 182–3, 191, 197, 213, 263
    Me 110/Bf 110, 71–2, 85, 92, 99, 105–106, 111
    Me 262, 238, 240
    Me 410, 205
Miles,
    Magister, 125, 137
    Master, 183, 249
    Martinet, 182, 243–4, 249
    Mentor, 120
    Proctor, 66, 181, 183

North American,
    Harvard, 183
    P51 Mustang, 162, 178, 183, 206, 209, 215–16, 218, 231, 232, 240–1
Octave Channel Glider, 32

Percival P.10 Vega Gull, 54
    No.7 Manuel Primary Glider, 33

RE8, 7
Republic P47 Thunderbolt, 175–6, 179–80, 187, 201, 211, 213, 217–18
Rhonalder Sailplane, 34
R101, 15–16, 45

Short,
    Stirling, 128, 156–7, 169, 183
    Sunderland, 183
Slingsby,
    Kirby Kite, 34
    T.21B Sedbergh, 255
    T.31B Cadet TX.3, 257, 260
Sopwith Snipe 7F.1, 20–2, 27
Stampe SV4, 231
Supermarine,
    Sea Otter, 135, 209, 215, 248–9
    Southampton Flying Boat, 38, 41
    Spitfire, 61, 71, 74, 76–79, 83–4, 92, 94, 96–108, 110-112, 114–32, 135, 137–8, 140–67, 169–78, 180–6, 191–8, 201–208, 210–11, 213, 215–16, 218–23, 225–37, 239–45, 247–9, 254, 260, 263, 265
    Walrus, 124–5, 131, 134–5, 137–9, 149–50, 153, 160–1, 165–7, 175–8, 184–6, 191–3, 195, 198–209, 211, 213, 215, 232, 234, 240

Vultee Vengeance IV, 243–4
Vickers,
    Virginia, 38, 50
    Wellington, 133, 158, 183

RAF HAWKINGE

Westland,
    Lysander, 59, 61, 66–8, 70–71, 116, 123, 125, 128, 132, 135–8, 146, 158, 161, 165–6, 169–70, 173
    Wallace Is, 51, 54, 66
    Wapitis, 35
    Whirlwind, 152–3, 183
    Widgeon, 30

V1 Flying Bomb, 198, 202, 210–11, 215, 218–23, 225–31, 235–6
V2 Rocket, 236, 238, 240, 242, 244

Zeppelin, 7
Zogling, 32

Buildings/Structures
Amaya, 215

Bijou Cottage, 2
Belfast hangar, 10
Bessonneau hangar, 7, 10

Chipdean, 101

Dover Castle, 36, 109, 218

Fairfield Court, 86

Hockley Sole, 98, 103

Linton, 236

Mimosa, 208
Meridian House, 98
    Hut Farm, 106
More Hall, 88

Pickett Hamilton Turret, 103

Reinden House, 80, 147, 196

Sunnyside, 215

Whitegate House, 117, 196

Hotels/Public Houses
The Danes, 32
The Grand Hotel, 205
The Majestic Hotel, 167
The Metropole Hotel, 8
The Plough, 167
The Red Lion Hotel, 124
The Queens Hotel, 34
The Valiant Sailor, 33
The White Horse Inn, 178

Engineering Companies
Airspeed Limited, 68
Armstrong Siddeley, 24, 27
Aster Engineering Company, 5

Burtonwood Repair Depot, 200

DeNapier Aircraft Engines, 200, 203
DH Aircraft Co., 200
Dowty Equipment Ltd., 203

Fédération Aéronautique Internationale (FAI), 256

Gloucestershire Aircraft Company, 24
GQ Parachute Company, 77
Green Engine Co. Ltd., 3, 5
Guncliffe Owen Ltd., 203

Hallicrafters Company, 65
Handley Page Aircraft Co. Ltd, 10, 12
Hawker Aircraft Co. Ltd., 48
Hele-Shaw Clutch Ltd., 5

Organisation Todt (OT), 200

Plessey Ltd., 200, 203

Roe, AV, 5
Rolls-Royce, 38, 178, 203

Short Brothers, 5, 74
Skoda, 176

INDEX

Stanhay Agricultural Engineers, 172

Webb's Radio, Ltd., 65

British Operations/Exercises
Big Ben, 242
Binge, 134
Black Violet, 69–70

Channel Stop, 120, 214
Convoy PQ17, 141

Dynamo, 72
Dover Patrol, 66

Jubilee, 144–6

King O, 164

Outward, 135
Overlord, 214, 216

Rutter, 144

German Operations/Exercises
Adler Tag, 88

Lion (Lowen), 76

Miscellaneous
Brenzett Aeronautical Museum, 106, 115, 201
British Gliding Association, 33

Channel Gliding Club, 31, 33–4
Cinque Ports Flying Club, 33, 74

Duke of York Military School, 208
Dutch Airways, KLM, 61

Entertainments National Service Association (ENSA), 146, 173, 242

Folkestone & Hythe Diving Club, 132

Gate Light Vessel, 88
Grosvenor Trophy, 30

Kent Battle of Britain Museum Trust, 106, 115, 122, 154, 265–6
Kent Flying Club, 74
Kings Cup Race, 30
Marshalls Aerospace, 98

National Gliding Contests, 34

Romney Marsh Wartime Collection, 115, 201
Royal Aircraft Establishment (RAE), 100, 181

Miscellaneous Units/Commands.
2nd Tactical Air Force (TAF), 158, 210, 216, 220, 233, 244
6th Wing Eastern Command, 9
No.1 (Anti-Aircraft Cooperation Unit) AACU, 68, 243
No.1 (Coastal Artillery Cooperation Unit), CACU, 104, 122, 150
No.1 Group (RAF), 20
No.1 Group (ROC), 63
No.1 (Pilotless Aircraft Section), 66, 68, 74
No.3 (Armament Practice Camp), 245, 249
No.3 Group Communication Squadron (GCS), 73
No.3 Recruit Training School, 63
No.4 Group, 132
No.6 Auxiliary Group, 58
No.8 Aircraft Acceptance Park (AAP), 9
No.9 Group, 166
No.10 Group, 150, 194
No.11 Group, 18, 79, 99, 103, 108, 134, 139, 147, 154, 163, 169, 202, 207, 218, 234, 242, 248
No.12 Aircraft Acceptance Park (AAP), 9
No.13 Group, 192
No.14 Group, 225

RAF HAWKINGE

No.14 Armament Practice Camp (APC), 207
No.16 Group (Coastal Command), 214
No.17 Armament Practice Camp (APC), 205
No.19 Aircraft Maintenance Unit (AMU), 66, 203
No.19 Group (ROC), 63
No.22 Group Technical Training Command (GTTC), 251, 257
No.22 Group (RAF), 258
No.24 Group (RAF), 63
No.31 WAAF Recruit Centre, 251
No.44 WRAF (OCTU), 257
No.46 Group Transport Command, 251
No.46 Reconnaissance Corps, 144
No.49 Maintenance Unit (MU), 117
No.53 Ferry Unit (FU), 200
No.56 Operational Training Unit (OTU), 74
No.58 Operational Training Unit (OTU), 225
No.71 Maintenance Unit (MU), 254, 257
No.83 Group, 177, 182
No.86 Maintenance Unit (MU), 160, 169, 178
No.99 (Folkestone) Squadron Air Training Corps (ATC), 147, 151, 173
No.149 Airfield, 211
No.312 (City of Canterbury) Squadron Air Training Corps (ATC), 173
No.354 (Dover) Squadron Air Training Corps (ATC), 156, 173
Acoustical Section, 22
Aeroplane Dispatch Section, 7
Air Sea Rescue, 110, 117, 119, 123, 125, 134, 138, 142–3, 146–7, 151–2, 154, 161–2, 167, 170–1, 175, 181, 183, 193–5, 201, 216, 219, 240, 259
Air Tactical Assault Group (ATAG), 62
Air Defence of Great Britain (ADGB), 29, 37–8, 46, 55, 88, 207, 209–10, 216, 222, 225, 233
Air Investigation Branch (AIB), 178

Air Ministry Experimental Station (AMES), 85
Aircraft Storage Section (ASS), 19, 35, 50
Aircraft Transport & Travel Ltd, 14
Air Training Corps (ATC), 254–5
Area Command No.22 Group, 55

British Army of Occupation, 12
British Expeditionary Force (BEF), 9

Central Flying School (CFS), 82, 253
Chain Home Defence (Radar/RDF), 61, 84–5, 87, 118, 155, 168, 190
Combined Cadet Force (CCF), 255

Directorate of Air Sea Rescue Services, 125
Directorate of Aircraft Safety, 126
Directorate of Military Intelligence, 206

Home Command Gliding Centre, 255
Hythe,
  Acoustic Research Station, 38
  Small Arms School, 41, 68

Oxford University Air Squadron (UAS), 74

RAF Airfield Construction Unit, 221
RAF Coastal Command, 214, 240
RAF Medical Service, 53
RAF Merchant Ship Fighter Unit, 141
RAF Signals Intelligence Service, 65
RAF Volunteer Reserve Training Branch, 256
RAF Volunteer Reserve (RAFVR), 35, 64, 74, 115, 117, 158
Royal Observer Corps (ROC), 62–3, 219

School of Army Cooperation, 58
School of Technical Training, 18

'Y' Service, 81, 104, 110

INDEX

Wessex Area Storage Unit, 19
Wireless Maintenance Section, 17
Women's Auxiliary Air Force (WAAF), 65, 81–2, 84, 116, 139–40, 147, 170, 173, 189, 208, 215, 236, 242, 249, 251–2
Women's Royal Air Force (WRAF), 86, 251–2, 254, 256–9

Luftwaffe Squadrons/Units

Erprobungsgruppe, 85, 103–104
JG 1, 185
JG 2, 142–3, 146, 182
5/JG 2, 142
2/JG 3, 70
3/JG 3, 94
6/JG 3, 71
JG 26, 79, 88, 119–20, 129–30, 135, 137, 148, 153, 155–61, 170, 176, 187, 191, 203
1/JG 26, 88
2/JG 26, 73, 111, 163, 165, 185
4/JG 26, 154, 181, 185
5/JG 26, 178, 193
7/JG 26, 165
8/JG 26, 111
9/JG 26, 135
10/JG 26, 163
JG 27, 177, 183
5/JG 27, 69
JG 51, 75, 83, 110, 116, 118, 120
1/JG 51, 69, 78, 84
2/JG 51, 78, 106
3/JG 51, 69, 77
4/JG 51, 110
5/JG 51, 77
JG 52, 84
3/JG 52, 81
2/JG 53, 123
JG 54, 83
2/JG 54, 118
3/JG 54, 72–3, 84
7/JG 54, 106
10/JG 54, 172

KG 1, 88, 109
KG 2, 88, 153
1/KG 2, 205
5/KG 2, 205
8/KG 2, 154
KG 3, 109
1/KG 3, 73
KG 4, 109
8/KG 6, 197
5/KG 26, 156
3/KG 27, 70, 73
2/KG 40, 205
6/KG 54, 205
KG 76, 90, 109
2/KG 76, 118
3/KG 76, 205
4/LG 1, 88
5/LG 1, 88
10/LG 1, 88
1/LG 2, 117
5/LG 2, 115
Luftflotte 2, 99
1/ZG 26, 92
2/ZG 76, 71
2/StG1, 88
ZG 1, 204

RFC/RAF/RCAF Squadrons/ Units

No.1 (RAF) Squadron, 7, 29, 40, 127, 177, 182, 204, 248–9
No.1 (RCAF) Squadron, 105
No.1 Photo Reconnaissance Unit (PRU), 119
No.2 (Army Cooperation) Squadron, 52–4, 61, 123, 231
No.2 Flight Training School (FTS), 22
No.2 (Cadre) Squadron, 51
No.3 Squadron, 37, 61, 66–7, 183, 185, 193, 219
No.4 Squadron, 70–1, 123
No.5 Flight Training School (FTS), 63
No.7 Squadron, 7, 169
No.8 Squadron, 7
No.9 Squadron, 38

No.11 Squadron, 20
No.12 Squadron, 8, 133, 182
No.13 Squadron, 70
No.16 Squadron, 66–8, 123
No.17 Squadron, 22, 27, 29, 68–70
No.18 Squadron, 17
No.19 Squadron, 128, 182, 200
21st Wing RFC, 9
No.21 Squadron, 206
No.25 Squadron, 18–22, 26–7, 29–32, 34, 36, 38, 40–1, 44, 50–1, 55, 57–9
No.26 (Army Cooperation) Squadron, 234
No.29 Squadron, 68, 112, 154
No.32 Squadron, 38, 69, 78, 84–5, 88, 94–5, 98
No.33 Squadron, 48, 51
No.41 Squadron, 104–106, 116–17, 141, 166, 172–4, 176–8, 180–1, 183, 200, 227
No.43 Squadron, 29, 40, 128, 138
No.46 Squadron, 54
No.49 Squadron, 109
No.50 (Home Defence) Squadron, 185
No.53 (Bomber) Squadron, 70–1
No.54 Squadron, 88, 117
No.56 (Punjab) Squadron, 22, 36, 55, 57, 137
No.57 Squadron, 71
No.59 Squadron, 68
No.64 Squadron, 74, 83, 92, 147, 193, 211, 231
No.65 Squadron, 55, 120, 141, 185, 200
No.66 Squadron, 100–101, 104, 107, 110, 150
No.71 Squadron, 130, 141, 144, 176, 179
No.72 Squadron, 99, 103–104, 110, 112, 117, 134, 141–2
No 74 Squadron, 115, 117–18, 122, 124–5, 249
No.74 (Signals) Wing, 118, 162
No.75 (RNZAF) Squadron, 232
No.78 Squadron, 132
No.79 Squadron, 70, 74–6

No.80 Squadron, 216
No.83 Squadron, 18
No.85 Squadron, 94, 197, 205
No.88 Squadron, 200
No.91 Squadron, 112–16, 118–21, 124, 126, 128, 131–2, 134–5, 137–8, 140–6, 148–50, 152–6, 158–61, 163–73, 175–8, 183–6, 200, 217–19, 228
No.92 Squadron, 71, 102, 108, 115, 128, 132
No.98 Squadron, 200
No.102 Squadron, 174, 176
No.110 Squadron, 16–17
No.111 Squadron, 73, 76–7, 90, 141
No.118 Squadron, 150
No.119 Squadron, 185, 214
No.120 Squadron, 12, 14–17
No.121 Squadron, 130, 179
No.121 Wing, 182, 198
No.122 Squadron, 249
No.122 Wing, 182, 200
No.124 Squadron, 149, 242
No.124 Wing, 213
No.125 Wing, 233
No.127 Squadron, 215
No.129 (Mysore) Squadron, 121, 209
No.130 Squadron, 231, 233
No.132 Squadron, 182, 231–5
No.133 Squadron, 130, 144, 179
No.133 Wing, 209
No.135 Wing, 225
No.137 Squadron, 152
No.141 Squadron, 77–8
No.145 Squadron, 121, 186, 227
No.149 Squadron, 156
No.151 Squadron, 89, 93
No.157 (General Reconnaissance) Wing, 185, 214
No.157 Squadron, 204
No.164 Squadron, 202
No.165 Squadron, 146, 154
No.168 Squadron, 209
No.174 Squadron, 198

INDEX

No.175 Squadron, 198
No.180 Squadron, 200
No.181 Squadron, 177, 198
No.198 Squadron, 173
No.201 Squadron, 41
No.207 Squadron, 20
No.210 Squadron, 38
No.222 Squadron, 106, 225
No.225 Squadron, 58
No.234 Squadron, 196, 211, 245, 248
No.238 Squadron, 122
No.239 Squadron, 134
No.240 Squadron, 134
No.245 Squadron, 73–4, 134, 198, 202
No.247 Squadron, 106
No.257 Squadron, 79
No.266 Squadron, 120
No.274 Squadron, 12, 229
No.277 (ASR) Squadron, 124–5, 132, 134, 137–8, 145–9, 152–6, 158–60, 163, 165–7, 169–70, 173, 177, 181, 183–5, 191, 193–6, 198, 201–202, 204–207, 209, 211, 213, 215–17, 220, 227, 234–6, 240
No.278 Squadron, 240–2, 248–9
No.302 (City of Poznan)) Squadron, 119, 195, 227
No.303 (City of Warsaw -Kosciusco) Squadron, 105, 118–19, 123
No.306 (Turunski) Squadron, 152, 209
No.311 (Czech.) Squadron, 192
No.312 (Czech.) Squadron, 128, 173, 192
No.313 (Czech.) Squadron, 192–4
No.315 (City of Deblinski) Squadron, 134, 209
No.316 (City of Warsaw) Squadron, 134
No.320 (Dutch) Squadron, 135, 200, 209
No.322 (Dutch) Squadron, 202–203, 205–207, 226–7
No.331 (Dutch) Squadron, 159–60
No.332 Squadron, 146, 165
No.341 Squadron, 227
No.345 Squadron, 152

No.350 (Belgian) Squadron. 141, 143, 196, 198, 200–202, 206, 208, 225–27, 230–1, 233
No.401(RCAF) Squadron, 135, 137–8, 144, 194–5, 205, 228
No.402 (RCAF) Squadron, 120, 150, 185, 197, 221–3, 229
No.403 (RCAF) Squadron, 167, 170, 198
No.411 (RCAF) Squadron, 191–2
No.412 (RCAF) Squadron, 134, 191, 205
No.416 (Army Cooperation) Flight, 66–8, 74
No.416 (RCAF) Squadron, 144–6, 163, 167
No.418 (RCAF) Squadron, 211
No.421 Flight, 104, 109–14, 116, 124
No.421 (RCAF) Squadron, 191
No.440 (RCAF) Squadron, 213
No.441 (RCAF) Squadron, 231–6
No.451 (RAAF) Squadron, 236, 239, 243
No.452 (RAAF) Squadron, 128, 134
No.453 (RAAF) Squadron, 154, 241, 243–4
No.456 (RAAF) Squadron, 236
No.460 (RAAF) Squadron, 188, 232
No. 485 (RNZAF) Squadron, 134, 196
No.486 Squadron, 202, 204, 219
No.488 9(RNZAF) Squadron, 205
No.500 (Kent's Own) Squadron, 66, 249
No.501 (County of Gloucester) Squadron,35, 78–81, 88, 93–5, 102, 105–106, 150, 186, 191, 193, 195–8, 200–201, 203–205, 207
No.502 (Ulster) Squadron, 50
No.504 (County of Nottingham) Squadron, 46, 50–1, 54, 58, 240–1
No.529 Squadron, 112, 162
No.541 Flight, 119
No.567 Squadron, 243–4
No.600 (County of London) Squadron, 34–5
No.601 (County of London) Squadron, 34–5, 68, 120
No.602 (City of Glasgow) Squadron, 38, 58, 146, 182, 204

301

RAF HAWKINGE

No.603 (City of Edinburgh) Squadron, 58, 111
No.604 (County of Middlesex) Squadron, 58, 215
No.605 (County of Warwickshire) Squadron, 69–70, 72–3, 106, 186
No.607 (County of Durham) Squadron, 57, 134
No.609 Squadron (West Riding of Yorkshire), 117, 123, 132, 134, 148–9, 153, 160, 181, 183, 195–6
No.610 (County of Chester) Squadron, 58, 74, 76-8, 83–4, 94, 96, 117, 121
No.611 Squadron (West Lancashire) Squadron, 154, 170, 198, 211, 237–41
No.612 (County of Aberdeen) Squadron, 58
No.613 (City of Manchester) Squadron, 63, 68, 72
No.614 (City of Manchester), 134
No.615 Squadron (County of Surrey), 83, 88, 115–16
No.616 (South Yorkshire) Squadron, 121, 128–9, 138, 144–6, 149, 151
No.653 (AOP) Air Observation Post, 164
No.1448 (Radar Calibration) Flight, 118, 162, 189
No.1474 (Wireless Interception Flight), 158
No.1624 (Anti-Aircraft Cooperation) Flight, 243

RAF Regiment Squadrons/Support Units.

No.2707 (Light AA) Squadron, 234, 243
No.2709 (Light AA) Squadron, 237
No.2733 (Light AA) Squadron, 220
No.2738 (Light AA) Squadron, 220
No.2740 (Light AA) Squadron, 220
No.2766 (Light AA) Squadron, 220
No.2767 (Light AA) Squadron, 232, 235
No.2797 (Light AA) Squadron, 220
No.2813 (Light AA) Squadron, 231
No.2826 (Light AA) Squadron, 158, 219, 231
No.2882 (Light AA) Squadron, 164
No.2889 (Light AA) Squadron, 220
No.2890 (Light AA) Squadron, 220
No.2891 (Light AA) Squadron, 220
No.2892 (Light AA) Squadron, 220, 231
No.2891 (Light AA) Squadron, 220
No.2955 (Light AA) Squadron, 231
No.3012 Service Echelon/Commando, 208
No.3210 Service Echelon/Commando, 200, 203, 206
No.3257 Maintenance Unit (MU), 116
No.3505 Service Echelon/Commando, 243
No.4029 (Light AA) Squadron, 164
No.4107 (Light AA Flight), 164, 181
No.4108 (Light AA Flight), 164
No.4187 (Light AA Flight), 182
No.4657 Works Flight, 235
No.6130 Service Echelon/Commando, 232, 235
No.6132 Service Echelon/Commando, 233
No.6402 Service Echelon/Commando, 232, 235
No.6504 Service Echelon/Commando, 241

8th USAAF Groups/Squadrons

4th FG, 176
44th BG 67th BS, 166
56th FG, 187
61st FS, 187
78th FG, 175–6, 179
92nd BG, 193, 210
93rd BG, 166, 210
94th BG, 193
303rd BG, 201
306th BG, 192
325th BS, 210
326th BS, 193
328th BS, 210
329th BS, 166
334th FS, 151, 176
335th FS, 179
336th FS, 179
352nd FG, 206
357th FG, 207
363rd FS, 207

INDEX

367th BS, 192
386th BG, 209
388th BG, 239
389th BG, 211
427th BS, 201
448th BG, 241
487th FS, 206
491st BG, 219
553rd BS, 209
563rd BS, 239
567th BS, 211

9th USAAF Groups/Squadrons

94th FS, 151
322BG, 210
323rd BG, 219
362nd FG, 211
378th FS, 211
406th FG, 213
450th BS, 210
454th BS, 219
513th FS, 213

RNAS/FAA Squadrons/RN Ships & bases

HMS *Erebus*, 234
HMS *Ganges*, 89
HMS *Holmes*, 241
HMS *Palencia*, 241
HMS *Wasp*, 173
No.790 Squadron, 162
No.819 Squadron, 185, 214
No.825 Squadron, 72
No.855 Squadron, 214–15, 221
No.854 Squadron, 214–15

Publications

After the Battle magazine, 96
Daily Express, 33
Daily Mail, 6
Flight magazine, 3
Picture Post, 270

Army Units

1st AA Battery Flight, 169
2nd AA Battery Flight, 169
3rdAA Battery Flight, 169
41st Army Division, 203
71st AA Brigade/Division, 144, 167, 219
131st AA Battery Flight, 144
Auxiliary Transport Service (ATS), 140
5th Battalion the Buffs, 63
6th Battalion the Buffs, 80
No.1 Defence Battalion Royal Engineers (DBRE), 68
No.560 Coast Regiment, 153
No.655 (General Construction Company) RE, 74
No.699 (General Construction Company) RE, 74
Home Defence Unit (HDU), 170
London Defence Artillery, 235
London Rifle Brigade, 103
Queen's Westminster's Regiment, 68
36th Infantry Brigade, 63
167th Infantry Brigade, 30
Royal Artillery, 107
Royal Engineers, 10, 37, 68, 89, 102
Royal Marine Siege Regiment, 83, 104
Royal Sussex Regiment, 85
YMCA Battalion, 6